THE TRAIL OF THE HARE

LIBRARY OF ANTHROPOLOGY

Editors: *Anthony L. LaRuffa and Joel S. Savishinsky*

Editorial Assistant: *Phyllis Rafti*

Advisory Board: *Richard Blot, Mary Ann Castle, Robert DiBennardo, May Ebihara, Paul Grebinger*

SAN CIPRIANO
Life in a Puerto Rican Community
Anthony L. LaRuffa

THE TRAIL OF THE HARE
Environment and Stress in a Sub-Arctic Community
Second Edition
Joel S. Savishinsky

LANGUAGE IN AFRICA
An Introductory Survey
Edgar A. Gregersen

OUTCASTE
Jewish Life in Southern Iran
Laurence D. Loeb

DISCOVERING PAST BEHAVIOR
Experiments in the Archaeology of the American Southwest
Paul Grebinger

REVOLT AGAINST THE DEAD
The Modernization of a Mayan Community in the Highlands of Guatemala
Douglas E. Brintnall

FIELDWORK
The Human Experience
Edited by Robert Lawless, Vison H. Sutlive, Jr., and Mario D. Zamora

DONEGAL'S CHANGING TRADITIONS
An Ethnographic Study
Eugenia Shanklin

MONTE CARMELO
An Italian-American Community in the Bronx
Anthony L. LaRuffa

MASTERS OF ANIMALS
Oral Traditions of the Tolupan Indians, Honduras
Anne Chapman

In preparation
CRISIS AND COMMITMENT
The Life History of a French Social Movement
Alexander Alland, Jr., with Sonia Alland

This book is part of a series. The publisher will accept continuation orders which may be cancelled at any time and which provide for automatic billing and shipping of each title in the series upon publication. Please write for details.

THE TRAIL OF THE HARE

Environment and Stress in a Sub-Arctic Community

Second Edition

Joel S. Savishinsky
Ithaca College, New York

GORDON AND BREACH
USA Switzerland Australia Belgium France Germany
Great Britain India Japan Malaysia Netherlands Russia Singapore

Gordon and Breach Science Publishers

820 Town Center Drive
Langhorne, Pennsylvania 19047
United States of America

Post Office Box 90
Reading, Berkshire RG1 8JL
Great Britain

Private Bag 8
Camberwell, Victoria 3124
Australia

3-14-9, Okubo
Shinjuku-ku, Tokyo 169
Japan

12 Cour Saint-Eloi
75012 Paris
France

Emmaplein 5
1075 AW Amsterdam
Netherlands

Christburger Str. 11
10405 Berlin
Germany

Library of Congress Cataloging-in-Publication Data

Savishinsky, Joel S.
    The trail of the Hare : environment and stress in a sub-Arctic community/ Joel S. Savishinsky. — 2nd ed.
        p.   cm. — (Library of Anthropology, ISSN 0141-1012)
    Originally presented as the author's thesis (doctoral—Cornell).
    Includes bibliographical references and index.
    ISBN 2-88124-647-8. — 2-88124-618-4 (pbk.)
    1. Kawchottine Indians.   2. Colville Lake (N.W.T.)   3. Stress (Psychology)—Case studies.   I. Title   II. Series
E99.K28S29   1993
971.9'3004972—dc20   93-38945
                                                                              CIP

To David, Kate, Ann, Susan, Max and Jacob

Contents

Introduction to the Series

One of the notable objectives of the Library of Anthropology is to provide a vehicle for the expression in print of new, controversial and seemingly "unorthodox" theoretical, methodological and philosophical approaches to anthropological data. Another objective follows from the multidimensional or holistic approach in anthropology, which is the discipline's unique contribution toward understanding human behavior. The books in this series will deal with such fields as archaeology, physical anthropology, linguistics, ethnology and social anthropology. Since no restrictions will be placed on the types of cultures included, a New York or New Delhi setting will be considered as relevant to anthropological theory and methods as the highlands of New Guinea.

The series is designed for a wide audience and, whenever possible, technical terminology will be kept to a minimum. In some instances, however, a book may be unavoidably esoteric and consequently will appeal only to a small sector of the reading population — advanced undergraduate students in addition to professional social scientists.

Our hopes for the readers are twofold: first, that they will enjoy learning about people; second, and perhaps most important, that they will come to experience a feeling of oneness with humankind.

Anthony L. LaRuffa
Joel S. Savishinsky

Illustrations

FIGURES

MAPS

Tables

Preface to the Second Edition

In the winter of 1841–1842, in the northern forests of the Canadian sub-Arctic, more than fifty Hare Indians starved and froze to death in the gray twilight of winter. It was not the first time that such an event had occurred among these people, and it would not be the last. Below the walls of the fur trading post at Fort Good Hope, and farther away, deep among the thick trees and frozen lakes of the spruce woods, men and women died, they killed and ate one another, and they consumed their children.

There is nothing political about such cannibalism when everyone else around you is starving and dying. Nor is it a religious act, or something sanctified by a mystique. It is a response to a threat without quarter, and as a stab at life, it is pure, and simple, and devastating. If the terrors of cannibalism and starvation have gradually disappeared from the North in the twentieth century, then they have been replaced by the traumas of change and modernization, and they have left in place the persistent dangers of an environment which still allows little room for error.

The northern world encompasses several different ecological regions, and it is important to understand their basic qualities and the terms used to identify them. The broad designation North, as used in this book, refers to two contiguous environmental zones, the sub-Arctic and the Arctic. I follow Helm (ed., 1981: 1) in defining sub-Arctic as "the Hudsonian biotic province (Dice 1943), which encompasses the northern coniferous or boreal forest and, as major resource mammals, moose, caribou, and varying hare." The term Arctic, in contrast, refers to the area beyond the tree-line or boreal forest's edge, and embraces a zone of tundra extending to the northern North American coast, its offshore islands, and the surrounding seas (Graburn and Strong 1973: 1).

Northern existence amplifies the stresses of life that confront us all, and there is a strain of fatalist wisdom among the native people who have survived both the aboriginal and the contemporary worlds of that region. This book is concerned with a small group of these individuals, and it focuses on a set of basic human problems which face them. It deals with the experiences of stress, kinship, and community among an isolated band of Kawchodinne, or Hare Indians, who continue to live off the land in the sub-Arctic region of Canada's Northwest Territories. The seventy-five people whose lives revolve around the tiny village of Colville Lake subsist as hunters, trappers, and fishermen, and in a subtle yet profound way, their collective existence presents us with a microcosm of the human condition. There is much that is richly distinctive and unique about their mode of living, but there are also some universal situations and predicaments which emerge from their way of life. By examining how the people cope with themselves, with their fellow villagers, and with their challenging environment, we can gain some fundamental insights into both the nature of these experiences, as well as people's experience of their own nature.

Collectively, the Indian people of the Northwest Territories are commonly referred to as Athabascans, which is the name of the language family from which they and the neighboring Indians of Alaska and the Yukon derive their various dialects. As a native nation within the nation-state of Canada, the Indians of the Northwest Territories now refer to themselves as Dene (pronounced Dèh-nay), which means "The People." In laying claim to their own name, the Dene have followed a path similar to that of another Northern people, the group once known as the Eskimo. Since "Eskimo" is actually a pejorative Cree Indian word meaning "Eaters of Raw Meat," natives of the high Arctic have insisted on their own ethnic designation for themselves, "Inuit" — a term which, like Dene, means "People" or "Human Beings."

Among the various cultural groups which comprise the Northern Athabascan or Dene people, the Hare of Colville Lake are characterized by a number of ecological and historical features which make them a very opportune group among whom to examine the problems of stress [1]. They live in one of the harshest environments in the world, and some of the most pervasive dangers and threats confronting them stem from their sub-Arctic ecology. The very name "Hare," ascribed to them by nineteenth-century explorers and missionaries, derived from their ancestors' extensive reliance on the Arctic or snowshoe hare for food and clothing. Extreme temperatures, long and severe winters, prolonged periods of isolation, hazardous weather and travel conditions, a precarious food supply, and the constant need for mobility during the harshest seasons of the year, continue to constitute major problems.

Survival has always been a crucial matter in the North, and even in modern times the Dene of Colville have maintained a semi-nomadic life style of hunting, fishing, and trapping which perpetuates these difficulties. As a consequence of their subsistence patterns, band members continue to lead a highly mobile existence, traveling thousands of miles each year by dogsled, snowshoe, canoe, and foot. Thus, despite a long history of contact with Western institutions dating back to the eighteenth century, the people of the Colville region have remained deeply involved with their natural environment, and that physical world persists as a paradoxical source of richness, identity, and challenge to them.

Beyond the severity and the ubiquitous pressures of their ecology, the people of the band are also confronted with a set of social and psychological stresses which are of equally profound significance for them. Their recent history and acculturation, their immediate social environments, their necessary involvement with white persons, their socialization processes, and the conflicting themes and orientations which compose their world view, all constitute sources of strain and fulfillment. Aboriginally and historically, Indian life styles in the North have presented an array of difficulties that have been met by native communities in both material and behavioral ways. The introduction of the fur trade and manufactured goods by Europeans, which occurred following initial contacts in the eighteenth century, led to a restructuring of Indian living patterns and ecological priorities. Trapping was added to hunting and fishing to form the central trio of native subsistence patterns.

Over the decades, economic changes were intensified by related social factors, including Indian exposure to European diseases on an epidemic scale, resulting in dramatic population decimation among indigenous groups. The nineteenth-century development of permanent settlements around fur trading posts, mission stations, and other Western facilities, had the effect of deepening and expanding the scope of outside influences: native peoples gradually became more sedentary, more involved with European persons, more conversant with Christianity and alcohol, and more reliant upon commercial commodities. Subsequent developments in the mid- and late-twentieth century, including the postwar economic growth of the North, the region's expanding population, and the increased Euro-Canadian involvement in the area's political affairs, have all become factors in the issues now facing the community. (For synopses of historical changes among Northern Indians, see Helm and Leacock 1971; Helm et al. 1975; and Helm, Rogers and Smith 1981; Brody 1987; McClellan 1987; Dickason 1992; Coates and Morrison 1992.)

The quality of life at Colville Lake reflects a confluence of these historical, social, and ecological forces. Across time and space, these influences have come to impinge on the way the Hare relate to one another and their environment. The pronounced physical mobility of the people during the course of every year is a major feature of their adaptation to life. The manner in which band members regularly shift the sites of their camps and their rhythmic moves between the village and the bush are primarily a response to their traditional survival requirements. They see their existence, in its broadest contours, as an alternation between *coyⁿ* ("the settlement") and *dešinta* ("the bush"). But this pattern of movement has also been developed by band members into a way of dealing with other sources of stress and anxiety. That is, provocative social situations, as well as ecologically threatening ones, are dealt with in part by leaving undesirable environments and shifting to more manageable or familiar ones. In trying to manipulate and control the context of their lives, the people consequently travel, or change their place of residence, as a primary coping strategy. Movement is not simply a strategic response to the environment, then, but also a kind of moral good: it embodies the value of freedom which the Dene prize so highly. It is one of my main purposes in this study to examine the relationship between the stress and mobility patterns which are such a basic dimension of Hare existence.

***

In the real life of Indian people, some things happen simultaneously: a man feels the cold, he senses his dogs are tired, he sees hopeful signs of fox tracks in the snow, he thinks about the cost of flour back at the village store. To list his experiences this way lays them out in a line, even though they may have overlapped with one another as he traveled. In this book, I have tried to explore this simultaneity in the people's life, even though the things I want to say must proceed in the linear fashion of print. What I learned from the Hare, and what I feel they can teach us, is necessarily arranged in a sequence — the one formed by the following seven chapters. The first of these, the "Introduction," considers how, as an anthropologist, I came to study and live in the Colville Lake community. The emphasis in this opening chapter is on the ways in which fieldwork was conducted and how I dealt with some of the problems I encountered, such as adapting to the cold, learning the technology, negotiating kinship, and making the best of the blunders I made. This section also considers how the concept of stress helped me to understand numerous aspects of people's lives, ranging from the way they drank to their manner of handling their dogs.

The second chapter, on "Ecology and Community," examines the cultural significance of the region's physical environment, focusing on how it has affected the people in both aboriginal and postcontact times. The nature of the resources, the rhythms of the year, and the Indian way of naming the land, the months, and the seasons are each considered. In the third chapter on "Kinship and History," I take up the fabric of values and personal relationships within the Colville band. This section shows how the Dene's web of blood and marital ties, and the people's moral emphases on generosity, restraint, interdependence, and freedom, have promoted the historical continuity and the recent resurgence of their community. The importance of kinship as a model for social life is reflected in the Athabascan term most frequently used by band members to refer to their fellow villagers: they are collectively designated as *sagot'ine,* "my people." The weaving together of kinship and values also involves the Hare in certain conflicts, however, such as the tensions between autonomy and reciprocity, and their desires for mobility versus those for togetherness. This chapter, therefore, also examines the stress of these contradictions, and outlines the primary coping techniques which the people employ to deal with them.

Chapter 4 on "Stress and Mobility" considers in detail the Hare's methods for surviving within their sub-Arctic environment: it does this by taking the villagers through the seasonal dispersals and reunions which make up the community's annual cycle. There are six major phases of band movement during the course of every year. Half of these the people pass in small, scattered bush camps in the boreal forest. These dispersals alternate with three other periods which band members spend as a reunited community back at their village. By discussing the social and ecological challenges of each season in the same rhythmic order in which the people experience them, the narrative here recreates the flow of the year and the sense of movement which runs through it like a current.

The fifth chapter on "The Missionary and The Fur Trader" explores how the Hare relate to the only two permanent, non-native residents in their settlement, a priest and storekeeper. These two white men at Colville Lake occupy crucial and dominant statuses on the local scene, controlling a good deal of the people's spiritual and material well-being. When I arrived at the village, however, I also found them carrying on a long-term feud with one another — a conflict that had deeply impacted on stress patterns and village social relations. In this chapter I examine the meaning of this feud to the Hare, and the way they play out and manipulate their roles within it. I argue that this conflict has become a constant source of gossip and strategy in the life of the community.

An equally pervasive presence in the people's lives turns out to be the large number of sled dogs they maintain. The relationship between Indians and canines — a subtle mixture of respect, aggression, and mutual dependence — is explored in the sixth chapter, "The Hare and The Dog." The importance of canines as extensions of human senses and the human family, and the way people treat their animals in physical and moral terms, gives dogs a multitude of meanings as members of the social order. One of the most intriguing of these lies in the parallels I found in how the Hare raise their pups and their children.

The fact that white men and canines prove to be constant sources of both gratification and tension for Indian people underlines the recurrent quality of ambiguity in Hare existence. The environment, the people, and the animals of the world are each a source of stress as well as satisfaction to them. The lessons to be learned from the ways the Dene cope with these contradictory meanings are summarized in a chapter of "Conclusions," which

suggests several hypotheses for extending these ideas on stress to other social and cultural settings. The models of stress, mobility, and sociability developed in the book are thus offered as a theoretical approach to comparable problems in other human groups.

***

The first edition of this book was based on two periods of fieldwork in the
Northwest Territories of Canada. The earlier of these took place from August of 1967 through August of 1968, and was supported by the National
Science Foundation; the second study occurred during the summer of 1971
with funding from the National Museums of Canada. While this revised version of the book does not include new firsthand research on my part, it
does draw on over twenty years of teaching about the North that I have done
since my last fieldwork there. As an outgrowth of that teaching experience,
I have sought in this revision to answer a number of questions that my students have raised with me about issues which they felt the first edition left
unanswered.

First, on a humanistic level, they have wanted to know more about the
process and experience of fieldwork itself: how I got to know people; what
band members felt about me; how I adapted to the sub-Arctic environment;
what role I played in the community; and what mistakes I made. Second,
my students have also seen connections between Hare Indian culture and
several controversial issues confronting their own society. In particular, they
have wanted to know how Indian feelings about the environment compare
with our own culture's newfound ecological awareness; and how the Hare
treatment of wild animals and sled dogs can be viewed in the light of ethical arguments advanced by the animal rights' movement. Finally, along with
anthropologists and social activists, my students have also been concerned
with questions of *human* rights, specifically the rights of indigenous peoples
in the Americas. They have wanted to know more about what has been happening to native communities in the North under the impact of oil pipelines, new political agendas, and changing economic priorities.

In this revised edition, then, I have added new material to address each
of these concerns. To enhance the book's readability, I have also extensively
rewritten many sections of it, and abridged a number of technical passages
that would be of interest only to specialists. The new material is concentrated in four chapters. The "Introduction" now has several sections explor-
ing how I carried out my fieldwork, and how I tried to create a role and a
place for myself in Colville Lake. The second chapter on "Ecology and Community" explores the people's environmental attitudes in greater depth, just
as chapter 6 on "The Hare and The Dog" examines the Indian treatment of

animals in comparison with animal rights' concerns. Finally, the last chapter of "Conclusions" contains a new section that looks at some of the major political and economic changes that have occurred in the North in recent years: native rights, Indian land claims, oil exploration efforts, and movements for regional autonomy.

In updating this book, I have retained the first edition's use of the late 1960s and 1970s as the "ethnographic present." My discussion of recent political developments in the North — including treaty and aboriginal rights, and land claims negotiations — covers the 1970s, 1980s, and early 1990s. It should be emphasized that the book's manuscript was finished at a time when Northern natives were working towards major changes in their control over their traditional lands, systems of self-government, and ties to Canada's federal authorities: the need to bring the writing to a close has meant that the following pages can only carry my account of these political events up to January 1993. Lastly, since so many of the issues considered here amplify the basic ecological concerns raised in the text's first edition, I have changed the book's subtitle from "*Life* and Stress..." to "*Environment* and Stress in a Sub-Arctic Community." By examining all of these matters in more detail than before, I hope the book now constitutes a more thorough attempt to grapple with the political, personal, and ethical dimensions of understanding another culture.

Acknowledgments

To the extent that I have succeeded in understanding the nature and significance of the people of Colville Lake, I must express a large debt to the work of certain other scholars from whose insights I have greatly benefited. While the published works of many of these people are cited in the text and references, I want to single out a few individuals because of their direct contribution to this book. When I was still a graduate student, Richard Slobodin of McMaster University encouraged me to go North, and provided invaluable suggestions and contacts to get me on my way. His own work has always stood as a model for me of informed, humanistic scholarship on that region. Two anthropologists who preceded me in doing research in Hare communities, June Helm and Hiroko Sue Hara, gave me good advice and generous access to unpublished field notes.

This book draws upon material which I first presented as part of a doctoral thesis at Cornell University, and hence it has benefited from the advice and teachings of a number of people with whom I have studied. I wish to express sincere gratitude to Burt Aginsky, Robert Ascher, Thomas Gregor, the late Allan R. Holmberg, Kenneth A.R. Kennedy, Bernd Lambert, and Morris Opler for their time and encouragement over the years, and for the patience with which they guided me. My colleagues and students in the Anthropology Department at Ithaca College have provided a very warm environment in which to think about the colder regions of the world, and their friendship and stimulation have helped me to focus on the contemporary issues raised in this new edition: Janet Fitchen and Garry Thomas deserve a special note of thanks for that. Acknowledgment also goes to Ithaca College, which provided me with released time from teaching in order to revise this book; to Fred Estabrook, for help with the maps; to Catherine McClellan, for many helpful suggestions on the revised manuscript; and to the National Science Foundation and the National Museums of Canada, for granting the funds that made my fieldwork possible.

I owe a special debt of gratitude to my wife Susan for all of her encouragement and assistance. Besides drawing several of the figures, and taking a number of the photographs, she shared with me a field season in the North, and helped me to understand a great deal about the life of Indian children. Without her support and companionship, this work would never have been realized.

The people of Colville Lake are the ones who have clearly contributed the most to this book, and I will always be grateful to them for their kindness and understanding. They showed me much of myself as well as of their own ways, and I hope they will appreciate the candor with which I have tried to write of their lives. I also trust that those of the people who may someday read these pages will find some truths here that will enable them to better cope with the modern problems of their existence. Because I have used pseudonyms throughout the book to protect everyone's identity, I cannot thank people directly by name for the hospitality and knowledge I received from them. My debt to all members of the community is nevertheless a very great and conscious one. *Mahsi šo.*

***

The first edition of this book drew on a number of my earlier publications (Savishinsky 1970a, 1970b, 1971, 1972a, 1972b; Savishinsky and Frimmer 1973). In this revised version, I have made use of material presented in a number of articles and book chapters which have appeared since that time (Savishinsky 1974, 1975, 1976, 1977, 1978, 1982, 1990a, 1990b, 1991a, 1991b; Savishinsky and Frimmer 1980; Savishinsky and Hara 1981). In addition, I have profited greatly from the rich body of anthropological writings produced by other scholars since the mid-1970s, much of which is cited in this edition's text and footnotes.

I would also like to acknowledge and thank the authors, editors and publishers of the following works for permission to quote from their publications — Edmund S. Carpenter: "Ethnological clues for the interpretation of certain northeastern archaeological data." *Pennsylvania Archaeologist* 31: 148–150 (1961); June Helm: *The Lynx Point People: The Dynamics Of A Northern Athabaskan Band.* Ottawa: National Museum of Canada, Bulletin No. 176 (1961). Reproduction authorized by Information Canada; June Helm: "Bilaterality in the socio-territorial organization of the Arctic drainage Dene." *Ethnology* 4: 361–385 (1965); John P. Kelsall: *The Migratory Barren-Ground Caribou of Canada.* Ottawa: Canadian Wildlife Service, Department of Indian Affairs and Northern Development (1968); and Robert McKennan: *The Upper Tanana Indians.* New Haven: Yale University Publications in Anthropology No. 55 (1959).

Lastly, I am grateful to Canada's Department of Indian Affairs and Northern Development for permission to reproduce, in Map 6, a section of their map *Comprehensive Land Claims in Canada* (Revised, June 1992), which shows the regions involved in the Dene/Metis land claims negotiations. This material is reproduced with the permission of the Minister of Supply and Services Canada, 1992.

A Note on Language

Though I recorded and learned a great many Hare words while in the field, I did not attempt to make my transcriptions in a rigorous, phonetic manner. In reproducing Hare words in the text of this book, I have tried to adapt my notes to the phonemic schemes presented by Hara (1980) and Hoijer (1966), both of which derive from the fieldwork done by Fang-kwei Li in 1929. A far more precise phonology for Hare, developed by Keren Rice, can be found in Savishinsky and Hara (1981: 314). My adaptation omits tones and is undoubtedly inaccurate in other respects, but it nevertheless seemed proper and necessary to utilize native words for concepts and relationships that had no English equivalent. Glottal stops are represented here with an apostrophe ('), as in *t'ine* ("people"); š is the equivalent of English sh, as in *dešinta* ("the bush"). My use of vowel sounds is as follows:

a as in mock (English);   Hare, *ason* = "grandmother"
e as in bet (English);   Hare, *bele* = "wolf"
ie as in pieta (Italian);   Hare, *bie* = "knife"
i as in meet (English);   Hare, *ni* = "moss"
o as in wrote (English);   Hare, *dzo* = "marten"
u as in food (English);   Hare, *uyalele* = "spring" (the season)

a^n, e^n, i^n, o^n, u^n are nasalized vowels.

Plates

PLATE 1 The village of Colville Lake, as seen from the southwest curve of the bay

PLATE 2 A dogteam entering a winter encampment

PLATE 3   Children at their family's mid-winter trapping camp

PLATE 4   Cleaning and
scraping a caribou hide
from which the hair has
been removed

PLATE 5   Unloading caribou after a successful hunt

PLATE 6   Beaver pelts being stretched at a spring hunting camp

PLATE 7   A trapper with part of his winter catch of marten at the trading post

PLATE 8   Old Joseph at the age of ninety

CHAPTER 1

Introduction

THE BEST LAID PLANS

Anthropology, while it is rooted in the Western tradition, departs from some of that culture's most fundamental ideas. Whereas Socrates urged people to "know thyself," anthropologists are more interested in knowing "others." In reality, however, in practice, most anthropologists come to realize that these two ideas are not so much contradictory as they are complementary: in the process of learning about others, thoughtful people do come to know themselves as well.

This reflective, and self-reflective quality, characterizes not just the student of culture, but the very way in which he first does his research and, later, the way he tries to make sense of it. In essence, Kierkegaard's insight that we "live life forward but understand it backwards" can also be applied to fieldwork: it is often only in retrospect that an anthropologist develops a clear understanding of how he came to know what he feels he knows. The process of writing and revising this book has helped me to appreciate *how* I went about trying to "know" the Hare, and one of my objectives in this chapter is to share some of what I experienced in living with them and learning their culture.

The data and the interpretations presented in this study derive from two field trips to the Canadian Arctic, the first of which was carried out from August of 1967 to August of 1968, while I was a graduate student at Cornell University. This initial trip grew out of an interest in human ecology and the problems of coping with extreme environments. I had first experienced such severity while doing archaeological work at Sardis, the capital of the Lydian Empire in Western Turkey: the summer temperatures there, where I was excavating human and animals remains, sometimes reached 120° F. Having been through the heat of the Middle East, I later decided that I wanted to do ethnographic research in a different sort of extremity. Though I had never been to the Arctic, the North appealed to me because of the challenge it presented to people who had to make the most out of life from the least promising of habitats.

I decided, however, that several conditions would have to be met in

1

order for me to carry out the kind of ecological study that I was interested in. First, I wanted to work in a small community, preferably a band of under one hundred people. This would enable me to get to know each member of the village personally, as well as afford me the opportunity to live and travel with most of the band's families over a long period of time. Secondly, the people's life style would have to be primarily focused on gaining a livelihood from the natural environment, rather than from other sources of income or subsistence. In the language of the North, they would have to be a "bush"-oriented band. Finally, I hoped to find a group that was physically isolated from large population centers and Western influences, and whose members were hence relatively less acculturated than most northern Inuit (Eskimo) and Indians.

It was not easy to find a community that fulfilled these conditions because social and economic changes in the Arctic since World War II had led to the collapse of many of the region's smaller and more isolated settlements. The native people who had previously lived in such villages were now residing, for the most part, in larger towns, where Western influences had caused them to abandon most of their traditional subsistence pursuits. It was not surprising, therefore — although it certainly was dismaying — that when I wrote to several Arctic experts to ask for advice on choosing a research location, most of the replies indicated that the type of group for which I was looking was now rare if not non-existent.

It was at this point in my search that I was fortunate to make the acquaintance of Professor Richard Slobodin of McMaster University, and it was he who first told me of Colville Lake. Although he had never been to the settlement himself, he had heard of it in the course of his own research in the Yukon and Northwest Territories, and an exchange of letters between myself and the local missionary at Colville confirmed Slobodin's opinion that the Indian band there had maintained the kind of traditional life style in which I was interested. Several months later, with the help of a grant from the National Science Foundation, the permission of the Canadian government, and approval of Indian leaders from the Northwest Territories, I travelled from New York to Edmonton, Alberta, and then, in August of 1967, I flew north to the town of Inuvik near the Arctic Ocean. From there, the only way to reach the community at Colville was by privately chartered aircraft, and so I secured a "bush" pilot and a small, single-engine plane equipped with floats, and early on a Sunday morning we flew the 220 miles into the village, landing on the bay of the lake around which the settlement was located.

Although I did not realize it at the time of my arrival, I was only to spend about half of the next twelve months in the village itself, for the people's nomadic life style would keep me on the move for most of the following winter and spring. By arriving during the summer, however, which is the most sedentary period of the year for the band, I had a good opportunity to first experience the people in a settled and collected condition: this facilitated my adjustment to them, and, equally important, their adjustment to me. At the very start, however, nothing went as I had planned: I realized, in fact, almost as soon as I stepped off the plane onto the village's dock, that part of my problem was that I *had no plans*. I had come to the North with a clear set of goals, but I had no clear idea about how to achieve them. Fieldwork, I sensed, was going to be a matter of trial, and error, and improvization.

MAKING A START

The first problem of fieldwork begins on the first day, and the problem is how to get started. More concretely, it means how to get to know people, and how to get them comfortable with your presence. Unfortunately, for anthropologists, there is no game plan, tour guide, or book of etiquette that tells you how to accomplish this. On reflection, how could there be? What has worked well in an African village may be inappropriate in a Chinese commune, and the best approach for a Mexican town may prove disastrous in an Indonesian city.

In my own case, having arrived at Colville Lake without a clear idea of what to do, I decided at first to do nothing. My mood, if not my philosophy, was decidedly in a Zen frame of mind. When I landed, the village's priest invited me to spend the next few days with him, and I accepted. While this seemed convenient, however, I soon found that the Indian people I met at the mission were very reticent in my presence. When I moved to my own cabin later that week, I expected things to improve. They did, but only slightly. I quickly discovered that while people were a bit more relaxed, they were still distant and proper. This concerned me, yet I was unsure how to break through their reserve. Furthermore, I had other things on my mind. Looking around at the cabin which had been put at my disposal, I immediately realized that I had enough to do just fixing up this 10' x 12' spruce log building so that I could weather the winter in it. While not forgetting the problem of rapport, at the moment it felt more compelling to worry about keeping my body rather than my anthropological soul together.

To create some order in my life, I established a few daily routines around getting water and wood. There were well-worn paths through the village to the nearby lake shore, and each day, as I walked these to carry back buckets of water for cooking and washing, I had brief encounters with my neighbors: we had short, polite conversations, which were limited by our uncertainty about each other and the lack of much of a shared language. There were also other trails leading out of the settlement: these passed through surrounding meadows of muskeg, and then threaded their way out into the forest. Following the advice of a young man from the next-door family, I found out which of these paths led to the best areas for standing timber and moss, and during that first week I began to cut and haul back wood for fuel, as well as meadows of moss to chink up the holes in my cabin's log walls.

Initial contacts with people during those opening days were decorous but superficial. I was meeting but not really getting to know my neighbors, and felt unsure whether my decision to first keep a low social profile would eventually work. Then, one morning, matters were taken out of my hands. I was sitting alone over a cup of tea, resting after several hours of cutting firewood, and looking out my one window into the open plaza in the village's center (cf. Map 1). For some reason I felt I was being watched, and glanced over my shoulder at the door, which was open to let in fresh air because of the August heat. Framed in the doorway I saw four children staring at me, their toes pressed up against the outer edge of the threshold. There was a girl of about seven, and three smaller ones who were perhaps four or five years in age. They were my first visitors, and I motioned them in, indicating that they could sit down in the only place available, the edge of my bed. Giggling and pushing one another, they seated themselves in a row, taking their lead from the older girl. I took down a tin of cookies and offered it around: without a trace of reticence now, four hands reached in and pulled out fistfulls of ginger snaps.

The sugar and the sharing broke the ice. In a few minutes the children were all over the small room, prying open my duffel bags, pulling out items of clothing and pieces of equipment. They asked the older girl what some of the things were, and when she was uncertain, she translated and passed the question on to me. Her command of English was quite good.

We began to talk, exchanging names and bits of biography, and then quickly moved beyond basics. Mehna, the seven-year-old, was full of the natural curiosity and candor of her age: she asked who I was, where I was from, why I was there, how long I intended to stay. Her given name, she explained, was actually Rose, which a German nun had once expanded into Rosemeena, and which the local people then shortened and re-shaped into Mehna [1]. She volunteered other things about herself: the names of her parents, her feelings about having a younger sister, her father's reputation as a hunter. Mehna told me some of the same kinds of family facts about her companions. Then, after an hour, and without much ceremony, they all left.

The next morning they were all back, but they brought reinforcements. Six children appeared, word about the bounty of cookies apparently having gotten around the village. While the younger children played, Mehna and I picked up our dialogue from yesterday. She asked me how many people in the settlement I knew, and when I confessed that there were only a handful of names I could put with faces, she took it upon herself to remedy my ignorance. She stood behind my chair and pointed out the window to people as they walked around the village. She told me their names, marriages and families, and also indicated which houses they lived in.

There were playful qualities to Mehna and how she related to me. The next day she quizzed me on what I remembered, clearly enjoying the role reversal of being a seven-year-old Indian girl teaching life's basics to a 23-year-old white man. Satisfied that I had learned my "who's who" in Colville Lake reasonably well, Mehna then began to add detail to people's identities. She rewarded my correct identification of Philip Ratehne by informing me: "Him, he's maybe the best trapper here. Over 200 traps last winter, close to 100 marten and fox.

"That woman?", she continued, pointing past the glass.

"Berona, the old woman in the cabin with the red door."

"Right," Mehna said. "Her, she and her daughters, you need clothes this year, they're really good sewers. Warm parkas, moosehide mukluks. You ask them."

A few weeks later, when I read over my notes from those first few days, I realized that I had never asked Mehna about these personal qualities: she usually just told me what she felt I wanted to know, or maybe what she felt would impress me. In my journal I recorded how one morning, when we had exhausted our stock of questions-and-answers, Mehna raised the stakes. She pointed at someone, I answered:

"George," I said. "George Ratehne. Philip's uncle. His wife's Christine."

"Yeah...," shot back Mehna. "You know what he did last night?"

I looked over at her, standing only a foot or two away. Mehna's face was on a level with mine, and I was unsure of her intent. "Do you?" she repeated.

"No. I don't know what he did."

"Well, he got real drunk on *kontweh*, you know that homebrew. And he got into a bad fight with Thomas, who he camped with last spring, and later he threw an old axe handle through Thomas' window."

She got what she was after: the shock on my face was not at what George had done, but at Mehna's blasé knowledge about such adult dealings. She broke stride only long enough to notice my look, register her success, and then continue:

"That woman with the young boy?"

"Mary Behdzi," I answered, " the one who is going to get married to Luke, and the boy, her son, he's Willy."

"Uh hunh. Right, but you know who Willy's *real* father is?"

Real father?" I said.

Mehna smiled.

She had me again.

***

Through the visits, the names, and Mehna's shock-value sharing, two things were happening, only one of which I was aware of at the time. The one that registered, because I dutifully wrote it down each night, was all of the information that Mehna was giving me. The basic facts of what people were called, where they lived, and with whom, were all credible and easy to check out. But I doubted Mehna's more intimate details, not because I felt adults were incapable of the virtues and vices she ascribed to them, but because I doubted a child could know so much about older people's lives. I nevertheless dutifully recorded these accounts along with my 'who's who' entries. It took me only a week or so to verify that Mehna's basic information — her names and kin ties — were correct: learning them from her, in fact, saved me a lot of awkwardness by allowing me to thread my way through the maze of kinship more quickly. But it took me months to appreciate the more "gossipy" parts of her summer-time stories.

It was only in late December, after I had been with the people five months, and had spent the first part of the winter out on the trapline, that I sat down one night during the Christmas ingathering and re-read my journal entries from those first few days at Colville. By that time I knew everyone fairly well — reputations, skills, foibles, and all. It turned out, in retrospect, that most of what Mehna had told me was essentially correct — a bit of embroidery here, yes; a touch of hearsay there — but no more imagined or imprecise than what other and older people believed to be true. At the age of seven, Mehna was still open about what she was able to share and, as I had come to realize, she also lived in a village with few secrets and little privacy. Only one or two dozen yards separated most of the buildings from those next-door, and practically the whole settlement could be seen from each family's front door: the entire community would have fit inside a small football stadium. As a child, Mehna could move about it with ease and, unhampered by the reticence that comes with maturity, she could speak of what she knew with little hesitation.

While I took note, those first weeks, of all the things that Mehna told me — whether or not I believed them — what I was *not* aware of at the time was a second process that was going on, this one relating to what happned to the children when they left my cabin. Months later, I heard from Paula, Mehna's step-mother, how the parents would ask the children about me when they were back at home: what I was like, where I had come from, how long I planned to stay. The children put the answers before their elders with the same openness they had used in telling me about the village. Less factual but probably more important in these family exchanges were the lessons people drew from what they heard of my behavior: I liked the children, and they liked me, and so whatever else there was to my character, that one merit was clear. And in a community where native people felt that anyone who likes children and dogs cannot be all bad, that merit went a long way in building me a decent reputation.

The initial lack of direct contact between the adults and I was soon eclipsed in importance because Mehna and her friends had done our communicating for us. The children were like informal amabassadors, diplomatically building ties between tentative allies. Within a few days after those initial visits, some of the young men my age stopped by my cabin to — as Philip Ratehne once put it — "check out all the stuff we heard you brought." Paula, Mehna's step-mother, brought me over two trout. One day I helped Philip's father Wilfred tar his roof. I came back from wood-cutting one afternoon to find a hind-quarter of caribou inside my front door, left there — I later learned — by Thomas. The cookies had paid off with interest. While there were still a lot of people left to meet even in this small village, I soon felt comfortable enough dropping in to see the people who had now come in to see me.

***

I slowly expanded my circle of acquaintances in the first weeks after my arrival, and I was greatly assisted in this by a voluntary and unwittingly portentous act of some of my closest neighbors. The members of one particular household included two young adult men, Adam and Philip Ratehne, with whom I initially spent a great deal of time hunting, and whose father, Wilfred, first instructed me in basic fishing techniques. One day Adam — who was three years my senior — half-jokingly referred to me as *sešile* ("my younger brother"), and the other members of the family followed suit by beginning to use appropriate kinship terms for me.

The consequences of this simple act were immediate, unexpected, and far-reaching. Up until that time, most of the people had been hesitant and reluctant to interact with me: this was not only because I was still an unknown quantity, but also because there were no standard behavior patterns that they could legitimately extend to me. Everyone in the village was a close or distant kinsperson to everyone else, and kinship was thus the language of interaction which defined community relations (see Figure 5). To be without relatives was to be in a social limbo, to live outside the norms that governed personal ties. Once I had been given a kinship status within one family, however —

even though it was a mock-serious one — I could then be placed by other band members within their own social networks, for the matrix spread out from Wilfred's household to encompass all of the village's fourteen families. Though no one seriously took me for the "cousin," "nephew," or "grandson" that they jokingly called me in *deneké* ("the people's language"), what *was* important was that the ability to extend these terms to me enabled people to figure out how to act with me. Thus, I suddenly found myself being accorded a sense of "fit" in the local community, and from then on the process of building rapport proceeded much more fluidly.

I spent my first few months in the Colville area both at the settlement proper, and in the neighboring fish camps, where people were putting up supplies of food for the forthcoming winter. I was fortunate to have a small cabin in the "native" part of the community to live in, for this set me apart from the village's missionary and trader: as my first walks through the village had shown me, these two white men had built their homes in locations that physically separated them from the people (and from one another), and they had thus established and enforced a "colonial" style of relationship with band members (cf. Map 3). The two of them had been carrying on a dispute with one another for a long time, and had not spoken in close to three years. Once the people realized that my attitude towards them differed radically from that of these two other individuals, and that I intended to spend a full year in the community — rather than being just another "government *mola*" (white man) passing through — they accepted my presence and my company with surprising readiness. I eventually found myself either welcome, or at least tolerated with amusement, in all of their homes, and the same was true when I visited or lived with people in their bush camps. In turn, many of the villagers came to feel comfortable with and curious about me, so much so that after a brief period of residence in the community, I began to receive a constant stream of visitors at my own cabin.

It was only much later that I realized how the feud between the fur trader and the missionary inadvertently benefited me during these initial weeks: it cast me in the role of a neutral and sympathetic outsider to whom the people could easily express their complaints and dissatisfactions without any fear of reprisal. It was safe and even cathartic to visit me. I thus found myself the recipient of a great deal of personal information and gossip within a brief period after my arrival. The trader and priest themselves proved to be equally hospitable and informative throughout the year, and though they each tried to win my support in their dispute, they eventually accepted (or, more accurately, learned to cope with) my proclaimed neutrality with good grace.

***

For the Indian people of the community, most of the long Arctic winter is spent in isolated hunting and trapping camps in the boreal forest, and I was able to travel and live with several different families during the course of this season. Initially, I stayed with households that contained bilingual members, for I had not had an opportunity, before going to the Arctic, to study any of the dialects of Athabascan — the language spoken by all of the sub-Arctic Indians in the Canadian Northwest. However, by the late winter, my understanding of *deneké* had progressed enough to permit me to spend several months with a number of monolingual families. I consistently found, however, that I could comprehend much more than I could express in the local dialect. And although my facility with *deneké* never approximated fluency, I discovered that a substantial vocabulary, combined with judicious use of body language, made it possible to relate to and understand people in a meaningful way.

Throughout the winter and spring I switched from one bush camp to another whenever good opportunities to do so arose. If the people with whom I was staying were shifting their area and travelling through the trapping region of another family, I arranged to live and hunt with the second group. Later in the year, when I obtained my own dogteam, I enjoyed much greater freedom of movement: I was then able to camp with many people whom I had previously not been able to catch up with. Altogether I travelled close to 600 miles between mid-October and early June. This constant contact with dogs, and the necessity of learning how to train, drive, and handle them, led to my recognition of the social and psychological, as well as the ecological, significance of these animals in the lives of the people. By staying with both traditional and acculturated — i.e., more Western-oriented — families during the various dispersals of the year, I was also able to observe different people in all their major economic pursuits, and I was thus in a position to study how they reacted to the many stresses which isolation in the bush presented. Experiences in different camps also enabled me to check and compare the observations I had made previously with other families. Furthermore, they revealed key differences in individual and family response patterns to the circumstances of winter life.

As was true in the bush, band reunions at the village were studied primarily through participant-observation, and the only times I payed informants was towards the end of my stay in order to get translations of the personal histories and folklore I had tape-recorded. The making of those tapes were the only occasions when verbatim statements were directly recorded, as most of the time I relied on a detailed field diary in order to preserve what I saw and heard of the community's life. Many of the personal quotes given in the text are consequently reconstructions, or close paraphrases, of conversations that I participated in or witnessed, rather than direct transcriptions of tapes or interviews. Within the first few weeks of my stay in the village, I tried to give people an idea of why I was there, explaining that I was a teacher who wanted to understand the Indian way of life so that I could write about it and better communicate it to my students. This was more meaningful to the Hare than my attempts to explain what "anthropology" meant. My main goals, couched in terms of learning and teaching rather than academic disciplines, were thus aspects of my presence that most band members could comprehend and accept, for they had all had at least some knowledge of the role of teacher and the institution of a school. So when people saw me squatting in the center of the village with a group of women, noting down the details of hide-tanning, or curled up in the corner of a tent after a day of trapping, filling up the pages of my journal, my actions were at least consistent with my purpose, and hence less disruptive or disturbing than they might otherwise have been.

If I had any lingering doubts about people's comfort with my note-taking, they were dispelled one December night when I was staying at a bush camp with Adam Ratehne. We had spent much of that day extending one of his traplines, and had come back to our tent quite exhausted. The area we had travelled through had been covered with a good deal of fresh snow, and so we had taken turns "breaking trail" for the dogs on our snowshoes. I felt quite played out after dinner, and warmed by the wood-stove and lantern-light, I curled up atop my caribou skin bedding and decided to indulge myself by reading a novel. Adam, who was repairing the webbing on his snowshoes, looked over at me after a while, and shot me a look of disapproval. "Hey," he admonished me, "you shouldn't be reading. You should be writing. Didn't we see some real bush country today? Good signs of fur? You learned how to recognize marten tracks, broke trail for the first time. Get out your notebook, lazy guy, write that all down!"

When I lived in the bush like this with a family, I did so as a full-time, working member of the household, and I shared with people the responsibilities for hunting, trapping, fishing, cutting wood, and travelling. I found, in fact, that it was impossible to live with a group in the bush and not be a productive member of the camp: the non-participating observer was a drain on already scarce resources, and hence a threat to everyone's well-being. It was with an understanding of my intention to contribute my labor that people agreed to let me stay with them in the bush. In the beginning they did so reluctantly, however, because I was very inexperienced, and they were worried about taking responsibility for me. When, eventually, my experience finally superceded my incompetence, the value of my presence in a camp was such that I was actually asked by the heads of several households if I would like to stay and work with them. Let me emphasize that I never became expert.

I never went native. What impressed people, I think, was not my skill but my willingness to try.

In the bush as well as at the settlement, I participated in the Dene ethic of generosity as best as I could. Rather than use money, I made gifts of meat, fish, wood, and labor to reciprocate the food, services, hospitality, and favors that I received from others. Though this form of participation was often very time-consuming and exhausting, it greatly enhanced my acceptance by the people, for it helped me to remain outside their stereotype of exploitative and dependent *molas* — white men who have little interest or competence in living off the land "the Indian way." Though it was a gross exaggeration of my abilities, Adam once complimented me by saying "now you're getting the hang of it just like the 'old-timers'."

BLUNDERS AND REFLECTIONS

Just as some religious believers hold that there is no life without sin, honest anthropologists confess that there is no fieldwork without error. Living in an Arctic environment and a Native American community gave me ample opportunity to make mistakes and, on occasion, make a fool of myself. I blundered from head to toe, from the way I butchered the language to my first, faltering steps with snowshoes.

Learning how to walk and talk are such fundamental human skills that I did not appreciate, before Colville, how hard they can be to re-acquire when you are in your adulthood. While I knew the language would be difficult, I unfortunately had no chance to learn any of it in advance since there were no modern grammars or dictionaries of the Athabascan dialect spoken by the Hare. The process of picking it up while I was in the community was slow because there were so many other daily tasks that also had to be done: getting fuel and fish, fixing the cabin, preparing food, trying to make acquaintances, figuring out the kinship system, these all cut into the time I could give to the language lessons that 68-year-old Leon Behdzi offered me.

Some of the other elderly men and women who, like Leon, knew practically no English, also helped me develop a basic vocabulary. I was actually able to speak to some of them in broken French, which they had acquired from the Catholic nuns who had nursed and taught in the North during their childhoods a half century ago. Colville's young adults, such as Adam and Philip, bilingual in *deneké* and English, took me through the thickets of grammar and syntax as best as they could. And each of my teachers, regardless of age, tried to get me to recognize and learn to make sounds unheard of in English, French, or any other European language. There were glottal plosives such as *k'*, which you made by building up a pocket of air behind your glottis and then exploding it; there were nasalized vowels, which rendered a word with the sound *iⁿ* different from one with plain, un-nasalized *i*; and there were bilateral fricatives too, such as *thl*, which you formed by tucking the tip of your tongue between the back of your top teeth and palette, and then letting the air vibrate out off of both sides of your tongue's surface.

One of the earliest examples I was taught which showed how sound and syntax went together was the name that the people of Colville Lake had for their own band. It was *K'apamituegot'ine* which, when "diagrammed," translates literally as:

> *K'apa - mi - tue - g'o - t'ine*
> Ptarmigan - net - lake - of - people.

Put into conventional English, the name becomes "The people who live at the lake where you catch ptarmigan in nets" — *K'apa-mi-tue* being the Dene designation for Colville Lake. The meaning refers to the fact that shoreline areas of *K'apa-mi-tue* are thick with the young willows that ptarmigan feed off, and that from aboriginal down to modern times, the local band of Hare have caught these birds by placing old fish nets among the thin shoots.

The feature of the language I found the most difficult to deal with was "tonality." Vowel sounds in Athabascan can be made with one of a number of different pitches or "tones" — such as dropping or raising your voice as you articulate them — and these changes in vowel sounds can alter a word's meaning. For example, altering the tone of the vowel "a" in a simple word such as *sa* can make it mean sun or moon or beaver or bear. To speakers of Western languages, the melodic quality of such Asian tongues as Chinese or Japanese derive from their tonal qualities; but an untrained, untoned set of ears like mine had trouble distinguishing such sounds in Athabascan. Thus, when I came back to the Behdzis' base camp after a day of hunting in the spring, I tried to convey the excitement I felt at having killed my first "beaver." But misplacing the tone, I ended up announcing instead that I had just shot "the moon." Once again, there were tolerant smiles. Leon's face told me that the heavens, if not the language, were still safe from my aim.

***

Walking was not as difficult as talking, but it still had its pitfalls, and on at least one memorable morning, I went out of my way to step into one. It was late October, just after the freeze-up, and there was enough snow on the ground for families to start moving away to their early winter trapping camps. Yen Behdzi, Leon's brother, had measured my height and made me a fine pair of snowshoes — sprucewood frames and cross-pieces, with thin strips of caribou hide *babiche* for webbing. The Hare rule of thumb was that the length of the shoe should be proportional to the wearer's size. Even for a short, 5'4" stature like mine, my snowshoes stretched for almost five feet from end to end. In their other dimension they were close to 15 inches at their greatest width, which was where my moosehide mukluks rested on extra thick plaits of *babiche.* Just standing still in such shoes meant that you could not put your own feet together, but had to adopt the bowlegged, caricatured posture of a cowboy.

Adam Ratehne had already shown me how to tie the snowshoes' thick, caribou skin lacings around my mukluks so that the toe area was anchored to the webbing below while the back of the foot, held by a strap that wrapped behind the ankle, could float freely in the air. When I stood outside my cabin that October morning, ready to put on the shoes and walk through the village to cut wood, the moment's excitement must have blinded both my vision and my judgment. Straddling the empty space between my knees, and looking down at the frames extending some two and a half feet both ahead and to the rear, I should have recognized the enormity of what lay below and before me. Perhaps I also should have given more thought to the subject of the preceding week's sermon from Father Claude — "Pride cometh before the fall."

My first few steps were cautious but flawless, and so I stopped watching my feet in order to strike a more confident pose as I walked ahead. Before I knew what was happening, however, I was tumbling to the ground, falling awk-wardly and heavily on my side. On that last step forward, the inside edge of my right snowshoe had come down atop the inner edge of the left one: when I went to lift the latter, my left foot was pinned to the ground, my balance gave way, and I toppled over. Embarrassed though unbrusied, I started to stand up, and then discovered how difficult *that* manoeuver was with five-foot lengths of sprucewood strapped to the bottom of my mukluks. Finally on my feet again, I took my first steps, and then the lacing of my right shoe came loose and the whole shoe fell off. I knelt down, re-tied it, and started out, but only got another ten yards before once more landing one shoe atop the other and tumbling to the ground. One blunder or pratfall followed another, and in fifteen minutes I had only covered about 60 yards and was still inside the village. Picking myself up again I sudddenly became aware of how quiet the whole place was, how odd it felt that no one else was around. Then I saw a curtain furtively move back across the corner of a window, and I realized at that instant where everyone was. They were inside, watching me, enjoying the one-man show: laughing at Chaplin of the North, a fool for all seasons.

***

Months later I made a different kind of mistake, one that had less hubris and humor, an error I was not even aware of at the time. It happened early in April, shortly after the end of Easter, when people were moving back to their bush camps for the spring hunt. I had arranged to spend this period with several of the Behdzi households, who were returning together to a site they had been using at *Tsoaytue*. After an early morning start from Colville and several stops to rest the dogs and make tea, we were heading across *Tsoaytue* on the last leg of the trip. It was late afternoon by then and in the clear light we could see — from a half mile out on the lake — the families' tents outlined among the shoreline trees.

We were five dogteams in all, stretched out along a well-marked trail: Yen was in the lead, followed by Yašeh and Michele, then their sister Mary, and finally my team in the rear. A good 50 to 80 yards separated each sled from the dogs coming behind. I was enjoying the cleanness of the sky, and the taste of spring in the air, and the clarity which the sunlight lent to all the distant forest's details. Closer to the camp and across our path there were several fish nets set end-to-end in a line under the ice. The poles which marked their locations stood up above the snow cover, and the teams of the three men in front passed between the upright sticks and over the nets as they approached the camp.

As Mary's sled and mine got closer, I looked back over my shoulder to see the lake in full, and watch the trail recede from under the back of my sled boards. For a minute or so, the experience of looking back in that way, with the rocking rhythm of movement below my feet, felt hypnotic. When I finally turned again to face forward, I noticed that Mary had taken her team off the path: she had driven her dogs around the outside of the last pole in line, thereby detouring away from where the nets were set. My own team obediently followed in the wake of her's, and then — once past the fishing spot — Mary and I picked up the main trail again for the last quarter mile run into camp.

By the time I arrived and had my dogs unharnessed and chained up, all the Behdzis were already having tea inside the largest of the tents. I stepped inside, poured myself a cup, and knelt down to rest. It was only then that I noticed how embarrassed and awkward people looked. Yašeh cleared his throat to break the silence and ask me why I had done that. Done what? I answered. I was really at a loss.

He and Mary said something to one another in *deneké* that I could not understand, and then everyone burst out laughing. Yašeh turned to me:

> Only women stay away from the nets. Only they have to do that. The fish, the spirit of the fish, would really be offended if a woman ever crossed over the net. Then the net wouldn't be good anymore. The fish wouldn't go near it.

He translated his words into *deneké* for his parents, and then turned back to me. "Yeah, you're pretty funny," he said, pausing for effect. "You drive dogs pretty good, you know, but you must think you're a woman. We know you want to be like an Indian but, hey, next time, just try to be like a man." They all laughed into their cups, which was all the encouragement that Yašeh needed for one last barb. "Yeah, take it easy, and pay attention. You know those old ladies back at the village have enough trouble trying to fix you up with a wife. They'd never be able to find you a husband."

I had to laugh too. By that point in the year I had made so many mistakes that of all the things I had learned, one of the most valuable was not taking myself too seriously. I had come to realize that a main reason why people put up with me was for the humor, the laughter, their curiosity about what I would mess up or fall over next. In retrospect, now, I think that this comic relief also helps explain why anthropologists are often the unexpected recipients of people's patience and forebearance. Whether it was the way I killed beaver or the language, my facility with snowshoes, or my unwitting care crossing nets and observing the wrong taboo, the people chose to take these and most other blunders on my part with good grace, which was more a reflection of their tolerance than of my own comic instincts.

***

The shock of being in another culture is standard anthropological experience, but one challenge that I had not expected to face was being questioned about my own society by the members of the "other" culture I had entered. Once my fieldwork was well under way and I had gained a decent level of acceptance, I tended to lose sight of how often I myself was asking people questions: Why do those men like to drink so much? How do you pick the places to set your nets? If you can't find a wife here, what will you do? In the midst of all these inquiries, I don't think I ever gave much thought to the position I was putting people in. That is, I'm not sure I ever asked myself what it was like for them to have to put their cultural ideas and practices into words, to articulate what was largely taken for granted. What finally raised my awareness about the dynamics of being questioned and having to answer was when the Hare turned the tables on me.

The first time it happened was so casual and conversational that I don't believe I fully appreciated its significance. It was Christmas: I was in my cabin after close to three months in the bush, sorting through an accumulation of mail which had just arrived. It had been sitting at Fort Good Hope since the freeze-up, waiting for a plane that happened to be going to Colville. Copies of magazines lay on top of my table while I read letters from home, and then Adam and Yašeh came in. They helped themselves to tea from the large kettle that was on my stove, and next helped themselves to some of the issues of *Time* and *Newsweek* that my parents had sent me. Yašeh, flipping pages that he could not read, seemed bemused by the ads and pictures. He came to one in particular that held his attention, and he pushed it across the table to me. "What is it?" he asked. It was a picture of the Manhattan intersection of 5th Avenue and 42nd Street on a workday afternoon. High-rise buildings towered over hordes of bubble-headed people crowding through the streets.

Well," I began, a native New Yorker about to explain his own hometown, "well... A lot of those people are shopping, or they're going to get a meal."

"Where do they eat?" asked Yašeh.

I put a finger on one of the minute storefronts peaking out from behind the mob. "In the bottom of those buildings," I began, "there are restaurants."

"What are those?"

"Places where people go to eat."

Adam interjected: "You mean they just walk in and there's food?"

"Hmm. Yes... but they have to pay for it."

"Pay who?"

"The people who work there," I started to explain. "They prepare, they cook the food."

"Where," asked Yašeh, "where do they get it? Do they grow it or kill it or catch it?"

"No," I replied and then stopped, suddenly realizing what I was up against. How could I make plausible the cultural food chain I was about to uncoil? The food is brought to the store in trucks, the truckers get it from wholesalers, who buy it from processors and packagers, and these in turn purchase the grain, beef, fish and vegetables from the producers, who are the real farmers, ranchers, and fishermen. The people in the photo eat food from far away, provided by people they never see, and brought to them by means which are almost as invisible.

Where to start, where to stop, what to leave in and out? Was a lunchtime meal in my culture so hard to explain? I began, condensed things, tried to make the process sound less Baroque than it was starting to sound to me. Adam and Yašeh listened, doing their best to hide a benign patience as I dug myself deeper into a morass of thick description.

Eventually, fed up perhaps with food, Adam turned the magazine to face him, and lay several fingers on the tall buildings. "What are these?" he wanted to know. "How big are they?"

To convey their height I reverted to trees, comparing the buildings' sizes to 20, 30 or 50 tall spruce trees stacked on top of each other. But when I tried to explain the skyscrapers' purpose — the business of business — analogy failed me.

"People work there," I began. "In offices. They sit at desks, and when they come in each morning there's a big pile of papers on one side of the desktop and they write things and change numbers and talk to people about the papers, and the idea is to have all those papers over on the other side of the desk at the end of the day..."

"And then?" Yašeh prodded.

"And then send them on to someone else."

I took a deep breath and laughed. Until that moment I never realized how lame or unconvincing I and my own culture could be. I learned then how hard it was to help others make sense of things that had never made much sense to me.

***

That first experience as a "native informant" humbled me. While I had had no trouble answering people's earlier questions about my own family — a concern with kinship that mirrored their culture's emphasis on social ties — I experienced an uncustomary loss for words when it came to deeper and broader inquiries about how my own society worked and thought. The most unsettling moments of this kind came in the late spring.

For most of April and May I had been absent from the village. Much of that time I stayed with the Behdzis at their camp at *Tsoaytue*: it had been a good season, with ample caribou and fish, and a successful harvest of beaver and muskrat. When we returned to Colville in June along with most of the community's other households, it was with a feeling of fulfillment. The seasons of ice and snow were over; I had managed to hunt, trap and travel with most of the band's families; and I felt I had learned a good deal about the people's past and present, their stresses and satisfactions.

Then, within a few days of our arrival, the news of the rest of the world — and its tumultuous spring of 1968 — reached us in a sudden rush. For the first time, via radio broadcasts and months-old magazines, we heard of what had been happening elsewhere: the escalating war in Vietnam; student protests in the United States; Paris, Prague and the rest of Europe galvanized by riots, barricades and social upheaval. Initially, the people's curiosity and questions about some of these events did not totally suprise me. By that time in the year I had come to realize that the Indians of Colville, despite their isolation and naivete about outside life, were notably aware of certain cultural and political developments in the larger world. On their radios they regularly picked up CHAK, the Canadian Broadcasting Corporation station in Inuvik, whose news programs were both local and global in scope.

At one extreme, CHAK broadcast personal messages between Mackenzie

River communities — my favorite being the one "To Johnny Frank in Akla-
vik from his brother Eddie: I'm at the north end of Horseshoe Lake, and
there are lots of muskrat here. Come join me, but don't tell anyone where
I am." But the more cosmopolitan programs that year not only played Beatles
songs and Buck Owens tunes, but they gave a lot of special attention to the
United States, particularly the presidential race and the civil rights movement. The most dramatic pieces of news we learned when we returned in June
— no less shocking for their late arrival — was that Martin Luther King Jr. had
been shot to death in Memphis on April 4th, and that Robert Kennedy had
been gunned down nine weeks later in Los Angeles. While we had been busy
killing caribou, America's assassins had been busy killing their country's
leaders.

I was too absorbed in my own confusion about these murders to anticipate
the questions that my neighbors were about to ask me. But my role in the
village as "native informant" for the United States was unavoidable. Adam,
Philip, and Yašeh came by my cabin one evening, and the assassinations
inevitably surfaced amidst our tea and talk about other topics. I turned to my
out-of-date magazines to answer who and when and where. But the printed
facts were no comfort or help when Philip asked me: "How does this happen
in your country? Why do your people kill their chiefs?"

How could I explain "my" country, "my" people, our decade's history of
making war on other nations while killing our own "chiefs"? I had no
answer for them or myself, only the confession of how sad and disturbed it
left me, and how others of *sagot'ine*, "my people," undoubtedly felt the same
as I did. Perhaps, I thought to myself, perhaps some parts of a culture were
beyond explanation or would never make sense. Or maybe it would take
more time to understand them. For the moment, at least, I was again at a
loss. Curiously, knowing how impenetrable parts of my own culture were
made me less anxious, less obsessed with trying to make every aspect of
their Dene life-way fit into some neat, academic scheme. And it made me
more patient with the people who could not answer every question that I
posed. After all, I had now been there myself. I decided that we would all
have to learn to be content with less.

STRESS IN THEORY AND IN PRACTICE

During that first year with the people, many stresses of life were revealed to
me as a result of my own exposure and reaction to them. Living off the land
in far-flung encampments, driving dogs, coping with the confines of small
tents and a small community, and dealing with brew parties as well as other

people's expectations, were difficult, demanding, and often aggravating tasks. Boredom, isolation, lack of privacy, gossip, the hardships of travel, starvation, knife-like cold, pressures for generosity, and drinking, all affected me directly. In most cases I was first aware of these on a personal level *before* I recognized them as larger issues within the community.

When the implication of these stresses began to dawn on me, however, I was at first wary of projecting my own tensions and problems onto everyone else in the band. It was quite possible that my own experiences were unique rather than universal, and that the people as a whole were not affected in the same way by the stresses and deprivations that weighed so heavily on my own mind. I therefore deferred any conclusions about the tenor and quality of the Hares' responses, but I did allow my own reactions to sensitize me to the possible recurrence of these patterns among other band members. I thus became more aware of interaction rates, avoidance patterns, minor complaints, the content of gossip, and the composition of day-to-day and long-term groups. In the months that followed, there were indeed a series of conversations, confessions, confrontations and encounters which confirmed many of my suspicions about stress and response modes.

These events also revealed several sources of tension, and an array of coping techniques, that I was unaware of initially. Although the people of Colville Lake can be characterized as an emotionally contained group, the repetitive, daily life of their bush camps was often as dramatic and informative as the more volatile and sometimes violent events surrounding their drinking parties and village ingatherings. The disciplining of children, the beating of dogs, and the shifting nature of personal reputations and trapping partnerships, each told a story of how people coped. Community members unveiled a great deal about themselves under a variety of circumstances, and verbal as well as behavioral clues ultimately revealed a picture of their life that possessed both system and dimension.

The concept of stress, which was central to these understandings, has often been defined operationally in terms of physiological and psychological changes. In its most general sense, it is used to denote "a perceived environmental situation which threatens the gratification of needs" or an organism's well-being or integrity (Pascal 1951: 177; Cofer and Appley 1964: 453, cited in Appley and Trumbull 1967: 7-8). In applying the concept to Indian culture, it became necessary to expand the notion of "environmental situation" to include the social and emotional as well as physical dimensions of life, for each of these was equally immediate, and they all contributed significantly to the nature and problems of existence. Well-being also had to be viewed in holistic terms, for people evaluated and responded to their situations on the basis of simultaneously social, psychological, and ecological criteria. In one sense, as Hans Selye (1956) has argued, all of life is stressful, and this necessitated a sensitivity to tensions, threats, and anxieties stemming from a multitude of sources.

Operating on this level of awareness, it became evident that band members were being confronted with stresses of varying specificity. Being caught in a "white-out at −45°F, or finding oneself unarmed in a winter encampment surrounded by hungry, baying wolves, were situations of unambiguous and clear-cut danger. On the other hand, a sense of distrust or suspicion directed towards one's neighbors — a feeling held by a few of the people — implied a stress that was less defined and more diffuse; it was, in fact, closer to "free-floating" anxiety, rather than being attached to a specific threat in time and space (cf. Slobodin 1960a: 122).

The people's ways of coping were as diverse as the tensions themselves, and responses varied with the nature of the stress source and the particular individuals or families involved. For example, exposure and susceptibility to stress differed according to such factors as gender and people's degree of cultural conservatism. Highly acculturated and very traditional Indians, for instance, responded quite differently to the distinctive stresses of *dešinta,* the "bush," as compared to village life. The isolation of the camps was much harder on people accustomed to living in town, while the concentration and drinking of settlement life was the more difficult situation for their conservative peers. Men and women similarly exhibited distinctive responses to the stresses derived from the band's sexual division of labor. Men had to deal more with the rigors of travelling and trapping, females with the daily demands of camp life and child care. Yet despite the differences rooted in such qualities as gender and acculturation, there were also features which many band members shared in the way they coped with life's problems: as these common qualities became evident to me, I eventually found I could characterize as well as simply inventory the people's repertoire of stress reactions. Some of these primary features, including an emphasis upon emotional restraint, an avoidance of direct confrontations, a respect for others' individuality, a recourse to moving away from tense situations, and the rechannelling or displacement of hostile feelings, constituted a behavioral set which the Hare have been found to share with other northern Indians [2].

***

While most theoretical and common-sense definitions of stress convey the sense in which this concept is used here, it is worthwhile clarifying how situations of stress were actually perceived and evaluated in the course of fieldwork. Operationally, stress has usually been defined by psychologists in terms if either disruptive stimuli or the responses that are made to them. Taking their analogy from physics and engineering, some scientists have viewed stress as the operation of a deforming force upon a body or person, and the outcome of stress as the strain or deformation which that body or person undergoes.

The physical metaphor of stress-and-strain has certain heuristic value, but like all analogies, its uncritical assumption may conceal more than it reveals (cf. Klausner, ed. 1968; McGrath 1970b). Certain dynamic aspects of the stress process may be obscured by it, such as the way in which the stressed person's responses may alter the source of his discomfort. Exposure to certain levels of tension and anxiety has also been found to benefit people by heightening their awareness of circumstances and of themselves, and by stimulating individuals to develop more varied approaches to life. An existence devoid of stress can become flat, unmodulated, and death-like in its monotony and lack of arousal or creativity (Selye 1956; May 1967; Bernard 1968; Marshall 1968; Bakan 1971).

In addition, stress is not always a threatening or negatively perceived condition. The people of Colville Lake actively sought to involve themselves in certain stresses of life, perceiving some of the conditions of bush existence, for instance, as challenging and exciting. They viewed the environment basically in very positive terms, seeing it not only as a place of difficulty but also as a source of meaning — the setting in which "real Indianness" could be realized. Their lives thus turned on a balance between the pursuit and the avoidance of different types of stress, their definitions of specific situations often being quite ambiguous and contradictory over time. Furthermore, as experimental and observational work elsewhere has shown, within and between groups there can be considerable individual variation in suscepti-bility and reactions to given stresses. As the gender and acculturative differences at Colville Lake themselves suggest, this limits the usefulness of operational definitions based on stimuli alone (cf. Langner and Michael 1963; Appley and Trumbull 1967; McGrath, ed. 1970a; Steiner 1970).

Operationally, therefore, I tried to deal with stress in a manner that recognized but also went beyond the idiosyncracies of personal reaction patterns. I attempted to derive a model from the villagers' over-all system of response to the wide range of disruptive, challenging, and threatening situations which confronted them. From the types of reactions displayed by the whole community, a basic set of response features emerged which could be distinguished from more individualized adaptations: mobility, avoidance, respect for autonomy, and emotional restraint and displacement, were among the coping techniques that stood out.

Some clues served as clear indicators of either positive or negative stress situations. Positively perceived challenges, for example, were often directly evaluated as such by the people in verbal terms. They freely expressed their sense of excitement and anticipation about returning to the bush, for example, or a forthcoming evening of cards or *udzi,* a native gambling game. They thus showed their desire to be tested by pitting themselves against persons and circumstances, whether it was within the context of the environment or a game.

I took as a general indicator of negative stress (or distress) the fact that the people's responses to certain situations constituted a disruption of their usual social and psychological equilibrium. Attempts to restore homeostasis, whether it was a balance in terms of emotional states, social relations, or physical well-being, were utilized as indices of such stressful circumstances. Residence changes, and alterations in the membership of trapping camps, for instance, often indicated the presence of social tensions or environmental threats. Outbursts directed at dogs and inanimate objects, or a person's sudden withdrawal from interaction and social visibility, similarly betrayed the experience of psychological stress.

As these examples indicate, Hare responses were not aimed at a strictly static equilibrium, for coping techniques sought to re-establish a balance at a new level or in a new social context: the techniques of withdrawal and movement, for example, reconstituted life at a new point in time and space. Rather than dealing with the kind of equilibrium model of stress that the medical and material sciences utilize — one that emphasizes a return to a prior state — I found myself involved in a process that was basically progressive rather than regressive. That is, people created or moved on to new situations rather than merely returning to old ones.

The emotional qualities of coping were sometimes transparent, and at other times opaque. In identifying stressful conditions, individuals often noted that certain behaviors by *others*—such as intense emotion or avoidance —were unusual or remarkable to them. Yet these same individuals were often unaware, or unwilling to admit of, their own participation in these same coping styles: people's consciousness of their own stress-reducing techniques was thus far from complete. Nevertheless, they were sensitized to the consequences of many of life's threats by their observations of others' conduct. It was by combining the Hare's insights about their neighbors with my own observations of the community that the nature of people's adaptive repertoire eventually became clear.

In the field, cues to the presence of disruptive states were noted in verbal, symbolic, and visual aspects of behavior. These often involved the delay or displacement of emotional release because of cultural patterns for repressing and restraining feelings. Verbally, for example, negative comments about a person's lack of generosity or helpfulness would be expressed to myself or a third party, thereby showing both the source of, and the response to, the specific tension at issue. Delayed and displaced responses were often exhibited in a highly public manner during drinking parties — events which constituted one of the people's few sanctioned outlets for aggressive release. Resentment over past slights or stinginess, simmering below the surface of relations, would suddenly boil over at such times. Anger, humor, and vindictiveness were also verbally displayed in the course of gossip sessions, and the content of the people's conversations and jokes often enabled me to link these delayed responses with their ultimate causes. Visually, variations of bodily and facial expresssion (such as indications of disgust, despair or disapproval), symbolic forms of non-verbal communication (such as the physical separation of persons through avoidance), and the mobility of individuals for non-economic or non-medical reasons (such as sudden trips to the village or other hunting camps), were also taken to indicate the presence of stress.

***

The various psychological states that researchers have included under the stress concept indicate the many forms that this phenomenon can take. These include "anxiety, conflict, emotional distress, extreme environmental conditions, ego-threat, frustration, threat to security, tension, arousal" and others (Appley and Trumbull 1967: 1). While a full discussion of psychological and physiological causes, symptoms, and adaptations is beyond the scope of this study, the Hare's major sources and means of resolving stress are considered in detail and in context here. Most importantly, an attempt has been made to understand their experience of stress as a process, linking it to other aspects of people's lives, and placing it within the context of their total existence. An extensive account of stresses and coping techniques is given in Tables 7 and 8 of Chapter 7, which indicate the full range of factors and responses which have been subsumed under the operational use of the concept. These tables summarize many of the insights gained during my first stay with the band, but they also reflect a number of subsequent refinements, most of which were made during a return visit to the North several years later.

In the summer of 1971, three years after I had concluded my initial stay in the Arctic, the National Museum of Canada gave me a field grant that enabled me to return to the village of Colville Lake. During the intervening years I had written, thought, and taught a great deal about the people of the community, and I had consequently become aware of some of the weaknesses and lacunae in my original work. It is always a good idea, while doing fieldwork, to interrupt one's research for a few weeks in order to escape, think over one's findings, and then return to the community with one's mind refreshed and one's ideas clarified. Unfortunately, I had not been able to do this during my first time in the Colville area, for there was no economical way to leave the settlement save by dogsled, nor was there any convenient place to go to except for Fort Good Hope — a Dene town of under 400 people — located on the Mackenzie River about 110 miles overland from Colville Lake. Good Hope was, and still is, a very important place for the members of the band, not only because it is the closest settlement of any size for them, but also because they have many friends and kin there whom they visit whenever possible. When a sizeable group of the people decided to travel to Good Hope by dogsled during Easter week of my first year, I consequently joined them for the trip. At the time, however, this journey was simply a continuation of my research rather than a break from it, for I was mainly interested in learning first-hand about the people's experiences in this larger, more "urban" environment. Since Easter week was primarily a time of intense sociability and drinking, I was occupied with the activities of the season, rather than with a review of my field notes or previous experiences.

The opportunity to return to the North in 1971 was therefore a very welcome and essential one, for it gave me a chance to re-examine the insights of my earlier trip after a suitable period of thought and reconsideration. I was equally interested in following up the changes that had occurred among the people during the preceding three years, and I had had some indication of these from an intermittent correspondence that I had kept up with several of the villagers. I knew from their letters that the fur trader had recently died, as had the band's eldest member, ninety-one year old Joseph Tehgu, who had been the community's main repository of folklore and mythology. Some people had also left Colville to go live or work in Good Hope, while a smaller number of others had quit the fort town and shifted their residence back to the settlement. In addition, several children had been born to members of the Behdzi, Yawileh and Bayjere families, and so — over all — the size of the village's population had not appreciably altered.

The main significance of the second trip to Colville lay in the re-evaluation and refinement of my earlier analyses of stress, kinship, mobility, values, and behavioral norms. I was greatly aided in this endeavor by my wife Susan, who had put up with me through the writing of a doctoral thesis and several articles, and who was therefore able to look at the village with the eyes of a neutral but well-informed newcomer. As a specialist in child development and early education, Susan brought a particular kind of awareness to bear on the village's family relations and socialization patterns. We spent most of

June and July together in the community, and during that time Susan recognized and reformulated several aspects of child-rearing and emotional expression that I had previously overlooked or misinterpretted. She also learned to insulate cabins, smoke moose meat, and filet fish: it pleased a number of my "adoptive" relatives in the community that I no longer had to live alone, and that I had a partner to take over some of the "women's work" of our household.

When I returned to the community I also learned about some political and economic changes that were taking place in the people's lives. As the presence of whites and government agencies increased in the North, it was prompting a heightened awareness, among Native groups, of their own ethnic identity. Politically, this new consciousness had taken several forms, including the development of Dene and Inuit advocacy organizations in some of the larger towns of the Northwest Territories. While the work of such groups was not much in evidence as yet at the small settlement of Colville Lake, another expression of this new native awareness was: some younger band members preferred to be referred to by the collective Athabascan term Dene ("The People") rather than the word "Indian." Similarly, instead of "Hare" as a designation for their own ethnic group, these young adults wanted more traditional Athabascan terms to be used: Ka-šo-got'ine ("People Among the Hares") and K'a-šo-got'ine ("Big Willow People") were some of the choices they were suggesting [3]. While I have chosen to retain "Hare" in this edition because of its wide recognition and historical precedent, I have also used Dene and local Athabascan names for the band where appropriate.

The political developments which helped to raise this new ethnic awareness were themselves the outcome of economic changes that were also affecting the people. During the last few years a number of the band's young adult men had obtained seasonal employment from the oil and mineral exploration companies that had become active in the Arctic during the late 1960s and 70s. Although this work was not carried out in the immediate vicinity of Colville Lake, it had nevertheless introduced some subtle influences which affected both the young men involved as well as — indirectly — the life of the entire community. These developments were a harbinger of far greater changes about to emerge in the areas of native rights, land claims, and environmental protection — issues which were to become major priorities among the Dene in the decades ahead. However, at the time of the fieldwork in 1971, none of these events had radically altered the life style of Colville from what it had been in 1967–68, and so I have chosen, in this book, to write of the community as it was during those earlier years. Though that time horizon constitutes the book's "ethnographic present," then, the direction and impact of social change are not ignored here. On the contrary, recent developments are introduced into the narrative wherever relevant, and they are considered more fully in the final chapter, where the political and economic issues that northern people face in modern times are taken up. I argue there that if the Hare and other Northern Dene are to preserve their culture and ecology, then they will need to master the modern political economy with the same ingenuity that they and their ancestors have brought to bear on the problem of survival itself.

CHAPTER 2

Ecology and Community

1. INTRODUCTION

To an outsider, the first sense is desolation, and the second a stab of unexpectedness. To travel over the northern forests is to be confronted with a landscape so seemingly devoid of animation that one is awed by whatever force or fate it was that first led to the peopling of this world. For the uninformed eye can describe no sign of life, and it sees no trace of passing. Nothing appears to move or be, except maybe the wind, and that stirs the spruce trees and ruffles the waters, but it touches nothing else. If there is any life to be sensed here, then its forms are obscure, and its trails are well-hidden.

Mysteries are a luxury for the uninitiated, but to the involved and knowledgeable native, their penetration is a secular necessity. The North may be an enigma to the *mola*, the white man, but it is a living, liveable, and necessary universe for the Indian and the Inuit, who have drawn their lives from its substance, spirit, and matter. In the millenia that have passed since the earliest Asian migrations to North America, few continental environments have gone unexplored by these people, and few life-supporting possibilities have been left undeveloped by them. The high Arctic of the Inuit, with its treeless stretches of northern coast, ice-choked seas, and island tundra, and the sub-Arctic of the Indian, which borders these barren lands with its lake-studded, forested regions, have been utilized as imaginatively and as creatively by native peoples as any area in the world. To Inuit and Indians, the land, water, and life-forms are constantly changing with the weather and the seasons. If the geography appears to be especially hostile, lifeless, and inhospitable to people of other latitudes, then perhaps this is a measure of our own comfortable inexperience with our physical and natural universe.

In contrast to our own visions and estimates, the sub-Arctic forests can often be rich with life, and in a sometimes erratic, sometimes bountiful fashion, they have supported small bands of hunters, gatherers and fishermen for thousands of years [1]. The Dene of Colville Lake are one of the few northern groups who continue to live off the resources of this land, and in an era when other northern peoples have gradually turned their backs on

27

such a life style, the people of the community continue to be adept, insightful, and expert at coping and surviving. Although they now have access to high-powered rifles, steel axes, metal traps, and other items of Western technology, the members of the Colville band also have a long cultural tradition at their disposal, and they have drawn from it a social and philosophical foundation that underlies and informs all their other adaptations. These ideas, which influence their social groups, their movements, and their relations with the environment and with one another, are foremost an outgrowth of the band's ecology and history: it is these latter forces which have molded the people's approach to life, and presented them with the major problems of their existence. The ecological and historical dimensions of the Dene world thus provide a necessary prelude to understanding their contemporary stresses, as well as clues for comprehending how the people deal with them.

2. THE SETTING

The settlement of Colville Lake is situated about fifty miles north of the Arctic Circle, and it is considered by Dene and whites to be one of the last "bush" communities in the Northwest Territories. The term "bush" refers not only to the boreal forest of spruce, tamarack, and willow which surrounds the village, but also to the settlement's isolation and small size. It encompasses the fact that the local people, the *K'apamituegot'ine,* derive most of their livelihood from the land, and that they have only limited access to such modern amenities as medical, schooling, transportation, and communication facilities. These and other services are available to band memebers only at some of the larger communities in the Mackenzie River area, all of which lie from one to several hundred miles distant from the settlement (cf. Map 1). Residents of the village consequently have only limited and intermittent contacts with a small number of white persons, for beyond the settlement's fur trader and missionary, there are no government services or administrative personnel resident in the community itself.

The permanent log houses of the people, which they have constructed from the spruce trees of the surrounding forest, are located on the shores of a bay whose edge curves in a quarter-moon arc around the southeast end of Colville Lake. The lake itself has an irregularly shaped outline which reaches some twenty-five miles from north to south, and about fifteen miles across its greatest width. Colville is one of several large bodies of water lying between Great Bear Lake and the delta of the Mackenzie River, and the community is only 165 miles south of the coast of the Arctic Ocean. Due east of the settlement, about 140 miles distant, lies the western edge of the Barren

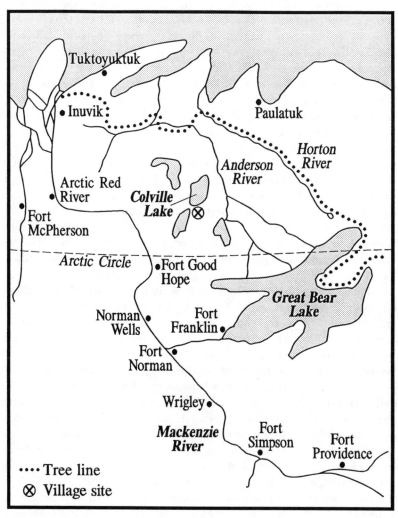

MAP 1   The Mackenzie River Area

Grounds, a zone in which the trees of the taiga (or forest) diminish in size and then slowly give way to the open tundra lands which stretch clear to the shores of Hudson's Bay. The edge of the forested region, technically known as the tree-line, generally follows the course of the Horton River, a waterway which traces its route along the very fringe of the Barrens. Far to the east of the village, the tree-line runs from south to north, but then swings in a westward direction as it passes north and northwest of the settlement. The community is thus well within the borders of the sub-Arctic forest, but it is also within reach of other environments as well. These widespread geographic features — the Barren Grounds, tree-line, Great Bear Lake, and the Mackenzie River — mark the informal boundaries of the territory that is currently travelled over and utilized by the people. Their domain constitutes the northeastern part of what was once the aboriginal range of the Hare [2], and the people have, in fact, constructed their settlement upon the site of an old camping ground. There is thus a strong sense of continuity in the life of the village, for its members are not only living "on native ground," but their numbers are also drawn from the descendants of those bands which once lived and roamed in this area in pre- and post-contact times.

While the *K'apamituegot'ine* have permanent houses and a home village at their disposal, the band is only at the settlement itself for about half of each year. Because most of the winter and spring are spent in dispersed bush camps, the people only experience one another as a social and physical community during certain holidays and seasons. When the fourteen native households of the band are reunited, the village's population may number 65 to 75 people, including the priest, the trader, and the latter's family. Such ingatherings are relatively brief, however, and the size of the local population often fluctuates for social, economic, educational, and environmental reasons. Young children, for example, are sometimes sent from the community to pass the winter at residential schools, and there is also a considerable amount of visiting and shifting of residences between Colville and Fort Good Hope. The village's missionary has opened up a fishing lodge which attracts a small number of wealthy summer toursists to the settlement, and throughout the year, the men and women of the community are constantly on the move in pursuit of wood, wildlife, and sometimes wage labor in order to further their own subsistence.

The isolation of Colville Lake is a major stress to certain local people, and this is a prime impetus for some of the travel they engage in. Band members strive to maintain an extensive network of kinship ties which encompasses not only their fellow villagers, but also a wide set of blood and marital relations in Good Hope. During the Christmas and Easter periods especially, a substantial number of the people go by dogsled to visit the fort town. While Colville, in return, receives its share of native visitors, as well as medical and administrative personnel from Good Hope and other Mackenzie area centers, the community nevertheless remains the most cut-off of all the settlements in the region, and for many of the younger and more assimilated people, this fosters a feeling of marginality.

One index of Colville's isolation is the village's relative inaccessibility. Most settlements in the Mackenzie River valley are located either on the river itself or one of its tributaries, but the people of Colville are without a direct water route to their community. The village can only be reached overland or by small plane, the former being arduous, and the latter both expensive and unpredictable. An overland route to the settlement from Good Hope involves 120 miles of walking and dogpacking in the summer and fall, or the use of a dogsled or snowmobile in the winter and spring. The winter route is somewhat shorter than the summer one because the people can cut across the frozen lakes rather than circumvent them, but the 110 mile journey is still a difficult and hazardous one.

Fort Good Hope is the nearest settlement to Colville Lake, and the only one with which the people have regular overland communication. With a population of about 360 people, the fort boasts a number of facilities and services — including a Hudson's Bay Company store, a nursing station, a Catholic church, a Royal Canadian Mounted Police (RCMP) detachment, a school, an Indian Agent, a Game Officer, an air-strip, and an electric power station — which give it a much more urban flavor than Colville, and which partially accounts for the force with which it variously attracts and repels certain of the people [3].

Much of the limited air traffic reaching Colville comes from Good Hope and two other settlements on the Mackenzie River: Norman Wells, the site of the Territories' only major oil refinery, and Inuvik, a large government administrative center in the Mackenzie delta. The flying distances from Good Hope and the latter two towns are 88, 124, and 220 air miles, respectively, and the flying times in the small, one and two-engine planes which usually make the journey can vary greatly with weather and travel conditions. Fog, rain, snow, strong winds, and low ceilings or temperatures often lead to the delay or cancellation of scheduled flights. Weather conditions in all seasons often change with dramatic suddenness, and can turn a short, routine flight into a long and pracarious one. Pilots departing for Colville have no reliable way of keeping up to date on local flying conditions there. Occasionally an aircraft must turn back in mid-flight or, having gotten as far as the village and finding the lake too rough to land on, the pilot has decided to return without depositing his cargo.

Since Colville is such a small and out-of-the-way settlement, it is also one of the few northern communities that does not have its own air-strip [4]. Small aircraft can land at the village during the winter by using hydraulic skis on the lake ice, and by using floats during the summer months on the open water. This situation, however, adds to the unpredictability of flying, because it makes the status of the lake's surface yet another factor to consider in planning and completing a trip.

A further consequence of Colville Lake's size and marginal location is that it is one of the last remaining communities in the North that still does not have a regularly scheduled airline run. Consequently, all flights into and out of the village have to paid for as personal charters, and because of the great expense this involves, it effectively puts air travel beyond the means of most native families. Such a situation has certain non-economic effects upon the life of the community as well: it essentially gives the priest and trader a local monopoly over the control of air traffic into and out of the settlement. This enhances their positions of power within the village, and Indian people, who are very aware not only of their isolation, but of their limited ability to overcome it, often feel manipulated by the missionary or storekeeper because of the latter's greater access to aircraft. People who want to leave or return to the village by plane thus experience the dominance of whites in this area of life as well: native resentment of this control is not only a "political" sentiment, but is also an indication of the value which band members place upon the freedom of mobility as a defining quality of fulfillment [5].

***

One gets a very keen sense of the village's isolation when flying out to it from one of the larger communities in the area. Coming from any direction, one passes over vast expanses of apparently lifeless country. Setting out from Inuvik near the Arctic coast, one first encounters endless stretches of flat muskeg. These are broken only by brush and scrub, lonely stands of isolated spruce or willow, and thousands of small streams, lakes, and ponds, which lay on the surface like drops of water spattered on a polished table. In the North, the table is not the earth's surface, however, but rather the permafrost (i.e., the permanently frozen ground and ice) which lies a few inches or feet just below the soil cover. The permafrost prevents the water — the rain, and the melted snow and ice of each year — from draining off, and so bodies of water collect in all the depressions and low areas on the land's surface.

As one travels further to the southeast, moving over the muskeg and closer to the village, one passes well within the tree-line: the forest becomes thicker and more extensive, and the coniferous trees stand taller. The landscape also loses much of its flatness and occasionally rolls up into small hills. The topography would continue in this way to the south and southwest of the community if one were to travel on towards Fort Good Hope. The trees in that direction get larger, and one begins to find stands of birch when passing south of the Arctic Circle.

In the summer there are few signs of life to be seen from the air: a moose or bear may be spotted if one is fortunate and flying low enough, and some waterfowl, or a trout breaking water, can be seen on the lakes. Otherwise, the land seems to sleep in muted tones of brown and green under the long hours of light from the midnight sun. But the whole landscape is really alive with small game and with the countless mosquitoes, gnats and insects which thrive on the wet summer muskegs and bodies of water. The lakes are full of trout, whitefish, sucker, loche, and other fresh-water species. Flying over Colville Lake towards the village, one can spot native fish camps along the lakeshore, and follow the wake of small canoes used by the men to check their gill nets.

In the winter, the colors, the fauna, and the lives of the people become transformed. The country becomes a sea of white, cut by the brown-black shafts of millions of spruce trees. Even in the dark, sunless days of late December, herds of grazing caribou can still be spotted from the air, as can the snaking dogsled trails which cut through the bush and over the frozen lakes. At Christmas and Easter times, sprays of clean, milky funnels of white smoke lift from the ground and announce the village. But during the rest of this period, from the winter's beginning in October to the thawing of the snow and lake ice in June, the people are scattered over a 100 mile radius in trapping and hunting camps of one, two, or three families. Except for the smoke from the missionary and fur trader's houses, and the tell-tale convergence of dogsled trails, the village is lost in the white for most of the year.

***

The dispersed camps of the Dene leave their own patterned imprint on the winter taiga. A December domesday chronicle would reveal eight or ten household clusters, far-flung and island-like throughout the forest, each with a ring of satellite tents at over-night trapline stops. Sixty miles to the north of the village one might find Wilfred Ratehne, his wife, and children, camped together with the family of Wilfred's brother-in-law, Maurice Bayjere. Down along the eastern shore of Colville Lake would be a likely place for the household of George Ratehne, Wilfred's brother, along with the family of George's daughter, Paula and her husband, Albert. Farther to the west, forty miles away at *Tueš̌o* (Aubry Lake), Albert's cousin Peter Dehdele frequently camps, and he and his wife Lena are sometimes joined there by the family of Lena's sister, Nora Godanto. South of Colville, along the eastern shore of Lac Belot, Leon and Pierre Behdzi have a favorite trapping area, while their brother Paul usually prefers to go after the marten and fox in the region just to the east and west of the settlement. Pierre's married step-son Charlie, however, is especially concerned that he and his wife Adele have good hunting during the winter, and so they are most often found to the southwest, either at *Wokatue,* or one of the other small lake districts favored by the caribou. To the northeast are a series of small hills and lakes where two other Behdzi households often camp together, those of Yen (Pierre, Leon and Paul's brother), and Yen's son Yašeh. Finally, far to the east, along the shores of the Anderson River, and sometimes as distant as the western Barrens, old Joseph Tehgu and his descendants can be found: their tents include the families of his daughter Berona Yawileh, and his married grandson Fred — a large clan whose members number 15 people from four generations.

These fourteen families of the band, alternately dispersed and united in successive seasons of each year, are a strongly independent people: they are as proud of their autonomy as they are conscious of their reliance on one another. André Yawileh, old Berona's husband, a deeply conservative, amiable man in his sixties, who was born in the Colville bush and has lived his entire life there, once observed that "the people belong together with this country, and what is best about our life is that it lets us be free." Old Joseph, André's father-in-law, a person with perhaps the deepest sense of tribal history, a man whose 90-year old face is carved and ridged like evergreen bark, once remarked that "these people have always needed one another," for as much as they may argue or quarrel, he noted, "who could survive here alone?"

As Joseph himself perceives, there is a tension in Indian life, a conflict between the ties that bind the Dene, and the impulses that force them apart. Band members need, respect, and look to one another, for they are kin, survivors, and fellow-travellers in this world, and yet the intensity of their shared existence back at the village occasionally divides and drives them from this very company. This is one of the greatest paradoxes underlying the people's life.

For the band as a whole there is another major ambiguity: that of their autonomy and commitment to the land on the one hand, and their depen- dence upon outside goods and services on the other. The residents of Colville continuously experience their reliance upon the government agents and facilities of Fort Good Hope, and yet their traditional culture has always kept the people at a social and psychological, as well as a physical distance, from the life-styles and amenities of the fort. While acknowledging the importance of the town in their lives, the *K'apamituegot'ine* have also attempted to contain some of its hold and its influence on them. Up through the first half of the twentieth century, for example, the more traditional families visited the fort as infrequently as possible, and kept their use of its expensive trade goods to a minimum. So when a mission and small store were finally established at

Colville in the early 1960s — over 100 years after such institutions had been inaugurated at Good Hope — these permanent facilities at the "bush" settlement bestowed on it a degree of independence from the fort that it had never known before. Over the decades, therefore, the band has been able to preserve its identity by drawing on diverse and anbiguous sources, including its history, its physical isolation, its fabric of kinship, and its ties to an environment where — in Joseph's phrase — "the people belong."

3. THE REGION

The resources and the rhythms of the North provide the framework within which Dene men and women play out the drama of their lives. The ecology of their world is complex because sub-Arctic Canada is a region that contains within it at least as many environments as it has seasons. In each locale, the different periods of the year create landscapes that are rich in contrasts and character. From mid-winter's darkness to mid-summer's midnight sun, from plentiful fall fish-runs to the silent, lean weeks of February, the people's life on the land is one of extremes.

This is apparent not only in the feel, color, and bounty of the earth, but also in the texture and quality of the water, for the North has more of its mass covered by lakes, ponds, swamps, streams and rivers than almost any other land surface in the world. Scientists have estimated that these bodies may account for as much as 25 to 40% of this region, and up to 60% of the "land" in some localities [6]. These liquid bodies draw their contents from the glaciers, snows, and rains of each year, and combine them to form a massive drainage system which eventually carries most of the Northwest Territories running waters into the Arctic Ocean.

Colville is one of the larger lakes in this drainage system. Although its surface is frozen for eight months out of every year, the lake is nevertheless continuously gaining and losing water from a number of sources and outlets. It empties out towards the Arctic Ocean at *Duta* ("Among the Islands"), a delta-like stream whose island-filled mouth lies at the lake's extreme northeast corner. Numerous other creeks feed into the lake on all its shores, including the one that the people call *Coyngeriwelin* ("The Stream That Runs by The Cabin"), through which the waters of Aubry Lake flow into Colville.

The members of the band have an intimate knowledge of the lake because of their daily involvement with it in all seasons. Colville is foremost a source of food for the people and their dogs, providing them with trout, pike, white-fish, loche, sucker, and grayling [7]. White-fish and pike average between three and four pounds per fish, while trout are sometimes taken at over forty pounds apiece. People fish the waters of Colville and neighboring bodies throughout the year, relying primarily upon nylon and rope gill nets, which have long since replaced the willow bark fish nets which the "old-timers" once made. The people's ancestors also constructed dams and weirs to barricade the channels of narrow streams, and then used dip nets to catch the fish that were blocked off in this way. Although none of the families have utilized these techniques for capturing fish in several decades, most of the older people can remember and describe their own youthful experiences with such activities. Leon Behdzi once recounted the excitement of life at a fall fish camp with such vividness, speaking of the shouting people running along the banks, and the scooping up of silver trout in the sprays of water and moonlight, that the young people listening to him induced Leon to build a spruce-and-babiche model of an old dip net, and they then used it to catch small fish in one of the tiny streams near the village.

While the people have abandoned much of their ancient fishing technology, they continue to utilize most of the knowledge that accompanied it. Leon and his brothers place their nets in the same locations that have proven most fruitful for generations, and every autumn, during late September and early October, a large group of families can still be found at *Tuešotadeli^n*, the mouth of *Coy^{n}geriweli^n* on Aubry Lake's south shore, awaiting the start of the fall fish migration. When the runs start, the people — working in concert with one another — first string gill nets across the stream's narrow passage. Then the men, paddling out in canoes, and illumined at night by the glow of gas lamps or moonlight, help drive the swarming shoals of fish into the waiting rope and mesh. In three or four nights' work, enough food can sometimes be gathered in this manner to last a household for several weeks.

Fishing is a year-round rather than a seasonal activity, for the people could hardly survive without this major supplement to their other sources of food. Gill nets continue to be used during the winter and spring, being set and then extracted from under the lake ice by a simple but arduous method (cf. Figure 1). Whenever possible, two men work together on these tasks, helping one another to first position and later check their respective nets, often dividing their total catch among themselves.

In mid-October, shortly after the lake had frozen and the ice was thick enough to support people, Leon Behdzi and *beša*, "his brother's son" Yašeh, showed me the basic way in which band members go about this work. Though the procedure they use is a detailed one to describe, it reveals the ingenius use of a simple technology — rope, rocks, and naturally shaped pieces of wood — to solve an important technical problem. First, back at their camp, Leon and Yašeh prepared their nets by tying sprucewood floats along the top edges and stone sinkers across the bottom. The men then hauled the netting and the tools that they needed out to their fishing location by dogsled. At the site, they began by chopping a line of holes in the lake ice, spacing the openings about twelve feet apart from one another. When this series of holes stretched out over a distance that equalled the length of one of their nets, Leon tied the end of a long coil of rope to the base of a fifteen-foot straight pole. He then introduced this stick into the first opening, and shoved it towards the second hole. Yašeh stood over the second opening with a carved *tehⁿehdiwoⁿ*, a large forked stick, which he used to catch and guide the pole under the ice when it reached this opening. The two men continued to advance the pole in this manner until it reached the final hole in the series, and they then pulled it out onto the frozen lake.

All this time, the pole had been simultaneously trailing the long rope in its wake: the latter now reached from the first opening, where several feet of it still sat unravelled on the ice surface, all the way to the last hole, where Leon held the rope's other end in his hand. Yašeh then got the prepared and folded fishnet out of the sled, attaching one end of it to a large stick from which a single, downward-pointing branch projected. Yašeh carried the stick and net over to the first opening in the lake, and having firmly tied the net's loose end to the coiled portion of rope remaining atop the ice, he signalled to Leon. The latter then began to haul on the rope end that was in his hands, and as he did, his pulling slowly unfolded the net at Yašeh's feet and carried it through the first hole and into the water. A minute later, Leon having literally come to the end of his rope, the entire net was under the ice, neatly suspended in the water between the first and last openings. Leon next attached a branched stick to his end of the net, just as Yašeh had done earlier on the far side. Each man then fixed an anchor stone to his end of the netting. A few moments later they each knocked a final pair of

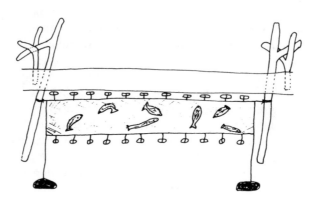

FIGURE 1   Winter Fishing Under The Ice

upright forked sticks — ones with upward-pointing branches — into the ice near their respective openings. That done, the two men poured ice chips and water around the bases of these last poles, which soon froze their bottom ends solidly into place. Finally, taking the branched sticks which they had earlier tied to the ends of the submerged net, Yašeh and Leon now hooked these by their branches onto the notches of the stationary, forked poles which they had frozen upright in the ice. This last step secured the net in place until it was time to check it for fish. By the time we were back in camp, all the holes we had cut in the lake's surface were starting to ice over.

Two days later we returned to the site, and set about freeing the branched poles at the net ends from the solid layer of ice which had since formed around them. Yašeh cut through the ice around one pole, and Leon worked to free the other. When both poles were loose from the surrounding ice, Yašeh pulled his end of the net out far enough to untie it from its stick and anchor stone. Then, in the place where the pole had been, he secured the tail of a long rope to the netting. When he had finished this task, Leon pulled out his end pole, and then slowly began to haul the attached net from the water. As he did so, he methodically extracted the thirty-one fish which had been caught; by stunning the ones which thrashed about with a sharp blow on the head, he made them easier to handle, and also spared the net from excessive tearing. As Leon did all this, he folded the emptied portions of the net into a careful pile at his side. In the process of checking the net, he had also been pulling along behind it — under the ice — the long rope which Yašeh had attached to the far end a few minutes ago. This cord was the means by which the men now re-set the net.

To do this, Yašeh simply picked up the free end of the rope which lay at his feet, and by hauling out the recently submerged section of it, he simultaneously pulled the piled up net at the other hole back under the ice. With Leon carefully feeding the netting back into the water, the net's entire length was soon back in position under the ice. Yašeh then untied his end of the net from the long rope and re-attached it to its original end-pole and anchor stone. Finally, he and Leon re-hooked their respective end-poles onto the stationary upright forks, which once again held everything in place until the ice was reformed around the end-poles themselves. The net was thus held in position to trap fish again, and throughout the rest of the winter it could be rechecked in this manner as often as necessity, the weather, and the men's inclinations would dictate. One change that would occur in the process over the next six months would be the increasing amounts of time and effort required to do it as the ice grew deeper: from an October thickness of four inches, the ice would grow, by March, to a depth of over four feet.

***

The waters of Colville and the surrounding lakes are highways as well as food sources for the people. Frozen and criss-crossed by sled trails during the winter, and plowed by paddles and outboards during during the summer, these direct and unobstructed water routes are utilized by band members whenever they are on the move. After the October freeze-up, people travel across the lakes with their dogs to traplines and hunting camps, and between the break-up of the spring ice and the following winter, they utilize boats to check their summer fish nets, as well as to haul in logs, hunt waterfowl, and locate moose.

There is actually a technological split within the community which reflects a key difference in how the Dene utilize the resources and advantages of the lakes. The main division is between men and women, for females almost never handle or make use of boats on their own. This gender-defined distinction in expertise is quite rigid: women do not make or paddle canoes, they do not operate or repair outboard motors, they never go hunting by boat, and they never check their family's fish nets from a watercraft. These separate areas of experience are not only an outcome of the sexual division of labor, they also stem from some deeply held beliefs that the older people still articulate. One afternoon, while I was helping André and Berona clean their fish nets in the village, André explained that:

> Women can do a lot of work with nets and boats on the land. They help us mend the old nets, and Berona sewed and patched the canvas cover on my hunting canoe. Certainly, they clean all the fish when they are brought in. But for a woman to paddle out on the lake to empty the nets would never happen. They just wouldn't do it. It's bad luck for fishing — very bad, the old-timers say. The boat would then be no good and the fish would leave the nets and not come back.

André smiled and threw a quick, rhetorical glance over at Berona, who just nodded her head in agreement. But I asked her anyway, and she raised her chin, pursed her lips, and laughed a quiet "no, I wouldn't do it."

There are some women who do visit their family's nets during the winter when the men are gone on the trapline, but this does not involve their use of watercraft. Fishing spots can then be reached via dogsled and snowshoe, thus maintaining the separation between women and boats. The only time that females can be found in watercraft is when an entire household is moving to or returning from a bush camp during a season of open water. Even during the winter — as I learned from my own, inadvertently feminine behavior — females in the more tradition-minded families avoid crossing directly over a net which has been set under the ice.

The limited access which women have to water transport is actually a key to a larger set of differences between the life styles of males and females. Men enjoy a much greater amount of mobility than women, and this pertains to a number of travelling modes, boats being just one case in point. Visiting patterns between camps, dogsled trips to the village, short-term residence changes, and the day-to-day subsistence pursuits of hunting and trapping all involve the men in far more travel than the women. Since the capacity for mobility is often used by the people as a means of avoiding stressful situations, the greater access that males have to movement becomes a basic difference in the coping styles and adaptations of the two sexes [8].

There is not only a stylistic and technological difference between the mobility patterns of males and females, but also a *de facto* divison among the men themselves. The younger adults make frequent and heavy use of larger, home-made skiffs powered by *klaso^n* or "kickers" (outboard motors), while the older, more conservative men rely primarily on the smaller, spruce-framed *alaiya* ("hunting" or "rat", i.e., muskrat, canoes), which are the traditional form of water transport in the area. While these "rat" canoes are now covered with canvas rather than bark, the village's elder and abler craftsmen, such as Leon and André, continue to construct their own hulls entirely from local materials. They feel safer and more comfortable in these craft for, as Leon once expressed it:

> I don't know anything about using motors like that... I can't fix one of them. If it stopped or broke, I couldn't do anything to it and I'd be stuck out on the lake. So all I know real good is my "rat" canoe. I'll leave those *klaso^n* to Yašeh, Adam and those boys.

The motor-powered skiffs of the younger men are, indeed, more complex, as well as larger, faster, and actually much more stable than the narrow *alaiya*. The males who operate these larger boats are able to afford the engines, tools, and equipment necessary for these craft because they pursue winter trapping far more assiduously than their fathers and uncles, and so earn more fur money. Like so many other Western items, however, their outboard motors also have some inherent — one is tempted to say purposely built-in — disadvantages. Not only is their obsolescence apparently planned, but — as far as the people can see — so are their constant breakdowns. Beyond being expensive to buy and fuel, then, the "kickers" are also unreliable and often frustrating. Since no replacement parts are sold in the village, any needed materials, like the engines themselves, have to be ordered from the "outside" (i.e., from outside the Territories), which can leave a motor idle for weeks or months, and its owner dependent on others for equipment. Outboards, as well as the gas-powered chain-saws which some young men have bought, consequently create a community of interest among their owners, who share their parts and expertise with one another, and often seem to spend more time fixing their equipment than actually using it.

A similar set of concerns binds the elder canoe-users together. Their fragile, exposed, and unstable craft require careful handling and decision-making, and a constant awareness of wind and water conditions on the lake. These men consequently set their fish nets within the bay which borders the village: its surface tends to be calmer than the more open waters, and it is protected from strong north winds by the projecting tip of land at its northeast entrance. Singly and in groups, one can often see the older men studying the condition of the bay as they go about their daily tasks, and much of their casual conversation turns upon the hazards and possibilities of that day's fishing.

Throughout the summer and fall, the senior men usually check their nets twice a day. Because they only like to go out on the lake when the wind is at its lowest, their trips are most often made in the morning and evening. Furthermore, just as the people of the band camp together in family clusters because they do not like to be alone in the winter bush, older males similarly gain security by paddling out to their nets in groups of two, three, or as many as six canoes at a time. Since the approximate time of day at which they go out is known to all of them, as soon as one man is seen heading towards his canoe, two or three others may also take up their paddles and join him. And since the men's nets are usually set in the same area of the bay, they can all travel out and back together. If the weather and the condition of the lake look threatening, a group of them may stand on the shore where their boats are beached, and then discuss the advisability of going out before they come to a decision. The process is an informal one in which casual remarks and the sharing of opinions slowly build into a consensus. Like other group decisions made by community members, there is neither a formal vote or an overt display of power. As in the sphere of politics, the consensus is binding because it grows from within rather than being imposed. It is rare to see one man paddling out on the lake when the others have determined it is too dangerous to do so.

The stresses and hazards which lake fishing present for elderly men are thus handled by them in a number of ways. In the first place they seek to minimize the dangers they face by fishing in the safest, most sheltered areas. Secondly, they visit their nets at the calmest times of the day, first conferring with one another when conditions on the lake are doubtful. They also keep from their nets and boats the only persons — their wives, sisters, and daughters — whose presence could conceivably bring bad luck and misfortune. Finally, the men enhance their security (and, equally important, their *sense* of security) by visiting their nets in groups rather than going out individually. Taken together, these simple strategies illustrate the kind of repertoire by means of which people cope with many of the stresses confronting them.

All the men of the village, regardless of their age, have an encyclopedic knowledge of the lake and its properties. The younger men, whose boats enable them to travel extensively, have each developed a detailed, mental map of shoals, sandbars, and shallow spots, and they share with their fathers and elder kinsmen an intimate familiarity with the lake's resources, their seasonal availability, and the dimensions and significance of the shoreline. This cognitive control of the environment, this internalization of its surfaces and content, is a hallmark not only of the people's spatial orientation, but also of their existential approach to the qualities of ecological survival. Their knowledge derives from relationships — with people and places and their properties — and so experience is invested with a strong consciousness of both the human and the natural environment.

Young Philip Ratehne, Wilfred's seventeen year-old son, first acquainted me with the richness and subtlety of the lake's contours by taking me with him on a hunting trip along its eastern shore. Every landmark that we passed drew forth some comment from him — "good duck hunting," "muskrats in the spring," "pools of grayling in the fall" — and, featured or unmarked, there was a Dene name for every major point where land and water met. Back at the village, the lake's identity continued to unfold, for Philip took the pen and paper that I offered him, and in one smooth motion, he outlined the entire shoreline shown in Map 2, and then proceeded to dot its borders with a score of native place-names (Table 1). As we read over and translated these from *deneké*, and as Philip — squinting through his one good eye — explained what he knew of their origin, a keen sense of history as well as geography emerged. Hunts, haunts, battles, deaths, the nature of the beasts and their seasons, encounters, and the real or more-than-real persons who have known this land were all evoked, turning Philip's map into an environmental almanac which recalled time while it described space [9].

***

The people of Colville Lake have access to a large number of foods during the course of every year, but their meals are nevertheless focused around a small number of basic items, particularly caribou meat, fish, and small game. Along with ptarmigan and snowshoe (or "varying) hare, both of which band members trap and snare at all seasons, fish are one of the few year-round food resources that Dene can count on. They are equally significant for feeding the several hundred sled dogs that the band supports, for without these canines the winter mobility and survival of the people would now be impossible. When families are able to accumulate a surplus of fish, they consequently preserve and store these against a time of future need. In the winter fish can simply be frozen by placing them atop an outdoor storage platform or *alahfi* ("stage"). In the summer and fall, when the temperature is too warm to permit this, the people dry and smoke the fish, a process which preserves them for the winter months to come. Even in the late autumn, when sub-freezing conditions have not yet begun, band members will take long willow branches, run them laterally through the gills of ten fish,

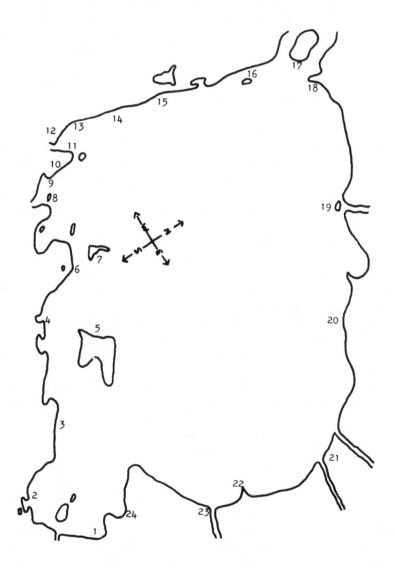

MAP 2   Colville Lake Native Place Names *(based on a drawing by Philip Ratehne)*

and then store several of these racks on an *alahfi*. While these "stickfish," as the Hare call them, will turn slightly rotten before the winter sets in, they nevertheless make excellent and convenient dog food.

One other storage and preservation technique that the people use for fish has a double purpose. The men in several families, including André Yawileh, Maurice Bayjere, and their grown sons, have dug dep pits near their homes, going down seven or more feet into the permafrost layer. These holes, with their walls of perpetually frozen material, thus constitute underground ice-houses with excellent storage potential. The tops of the pits are covered over with moss and brush, and just a small opening is left at ground level. Fish are thrown into these holes in the fall and early winter, and although a certain amount of decay occurs, the coldness of the pits slows and retards the process of putrefaction so that the fish do not fall apart or lose their nutritive value. While their powerful stench prevents the people from eating these fish, no such inhibition affects the dogs, who thrive on such food during the winter. Their penetrating odor also lends the fish added value, for the long distances over which their stench is broadcast makes them excellent bait for winter traps. Marten, fox, and other animals are attracted by their smell, and so when the people move out into the bush to pursue furs, they try to take a supply of this "pitfish" with them for use as bait on their traplines.

The main source of meat in the people's diet are the large, migratory herds of caribou which move into the Colville area from the Barren Grounds each November. The herds break up into smaller, roving units of several dozen animals once they reach the Colville vicinity, and they remain in the region until late May or early June, at which time they reform into larger groups to migrate back to the Barrens for the summer months. The people hunt the caribou throughout the winter and spring, preserving their meat for the summer either in underground ice-houses or in the form of drymeat, smoked meat, or pemmican.

The snaring and spearing of caribou, the use of bows, arrows, and deadfalls, the construction of pounds, pits, surrounds, and drift fences, and the utilization of large communal drives to take great quantities of game, were all once prime hunting techniques in the region. However, under the impact of modernization and new technologies, they have long since disappeared from the band's repertoire. Instead, men now take large game with high-powered rifles, pursuing them either individually or in cooperation with the other hunters in their encampments. The scattering of the caribou into small herds during their winter stay, and the people's intense dependence on them for their own survival, are factors which necessitate the band's corresponding dispersal during much of every year. And since the fish, fur, and fuel upon which the *K'apamitueg'ot'ine* also depend are similarly dispersed over the landscape, Colville's families experience their yearly separation from one another as a stressful but necessary dimension of their ecology.

The importance of the caribou in the people's lives includes the utility of the animals' hides and bones as well as the edibility of their meat. An adult, depending on its sex, its age, and the season in which it is killed, not only weighs some 150 to 450 pounds (Burt and Grossenheider 1952: 234; Kelsall 1968: 29), but its skin, hair, antlers, and skeleton also provide the people with materials essential for their survival and well-being. The hides, which the women laboriously clean, scrape, soak, stretch and tan, are made into

---

TABLE 1

Colville Lake Native Place Names

1. *Sanefíga* .... "White Hair of An Old Man"
2. *Mits'airmošontin* .... "Mits'air's Mother is Buried Here"
3. *Ala'inurat'adu* .... "Airplane Point"
4. *Óndahwadon* .... "Sitting Jackfish"
5. *Duga* .... "White Island"
6. *Nofayfïwehon* .... "Loche Skull Point" (actually a hill)
7. *Fólehdúway* .... "Sawbill Duck Island"
8. *Duehtséhgay* .... "Between the Island" (an inlet)
9. *Ehgoneriwelin* .... "Fish Scale Stream"
10. *Behguhulehsonti* .... "Toothless Old Lady Buried There"
11. *Gok'ayéh* .... "Blackbird Eddy"
12. *Coyngeriwelin* .... "The Stream That Runs by The Cabin" (the stream that connects Colville and Aubry Lakes)
13. *Bayrehhohéjin* .... "Hooked a Big Trout"
14. *Ehjirihofïwehnewehun* .... "Musk Ox Skull"
15. *Wonraglin* .... "Alone Again"
16. *Fiziahdá* .... "Spruce Gum Point"
17. *Duta* .... "(The Stream) Among the Islands"
18. *Ahdahdahwelay* .... "The Island at The End of a Point" (this is actually part of the point, being connected to it by a thin strip of land)
19. *Bahkahdúweh* .... "Sea Gull Island"
20. *Behk'áhrehedah* .... "Sea Gull Point"
21. *Dedélilin* .... "Sucker Creek"
22. *Sehléhrahdah* .... "Sehlehr's Point"
23. *Sehléhrriwelin* .... "Sehlehr's Creek"
24. *K'apamí* .... "Ptarmigan Net" (the village itself)

moccasins, mukluks, and mittens; the untanned skins are cut into cord-like strands of rawhide *babiche*, the sinews become thread; and the softened hides whose hair is left on are utilized as sleeping rugs. The pelage of the caribou provides excellent warmth, not only because of the thickness and length of the coat, but also because each caribou hair is hollow inside, and thus carries within it a highly insulative pocket of air. Some of the more assiduous and practical women in the band, such as Lena Dehdele, Bertha Ratehne, and Berona, also sew winter socks and slippers out of caribou hides and hair. These pieces of footwear are made with the hair turned inwards against the wearer's skin, and when worn under a pair of well-sewn mukluks, they enable a person to withstand some of the coldest weather that the North offers. In the midst of a seventy-degree-below-zero spell one February, Peter Dehdele and I were camped out on his trapline, and he held up a pair of caribou slippers that his wife had made him:

> I don't think I could take it for long out there without these. Two weeks ago all I had were those lousy woollen ones from the store, but they weren't worth a damn. It was forty or fifty below and my feet were freezing. Then I had Lena make me these. That's some difference I'll tell you. I put these on and I don't care if it's sixty below — it's like I don't feel anything and my feet never hurt.

There are thus some traditional native materials for which there are still no adequate Western substitutes. The *babiche* which the people make from caribou hide is another of these highly versatile resources. It is not only essential for constructing the webbing of snowshoes, but is also used to make or fix a wide variety of other items, including ice-scoops, sleds, dog harnesses, snares, and whips. I have seen men who could not secure parts for their chain-saws, "kickers," and snowmobiles make inventive use of *babiche* and spruce wood to do temporary repairs on their engines.

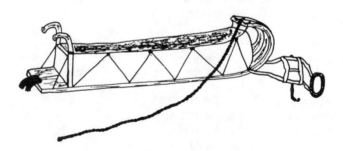

FIGURE 2   Native Dogsled with Wrapper (Cariole), Backboard, Braker, Head-Line and First or "Wheel" Harness

The people have, of course, abandoned a great many aspects of their old life style. Caribou are hunted quite differently from aboriginal ways, and the animals are not utilized as fully as they once were. In the band's low carbohydrate diet, however, the large quanitites of back-fat that caribou provide still allow the people to generate the body heat that they need to withstand the winter cold (Symington 1965: 49-50; Kelsall 1968: 41, 209-211). The women continue to smash and boil the caribou bones in order to get the fat and tallow, and they also split open the larger leg bones and use their sharper edges — as well as scapulae — for hide scrapers. But neither bone or stone are utilized now as needles or knife blades, nor are antlers employed as ice chisels any more. Iron and steel have superceded these latter uses of caribou, just as modern containers have replaced the intestines and stomachs of caribou as convenient storage pouches for fat and liquids. Similarly, curved and frozen caribou leg skins, which were once loaded up with food, and then dragged from camp to camp like toboggans, have given way to the bent wooden planks, backboards, and canvas sides of the modern cariole or dogsled (cf. Figure 2).

The people's ancestors also made much more use of caribou and hare skins for clothing by making parkas, ponchos, capes, leggings, moccasins, mittens, pants, hoods, and entire head-to-toe outfits from these materials. In the "old days," as well as in modern times, these tasks have remained the specialized occupation of women, and it is usually the oldest females who have been the most skilled at tanning, sewing, and manufacturing techniques. In the past, hare pelts were cut spirally to make a single, continuous strip, and then several of them were plaited together by the women to make a garment. Caribou skins, generally with the hair left on, were sewn together with babiche and sinew to produce a garment. As was true of neighboring groups like the Chipewyan, eight to ten caribou pelts were probably needed to make each person's winter outfit in the old days (Oswalt, 1966, p.25) [10]. Nowadays, women continue to take great pride in their sewing abilities, as well as aesthetic pleasure in the embroidered, floral patterns they create out of colored thread and beads on the surface of parkas and mukluks.

A commitment to traditional types of caribou clothing actually affected the mobility and territoriality of the Dene in earlier times. This is because the kinds of caribou skins that were most useful for clothing could only be gotten at certain seasons of the year, and only in certain locations. Ironically, the winter pelts of caribou, despite their long hair, were really not suitable for large garments. Rather, it was the late summer and early fall hides which were in optimum condition, and this necessitated that the people pursue the large herds out onto the Barren Grounds at those times in order to obtain these pelts. The seasonal quality of caribou hides has to do with two features of the animals' biology. One is that the long winter hairs easily break and fall out after continuous use in a garment, which would require that such clothing be replaced regularly. And second, the underside of almost every mature caribou's skin is infested and pockmarked by large numbers of warble fly larvae. This infestation, from which the caribou are never really free, follows an annual cycle in which the flies pupate in early summer, and then reinfest the caribou before the onset of winter. The flies burrow down to the underside of the pelt on the animal's legs or rump, migrate to the back area, and then, after cutting breathing holes, utilize the surrounding skin as food during the coming months of cold. Such infested hides can be decimated by the following spring, making these animals of very limited utility for clothing [11].

The caribou who offered the people the best cothing pelts available, then, turned out to be the newborn calves of each summer — animals who accompanied their mothers to the Barrens, but whose skins had not yet been populated with flies. Adult hides were also in optimum condition at this season because the breathing holes of last winter's larvae had healed over with scars (Kelsall 1968: 274). In the late summer and autumn, the hairs of both calves and adults were short but firmly rooted, and their skins were thin, relatively unmarked, and very pliable. Members of the various Indian bands which bordered the Barrens therefore made an annual trek to the summer grounds of the caribou to hunt them on the tundra. The Hare and neighboring Dene groups to the southeast — especially the Chipewyans, Yellowknives, and Dogribs — were literally "edge of the woods people," as much at home on the tundra as they were in the taiga [12]. The Hare who went on these late summer hunts dried and smoked the meat they obtained there for easier transport back to the forest, and also brought with them enough hides to make new sets of winter clothing. In the Colville area, these summer hunting expeditions were still being made into the first decades of this century. Although nowadays the people rely heavily upon the commercially made clothing found at the local trading post, the elder Yawilehs, Behdzis, Ratehnes and Bayjeres can all remember these trips to the Barrens in their own youth, as well as the caribou hide clothing which they once wore [13]. Their memories and experiences are thus a direct link with the band's past, a reminder of the vast geographic areas over which the Dene have always wandered.

The earlier travels of the people out onto the Barren Grounds also brought them within reach of the musk-ox herds, which were once a significant part of the food supply and trading economy of the northeasterly Hare. Unfortunately, under the impetus of the fur trade in musk-ox pelts in the latter part of the nineteenth century, the herds to the north of Great Bear Lake became severely depleted, and so musk-oxen have not figured prominently in the people's economy since the early 1900s (Kelsall, Hawley and

Thomas 1971). Besides the caribou, then, there are only two other large mammals — moose and bear — from which band members now obtain meat and hides, and neither of these is as plentiful for them as the caribou have been. Bears are actually feared by many of the villagers, and everyone in the community knows the stories of the close encounters which André Yawileh and other men have had with these animals. The browns, blacks, and grizzlies of the region are only hunted infrequently, and more have been killed in the last few years because of chance and circumstance than by design or tracking.

Moose, however, are regarded in a totally different manner by the people. Though scarce, they are unquestionably the most highly valued animal in the area, not only for the great amount of meat that they supply, but — most important of all — for their tough, thick hides, which provide the Dene with the best possible material for mittens and mukluks. In the depth of winter, these pieces of foot and hand wear protect the most vulnerable parts of the people's bodies from frostbite, and so their quality and manufacture are a prime concern. No other material available to the band can compare with moose hide for these purposes, and so there is considerable excitement whenever one of these animals is shot, and its meat and hide divided up among the hunter's kin and friends.

Moose hide is so scarce — and so valuable — that the people of Colville carry on a very active trade for it with the families of Good Hope. Due to the fort's distinctive forest ecosystem of willow, poplar, and birch, the area around it still abounds with moose, and the members of the Colville band receive several hides each year from their friends and relatives in the town. This trading relationship is one of reciprocity, however, for there are also some key resources to which the villagers, in their turn, enjoy greater access. The caribou, for example, restrict their winter movements to the climax spruce-lichen forest characteristic of the Colville area, and because the herds therefore do not migrate as far to the southwest as Good Hope, the townspeople often look to their more isolated northeastern kin for seasonal gifts of caribou meat [14]. The fishing around Colville also surpasses that found in the vicinity of Good Hope, and it is a rare dogsled or plane that leaves for the fort without several bundles of smoked trout, as well as a pile of caribou quarters. There is thus a regional trade network, operating along kinship lines, which redresses certain ecological imbalances, and gives people access to bush foods and materials that would otherwise be scarce commodities for them.

The importance and precariousness of game in the people's lives is reflected not just in efforts at trade, but in acts of taboo, reverence, and generosity. In regard to the latter behavior, band members share meat, fish, and dogfood with one another as part of a cultural ethic of mutual aid. In their small, kin-based community, this moral attitude also extends to the loan of equipment, tools, and sled dogs, as well as the offering of labor and hospitality to needy neighbors and travellers. These qualities of kinship and reciprocity in Hare social life also manifest themselves in the people's relationship to the animals they hunt and fish. All creatures are believed by the Dene to have a "spirit" or "soul" which controls whether humans will be allowed to capture them. To respect these animals' spirits and show reverence for them, the Hare observe a series of taboos. For example, women — as noted before — stay away from fishing nets and boats, and they are also careful not to step over the hunting weapons of their men so as to avoid offending the game. For the same reason, females refrain from touching certain parts of the fur-bearers that are trapped. There are, in addition, still other events in daily life that express a similar pattern of concern and regard. In the bush, for instance, when a pocket of sap in a burning log bursts with a long hiss, the people hear in this a cry of hunger from an animal's soul. A man will then take a piece of caribou or moose fat and throw it in the flames, returning to that creature's spirit a part of the gift which it has bestowed on the hunter. In the old days, when Hare *ehtseneg'oⁿt'ene* (medicine men) had the abilities to protect and cure the people, and help them find game, their medicine powers derived from "knowing" animals who bestowed these special gifts upon them. Such a pattern of respect for animals, and of spiritual relationships with them, is found throughout the sub-Arctic, from the Naskapi and Cree in the east, to the Chipewyans in the center, and the Koyukon in the west [15].

***

Besides the fish, moose and caribou that the people harvest each year, there is now a large array of Western foods which are also available to band members. These commercially produced foods only account, however, for some thirty percent of their overall diet, and most people, in fact, continue to prefer meals built around *denepere* ("Indian" or "bush food") rather than *molapere* ("white man's food"). The Hare, therefore, continue to go to considerable effort to secure small as well as large game for their subsistence. For example, a constant occupation of women throughout the year is setting and checking hare snares, which provide a modest but steady supplement to the family larder. Aboriginally, and throughout the nineteenth century, hares were a very important source of food and clothing for the people, and their pronounced dependence upon this animal in some areas led to the tribal name by which non-Indians have come to know them. Other English, French, and Athabascan terms for regional groups also reflect this fact by incorporating rabbit, *lièvre,* and *k'a, kha,* or *gah* ("hare") in their designations, such as in Hareskins, Rabbitskins, Peaux-de-Lievres,

and K'a-tcho-gotinne ("People Among the Large Hares") [16]. This historical dependence was so pronounced for some bands, that when the natural
cycle of the hare population reached a low point, as it did every six to ten
years, the Indians were struck with widespread starvation and cannibalism
because other food sources were not sufficient to make up for the decrease
in their diet (cf. Rand 1945: 74, cited by Hara 1980: 14) [17]. Even
nowadays, when the people are still faced with periodic hunger in the heart
of winter, they survey the land and its seasonal poverty, and tell one
another, in Wilfred Ratehne's words, "Well, it's back to choking rabbits."

Of the various birds that band members utilize, only ptarmigan and grouse
are available at all seasons. During the late spring, summer, and autumn of
every year, however, the Colville area swarms with a variety of ducks, geese,
and swan who have come north to breed. The people both hunt these species
and they gather their eggs. As soon as the shallower ponds begin to thaw in
mid-May, hunters can be found among the shoreline brush and willows,
waiting in these natural "blinds" for the birds to land. As the open waters
expand and spread to the larger lakes, the waterfowl eventually become more
dispersed, but the people continue to hunt them by boat during the few ice-
free months of their stay.

Coinciding with the appearance of the waterfowl, the open waters of the
spring also allow the people to hunt the beaver and muskrats which now
emerge from their winter lodges to swim on the surface of the region's ponds
and lakes. The meat of these animals is considered a delicacy, but they are
primarily sought for the value of their furs. The northern forests of both the
Eastern and Western Hemispheres are rich with fur-bearing animals, and at
Colville Lake, a major part of native income derives from trapping them. The
most plentiful local species is marten, but the people also take red, cross and
white fox, squirrel, ermine (weasel), mink, wolverine, wolf, and lynx, as well
as the seasonal beaver and muskrat. While the latter two animals are largely
hunted with small-gauge rifles, all the other fur-bearers are taken with
variously sized traps during the winter. The pelts are in optimum condition
during these months, and so from October until early June of every year, the
search for furs keeps the people of the community in the bush. The band's
traplines extend over an area of thousands of square miles, and setting them
out disperses and spreads the people to the limits of the forest. Fur trapping
thus structures a major part of the community's annual cycle, and the sparse,
scattered distribution of the animals creates a parallel pattern in the band's
social organization.

While fur is central to the economy and life-style of the people, the
importance and pursuit of trapping is actually a modern consequence of
early Western contact. Aboriginally, fur was primarily of value for clothing
and insulation, and people still use wolverine, beaver, and other pelts to trim

their parkas, mittens, and foot gear. However, after the fur trade's introduction to the Hare in the late eighteenth century, it became the natives' main means of access to the European goods which people came so quickly to value. At present, for example, a wide variety of Western commodities, including fish nets, traps, ropes, pots, tents, stoves, axes, ammunition, clothing, canned goods, flour, sugar, matches, packaged fruit (for making homebrew), lard, and tea are all available both at the settlement's fur trading post, and at a small store maintained by the local priest. While these facilities, and the village's Catholic mission, have developed into focal places for the band, their presence in the settlement is actually quite recent, and they only alleviated the people's long-standing reliance upon Fort Good Hope in the 1960s. Until that time, band members had been travelling to the fort each year for trading, religious, and medical services: prior to that, and going back to the early 1800s, Fort Good Hope had been the only convenient, permanent community and fur outlet available to them. While trapping has thus involved the Dene in a necessary dependence upon the outside, it should be emphasized that the fur trade has also kept the people involved with the land over the centuries: by fostering the Hare's autonomy and identity, trapping has enabled the band to support itself and thereby maintain a life-style which still draws its substance and spirit from the forest.

It should be noted, too, that while the significance of the fur trade for native people has clearly been considerable, it has also been misunderstood and politically distorted at times by outsiders. In recent years, some non-Indian interpretters of Indian life have argued that the native use of high-powered rifles, steel traps, and nylon netting — equipment whose purchase depends on the sale of furs — is proof that indigenous communities no longer utilize their environment in traditional, respectful, or authentic ways. Such arguments have been used as ammunition in attempts to ban the trapping and sale of furs. This line of reasoning, however, is a serious misreading of contemporary Indian cultures. In the modern world, in fact, it has been the Dene's adoption of these new technologies which has enabled them to stay on the land, and thus live off and harvest its resources. The new tools and weapons being used by them effectively allow their traditional pursuits to remain economically viable occupations (Berger 1977: 100-113). When harvested by native people, the numbers of fur animals have remained at a viable level. The only time when populations of fur-bearers have been seriously depleted in the modern Northwest was when white trappers — often using poison — were allowed in to take large numbers of animals in violation of Indian Treaty agreements (Fumoleau 1973: 235-250).

Nevertheless, some extremist voices in the anti-fur and animal rights movement have equated technological changes among Indian people with cultural and ecological decay [18]. Esther Klein, past president of the Animal

Defense League of Canada, has also asserted that "We do not believe that supporting [indigenous peoples] in trapping is going to make them happy" (1986: 16). Both these arguments are contrary to the realities of Indian life. As noted before, the Dene continue to regard the animals they take with reverence, and show their respect in the various taboos and practices which express gratitude to the spirits which control the game. It is in the very areas where hunting and trapping continue that Indian people have been most effective in preventing development interests from destroying the ecosystem with extractive industries. Where native communities continue to trap, hunt, and fish, then, their environments are well maintained, their cultures are alive, and the new materials being used have helped to preserve both land and society by keeping people engaged in the natural world.

***

The most evident feature of that natural world are the trees of the taiga, and these have supplied much of the material out of which the Hare have literally built their lives. Their ancient shelters consisted of moss and hide-covered poles, and in the modern era, snowshoes, dogsleds, caches, fur stretchers, tent floors, axe handles, ice scoops, canoe frames, and paddles are among the handmade items which people continue to manufacture from local woods. Their homes are constructed from spruce trees — the dominant conifer of the boreal forest — and band members also make use of tamarack (larch) and willow, as well as moss and lichens for insulation, and summer berries for food. Although birch trees can rarely be found as far north as Colville, the people can still obtain this wood when they travel further to the south and west near Good Hope. As is typical of the northern forests, with their thin soils, harsh temperatures, and short growing seasons, the local trees do not attain as great a height as they would in more southerly regions, and this makes their utilization that much more precious. Spruce trees in the Colville region rarely exceed forty feet, and the thickness of the forest cover itself is highly variable. Numerous lakes and wide stretches of swampy muskeg break up the wooded areas, and wherever fire has destroyed the climax forest of spruce and softwoods, thick enclaves of willows and brush have succeeded them.

The high pitch content of coniferous trees makes them very susceptible to destruction by fire (James 1951: 334), and this, along with the extremely dry conditions which prevail during the long, hot days of constant summer sunlight, make forest fires a constant threat during that time of year. In snowshoeing through the bush with Peter Dehdele, I travelled over a wide radius from the village, and saw the evidence of many such blazes. There have been a few fires within the vicinity of the village itself in recent years, but as

Peter observed, since these have left behind them a good supply of firewood, especially in the form of dead standing and fallen timber, the people have not been particularly worried about them.

Of greater significance than this firewood, however, are the large swathes of ground cover and foliage which these fires destroy. The spongy, tufted growth of moss and lichens, which rolls like a carpet across the forest floor, is the prime winter food of caribou, and an area denuded of lichens soon becomes an area bereft of caribou. The herds divert their migration and wintering habits to avoid these barren tracts, and the situation is a long-term proposition, for the slow pace of growth and re-growth in the northern taiga may require several decades to a century or more for the supply of foliage to regenerate itself (cf. Symington 1965: 45-46; Kelsall 1968: 263-268). Fires thus affect the carrying capacity of the environment, and this, in turn, limits the places and possibilities within which the people can support themselves.

The village site at Colville Lake has been cut and hacked out of the wooded growth which once covered its ground, and though there are no trees left within the community itself, a quarter of a mile away one is already deep within the forest. From the shores of the bay where the settlement stands, the land rises abruptly to the east and southeast, and then presents a level surface which overlooks the water. The elevation of the village site exposes it to summer breezes, which keep down the mosquitoes, and also protects the settlement's homes from floods at break-up time. This parcel of land, upon which Wilfred Ratehne and Maurice Bayjere built the first cabins back in the 1930s, parallels the curve of Colville's southernmost bay, and extends inland to a distance of fifty to eighty yards. The tract slopes downward towards its northern end, and it is on this abrupt plateau — reaching from its northern extremity to the deep curve at its southern belly — that all the people have since erected their logs homes (cf. Map 3).

Over the years, band members have cleared away the trees and bush from the vicinity, although some willows have been left between the houses and the shoreline. Several paths now cut through this brush to the waterfront area, where people draw their drinking water, beach their boats, and tie up their dogs during the summer. At other seasons, canines are kept chained up to stakes behind each family's home, leaving the central part of the village free for walking, playing, communicating, and travelling into and out of the community by dogsled.

There are many well-worn trails which wind out of the village in various directions, their routes either a path to resources, or a road of escape from the pressures of communal life. Some routes are used for getting to firewood, while others lead to hunting, trapping, and fishing camps. In winter the people cut across the frozen bodies of water, as well as the tree-less, marsh-like region of scrub, willows and streams which lies to the east and southeast

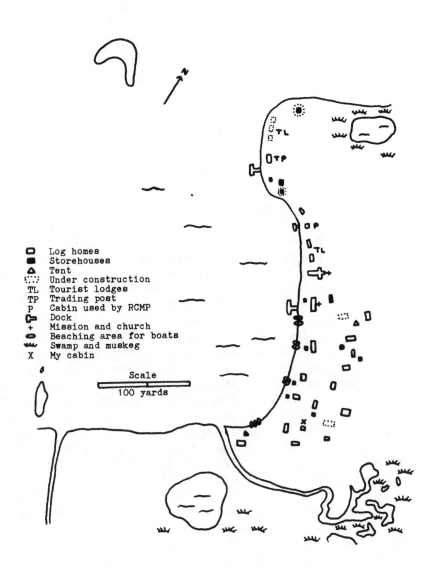

Log homes
Storehouses
Tent
Under construction
TL   Tourist lodges
TP   Trading post
P   Cabin used by RCMP
     Dock
+   Mission and church
     Beaching area for boats
     Swamp and muskeg
X   My cabin

Scale
100 yards

MAP 3   Colville Lake in 1967

of the settlement. Directly behind the community, the land immediately drops, and because the village's plateau blocks this low area from draining into the lake, the resulting muskeg provides a large breeding ground for mosquitoes and insects in the summer. However, because the region's prevailing wind blows in off the lake, breezes often keep air-born pests away from the village site itself. The swampy region behind the community is also an asset. Its shallow ponds thaw out earlier than the surrounding lakes in the spring, and thus furnish an excellent duck hunting area for the band as well. Beyond this marsh, the land rises once again, and the boreal world of hills, lakes, muskegs, forests and streams emerges, which is the people's true living environment, and the earthly heritage of their ancestors.

4. THE YEAR

Although the force of history is rarely an immediate presence in the North, the rhythm of time is. Historical events have indeed altered the lives of the Dene and their institutions, and yet if the impact of change is not pressing, its effects are more often implied than directly evident. Ecological time, however, the flow of forces in life's context, is unavoidable; it is, perhaps, the key dimension of relation and being in the Arctic. No one escapes or ignores the seasons, for too much is at stake, and literally everything is involved. Fur, food, and fuel, shelter and movement, people's relationships and moods — these each change and transform with every phase of the year. The seasons' cycles punctuate the rhythms of existence, and they provide a sense of continuity and depth that linear time so often deprives us of.

In the pulse of every year, the people of Colville confront dramatic extremes of temperatures, as well as stark variations in the relative length of day and night. The annual temperature range often covers a span of over 160 degrees, and during the first seven months of one year (1968) it went from a low of −75°F in early February to a high of +88°F in mid-July [19]. Snowfall and subfreezing temperatures begin in late September, and the southern bays of Colville Lake are completely frozen over by the second or third week of October. This "freeze-up" marks the beginning of real dogsled travel and the commencement of winter trapping. The heaviest accumulations of snow usually occur in November, December, and January, and while smaller amounts continue to fall through May, the sub-Arctic actually has a much lower level of winter precipitation than more southerly regions. Winter snowfall averages forty to fifty inches, and the total amount of water, in fact, "is within the limits usually associated with deserts" (Kelsall 1968: 47). Although there are no statistics available for Colville Lake itself, total yearly precipitation, if "calculated on the basis of ten inches of snow equalling one inch of rain" (Phillips 1967: 14), amounts to ten to fourteen inches for most of the boreal forest (Kelsall 1968: 47). It is the poor drainage caused by the permafrost, and the meager evaporation of the summer, which keeps most of the year's precipitation at, or just below, the surface of the land, and produces a situation in which up to forty percent of some regions are covered by water bodies and muskeg.

During the long winter in the Colville area, temperatures are usually between –20°F and –50°F. The coldest months of the year are January and February, during which readings in the –50°Fs and –60°Fs are common. Between January 28th and February 7th of 1968, for example, the approximate mean daily temperature was –53°F. Yet the depth of the cold is also highly variable during this severest part of the winter. Following a week of –38°F to –75°F readings, there were six days of –5°F to +10°F. After that the thermometer dropped back into the –20°F to –50°F range, only to rise again after two weeks to an unseasonable high of +45°F on February 29th. No temperature that high was recorded again until April 28th.

It was remarkable to witness the sense of relativity with which people responded to some of the more dramatic temperature reversals during this period. On days when it was –50°F or colder, most activities in the bush camps were curtailed. No long hunting or trapping trips were taken, and fishnets were rarely checked. Some wood might be cut, and of course the dogs would be fed and cared for, but otherwise people stayed inside their tents and skinned pelts, sewed clothing, and repaired equipment. Once, when the temperature shot up to –30°F a few days after a cold spell, everybody resumed outdoor work, commenting on how *goweleh* (warm) it had become. About a week afterwards my outdoor thermometer rose to –10°F, and everyone in our camp ran outside in the morning, dressed only in thin pants and shirts. We squinted into the feeble sunlight of mid-February, observing to one another how much like spring it seemed, and then worked outside for the rest of the day without putting on any additional clothes. Yet three morning later, when the reading again fell to a more seasonable –30°F, we were all shivering and complaining, despite the fact that exactly one week previously we had greeted the identical temperature with expressions of warmth and gratitude. Regardless of what biological resistance the people have developed to cold through diet, training, and heredity, then, they still must obviously readjust themselves to the constant changes of every season.

Wind can be an even more crucial weather factor than temperature in the Arctic, and a consideration of just one of these features without the other — as Peter Dehdele once said — would be like trying to walk cross-country with only one snowshoe. One observer of the North has written that:

> For human — or animal — comfort, temperature is of far less consequence
> than the wind. An intensely cold, calm day is infinitely more tolerable than a

moderate one with winds of gale force. The effect of wind-chill, the rapid loss of the body's warmth through radiation, is keenly felt (Phillips 1967: 13-14) [20].

I can remember the time when Leon Behdzi set out with perfect equanimity on a calm, −40°F day, whereas four mornings previously, he and Yašeh had been immobilized at Aubry Lake by −5°F air propelled by thirty mile per hour headwinds.

Leon and all the people showed an exquisite sensitivity to subtle changes in both wind and temperatures, and without any reference to thermometers, they could, from day to day, recognize drops or rises of five degrees. Their consciousness of wind conditions — including strength, direction, and consistency — was pervasive, as was their constant awareness of the quality, depth, and compactness of snow and ice. Like a computer digesting a dozen sources of raw data, the people could process the environment with simultaneity, precision, and a flexible view to multiple outcomes. When living in the bush with them and confronting these forces every day, one could not help but sense and respect the experience, balance, and judgment that went into every hunting and travelling decision. Yet it was all done by the Hare with an outward quietude — a few words, silence, a nod or two — and the men had reached a consensus on a good route, a reasonable timeframe, and a fruitful objective. Within the limits of their knowledge, people tried to maximize the safety and utility of their efforts by sharing the lessons of experience and by respecting the dangers that they were up against. Peter Dehdele once expressed this attitude to me by using one of the *K'apamituegot'ine's* favorite — and most oblique and understated — aphorisms: "*Elegu go^n raetseh dloleh,*" he said, "don't ever laugh at the cold.

> If you try to ignore it or take it for granted, if you don't dress right and stay alert when you travel, then you're headed for trouble. The cold gets angry when people laugh at it, and so it strikes out at them. It can remind you by killing you.

The Hare's ability to adapt their behavior to extreme environmental challenges is shown dramatically in their response to the rigors of winter travel. One of the most threatening of these circumstances is that of a "whiteout," which occurs when a traveller gets caught in a winter storm while out on a frozen lake. The swirling, wind-blown snow quickly obliterates the trail, and also wraps a person in a uniform, colorless, and featureless envelope of flakes. In the sun-less days of mid-winter, where there is little enough natural light to see by, the storm "whites out" whatever clues there might have been to guide a person to safety.

When I stayed with Peter Dehdele in February, he showed me how his own father had taught him to cope with such a situation. On the morning after a night of wind and snow had covered over the trails near our camp, Peter took me out to the lake on our snowshoes. We stood in the area where yesterday's paths had been, and Peter first let me walk around aimlessly for a moment. Then he suddenly asked me to stop and shut my eyes.

"Which direction is the wind coming from?" he asked.

I didn't know. I could feel the air hitting my right cheek, but wasn't sure which direction that was. When I admitted to not knowing, Peter admonished me:

"*That's* what you should pay attention to. You leave camp and you say to yourself: 'I hear it. I feel it. The wind's from the west today.' Why do you want to do that? So that if you get caught in a storm, with nowhere to see, you feel the wind, you listen to it, and you know where 'west' is. Then at least you know which way you want to go, even if you can't see anything there."

Peter next positioned me facing out towards the lake, and then told me again to close my eyes. "Now take a step with your left foot," he instructed. "What do you feel?"

I hesitated, sensing I was again on the verge of foolishness. "Snow," I answered lamely.

"Listen," he responded. "Move your foot further to the side. Press it down. What's that like?"

All I could think of was "it's still snow."

"No," he said, "*feel* the snow. How does the snow *feel?*"

Peter had to repeat his directions and re-phrase his question several times before I finally caught on. He was trying to get me to pay attention to the texture, the compactness, the depth of the snow, how it's feel differed when I put my foot down in different spots. Where the trail had been, the wind-blown cover was soft on top, more dense as I pressed deeper. To the sides, the older surface was harder from the start.

These were differences that no eye could see, and even to try to see them only invited the visual illusions of wishful thinking. You would end up imagining a trail where there was none, and then — fully sighted — would blindly follow it. Peter had made me close my eyes, then, not only to mimic the blindness of a real white-out, but also to close out the temptation to "see" what was no longer there. The key senses here had to be touch and kinaesthesia, the ones a blind person in our culture elaborates to compensate for the lack of sight. With the Hare's finely tuned and culturally trained sense of feel, Peter stressed, you could still follow a trail that you would never be able to see again.

***

As the threat of a white-out suggests, the stresses and dangers of winter are very real and intense for the people, and while they do not exaggerate them, neither in their thoughts and words do they try to minimize them. Too many of their own kin and friends have frozen or starved to death in this century — the Behdzi brothers' elderly father, Wilfred and George Ratehne's younger siblings — for the Dene to dismiss such anxieties as historical artifacts. The environment and its rhythms are still too immediate for that. Yet seasonal stresses also abate with time, and there is a perceptible lightening of mood when the harshness and solitude of winter have passed. To band members, the end of February marks the finish of the most difficult part of their year, and they made a point of emphasizing this to me. "If you can make it past the end of February," Maurice Bayjere once confided, "you can stop worrying. You'll be okay after that. That's the end of *xai,* the real Indian winter."

True to Maurice's words, March did witness a number of important transformations. Daily temperatures gradually rose, sunlight and day length increased, and by the end of the month, readings above 0°F were fairly common. Each of these changes had been in process for several weeks. Back in December, the sun had dipped below the horizon one day, and then had not been seen again for close to a month. There was a pale, gray light, dim and weak, which had lasted but a few hours. That was all that one could travel or work by in early January, although there had been a few nights of moonlight, as well as the milky, colored ribbons of the aurora borealis. But the mid-winter dark had been mercifully brief, for Colville is not too far north of the Arctic Circle, and the rainbow hues of northern lights were soon diluted by the growing daytime hours of February. Light brought warmth and glare as well, and by April and May the reflection of the sun off the snow and ice — crystalline, sharp, and dazzling — brought the ever-present danger of snowblindness. In the Dene's own lunar calendar, in fact, their names for the months that correspond to Western culture's "spring" mean "the moons of snowblindness" (Table 2). When the people travelled during daylight hours at this season, they wore sunglasses and smudged the rims of their eyes with soot to cut down the glare. By late April there were no more "minus" degree days, and afternoon temperatures were around or above the freezing mark. In early May, when the band dispersed once again for the final weeks of spring caribou and beaver hunting, the days were consistently sunny and warm, and the snow was fast disappearing from the land.

The heat of the long and lengthening days was also melting and rotting the lake ice, and waterfowl were reappearing on the open ponds. As the thaw continued into June, the "break-up" of the ice on the larger lakes occurred, ending the frozen period begun by the mid-October "freeze-up." The people returned to the village from their hunting camps, and settling in for a summer of relative ease and communality, they once more set their fish nets in the open waters of the bay. The warm, unending days of midnight sun continued through July, providing an uninterrupted backdrop for the band's affairs and pursuits. But in August the temperature started to drop, and brief periods of rain and nighttime began to invade the daylight. By September, the air was chilled around the freezing point, and a foretaste of winter was in everyone's mouth.

***

These rhythms in the people's lives — the swings between seasonal extremes, the cyclic movements from village to bush, warm to cold, light to dark — create an annual cycle alive with ambiguity and the particular satisfactions that competence and community can bring. Dene experience

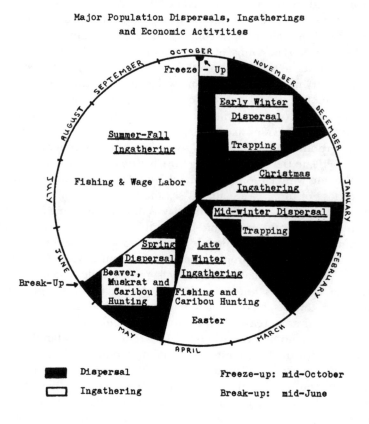

FIGURE 3   The Annual Cycle

alternates between intensities of people and textures of environment, demanding a protean ability to cope with both physical and social nature. If band members are sometimes ambivalent about the dimensions of their existence, it is be-cause these stark contrasts in life are simultaneously a source of both un-deniable demands and a welcome degree of variety, release, and stimulation.

The people's existence is quintessentially mobile, for movement characterizes every phase and transition in the band's experience. The annual cycle falls into six alternating periods of community dispersal and social ingathering, resulting in a life-style of semi-nomadism (Figure 3). The lengthy winter and spring, demarcated by the yearly freeze-up and break-up, encompass three major separations, during which the people live in canvas tents, and move through the forest in small hunting and trapping groups. These three periods, when all travelling is done by dogsled and snowshoe, are in the early winter from mid-October to mid-December, in the mid-winter months of early January to early March, and in the spring from late April to mid-June. Between these dispersals, people congregate at the community for brief holidays, but they must pass most of their year in the scattered encampments of the bush in order to subsist. Altogether, a contemporary family which is conscientiously trying to live off the land will actually spend at least half of every year in the forest, and experience — during these dispersals — the company of only two or three other households for much of that time.

The settlement at Colville Lake is the scene of three annual band reunions, which counterpoint these phases of social atomism in the bush. One ingathering is in late December, during the Christmas period, and a second comes in the late winter months of March and April. The latter reunion follows the close of the area's main fur season, whose dates are set by the government, and includes the Easter holiday. A third ingathering covers the summer and fall months from mid-June until late September or early October, during which time the people often spend several weeks in nearby fish camps and make their preparations for the coming winter. There is usually some wage labor available from the village's fur trader and missionary in the summer, and at this time the settlement also receives its seasonal visits from the police, tourists, medical personnel, and local administrators. The village's size is further increased by the return of the children who were sent away to residential schools the previous fall, thus reuniting both families, and the entire band, for the lengthiest communal period of the year.

In its totality, the current annual cycle of the people is a mixture of ecological, governmental, and religious time schedules, and these diverse features reflect the combination of traditional and Western elements which affect band members. The Dene are simultaneously oriented to a range of expectations and timings, including Church holidays, trapping regulations, and school terms, and yet the environmental dimensions take precedence over all of these for they are the ones most intimately connected with the dangers and possibilities of survival. While the people have taken on some of the external trappings of Western time-keeping, such as clocks, watches, and calendars, in a more fundamental sense they continue to operate on an ecological rather than an artificial model of life and scheduling. They still think of the year in terms of *xai, golu, uyalele, inpe*, and *k'atan*, the five seasonal divisions that their ancestors recognized. These were explained to me by André Yawileh and some of the other people, who defined these periods in terms of their environmental features, as well as their calendrical equivalents.

xai: "winter"; the period following the freeze-up of the lakes in mid-October and lasting until early May. The Dene also speak of a period toward the end of the winter called *golu* or "crust." As André described it:

> This starts in March when the sun really comes back strong. When it's warm during the day and the snow on the lake melts, then in the evening it gets cool and it freezes into a hard crust on the snow. That makes it real good for travelling.

Yen Behdzi added:

> It's the strong winds in March that make the snow on the lakes so hard on top. They blow it hard like it was ice.

uyalele: "the melting of the ice." André's son Martin described it as "the time when ducks fly north and water starts to come on top of the lakes; this is the Indians' 'spring'." It begins in early or mid-May and ends with the break-up of the ice in mid-June.

inpe: "summer" or "the time when it gets warmer" (Sue 1980: 56). This begins with the break-up of the lake ice in mid-June and lasts until mid-August, when the temperature starts to drop again.

katan: "autumn"; this starts around mid-August and concludes with the freeze-up of the lakes in mid-October. In Yen Behdzi's words: "Then bush life and real winter start again for us."

Freeze-up and break-up, the presence or absence of snow and ice, and the types of mobility that are feasible, clearly dominate the people's vision of the year. Their persistent concern with ecology rather than clocks is indicated not only by their seasonal scheme, but also by some finer distinctions that they make within their annual cycle. While they are familiar with the names of Western months, many of the people continue to conceive of time as a series of "moon" divisions, thus perpetuating a type of aboriginal lunar calendar which was once ubiquitous in the sub-Arctic [21]. Yen and Yašeh Behdzi once named and translated for me the following *sa* or "months,"

TABLE 2

Native terms for lunar months

Approximate Gregorian equivalent	Athabascan Name	English Translation
January	*Delederahodedele*	"The Month of the Sun Coming Back"
January-February	*Li^{n}šayduwesa*	"It Is So Cold that When the Dogs Piss, They Piss on Themselves"
February	*Akaradetsisa*	"The Month of The Wind"
March	*Raxonraselsa*	"The Month of A Slight Touch of Snowblindness"
April	*Raxo^{n}radesa*	"The Month of Very Bad Snowblindness"
May	*Li^{n}yatisa*	"The Month of The Barking Dog"
June	*Bemetegoxay*	"The Month of The Ice Melting"
July	*Ehgaygo^{n}sa*	"The Month of Eggs"
August	*Ehšuwego^{n}sa*	"The Month of Ducklings"
September	*Bekarabeh^{n}deri^{n}daygo^{n}sa* ..	"The Month of The Ducks Going Back South"
October	*Tayaahgo^{n}sa*	"The Month of The Caribou Migration Coming Back from The Barrens"
November	*Ehseh^{n}go^{n}sa*	"The Month of Caribou Rutting"
December	*Begetei^{n}aisa*	"The Month When The Sun Disappears Below The Horizon"

which demonstrate how deeply the events and migrations of every year enter into the Dene vocabulary of time (Table 2).

5. CONCLUSION

The fact that the people's calendar is a description rather than simply a demarcation of time reflects their concern with the natural world, and serves as a mirror of their own participation in it. Their ecology embodies some of the most visible threats and anxieties with which they have to contend, and these dangers are more consciously perceived of by the people than are the subtler stresses of their social life. In a community where death by starvation and freezing have occurred within living memory, survival is a challenge rather than an assumption. When one adds to this the hazards of hunting and dogsled travel; the dangers from bears and wolves; the possibility of accidents with guns, axes, and knives; and the frustrations of perverse weather and unpredictable caribou migrations, then one be-gins to sense the full dimensions of human ecology in the North.

The sub-Arctic is often considered to be the harshest environment in the world, but few people get beyond temperature, ice, and wind when they think of it in these terms. They forget that there are hunting-fishing-and-gathering groups in other regions who have also occupied, into modern times, equally "marginal" ecologies, such as deserts, jungles, and rugged coastlines. Having been pushed or kept from seemingly richer areas on their continents by the expansion of agricultural and herding societies, hunters-and-gatherers in most parts of the world have nevertheless been able to maintain a viable lifeway. In fact, recent studies of extant foraging populations have revealed how secure and often leisurely their lives can be, despite the apparent severity of their surroundings (cf. Lee 1968, 1969; Lee and DeVore 1968; Service 1966; Sahlins 1968).

What underlies the security of most of these groups is the access that they enjoy to abundant, wild, and edible plants or shellfish, with the result that the "gathering" of these resources supercedes "hunting" and "fishing" as means of acquiring food (Netting 1977). In this respect, the sub-Arctic appears to be doubly damned in an ecological sense, for not only do natives there have to deal with extremities of weather, but they are also faced with a paucity of edible vegetation. Berries, certain boiled mosses, and rose hips are the only wild plants which the people of Colville employ as food, and these make up a small and very seasonal component of their diet (cf. Hara 1980: 135-141) [22]. Also, lacking access to the sea mammals and salmon enjoyed by natives along the Northwest and Arctic coasts, Hare subsistence thus turns predomi-nantly upon the availability of meat, fowl, and fish. The people's survival is therefore a function of their ability to understand, stalk, and keep up with animal movements — a much harder task than collecting sedentary food-stuffs or harvesting fish and game that exist in abundance.

Certain behavioral characteristics of the animals upon which the people depend make it difficult for them to lead a secure and predictable life during the winter. As noted, caribou are in the area for only seven months of the year, and they remain nomadic throughout their stay in the forest zone. A neighboring "edge-of-the-woods" people — the Chipewyans — compare themselves to wolves because of their need to follow the caribou herds season to season (J.G.E. Smith 1976: 13). For the Hare, too, hunting caribou necessitates a comparable level of mobilty, though an equally stressful aspect of these animals is the unpredictability of some of their seasonal moves. Caribou are notorious for the erratic nature of their migration habits, and herds which have regularly come to a particular region for many years may suddenly fail to turn up one winter. The forest fires of the preceding summer — many of which are caused by lightning — may be responsible in some cases, but more often there is no discernible reason for the change, and both native hunters and Western scientists remain baffled by these shifts in movement [23].

Hunting possibilities within a given locale can also radically alter from week to week as the caribou shift their grazing range, forcing families either to move or to rely upon fish and hare for their food. There is evidence to indicate that many sections of the aboriginal range of the Hare were periodically devoid of caribou, which would have necessitated the people's dependence upon smaller game in earlier times as well. The writings of 19th and 20th century observers graphically describe starvation among Dene and Inuit deprived of their usual supply of caribou [24]. Since aboriginal families would have needed 100 to 200 caribou per year to maintain themselves and their dogs, this fluctuating situation would have intensified their reliance upon other sources of food and clothing [25].

Fish also present a problem of movement to the people because they change their primary locations during the winter as a result of varying temperature, nutrient, and ice conditions. Nets which have been coming up full may suddenly yield a very small harvest, impelling either a shift in fishing sites, or perhaps the move of an entire camp to a new lake. If such a move must be made in the latter part of the winter, there is the added hardship (and occasional impossibility) of having to re-set one's net under a five to six foot layer of ice.

Waterfowl and moose embody some of the same dynamic problems as caribou and fish, being in the first case migratory and seasonal, and in the second both sparse and dispersed. The variously scattered, mobile, or erratic nature of these food sources is complemented by the cyclical nature of other important species. Snowshoe hare, mice, and lemmings go through population cycles in the Hare's part of the sub-Arctic every few years, and these affect the people in a double manner. The hare is still an important food resource for the band, and as a reminder of earlier centuries of starvation and cannibalism, the years in which the numbers of hare reach a low point continue to mean winters of exceptional hardship. Furthermore, a decline in the population of hares, mice, and other small mammals leads to a corresponding decrease among the marten, fox, lynx, and other fur-bearers which feed off these smaller species. The people may thus find not only their food supply threatened, but also experience a simultaneous decline in their trapping income. This combination of population cycles and local fluctuations in the abundance of game is characteristic of what some other sub-Arctic groups face (eg., Nelson 1973: 68, 80, 131, 166, 274-276). In modern times, these vulnerabilities have made the Dene especially sensitive to any proposals — ranging from government registration of traplines to corporate efforts to build oil pipelines — that pose a threat to the people's freedom and their environment's integrity (see Chapters 3, 4 and 7). They know better than anyone how fragile the sub-Arctic ecosystem is, and how precarious life can be for those whose livelihood depends on its resources.

***

Over the centuries, the fur trade — besides giving the Dene increased access to many Western goods — has also altered and intensified certain of their ecological patterns. While it has made available a more sophisticated technology, the steel traps, rifles, and commercial fish-netting it has offered have not changed the nature or habits of the fur and food-producing species which the people pursue. It is true that these may all be taken now with greater efficiency and more individualized effort, but one can still only live off the animals that are immediately at hand: if game is scattered in time and space, if migrations and cycles continue to create seasons of plenty and winters of discontent, then all the steel, rope, and fire-power in the world will not produce food.

In the course of hundred of generations, the Hare have developed many ways to meet the particular challenges of their existence. Social, cognitive, psychological, and material techniques are all involved. What is perhaps most striking to the Western observer is that native individuals deal with the ambiguities of experience by accepting and participating in them, rather than by trying to reconcile or eliminate life's contradictions. There is an element of what the poet Keats called people's "Negative Capability," which emerges "when man is capable of being in uncertainties, Mysteries, doubts, without any irritable reaching after fact and reason" (1817: 261). One anthropologist has related this pattern among the Dene to the qualities of their language: "Motion, process, and change are the very nature of the Dene universe; state is a momentary aberration, and 'nouns' are very often verbs in disguise. Moreover, unity or wholeness is the very nature of things, a unity in process and constant unfoldment... Dene dualities or oppositions tend to resove themselves into unity and possess fluidity and even a transposing nature" (Christian 1989: 653).

By rhythmically moving between poles of existence and styles of experience, the Dene of Colville Lake share in qualities that a more narrowly-defined and consistency-oriented lifeway would deprive them of. Life is indeed stressful for the Hare because of the extremes to which the people are subjected, but stress per se is not necessarily or entirely negative in its implications, for it also operates as a stimulant which invests their lives with motion, motive, and awareness. The people actively seek to experience some of the most challenging circumstances of their world, and they derive some of their deepest satisfactions from the sense of competency and harmony which these social and environmental involvements provide. It is these contrasting and ultimately creative qualities of stress which impart a uniqueness to the people's existence, and it is to an exploration of these dimensions that the remainder of this book is devoted.

CHAPTER 3

Kinship and History

1. INTRODUCTION

The idea that people are social animals is a reflection on human nature, but in the North, necessity is even more immediate than propensity. There is too much to be contended with for a person to exist without a partner, or for a family to survive without kin. Lone individuals are actually pitied and feared, and if isolated too long, the Hare believe they may become the freakish and mysterious *lariyin* ("bush men;" literally: "he hides") who, when cut off from society, lose their humanity, and take to roaming the forests with cannibalistic intent. For the Dene, isolation *in extremis* is dehumanization in earnest, for people need one another both to insure their survival and preserve their identity. As the band's "bush man" belief implies, life is indeed *with* people and *within* nature, and necessity — as well as history — becomes the mother of kinship.

Relationships bind the Colville Lake community into an intimate fabric. But since kin can quarrel as well as cooperate with one another, the band's social life is also home to many ambiguities: there are tensions between dependence and independence, generosity and mistrust, and restraint and honesty. People cope with their attachments and ambivalences about one another in many ways, and a key approach is to shift between intimacy and avoidance with different relatives at different times. This rhythm of separation and togetherness, as a way of dealing with relationships, is one of many dimensions of existence in which fluidity and alternation characterize Indian life.

Kinship patterns in the band involve individuals with both their maternal and paternal relatives, reflecting what anthropologists technically call a "bilateral" (two-sided) social system. That is, in a person's social life, there is a complementary or bilateral emphasis in which an individual considers all of his or her kin to be of potentially equal significance, regardless of whether they are related through the mother's or the father's side. This local pattern differs from the "unilineal" social systems of certain Yukon, Alaskan, Algonkian, Siberian, and Sami (Lapp) groups, where people are organized into more complex clans, sibs, and moieties in which either the mother's *or* the father's relatives are, in many situations, more significant than other kin. These differences demonstrate the great diversity of social organization that can be found within northern cultures [1].

Beyond such diversity, however, a strong case can also be made for some basic similarities which cut across the circumpolar regions, and which give to the peoples of the North a set of common cultural denominators. Specifically, there are several dominant orientations shared by many Arctic and sub-Arctic groups, and these involve strong emphases upon (1) kinship ties, (2) generosity, (3) emotional restraint, and (4) behavioral flexibility. These four themes have great adaptive value in rigorous environments where they bring elements of security, stability, and adaptability to life. This argument is a simple but nevertheless compelling one, especially for those persons who have experienced at first-hand the exigencies of survival in the North. Though these emphases are expressed in diverse ways by different groups, their ubiquity — including their presence at Colville Lake — underlines their significance for a wide range of native peoples.

Recent workers in some of the North's larger settlements have pointed out that these traditional social values have persisted into many areas of contemporary community life. In some instances these four themes have been modified by native people to suit new institutions and conditions, while in other cases their continuance has produced stress because of their inconsistency with certain demands of modern "urbanized" life in the North. These values have a considerable historical depth to them, and as they are participated in by the Hare and other groups, they show an elaboration and integration with many other aspects of existence.

The focus on social relations and social values in this chapter reveals the historical significance of kinship in the lives of a northern people: it examines how kin ties have promoted the survival of the Colville band in the face of ecological disasters and social change, and it explores how the Hare's concern with reciprocity, restraint, and adaptability have bound them into a community possessed of its own consistencies and contradictions.

The relevance of Colville Lake for such an analysis lies in the fact that its people represent a transitional stage between an aboriginal style of life and the more settled existence of present-day towns. The small size and isolation of their village, their "bush" orientation, and their limited contacts with white outsiders, resemble the living conditions that most Indians and Inuit experienced during the bulk of the post-contact era. The current life style of this small community was widespread in the North as recently as the mid-twentieth century, and most native peoples abandoned it only in the post-World War II period. An analysis of this band can thus provide us with insights into the past and the future, as well as the present, of the Dene and their neighbors. By emphasizing the cultural values governing kinship, sharing, emotionality, and generosity, we will be highlighting key aspects of the social transformations that these people are currently undergoing.

2. HISTORY AND IDENTITY

A crucial dimension of Colville Lake's life is the complex, bilateral network of social ties that links its native people. The band is comprised of fourteen separate families, and the members of every household can trace blood and marital relations to persons in several of the villager's other homes. The cohesion and unity of the band is significant because Colville Lake is, as we have seen, something of a satellite to Fort Good Hope, a town which has been the economic and social focus for the Indians of the region since its founding in the early nineteenth century. This area of the northwest was first opened up to the European fur trade by Alexander Mackenzie who, in 1789, explored *Deh-cho,*"The Big River" that now bears Mackenzie's name. Prior to this, trapping and trading activities had been steadily expanding westward from the southern Hudson's Bay region since the early eighteenth century. During this period, Cree, and eventually Chipewyan, Yellowknife, and Dogrib Indians, had operated as intermediaries between the white traders and the northwesterly Dene groups of the Arctic drainage. But after Mackenzie's explorations, more direct contact was opened up with these interior Indians through the establishment of forts in their own territories.

Fort Good Hope was founded in 1806 as a fur trading post by Alexander Mackenzie's nephew for his employers, the North West Company. After the Hudson's Bay Company absorbed the North West Company in 1821, the fort's location was changed several times in attempts to increase trade not only with the Hare, but with Kutchin (Gwich'in) and Inuit groups as well. The present site of the town was settled on in 1836. Well into the latter half of the twentieth century, the various Hare groups that lived in the forested regions to the northeast of Good Hope travelled to the fort periodically to trade, socialize, arrange marriages, seek medical assistance, and, after the establishment of a Catholic mission in 1859, to participate in religious holidays and observances there. The Catholic priests inaugurated an annual religious cycle in which three major holidays were emphasized — Christmas, Easter, and the Feast of the Assumption in mid-August — and these have influenced the timing of community reunions right down to the present day.

The Canadian government did not begin negotiating treaties with the country's western and northern Indians until the 1870s, and it wasn't until 1921 that federal representatives finally concluded treaties with Dene groups in the Mackenzie area. At that time all of the Hare were administratively joined together as "Band Number 5." The people who now make up the

Colville Lake community are drawn from the various groups that have traded into Fort Good Hope since the early nineteenth century — a time period that has witnessed many intermarriages and migrations among the native peoples from this region. The people of the Colville area thus have a long-standing set of social and economic relationships with the town of Good Hope and, until recently, the smaller settlement lacked even a semblance of self-sufficiency. It had thus persisted over many years of the "fur and mission era" as a "contact-traditional all-native community," viz., a village without white personnel or institutions, but one which was

> itself oriented toward a focal center of White institutions in the region, a settlement that may be characterized as a "Point of Trade" (Helm and Damas 1963: 10).

Prior to the European presence in the Northwest, aboriginal groups lacked the kind of unity that is implied by the tribal names (such as "Hare") which Westerners later applied to them. Most of the indigenous groups simply identified themselves as *dene* or *t'ine* ("people"), and they referred to themselves and their neighbors by terms which described bands as ...*godene* or ...*got'ine* (i.e., the people of a given place or area), such as the *Dutagot'ine*, "Among the Islands People". Social structure was fluid, and it was based upon a multiplicity of kinship ties which individuals could utilize as circumstances warranted. For the "Hare," as for other Dene in the region, intermarriage, trade, and economic interdependence during times of scarcity were factors which linked local groups to one another. The flexible nature of social organization thus allowed people to shift their group membership and place of residence as social or economic conditions necessitated (Helm and Leacock 1971: 347).

> Kinship was the basis for membership in both large and small groups, and each household joined larger groupings on the basis of wider kinship connections, personal relationships between male household heads, and other haphazard factors. In spring and summer most of the Hare were on the Mackenzie River, but in winter and late fall they broke up into small camp groups of not more than two or three family units which were spread throughout the bush. There were no family hunting territories (Cohen and Osterreich 1967: 4).

While there were cultural, linguistic, and geographic differences which gave identity to regional bands, there were no formal leadership patterns to bind different groups together aboriginally, nor were there any "tribes" to explicitly distinguish larger groupings from one another. Social organization, in many respects, was thus not political in nature. Nevertheless, the regional bands who were collectively designated by the term "Hare" did gather several times a year for ceremonial purposes, for arranging marriages, for cooperative fishing during the summer and fall, and for joint hunting expeditions during the caribou migrations [2]. In small and large numbers, they were in contact with many neighboring peoples, including Kutchin (Gwich'in or Loucheux) groups to the west, Inuit to the north, Satudene (Great Bear Lake Indians) to the east, and Mountain Indians to the southwest [3].

Folklore and historical accounts reveal contacts with the more southerly Cree, Slaveys, Chipewyans and Yellowknives as well. Hostilities and contacts with many of these groups may have been intensified in the eighteenth and early nineteenth centuries as a result of the "middleman" position in the fur trade that some of the latter people occupied (Rich 1967: 97-98). The geographic position of these other peoples placed them between the most advanced European outposts of the time and the more isolated, interior groups such as the Hare, giving them a trading and material advantage over the latter [4]. "Middleman" tribes thus involved more distant Indians in the fur trade long before there was direct white contact with them, and they may in fact have pushed certain groups, including the Hare, into more northerly regions than they had previously inhabited. Although it may not be histori-cally definitive, André Yawileh can remember his grandparents telling him how the Cree (*A'da*, "The Enemies") and the Chipewyans (*Gasehletin*) used to raid and cheat the people for their furs "long ago." As André expressed it:

> There used to be lots of marten around here. Some guys were taking them with deadfalls and they were getting so much fur they just kept them. And the Chipewyans knew about the white men to the south, the whites were already down there. The Chipewyans used to come up here (to raid the people) for the furs. The Chipewyan didn't tell these people there were whites to the south [5].

The nomadic, aboriginal life style of the Hare periodically brought them into touch with neighboring groups in other contexts as well: to the east and northeast, for example, the seasonal pursuit of caribou by Satudene, Dogribs, Hare and Inuit brought all these peoples in contact with one another on the Barren Grounds. In their own oral traditions, the people of Colville Lake portray their ancestors as being defensive and fearful about these encoun-ters. Many of their tales involve the powerful *ehtseneg'oⁿt'ene*, (medicine man and shaman) *Asoneh* ("Caribou Dung"), who is usually called upon in the narrative to save the people from their enemies, or to avenge them upon some raiding group. The act of telling these stories is a real art-form to the Hare, one that combines words with dramatic body language, well-timed pauses, the imitation of sounds and songs, and the acting out of key events as the narrative unfolds. Old Joseph Tehgu — the most accomplished story-teller in the community — recounted some of these tales to me, and Philip Ratehne translated them in the following way:

Asoneh was travelling with these people down by the Anderson River (*Seholilinne*, "Connie River"). They were always afraid of meeting Eskimos [Inuit] so they told everyone not to go too far. Asoneh was walking along the shore, and while he was walking along there, he saw three Eskimos coming towards him in kayaks. Asoneh walked poorly, trying to make himself look like he was weak.

Then the three Eskimos came to the shore and went to Asoneh. They never know him {i.e., did not recognize who he was]. The Eskimos chased him and Asoneh ran crying: heeee yeeeeee, heee yeeeeee! Just like that. They were chasing him and hitting him with mud. And Asoneh was running a little faster than they were running. Then Asoneh jumped right to the top of a cliff and these Eskimos were running back for their kayaks [in fear]. Asoneh ran after them and knocked them on the head. He killed them and threw them in the river. He threw their kayaks in the water too.

***

The people were still on the Anderson River. Asoneh went back again. He had seen real lots of Eskimo camps. The Eskimo saw him and said: "There's a little kid coming." There were four boys who ran faster than the other ones. They were running just behind Asoneh and throwing mud at him. They kept on throwing mud at Asoneh and Asoneh kept running.Asoneh jumped to the top of a cliff again. Then these Eskimos remembered about Asoneh and started running back. But Asoneh was faster. He knocked their heads off. Asoneh threw them in the river and then went to their camp. There were still lots of Eskimos yet and they were saying that there's a kid coming. They were telling each other to kill him just with mud. Four big boys ran after him and Asoneh was crying while he was running away. Then he did the same thing again. He turned back and killed them all. He killed all the Eskimos that were there in the camp, and after that he went back to the people.

***

Some Eskimos were staying along the Anderson River. Once in a while caribou came acrosss the river and the Eskimos killed some of them. These people [our ancestors] and the Loucheux [Gwich'in] couldn't go near there because the Eskimos always killed them. Asoneh was travelling with the people from around here. These people travelled way down and they didn't want to get closer to the Eskimos. Then Asoneh told them he would walk and hunt around and so he was gone.

When Asoneh came back, they asked him, "Where were you?" And Asoneh said: "Walking by the sand." They asked where the Eskimos were and Asoneh said that there were no Eskimos around. These people decided to go across the Anderson River because there were no Eskimos there.

Before, when Asoneh went around, he saw Eskimos and he came to the Anderson River just near them. They chased Asoneh and he started crying.

They kept on chasing Asoneh, and then he turned back and started fighting. The Eskimos were sorry because they didn't know it was Asoneh.

After he killed them all he went to their camp. When he went into it he saw an old lady who was blind. This old woman told him that the Eskimos said there was one boy around and they all went to chase him. Asoneh said: "Yes, I know." Asoneh didn't want to kill the old lady: he only wanted to take the tobacco and the flints which she used to make fire with.

After that he left the old lady alone and went back to the people and told them that there were no Eskimos. The people wanted to see what Asoneh did, so they went on a hill and saw the camp and it was empty. They thought the Eskimos had gone some place. Asoneh was walking way behind. When the people went around the camp, the old lady was still alive. This old woman told the people that her people had gone away: there probably were some caribou that they were hunting. These people never told her anything. She said they might be back any time.

But they were all lying outside dead. Asoneh had killed them all. These people left that old blind lady alone and they never said anything to her. The old lady finally died: she was blind and just crawling around and finally died.

***

Warfare and trading were not carried on by the Hare in an organized manner for, like other Northern Athabascan peoples in the Mackenzie aea, the Hare lacked any centralized authority and did not "consider themselves as composing neat political or cultural units" (Osgood 1936a: 3; cf. also Keith 1890: 123) [6]. This decentralization was a cultural quality shared by all the Arctic drainage Dene groups (MacNeish 1956), with the main distinguishing feature of the Hare being their widespread reputation for timidity (Richardson 1851i: 211-212; 1851ii: 3-32; Mackenzie 1801: 44, 50; Jenness 1967: 392-395). When Mackenzie compared the Hare with other Athabascan peoples he had encountered on the Mackenzie River part of his journey in 1789, he remarked that: "Several of them were clad in hare-skins, but in every other circumstance they resembled those whom we had already seen" (1801: 44). Half a century later, the explorer John Richardson made a similar comment based on his own experiences:

> Various tribes have been distinguished by peculiar names, but there is little variety in their general appearance, and few discrepancies in their dress, customs or moral character. The Hare Indians (*Ka-cho-'dtinne*) inhabit the banks of the Mackenzie, from Slave Lake downwards, and the Dog-ribs (*Thling-e-ha-'dtinne*) the inland country on the east, from Marten Lake to the Coppermine. There is no perceptible difference in the aspect of these two tribes. They meet in the same hunting grounds at the north end of Great Bear Lake, intermarry, and their speech scarcely differs in accent. The Hare

Indians, frequenting a thickly wooded district in which the American Hare abounds, feed much on that animal, and clothe themselves with its skins, while the Dog-ribs depend more upon the rein-deer [caribou] for a supply of winter dresses, but in all essential respects, they are the same people... (1851ii: 3-4).

Jenness noted that the nearest neighbors of the Hare, i.e.,

the Kutchin, Eskimo, and Yellowknife, rather despised them on account of their timidity, for they often concealed their camps under fallen trees some distance back from the river and fled at the slightest indication of strangers (1967: 394) [7].

In most other regards, however, including technology, social organiza-tion, shamanistic practices, and ritual, there was little to differentiate the Hare from surrounding peoples (Jenness 1967: 394-395). In historical perspective, therefore, the term "Hare" has been used to designate a number of bands which shared linguistic, cultural, kinship, and territorial ties that only partially distinguished them from other such loose groupings in the Mackenzie area [8].

It is probable that whites (including anthropologists) have imposed a much greater sense of tribal identity upon the Northern Athabascans than they themselves possessed aboriginally. This stems not only from ethno-graphic and administrative convenience, but also from the Western pen-chant for thinking of peoples in political and corporate terms. In more recent times, however, these modes of identification have actually gained some historical validity as a result of the collection of large and increasingly settled native populations around the trading forts (cf. Osgood 1936a: 3-5; MacNeish 1956). This increased sedentariness, along with the Dene's growing identi-fication with a "home town," and their restricted travel over a more limited territory than in the past, have all intensified the sense of separateness among formerly contiguous and geographicaly overlapping groups. The same process has occurred in the eastern sub-Arctic (Salisbury 1986: 8-9).

In the period since the beginning of European contact, several observers have tried to describe the number and location of native bands among the Hare. The Oblate missionary and explorer Emile Petitot, who lived and travelled in the Fort Good Hope area in the latter half of the nineteenth century, published a number of band lists during that era. In the twentieth century, several recent scholars have performed a similar service (Osgood 1932; Hurlbert 1962; Hara 1980). What is most striking about these band inventories is the repeated inconsistencies they display, a feature which suggests some corresponding attributes of Hare social organization and fluidity. Petitot, for example, gave differing band designations on each of three occasions in the nineteenth century (1876, 1889, 1891), and these, in turn, differ considerably from those offered by Osgood in 1932. These discrepancies led Osgood to remark:

> The frequent lack of correspondence in lists which designate divisions sometimes called bands, such as exists between mine and Petitot's, or the inconsistencies of Petitot's several lists, or the inconsistencies of my own informants, all these lead me to suspect that the reason lies in the *mutability* of these so-called bands (1936a: 12; emphasis added; cf. also McClellan 1975b: 14-16).

There is considerable evidence from recent studies of Fort Good Hope (Hurlbert 1962; Hara 1980), and from the personal histories of the people at Colville Lake, to support and clarify Osgood's contentions on the fluidity of Hare social structure. Part of the confusion stems from the native custom of designating people in terms of the area in which they camp and hunt. Although families develop preferences for camping in certain areas — and thus become identified in terms of these locales — the descriptions so used to identify people can vary in their geographical precision (cf. Hara 1980: 26). A family, for instance, may be identified simultaneously in three different spatial contexts, including (a) the general region they are in, (b) the particular lake they camp at in that region, or (c) their specific camping site on that lake.

> Thus, Antoine can be described as *Dala-go-t'ine*, showing the audience that he migrates and camps mostly in the eastern half of the present Hare Hunting Area; as *Tu- o-go-t'ine* (Man of Aubry Lake), Aubry Lake being his most favorite region; or *Tu-hota-delin-go-t'ine* (man of the spot called *tu-ho-tadelin* on Aubry Lake where he is currently camping) (Hara 1980: 26).

This pattern of identifying and grouping people geographically can give the impression that there are many more "bands" than actually exist [9].

Furthermore, although specific people tend to frequent some areas more than they do others, membership in geographical groupings is fluid, and camping preferences can change over time. Mobility, interpersonal frictions, post-marital residence changes, and attempts to make the maximum use of scattered resources, all underlie the kind of "mutability" referred to by Osgood. Each family at Colville Lake, for example, tends to alternate among a number of preferred camping spots, and this type of fluctuation may occur from year to year or over a number of years. A primary reason for this is the people's "conservationist" awareness that such periodic shifts allow local animal populations to replenish themselves (cf. also Nelson 1973: 155, 311). Families also use different campsites for different seasonal activities, and so population distribution is constantly being altered from month to month. Since each of these moves may bring a household into contact with other named groups, multiple camp memberships can yield a corresponding complex of identities. In addition, a geographical grouping may cease to exist if people stop using the area, or if the regional population declines. According to Osgood (1932) and Hara (1980), for example, this has been the case with Petitot's *Bâtards-Loucheux* or *Nne-la-gottine* ("End of the Earth People") band of the Hare, which had disappeared by the 1920s as a result of population depletion and shifts by survivors to other areas.

Finally, specific post-contact conditions, especially disease, starvation, and the concentration of people around forts, have continually affected the nature of Hare geographical groupings throughout the nineteenth and twentieth centuries. Starvation has occasionally occurred into modern times, and smallpox, measles, influenza, and other epidemic diseases introduced by Europeans have periodically decimated the Hare and their neighbors since the eighteenth century (Krech 1978a, 1980b, 1983). The combined effect of these factors is illustrated by the history of the various nineteenth century bands which once inhabited the northern part of the Hare's territory. During the twentieth century, these groups have declined, coalesced, and collected at Fort Good Hope and Colville. Families from the former Anderson River and Mountain bands, for instance, were absorbed into the Colville grouping as late as the early 1960s (Hurlbert 1962: 25). The bush community at Colville is thus an amalgamation of the members and descendants of several local groups who have focused their activities in this region in recent decades. The over-all picture, therefore, is one of fluctuation in band composition and terminology over time, and a general fluidity in the people's social structure across space [10].

3. KINSHIP AND THE CONTINUITY OF THE BAND

The Hare and their neighbors have now experienced over 200 years of contact with Euro-Canadian culture. The earliest form of this relationship — the fur trade — began to penetrate into the Northwest Territories in the 1770s. In the following, first century of significant relations between indigenous people and whites, it was fur trade companies, rather than governments, that represented the major outside influences on native communities. The dominant commercial enterprise during this period was the Hudson's Bay Company which, in a royal charter granted to it in 1670, was given a monopoly over all trade in the vast area that drained into Hudson's and James Bay. Though competing groups and independent traders did subsequently arise to challenge the Bay Company in this region, "The Bay" eliminated its most serious rival by absorbing the Montreal-based North West Company in 1821. The Hudson's Bay Company's hegemony in the North ultimately came to an end a half century later when political events finally caught up with commercial ones. In 1867, the British North America

Act united the various provinces and territories of Canada to form a new nation: this process of Confederation created the Dominion of Canada, which took over the lands formerly controlled by the Hudson's Bay Company, and thereby ended The Bay's monopoly of trade.

The government of the newly created Dominion of Canada inherited and recognized certain legal obligations towards aboriginal people that had been enacted during the country's colonial past. Over a century before Confederation, the British and French rivalry in northern North America had formally ended with the Peace of Paris (1763). In that same year, the British Royal Proclamation of 1763 established certain guarantees for Canada's indigenous groups. It reserved for Indian people their unceded lands; gave them royal protection from being molested or disturbed; and reserved for the Crown the exclusive right to purchase, or control purchases, of Indian lands. The Proclamation was meant to avoid conflict and fraud between Indians and land-hungry settlers. Over 200 years later, in twentieth century land claims disputes, the Royal Proclamation has been invoked by Indian people as a major legal precedent for — and acknowledgement of — aboriginal rights in the land (Miller 1991: 71-73).

The legal views of Canada's modern federal government have had a different emphasis. In the first two decades after Canadian Confederation, the government of the new Dominion took several decisive steps which, in its view, alienated Indian title to much of the land in the Canadian prairies and the west. These steps took the form of seven "numbered treaties," Treaties 1 through 7, which were signed between 1871 and 1877 with Indian peoples in Alberta, Saskatchewan, Manitoba, and western Ontario. During this time, and throughout much of the nineteenth century, Canada's major policy towards its Indian people was one of assimilation. In eastern and western Canada, and in the prairies, this policy took the form of schools, reserves, missionary work, and the encouragement of a family-based agrarian life. It has been summed up as an approach centered on "the Bible and the plough."

But government action and policy of any sort did not really come to the Indians living in the Northwest Territories until the very end of the nineteenth century and the early decades of the twentieth. The two treaties that finally involved the indigenous people of the Territories — Treaties 8 and 11 — not only came late, but they were also prompted by a different set of causes than previous negotiations. Whereas Treaties 1 through 7 were designed to make way for white settlers, the precipitating factors in the case of the northern treaties were the discoveries of gold and oil on native soil. First, the Klondike gold rush in the late 1890s suddenly brought large numbers of outsiders to the North. In 1899, this pushed the federal government to negotiate Treaty 8 with Indian people in northern Alberta and

Saskatchewan, northwestern British Columbia, and that part of the North-west Territories which lay to the southeast of Great Slave Lake. Further to the north, however, nothing official was done until the discovery of oil on Indian land north of Fort Norman in 1920. Then, in the following year, Treaty 11 was finally negotiated to establish Canadian title to Indian lands in the rest of the Territories. This last treaty was the one signed by the Hare, and it led to their collective and official designation as Band Number 5.

Though the factors precipitating the two northern treaties were different from the motives behind the earlier ones, the treaties' basic provisions were similar to those in the agreements that preceded them. The government has interpretted all these documents as alienating Indian title to the land in return for a promise of continued native use of the land's resources, and the receipt by Indians of gifts, services, and annual treaty payments. In later years, government officials have also viewed the treaties as legitimating their creation of game laws and resource management policies in the North. But, as has also been true in more southerly areas, Indian communities have understood the treaties to have a different set of meanings (eg., D.M. Smith 1976: 38n). Native peoples, who had no concept of property rights in the land, have thought of these treaties as compacts of peace and friendship in which they simply agreed to allow whites to use their land: they feel they could not have surrendered "ownership" of their territories, for that was something which was never their's to relinquish in the first place.

The Dene have also had a very different understanding of the treaties' significance for their hunting, trapping, and fishing rights. Oral promises made to them by government negotiators clearly indicated that their ability to live off the land would be unimpeded; that they would be exempt from game laws; and that they would be protected from the inroads of white trappers. But unbeknownst to them or their leaders, the actual treaty documents that Indians signed — or more often simply put their mark to — had none of these provisions written into them. In the decades that fol-lowed Treaties 8 and 11, the Dene found themselves increasingly subjected to game regulations, fur taxes, and the encroachments of white trappers who stripped the land of animals in pursuit of quick profits.

Just as the government's oral assurances about land and resources were not kept, some of the treaties' written commitments — such as those to provide adequate schooling and medical care — were not fulfilled. These failures to address what Indians believed were basic social and economic guarantees unfolded during some of the most difficult decades of modern times for the Dene. In the years after Treaty 11 was made in 1921, fur prices collapsed, white controlled mining and mineral exploration boomed, and influenza, tuberculosis, and other epidemic diseases took thousands of native lives in the North. Repeated appeals to the government by Indian leaders, church officials, and other white advocates to respond to the plight of the Dene generally went unheeded. It was only in the late 1940s and 1950s that a Northern Development policy began to provide more substantial health and human services to Indian communities. But by then, in the wake of recent economic and demographic losses, the smaller native communities had disappeared, their remaining members moving to the larger towns [11].

The modern and very minimalist meaning of "treaty" to the Hare and other Dene can be heard in their continued use of the *deneké* word coined for "Indian agent," viz., *sampa-alle*, which means "he who gives money." True to the literal language of Treaty 11, for example, the current *sampa-alle* visits Colville Lake each summer to pay the people the grand sum of $5.00 per person. He also dispenses fish netting, bullets, and other supplies in fulfillment of the treaty provision which states: "There shall be distributed annually among the Indians equipment, such as twine for nets, ammunition and trapping to the value of three dollars per head for each Indian who continues to follow the vocation of hunting, fishing and trapping" (Fumoleau 1973: 168). Given over 70 years years of inflation since Treaty 11's passage in 1921, the people of Colville now find the money and supplies laughable. When they gather on the steps of the mission each year to "take treaty," their mood has an undercurrent of resentment and derision. Behind their feelings is a growing awareness of what they and their ancestors have lost, and what they themselves might hope to regain. These historical developments, these modern reactions, and these profoundly differing interpretations of the treaties are — as Chapter 7 shows — at the very heart of current controversies about the rights and future of the North's Indians and their homeland.

***

Every native community in the North is the product of a number of historical forces, and Colville Lake is no exception. As noted earlier, several bands that once lived in the vicinity of Colville have contributed their members and their descendants to the current make-up of the settlement. The composite origins of the village are submerged now under their current status as a single community. The various names by which the people are known, however, and the designations which they themselves acknowledge, indicate their affiliations with several earlier groupings. They continue to be called the *Dalagot'ine*, which indicates their identity and affinity with the major band which hunted in their region in the late nineteenth and early twentieth centuries (Hara 1980: 36). Some of the people similarly recognize the terms *Khachogot'ine, Nelagot'ine,* and *Dutagot'ine* as applied to themselves, all of which are earlier band names for north, east, and northeasterly groups (Petitot 1875, 1876, 1889, 1891; Osgood, 1932). The residents of

Good Hope also call them "the Lodge People," a term being derived from the fact that some of the band's ancestors were the most northerly and isolated of the Hare, which led the early priests and traders to refer to them as the "gens du Large" (Petitot 1891: 362) "Lodge" is thus an English corruption of this earlier French phrase [12]. All these names reflect the local, geographic nature of Hare groups, rather than a larger tribal identity.

The recent history of the Colville community graphically illustrates the role that kinship and fluidity have played in the survival and adaptability of the people. Prior to the 1960s, the groups in the Colville area had undergone a fifty year period of slow attrition, during which their total population was reduced from a size of about 200 in the first decade of the twentieth century to a core of only twenty-eight people in the mid-1950s [13]. Several factors contributed to the decline of the community, primary among which were

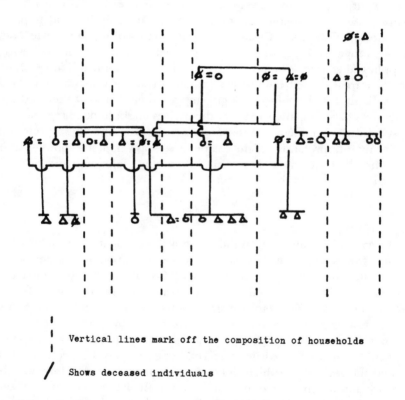

Vertical lines mark off the composition of households

Shows deceased individuals

FIGURE 4   The Composition of the Colville Lake Bandin The Winter of 1956–57

influenza and cholera epidemics, and a high incidence of tuberculosis which had persisted over a period of many years (Hurlbert 1962: 13-14). The Colville band also lost many of its members through migration to Fort Good Hope as the expanding population and facilities of the town attracted more and more native people to it. High fur prices during a brief time in the 1930s induced and enabled many Dene to build houses around the fort, and it was also during this time that the first permanent trapping cabins were erected on Colville Lake's south shore. When a sharp decline in fur prices occurred after the Second World War, however, and the tuberculosis rate increased, bush life suddenly became less economically and physically viable, and the movement of people to the fort was augmented. This was spurred on by the opening of a nursing station and school there, an increase in government transfer payments and financial assistance for Indians, and the availability of more wage employment in the Mackenzie valley region in conjunction with DEW line (radar station) construction and the federal government's Northern Development policy. Similar factors also led to more settled and nucleated Indian communities elsewhere in the western and eastern sub-Arctic (cf. D.M. Smith 1976; J.G.E. Smith 1978; Jarvenpa 1980; Salisbury 1986). As a consequence of these changes among the Hare, by the winter of 1956-57 there were only seven households still spending most of their year in the Colville area, and the bilateral composition of the reduced band at that time is illustrated in Figure 4.

For the handful of people who continued to live and hunt in the Colville region during this era, there will always be a clear distinction between the continuity of their own life style in the bush and the new patterns which lured other families to the fort town. They see themselves as the people who "resisted the gradual abandonment of their traditional lands by the majority of the Gens du Large" (Helm 1965a: 374). To these elderly villagers, possessed of a strong sense of pride and history, there is a deep feeling of affinity with the outlook and ways of the "old timers" who coped with the northern forests in an earlier period — just as they themselves have done in the modern one. This sense of nostalgia and kinship, so real and immediate for many of them, was expressed by old Joseph when he recalled the years of his own youth in the late nineteenth century.

> When I was a young boy, we never knew about a store. We used to wear caribou clothes. We always made open fire. Sometimes we had fire inside a caribou hide tent. It's real funny. It's bad. The smoke goes in your eyes and it's real sore, real bad. We used to laugh at each other. If the smoke goes in your eyes you want to get it out. It's almost like snowblindness. We used to wear just caribou hide clothes. It was real warm in them. A guy will wear warm clothes if he's smart. If he's not smart he'll be cold in the winter, just shivering. If a person's smart, most of the people will stick with him during the winter.

We went to the Barren Grounds four or five weeks before the Feast of the Assumption. We passed the Horton River and there's no trees; just willows real low, like blankets thrown on the ground. Those willows, that's what we used for wood, to make tea or cook food. Once the water boils we keep throwing meat inside. We have no tent that time. The people bring poles along with them and put caribou hides over them and sleep under that.

A guy who really traps hard, who gets lots of marten, that's the guy who gets a seven-by-seven foot tent. All the rest of the guys use caribou hide only.

If we go to the Barrens we kill the first caribou and use the hides for a tent. Sometimes we go for five weeks with no wood. Just use willows. We go down there just for clothes and tents.

When I was a little bigger than Daniel (i.e., around eleven or twelve years of age), my parents wanted to go to Good Hope. The people out here used to go there. It was my first time and when we hit the high hill near Good Hope, we could see big houses and look at them. In the store was tobacco; sometimes no tea, no matches that time.

There were no matches and we used flint: that's what we used for lighting fire and lighting pipe. That time we really suffered. I was raised up when the white man came to this country. The people before me really suffered hard. The people before me, they're the ones who used to live on arrows only. The people in my time were raised up with guns so it was a little bit okay. The first gun wasn't like these kinds of guns — it was a muzzle-loading gun. At that time I used to be real strong. If I run I'll never stop for a long ways.

Now there are not enough people. When I was little there were lots of them, some of them real old. When I was as big as Antoine, some of them were even older than I am now. There was an old man Eh-ga, and Da-šey, Bele-ahn- u, Si-geh-ho, Luzon. There were more old men; their hair was real white. They can't even walk good. They were the people who lived on arrows. Some of these men had strong power, "hay aay, yaay aay," and that's how they sing when they do magic. That time even the young boys get strong magic power, and now these boys don't get them.

When there was no food, no meat to eat, some of them used to sing. Now people are just like white men, they have no magic. Even me I don't have any left.

***

While the true past of which old Joseph speaks can only be recaptured in words and memories now, recent events have wrought certain changes which, to an extent, have re-established a modern version of this earlier reality. In essence, the fate of the Colville band has undergone a dramatic reversal since the community's low point in 1957. This has been primarily due to the fact that since the late 1950s, the rapid expansion of Fort Good Hope was manifesting itself in the form of some pervasive social and economic problems. The town's population was outstripping the natural resources of its environment, and wage labor opportunities were not increasing sufficiently to keep pace with the demand for them. People who had received some education, and those who had become used to paid employment as a new way of life, were reluctant to return to living off the land. Combined with alcohol and other aspects of Westernization, these factors were producing a situation in which transfer and welfare payments, along with drinking, were taking on the dimensions of a new life style for a large segment of the fort's population.

In reaction to these developments, the Canadian government personnel responsible for the Good Hope region undertook a program to encourage people to make greater use of the abundant fish, game, and fur resources of the Colville area.

> In the fall of 1959, a winter road was cut through the woods between Fort Good Hope and Colville Lake at the cost of $5,000 to facilitate easier and faster travelling for trappers. In 1960, a private trader opened an outpost at the southern shore of Colville Lake which saved... long trips to town for supplies (Hara 1980: 49).

The establishment of this trading post marked the beginning of the revival of the community at Colvile Lake. The immediate effect of the store was to encourage more of the original band members to spend a greater part of their year in the Colville area. With supplies available locally, shortages of goods and mid-winter trips to Good Hope for re-stocking were no longer necessary hardships. Many of the Hare took advantage of this opportunity to shift their residence back to Colville Lake. The chance to return to their original territory on a more permanent basis, coupled with the better subsistence and fur resources of the region, and the absence of the drinking and welfare problems of the fort, were strong inducements. In the next few years, some of the people began to construct new homes at the village site, and the government assisted and encouraged them by supplying building materials. Within a few years, the community had achieved a high degree of economic self-sufficiency from Good Hope, and trips between the two settlements became more of a social matter than a survival one.

In the summer of 1962, a Catholic priest was assigned to Colville Lake and a church was built there. The missionary's presence in the village enhanced its appearance of permanency and made it that much more attractive to people. It also obviated the need to go to Good Hope for major Church holidays. More of the band's original families moved back to Colville, and summer trips to the fort declined. The last family to make this seasonal journey by dogpack did so in the summer of 1964. Some families and individuals who had never lived at Colville also relocated there, although several of the latter, plus a few of the old families who had considered

returning to the village, eventually decided against it. At present, consequently, twelve of the settlement's fourteen native households consist of
persons from what the people call "original Colville Lake families" [14].

The blood and marital ties which connect these households provided the
kinship network around which the re-formation of the community was based.
New members of the settlement joined it through relationships with close kin
who were already residing there. The latter people served as the newcomers'
sponsors for community membership. Ties to brothers, sisters, parents, and
spouses' families in the band each served to draw people into or back to the
settlement. In relocating to Colville, people's decisions have revealed two
particular trends: one has been for the reunion and solidarity of groups of
siblings; the other has been for the affiliation of incoming families with either
the husband's or the wife's kin at the settlement. Once people have moved
to Colville, however, their choice of whom to camp with in different years or
at different seasons is quite variable. A family may stay with the husband's
brother for fall fishing, the wife's parents for winter trapping, and close
friends for the spring hunt. Thus, there is really no consistent or dominant
pattern in the people's residence choices. In the long run, flexibility and

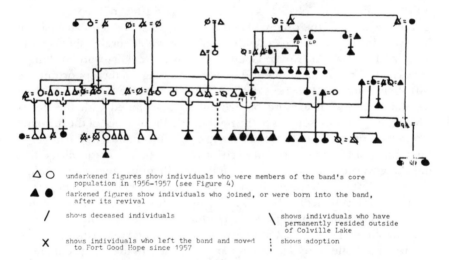

△ O   undarkened figures show individuals who were members of the band's core
      population in 1956–1957 (see Figure 4)

▲ ●   darkened figures show individuals who joined, or were born into the band,
      after its revival

/   shows deceased individuals   \ shows individuals who have
                                                       permanently resided outside
                                                       of Colville Lake

X   shows individuals who left the band and moved ⋮ shows adoption
      to Fort Good Hope since 1957

FIGURE 5   The Composition of the Colville Lake Band in 1967.*

* It is important to emphasize here that this figure provides only a partial
presentation of the kinship links within the community, and a more detailed picture,
i.e., one which was extended vertically and laterally to show ties through deceased
ascending generations and additional intermediary collateral links, would be so
complex that only a three-dimensional model could adequately portray it. This
figure merely attempts to indicated the magnitude and complexity of band
interrelatedness.

bilaterality emerge as the over-riding features of the social system [15].

The fluidity of the kinship system becomes especially evident when one examines the connections through which people joined the re-formed community. The recruitment process can be analyzed visually by taking the social structure of the band at its nadir in the mid-1950s (Figure 4) and contrasting it with the social structure of the settlement ten years later (Figure 5) when the band's revival had been fully accomplished. The darkened individuals in Figure 5 show the new members of the community who moved to, were born into, or rejoined the band after the establishement of the trading post and mission. Each of these individuals shows one or more ties to members of the core population, and several people show numerous links with this group. It is important to note that this figure provides only a partial presentation of kinship links within the community, and a more detailed picture, i.e., one which was extended vertically and horizontally to show ties through deceased ascending generations and other distant kin, would be so complex that only a three-dimensional model could adequately portray it. This figure does serve, however, to indicate the magnitude and complexity of band interrelatedness, and to convey the more visible features of the system.

The way in which people joined the community can be illustrated by two brief case histories, those of the families of Peter and Lena Dehdele, and Fred and Thérèse Yawilweh (cf. Figure 5). Fred left his parents' home at Colville in the late 1950s and moved to Good Hope, where he began living with his future wife Thérèse. They camped with their various kin from the fort over the next few years, and raised a number of children. When they finally married, Fred's family of orientation — including Andre, Berona, and old Joseph — came to town from Colville for the wedding, and soon after that Fred, Thérèse and their children moved back to the bush community with them. The new couple eventually built a cabin for themselves, and they have been living in the village ever since.

Lena and Peter Dehdele, on the other hand, are originally from the Good Hope area, but in the early 1960s Lena's sister's family took up residence at Colville Lake, and soon after Lena's parents did the same. At around that time, Lena and Peter — whose marriage had always been a stormy one — separated from each other. Lena then moved to Colville to join her sister and parents. She also had another kin tie in the village, a young daughter Suzanne, who had been adopted by Wilfred and Bertha Ratehne several years previously. That adoption had occurred because Suzanne had been born during an earlier separation between Lena and Peter, and Peter was dubious that he was really Suzanne's father. A year or two after Lena's move to Colville, she and Peter reconciled their differences, and he then joined her at the community. Peter had some relatives of his own in the village as well,

The Trail of the Hare

including Albert Limertu, a cousin, and Thérèse Yawileh, who was the daughter of one of his older brothers.

***

As these two cases illustrate, a married couple has considerable flexibility in choosing who to reside near because of the options which a bilateral system presents to them. Personal sentiments, likes, dislikes, and other non-kinship factors can thus be incorporated into decisions without violating a kin-based system of affiliation (Helm 1965a: 371-372). The over-all structure of the rejuvenated Colville Lake community, which is summarized in Figure 6, shows some of the primary kinship ties that currently connect the adult men and women who head the village's native families [16].

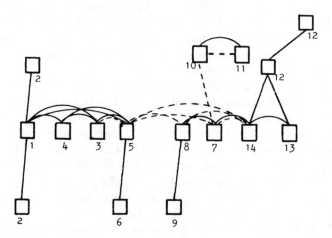

Numbers refer to households discussed in the text

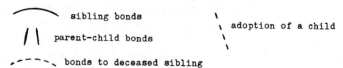

FIGURE 6   Primary Kinship Links Among Village Households.

The term "primary" refers to parent-child and sibling bonds between households. Some households have more than one primary tie between their respective members: e.g., in numbers 3 and 5, two brothers married two sisters; between numbers 7 and 14, there was a sister-exchange marriage. A child from household number 10 has been adopted into household 7, and a second child from household 10 has been adopted into household number 11.

A social feature which is consistent with the settlement's bilateral structure is that ties through one parent are not especially emphasized by the
people over those through the other parent. Individuals associate and
affiliate as much with their mother's kin as they do with those of their father.
Philip Ratehne, for example, variously fishes with his father's brother and
drinks with his mother's brother, just as his parents, Wilfed and Bertha,
alternate camping alliances between their respective siblings. Furthermore,
and despite the prevalence of bonds between brothers in the community, the
fraternally-linked families in the settlement do not join and cooperate on a
permanent basis. Rather, they each maintain separate households, and while
they sometimes camp and hunt with one another, the degree to which this
is done is highly variable. Only the two sets of parent-son related households,
Yen and Yašeh Behdzi's, and André and Fred Yawileh's, regularly stay
together; but even these go their separate ways for at least part of every year.
Underlining the flexibility of the entire system, therefore, is the autonomy
of the nuclear family as a social unit. The history of the band's families, when
they are looked at as affiliating groups, reveals that they all utilize multiple
ties with different kin at different seasons each year. Beyond the nuclear
family, therefore, the more extended, bilateral ties which each person traces
in the community constitute loose kindreds rather than formalized or
defined groups (cf. Freeman 1961). Thus, the Hare extend the value-laden
term *sagot'ine* ("my people") to include all of their kin, and they make no
sharp distinctions between their paternal, maternal, and marital relatives.
Cognate words among other Dene groups — such as *silot'ine* and *ellotine*
among the Chipewyans — indicate bilateral kindreds "with whom one lives
and cooperates over time" (J.G.E. Smith 1976: 22; Jarvenpa and Brumbach
1988: 602-606). To the Hare and their neighbors, then, the idea of *sagot'ine*
consequently describes a social universe *in* which all people are potential
allies and *from* which each individual creates a personal world.

Flexibility is also evident in the way the kinship terminology itself is used:
kin terms are sometimes extended (jokingly or seriously) to non-kin to
indicate the way people perceive the closeness of their interpersonal relations, regardless of real geneaological ties. Adult male friends who are not
actually related by marriage nevertheless address one another as *sala*, "my
brother-in-law," to verbally demonstrate their sense of affinity [17]. When
Wilfred Ratehne's family "adopted" me as a fictional "son" and "brother,"
the understanding was that I had acquired the rights and obligations that
went with that status. Thus, although the people associate certain norms —
such as intimacy, aloofness, reserve, joking, respect, and deference — with
particular kinship ties, real patterns turn out to be very loosely defined
beyond the range of the nuclear family and lineal kin [18]. This supports
Helm's argument that

...one trend of the "internal adjustment to altered conditions of life" (Murdock 1949: 199) by the Northern Dene has been toward the loss of significant behavioral distinctions between certain categories of relatives, [and] toward less correspondence between terminology and behavioral patterns... (MacNeish 1960: 287).

The structure and relationships found in the community, therefore, echo the fluid kinds of social organization that characterize other Athabascan groups in the Arctic drainage region.

***

If we step back in time for a moment and expand our perspective beyond the twentieth century, we find that a dual emphasis on the nuclear family and some sort of flexible, bilateral system was evidently operative in the aboriginal and post-contact periods as well as the modern era. Helm (1965a; Helm and Leacock 1971) has argued persuasively for the adaptive significance of such a social pattern under the environmental conditions prevailing during those earlier times. In previous centuries, the Hare and other Northern Athabascan bands were subject to periodic and widespread starvation, as well as population decimation from epidemic diseases and the raids of such neighboring groups as the Inuit, Kutchin (Gwich'in), Chipewyans, and Cree. Starvation was due to the people's dependence upon migratory and cyclically fluctuating animal populations, such as caribou, hare, fish, and waterfowl, and the literature of the nineteenth century is replete with descriptions of cannibalism, hunger, and death among the Hare and other Mackenzie area peoples [19]. In late April of 1811, for example, the fur trader W.F. Wentzel wrote the following account from the site of Fort Simpson in Slavey country on the Mackenzie River:

> This last winter has been the most melancholy and disastrous that could ever have befallen to any one single man to support without becoming torpidly stupid or totally senseless. Our distresses and sufferings have been so great, that, of four Christians who were left at this establishment last Fall, I am the only survivor... all my men are dead of starvation... I am unable to describe my own position; all my Indians have starved more or less; from one small band only, I received news yesterday evening that five were dead of hunger; but of the majority of the Natives, I have not heard of since the month of November, they were already at that period gnawing the clothing they had upon themselves.
>
> Hares have totally failed throughout all parts of the country and large cattle [i.e., large game] have been uncommonly scarce at this place in particular, and the cold has been, this winter, the severest I have ever yet known. The ice on the Grand River [the Mackenzie] is no less than four and a half to five feet

thick, and at this late date none of the snow has yet disappeared in the woods (1889: 106-107).

According to another nineteenth century observer, John McLean, conditions of starvation and cannibalism were more prevalent among the Slaves and Hares "than any other of the kindred tribes" (1932: 343). William Hooper (1853: 305), writing of the 1840s, reported that the Indians around Fort Good Hope were "dying in crowds." The Hudson's Bay Company records at Fort Good Hope for the winter of 1841-42 report that "52 men, women and children had fallen victims and perished by famine all within 200 yards of the fort... and the survivors of them were living on the carcasses of their relatives" (quoted in Krech 1980b: 4).

Two years later, in 1844, the explorer Henry Lefroy recounted the following incidents among the Hare at Forts Simpson and Good Hope:

> As it was, there had been great scarcity for three or four years, and a frightful famine only the previous winter, accompanied by numerous acts of cannibalism. The Hare Indian woman who washed for me, known as the "*Femme du Diable*," was protected from her husband at the Fort, because he had killed or eaten one or two other wives. Some starving women, who had already eaten their husbands, fell upon the Scotchmen who were carrying a mail, killed them as they lay asleep, and devoured them. They told me at Fort Good Hope that the scenes enacted just outside their palisades were harrowing. The cause of it all was the failure of rabbits from some epidemic, and of reindeer [caribou]... (1938: 88).

These conditions continued not only well into the post-contact period, but up through the first decades of the twentieth century as well (Fumoleau 1973: passim). One woman at Colville Lake is the sole surviving member of a family whose other members starved to death in the area north of Aubry Lake in 1905. Yen Behdzi, who was born in 1898, described one incident of starvation in the early years of this century in the following words:

> When I was young, four men and two women and seven children starved to death. At that time they were getting no rations [from the government]. Now old people get rations. They're lucky. When I was small these guys starved to death because there was no food. When we were going after them, two men were already dead and two women buried them. They were wrapped in blankets and had spruce piled on top of them and had a ribbon tied up on a tree to show that these two guys were dead. There was one guy at the north end of the lake and one guy at this end. They both starved. That's what I know.

Other elderly people in the village recount similar stories of deaths from exposure, cold, or starvation from around the same period, and Hara reports that in 1904, "20 people who were hunting in the Mountain area died from hunger" (1980: 36).

Traditional spiritual beliefs may have eased the stress of the people's hardships and shortages in earlier times. Their relationship with personal guardian spirits, and their former reliance upon medicine men (*ehts'ehgont'ene*), divination, animistic procedures, and shamanistic curing, gave them means of communicating with natural and supernatural forces. But even later, with a modern technology at their disposal, death by starvation has occurred within the Colville band as recently as 1921 (Hara 1980: 144). Martin Yawileh, whose grandfather old Joseph is supposed to have been a very powerful medicine man in his youth, explained that:

> The medicine men knew about animals, ground, trees, anything on the earth. Anything that is on the earth could sing to the medicine man and then he would have it for his helper. That's how he got his power and how he made people well. A man who knows about plants, or other things, for instance, could grab a person, sing over him, and make him well.

Martin's father André added:

> a man would sometimes just know that he had the power to sing certain animals. He may have been out hunting or travelling and then wolf or caribou or some other animal would speak to him and then he had it for life. A man would also know sometimes because these things happened in a dream.

The Hare continue to place a strong emphasis on the predictive efficacy of dreams, and they stress this as an important source of the old medicine men's power (Hara 1980: 220-223).

In times of extreme hardship, it was these powerful *ehts'ehgont'ene* who would go into a trance and sing to their spirit helpers to aid the people in securing food. "If a man knows about caribou," André continued, "he can sing to the caribou and a big herd will come if he is really strong and has strong medicine." The *ehts'ehgont'ene* of the Hare "also permitted themselves to be suspended in the air to facilitate communion with their guardian spirits" (Jenness 1967: 395), and they had a powerful reputation among their own and other people which only began to decline in the mid-nineteenth century as a result of white contact (Franklin 1824: 261; McLean 1932: 324; Richardson 1851ii: 22; Hara 1980: 223-227) [20].

Another facet of the Hare's earlier reliance upon medicine men is reflected in one of the tales in the Asoneh cycle. It shows that even when surplus food was cached as a hedge against times of need, raids by enemy bands, or the depradations of wild animals, were crises that could still threaten the people's existence. In Paul Behdzi's version, this story involves the neighboring Loucheux (the Gwich'in or Kutchin), but Paul and the other band members emphasize the tale's similarity to their own ancestors' plight.

Asoneh was northeast from here in the mountains. The Loucheux buried some drymeat (*inyego^n*) for the winter under the ground. There was a grizzly bear (*sašo*) near there, just near the ice house. The grizzly was killing lots of people.

The Loucheux were coming back to the place where the meat was buried without anything. They were starving. Two boys went to that place. But they were killed; and two older boys went and they were also killed.

So these two boys also never came back. Then they sent two older men to get the meat. They didn't know what had been happening there. So the two men were coming to the place. They saw a big mound near the place and it was the grizzly. The grizzly ran after them and took one of them away. So the other one came running back home and said: "There's a grizzly here who took my friend." Everyone said: "We are going to starve because the grizzly is right on the food we buried." The Loucheux said it was too bad that Asoneh wasn't there.

The year before Asoneh had been staying with an old man, and the old man was now staying with these people. The old man thought of Asoneh. Just when they were thinking about him it was getting dark and they heard someone coming. It was Asoneh who came to that old man. And the old man said: "Is that really you Asoneh?"

Everybody said to him: "We're just starving because the grizzly's on the buried meat." They told him that nearly everyone had been killed by the grizzly. After a while Asoneh went out and met a little boy. He asked the boy which way the people went for the grizzly bear. The little boy pointed and said: "This way. There are two roads. They go on one and after a while they cry and come back. The grizzly took one or two guys each time."

It was getting dark. There was moonlight. The old man went to sleep. So Asoneh went out and went on the road. He saw a big thing on the hill where the Loucheux buried the meat. The grizzly came running after Asoneh. He was coming right near Asoneh, and so Asoneh jumped right over the grizzly bear with his snowshoes. He jumped back and forth over the bear and each time he hit him over the head with a stick. He wanted to tire the bear out. He kept jumping over him and hitting him between the eyes. Both of the grizzly's eyes came out.

Asoneh was sitting, resting beside the grizzly bear. Asoneh was wondering: "I can't leave the grizzly like this." So he broke up a lot of wood. He propped up the grizzly with the pieces and he also propped his mouth open with a stick. He faced the bear, on the road, to where the people would come from. Then Asoneh went back home. When he got back he went to sleep. The old man knew nothing about what Asoneh did.

The old man said to Asoneh: "Please go with those men when they go to the grizzly." And Asoneh said: "When they go, I'll go with them." So the old man said to the men: "Asoneh will go with you, so you had better hurry up." Everyone said "Yes" and they went. Asoneh was walking behind and those men were walking ahead of him. They yelled: "The grizzly is coming already!" Those guys then ran back. The old man ran back too. Asoneh was still walking towards the grizzly and the old man saw him. He said to the other men: "You don't have to run because Asoneh is still walking toward the grizzly. What's the matter with you?"

The men saw Asoneh walking right up close to the grizzly. So Asoneh took his stick out and the grizzly fell down. He was frozen up. Asoneh asked these men: "Why do you run away? This grizzly is frozen."

Then they went to the place where they buried the drymeat. They threw away the meat with the blood on it from the men that the grizzly had killed and they took only the good meat. Some of them had already died from starving. They gave the meat out to the people.

The old man said to give Asoneh two girls and he can camp with us three times. Everybody said yes. They were looking for two good, cute girls.

Asoneh was camping with the old man. Those girls came into the house and sat down waiting for him. But Asoneh was a really good guy. Asoneh told them: "Go out. Me and the old man are going to sleep. We don't need you here." He chased them out.

The next morning Asoneh was gone when the old man woke up.

***

Another story, told by Joseph Tehgu, shows the special relationship between a man with strong medicine and his guardian spirit, and it also recalls the stresses of warfare and raiding by the Chipewyans in early historic times.

The people were staying at *Lugewatue* (Whitefish Lake), and everyone was visiting nets. They said visitors were coming from *Denedigontue* (Those-men-were-killed-there Lake). Everyone was just excited because visitors were coming. They were survivors from the Chipewyans who had been killing people at *Denedigontue*. The people at *Lugewatue* saw the smoke from there.

Everyone was killed at *Denedigontue*. The Chipewyans took off for *Sasoyetue* (Great Slave Lake) and the *Lugewatuet'ine* (The Whitefish Lake People) went out after them. They got to Great Slave Lake. The Chipewyans ran on the lake and these guys were crying because their parents had been killed by the Chipewyans. The people asked each other: "Someone of you has to do magic (*ehts'ehneh*)." Some of them said no. But one of them knew about Crow and so Crow came to him. The man took a little piece of ice and put it in Crow's mouth. Then Crow took off on Slave Lake.

The Chipewyans were in the middle of the lake and a big cold wind started blowing. They all froze to death. There was one guy named Tsurayule who made it cross Slave Lake. And one other Chipewyan made it across after Tsurayule. So there were two Chipewyans. They made fire. The second one was a young boy: when he got warmed up, he just fell down dead. Tsurayule almost froze to death too. His eyes were getting blurry. He saw things. He said: "There are too many mice around here." Tsurayule was sitting down and then he fell backwards dead. One other man was saved of the Chipewyans. He was the only one who did not freeze to death. He had no food. He cut off his parka and he was wearing caribou hide. He took his belt off and made a hole in the ice and tried to fish with his belt and some caribou hide at the end of it. He pulled a loon up out of the lake. He knew something this man: he was a magician. Old-timers magic is strong. He ate the loon up and then took off. Then he met some of his Chipewyan people leaving to come after the people from around here. He said: "Don't go because all your people were killed by a big wind on the lake." So everyone quit. All the Chipewyans gave up the idea.

In those days, the people weren't afraid of killing each other.

***

The assistance that the Hare received from "people with strong medicine" may have mitigated their plight in former times, but more drastic measures were sometimes necessary to cope with serious and ubiquitous privations. Aboriginally, as well as during the nineteenth century, the people's recourse to such population control devices as infanticide, especially female infanticide, and the abandonment of the aged and infirm, testify to the severity of environmental pressures (Petitot 1889: 154-157; Keith 1890: 119; Hooper 1853: 319; Helm 1980). The Hare's resort to these measures added flexibility to their social system by giving them options for dealing with economically marginal individuals who also inhibited their mobility. These ecological stresses, and the people's consequent efforts to control the size and composition of their groups, gave to the Hare and the other sub-Arctic Indians one of the lowest population densities of any indigenous people in the New World. Scholars have placed the aboriginal Hare population at 700-800 people, occupying an area of approximately 45,000 square miles (Mooney 1928: 26; Osgood 1936a). The density for all the boreal forest groups — which totalled 30-35,000 individuals over some 1,500,000 square miles of the Shield sub-Arctic — has been estimated at only one person for every 50 to 70 square miles (Kroeber 1939: 141; Rogers and Smith 1981: 141) [21].

Given the recurrence of starvation, disease, and other disasters for northern natives, it is likely that it was the basic fluidity of the kinship system itself which allowed people to first respond to and ultimately recover from these decimations by shifting residence, requesting hospitality, affiliating with other kin, and then reconstituting communities of the survivors and the unafflicted. As one anthropologist has summed up the social implications of the northern Dene's ecology:

> We know from reports in the last century that the Mackenzie River Dene, although in possession of iron ice chisels and firearms, nevertheless periodically suffered from drastic depopulation through starvation... The concurrence of the low point in the rabbit cycle, of severe ice conditions not permitting net setting, and/or fish failure, and of regional failure of moose or

of caribou migration would impose absolute starvation for several or many weeks. Severe starvation and population loss under exactly such circumstances were described by Wentzel... in 1811. Could conditions in truly aboriginal times have been better? What I am stressing is not merely that aboriginal Dene populations were small in size and low in density, but that population was unstable, with decimation through famine occurring at what may have been rather cyclical intervals. When such disasters struck, "multiple kinship avenues" (Goodenough 1962: 11) to new affiliations as old ones collapsed may well have been crucial in permitting quick regrouping of survivors... (Helm 1965a: 381-382) [22].

The decline of the Colville Lake band through economic and epidemic factors in the twentieth century was a crisis whose nature and magnitude were similar to those described for earlier periods. Initially, bilateral networks allowed most of the group's population to be successfully re-integrated into Fort Good Hope. Later, when the opportunity to revive the bush community arose, "multiple kinship avenues" were again utilized to re-form the band in accordance with this underlying principle. The fluidity of population movements, and the adaptability of the kinship system in allowing the Hare to relocate and reconstitute their groups in this fashion, thus stand out as social features with both historical depth and contemporary importance for Indian people.

4. KINSHIP, GENEROSITY AND EMOTIONAL RESTRAINT

Another flexibile feature of Colville's kinship system is the variable way in which band members treat different kin. There are marked disparities in the extent to which attitudes and behavior are standardized for close and distant relatives, or for people connected by marriage. This degree of latitude in kinship patterns, and in the kinds of expectations and obligations associated with them, also reveal how the Hare participate in cultural values of generosity, equality, concensus, and emotional restraint.

Although members of the Colville Lake community use extended kin bonds to form camping and hunting alliances, the nuclear family remains the basic social division in their lives. It is the residential unit, the main place for economic cooperation and the division of labor, and a source of material and emotional support. Since the family contains each person's closest kin, it is also the center of the strongest affective ties in each individual's world. It is among family members that the bonds of generosity, interdependence, and mutual aid are the strongest, and the social relations people create with one another there exhibit a combination of warmth, respect, and restraint. The respect that children show for their parents, and the ties that siblings establish among themselves, ideally continue into the children's own adulthood, thus perpetuating the family's cohesiveness over time. Relations between grand-parents and grandchildren, and parents and their young offspring, are especially warm, and the display of affection by and towards children is one of the most open and culturally permissible forms of emotional expression shown in the community. In contrast to this, adult siblings of the opposite sex, as well as husbands and wives, often mute the demonstration of their sentiments for one another – even though the underlying feelings are commonly quite affectionate. While social bonds remain the closest within the nuclear family, then, their low-keyed warmth is often hidden from the observer by a demeanor of restraint and a sense of mutual respect.

The modern emphasis upon the nuclear family is probably a point of continuity with earlier forms of Hare social structure. Historically, it has been shown that the introduction of a trapping economy among native peoples has led to an increased emphasis on the family at the expense of wider band ties (cf. Murphy and Steward 1956; Leacock 1954; Jenness 1967: 257; Helm and Leacock 1971: 365). This is because trapping necessitates the fragmen-tation and dispersal of communities into small social units for the effective exploitation of widely dispersed fur resources. During most of each year, therefore, especially the winter and spring, larger groupings become eco-nomically inefficient, and dispersal becomes more pronounced and more prolonged than under previous conditions.

The crucial economic role of the family, combined with the premium that survival in the bush places upon smooth-working, cooperative social units, are factors conducive to an emphasis upon emotional restraint. Strong outbursts could seriously disrupt the harmony which is necessary to camp life. The pervasiveness of emotional containment at all social levels in the band lends strong support to such an interpretation. This argument is also strengthened by the fact that most cultural means for coping with stress and tension – such as mobility, the withdrawal from unpleasant encounters, the frequent participation in gossip, and the redirection of aggression towards dogs and inanimate objects – are essentially techniques which allow the people to avoid direct emotional confrontations with one another [23].

***

Beyond the nuclear family, extended kin ties persist as a very important part of community life. In the reunions of each annual cycle, and in the changing bush partnerships that people form, the Hare activate their extensive social networks. The Dene continue to stress their interdependence with kin and fellow band members, and they look to one another for mutual assistance, sharing, and companionship. Beyond a certain range of kin, however, interpersonal ties tend to be loose and diffuse. Outside of a married adult's immediate in-laws, who usually warrant deference and respect, a person's other relations do not elicit uniform attitudes or behaviors. They can be turned to, camped with, borrowed from and called on as conditions necessitate, just as they can expect you to reciprocate. But this is done in an ad hoc way that reflects current needs and opportunities. The fact that large kinship networks are not "corporate" in nature – i.e., they are not formally organized to own property or to live and work together – permits them to be utilized with the same kind of flexibility that occurs in other areas of life.

The diffuseness of expectations and obligations beyond a person's immediate family and parents-in-law allows for a high degree of fluidity in establishing camping alliances and other social ties. Such variables as age, gender, personality, degree of assimilation, allegiance in local disputes, participation in drinking, and the size of economically viable groups, all affect the actual relationships found within the community. In many cases, these non-kin factors supercede kin ties in the development of close bonds. Heavy drinkers, for example, camp and trap together more frequently than they do with non-drinkers, even if the latter are close relatives. Kinship considerations may also become secondary if shared acculturative experiences — such as the time two people spent together at school, living at Good Hope, or working at outside wage employment — have bound non-kin together in a long-standing friendship. Furthermore, because of the cultural emphasis upon avoidance and restraint among adults of the opposite sex – especially if they are kin — young men and women often establish their closest ties with non-related age mates of the same sex. This is evident in some of the community's best friendships, such as the one between teenagers Philip Ratehne and Gabyel Behdzi; the tie uniting Monique Yawileh and Yerimen Behdzi, both traditional, unmarried women in their twenties; and the bond between Lena Dehdele and Paula Limertu, each of whom is a bilingual, educated, and relatively Westernized mother of young children. Personal affinity — along with similarities of age, gender, and outlook — underlie each of these friendships.

Ties are also affected by the type of relationship that a linking kinsman or kinswoman has with a particular relative of a given person. In relationships between a father's brother and a brother's son, to cite one such instance, each of the cases in the village is strongly influenced by the kinds of bond maintained by the connecting brothers, as well as by the relative cohesiveness of their households. Leon Behdzi and his brother Yen, for example, are both tradition-oriented, non-drinking, and monolingual individuals, who are drawn together by their quiet, conservative philosophy, as well as their relation as siblings. They are much closer with one another than either of them is with Pierre, their heavy drinking, more assimilated brother. When

Leon, who has no adult sons in the village, needs help or assistance, he and his daughter Yerimen usually call upon Yen's son Yašeh rather than Pierre's boy Gabyel, for it is with Yašeh — and with Yašeh's father — that they share a common outlook and strong sense of affinity. Not surprisingly, Leon and his daughter camp much more frequently with Yen and Yašeh's household during the winter than any of their other — and equally closely related – village kin.

***

The ad hoc, fluid nature of each individual's social network leads to a certain amount of tension among the people as a result of their wide-ranging and pervasive expectations for generosity among kin and *sagot'ine.* In cases where non-kin are more closely connected to a person than some of his own relations, there can be a lack of clarity wherever the issue of that person's responsibility to kin and friends is raised. Band members are very conscious of their own and other people's behavior in the areas of hospitality and reciprocity, and they are anxious both to receive their share of others' largesse, and also to maintain their own status and reputation for magnanimity. When the actions of individuals do not coincide with what others expect of them, strong sentiments are raised which must be dealt with in some way. Stinginess, and the failure to cooperate and provide hospitality, thus put the themes of interdependence, generosity, and emotional containment to an acid test. The way in which these values are elaborated and reconciled with one another, then, is crucial to an understanding of the nature of social and ecological adaptations within the band. It is therefore worth examining here how the people cope with these moral ambiguities.

One of the primary functions of a cultural emphasis upon sharing is that it serves to relieve aspects of environmental stress by insuring the distribution of scarce resources among kin and fellow villagers. The corollary of reciprocity means that each person has a claim upon the fish and game taken by the people to whom he is obliged to distribute his own kill. Ideally, things should balance out in the long run, while in the short-run the chances for the well-being and survival of group members are increased.

The value of such an ethic under aboriginal conditions is manifest, and currently the successful hunter or fishmen is still expected to share part of his food catch among kin and other band members. This obligation is particularly strong in the case of moose, caribou, and fish. Moose are rare in the Colville area and they are hunted mainly in the summer and fall, viz., seasons during which meat is at a premium since there are no caribou herds in the area. The successful hunter usually gives the moose away to another person, such as his father or a close friend, and the latter is then expected to supervise the butchering of the animal and the distribution of its meat among the people. Upon receiving news of a successful moose hunt, the men of the village, along with some of the adult females, go to the site of the kill by boat or on foot, and the meat is then shared out among them by the person to whom the moose has been given. The man who shot the animal receives his share as well, and both he and the person to whom the animal was given usually retain a good portion of the meat, in addition to keeping most of the much-valued hide.

Gross inequities in hunting luck can be a source of stress and envy within the community, but the fate of a slain moose illustrates the subtle way in which these potentially disruptive emotions get handled. At a material level, disparities in the good fortune of hunters are redressed by redistribution mechanisms. Although envy may be repressed or rechanneled rather than annihilated by these means, the feeling's immediate impact is dulled. At a social level, since the meat and hide received by the successful hunter ultimately come to him as a gift from the distributor rather than as a direct windfall, envy of the hunter himself is less concentrated. The distributor, who also retains a sizeable percentage of the animal, similarly comes off in a good light as a man who is generous with other people's largesse. This variation on redistribution, by deflecting envy, dilutes it. The egalitarian outcome of the situation maximizes band survival by guaranteeing people a minimum level of access to food. One can thus argue, as others have done for such a negatively experienced phenomenon as anxiety (Hallowell 1941; Slobodin 1960a), that the fear of envy, when its manifestations are culturally institutionalized, can be made to serve some important and unexpected social functions [24].

Generosity involving fish operates differently in the band. Each household has nets set the year round to get food for human and dog consumption, and no one is expected to distribute his daily catch on a regular basis. If a particularly "meaty" fish (eg., a large trout), or several especially favored ones (such as loche) are caught by a person, some of this fish may be given to that man's parents, or to a married son, daughter, or sibling. Such distribution occurs on a small scale, however, and it does not involve the obligatoriness, the amount of food, or the number of people that are affected in sharing out a moose-kill. Methods of storing and preserving fish allow surpluses to be kept for future use, which is important in view of the people's continuous and daily need for dogfeed. More intensive generosity with fish occurs when a close or distant kinsperson, or a friend, has run out of fish for dogfeed on some particular occasion.

The latter situation can come about in a number of ways. Some people, for example, are much less assiduous than others in laying up a large cache of fish. This can leave them without dogfeed at those times of the year when fish are hard to get: this occurs most often during fall freeze-up and spring break-up, as well as during January and February, the coldest months of the winter. At such times, the persons in question may have to turn to kin and friends to fill their need, and people are expected to respond positively to such requests for help. A second scenario involves people who have just returned to the village from the bush or switched winter campsites. Under these conditions they are often without dogfeed for a few days until they can reset their nets and get their own fish. During this interval, they rely upon the generosity of others to feed their families and dogs. Other instances involve men who have had bad luck in their fishing, as in cases where the fish have moved from the part of the lake where their nets were set. They, too, can count on the aid of kin and friends in such times of need. Travellers are another group who can expect to benefit from the hospitality of others: people are expected to feed the dogs of any person who visits their bush camp, as well as offer generous treatment to the traveller himself.

The sharing of caribou meat presents yet a third pattern of distribution. At the present time, caribou are generally plentiful in the Colville region during the winter and spring. Most households, therefore, have an equally good chance of acquiring sufficient meat for themselves, and there is no binding obligation or expectation that band members will distribute most of their meat among other families on a regular basis. Persons sometimes present one another with caribou heads, tongues, and fetuses – all of which are considered delicacies by the Hare – but this is only an occasional and unformalized type of prestation. However, there are also some serious circumstances in which entire families may be without meat for a considerable period of time. Some households contain better or more hunters than others, and some families may find themselves camped in an area where the caribou did not come that particular winter. In such cases, the people without meat generally do ask for some from those who were more fortunate. Their request is stated in an oblique and stylized manner, however, the needy person simply stating his lack of meat to the other party, who is then expected to understand this as a request for caribou [25]. The people without meat may actually offer to buy some from the others, but this is rare: rather, there is a tacit expectation among villagers that the families who have had greater luck at the hunt should offer some of their kill to those with little or no meat. This is especially the case if the men of one household have killed a very large number of caribou at one time.

The concept of generosity is not extended to cover the distribution of fur-bearing animals or small game, such as beaver, muskrat, hares, or waterfowl, but it does include liquor, homebrew, and invitations to brew parties. Non-edible items which are considered to be personal or family property by the people, such as dogs, sleds, household supplies, sewing materials, rifles, and traps are similarly the subject of claims by one's fellow band members. Such goods are loaned out rather than given away, however, and reciprocity may ultimately take the form of a loan of a different piece of property or a direct gift of food.

***

In addition to the sharing of food, drink, and supplies, the people's concepts of interdependence and reciprocity also extend to matters of hospitality, cooperation, and mutual aid. The Hare adopt and care for one another's children; they help each other in moving to and from bush camps; they get one another firewood in cases of illness or incapacity; they do sewing for each other; they camp with one another for varying periods in the bush; and they also offer each other assistance by lending and operating boats, motors, and other equipment. Generosity therefore covers both goods and services, and these two aspects are often interchangeable when it comes to reciprocating the helpfulness of others. When Wilfred Ratehne's son Philip, for example, had camped with some relatives for an extended period of time one spring, he brought these people several quarters of caribou meat the following winter. After Leon's daughter Yerimen had done a great deal of sewing for Maurice Bayjere's son Luke, Luke cut several cords of wood for her family when Leon was taken ill a few months later. I found that my own attempts to reciprocate rather than pay people cash for the services they provided me with were warmly received and appreciated by them – much more so than the money with which the trader and missionary usually paid villagers for food and labor.

Adoption is another process which throws key cultural values into bold relief. The motives for giving or taking a child in adoption are diverse, and in their variety they exhibit some of the basic social, psychological, and survival considerations which concern the Hare. A family, for example, may offer a child to some kin to raise if their own household already has more members than can be successfully maintained. Berona and André Yawileh have brought up a grandson of theirs from Good Hope because the boy's parents could not manage with the large number of offspring they had already produced. If a man or woman dies or is taken seriously ill, young children may also be given in adoption to ease the other parent's burden. Wilfed and Bertha Ratehne provide a case in point, for they have brought up Suzanne Dehdele, one of Lena Dehdele's daughters, partly because this child's mother was stricken with tuberculosis soon after Suzanne's birth. There are also adoption cases involving children whose paternity is in question, or who were conceived outside of a marriage. Such individuals may be given to another family to bring up in order to relieve the tensions that are developing between a husband and wife. The difficulties surrounding Suzanne Dehdele's birth, for example, were compounded by her doubtful paternity, and this threatened to precipitate a crisis between her parents. A second case involved a son whom Albert Limertu had fathered in a common-law union prior to his marriage. The boy, who was living with Albert at the time, was eventually returned to his natural mother because the child's presence was creating constant friction between Albert and his new wife Paula.

People ask for or accept a child for a variety of reasons as well. Infants and youngsters are loved and valued, and kin and close friends are anxious to help a child, and his or her parents, in times of distress. Adopted children are raised with great warmth and affection, and Western notions of legitimacy and illegitimacy are irrelevant in influencing the treatment that a child ultimately receives in his adopted home. No person is permanently stigmatized because of the conditions surrounding his conception or upbringing. Adopting a child is also an excellent opportunity to publicly display one's generosity and good-heartedness, and it simultaneously demonstrates to everyone the competence and self-sufficiency of a couple in their ability to provide for an extra person. Adoption, then, is not always an entirely altruistic endeavor. Childless couples are especially anxious to adopt, not only for the companionship, but also so that there will be someone to take care of and support them in their later years. While old age pensions have increased the economic security of the elderly in modern times, such transfer payments have not always enhanced the social ties or standing of those who receive them. People are still valued for their strength and physical productivity, so while an older individual's money can buy things at the store, it does not necessarily purchase that person esteem. Being able to count on the help and hospitality of a grown child thus remains a strong motive for adopting a youngster.

Adoption, then, is a social relationship which embodies the themes of kinship, flexibility, and generosity. It is a process which distributes children among the people who most need or can best care for them, and it solidifies and extends community ties while enhancing specific reputations. When families discuss the possibility of a child being raised in another household, no one makes a highly formalized decision to offer or accept the child in question. Rather, a series of informal conversations occurs among the adults involved, out of which a sense of overriding sentiment and willingness emerges. Underlying the process, then, is not the exercise of authority, but — once again — the creation of consensus.

As a source of interest, children also become a medium of exchange and expressiveness under other circumstances. Not only are they adopted with great ease, but they are also sent, from time to time, to live temporarily with relatives in different settlements and encampments. They thus experience, during their early years, periods of residence with aunts, uncles, and grandparents, and they consequently share life with a substantial range of their *sagot'ine* as they mature. They come to define their social world, and its values, in a broad manner, and this prepares them for coping with a diversity of people and expectations in their adulthood.

***

This summary of emotionality, kinship, generosity, and adoption in the band, while it omits some features of this complex, does serve to indicate its central place in the community's life. Since it is among a person's *sagot'ine* that tensions over reciprocity may also threaten to erupt, social mechanisms for avoiding, displacing, or diffusing disruptive feelings become especially important. In the emotional economy of the band's life, then, the ethic of restraint, the safety valve of gossip, and the escape mechanism of mobility, are crucial devices for maintaining peace and order within the community.

A significant corollary to these social and emotional themes is the emphasis on flexibility. If one compares the way in which the generosity ethic operates in regard to moose, caribou, and fish, to take just three examples, it is evident that the moral system is flexible enough to allow different kinds of expectations to be in force according to the degree of scarcity of these various commodities. The system allows adjustments not only in response to the availability of these foods, however, but also in response to the level of need that people have at different points in time. Since a person's possession of surplus food, time, or equipment is partly a function of his luck in a somewhat unpredictable environment, a rigid set of rules that bound him to dispensing his goods and services through a rigid network of kin might not benefit those who were most in need at any particular moment. Conversely, again, a family that could only rely upon specific relatives in order to obtain assistance might find themselves, at certain times, without access to those persons in the band who could help them most in their current distress. Given the persistence of a bush way of life and its ecological stresses for the people, a flexible implementation of generosity as a cultural value allows for the distribution of scarce goods and services in a way that maximizes the well-being of all concerned.

What makes the flexible elaboration of this theme possible is the people's emphasis on equality, their consciousness of their interdependence with one another, and the inherent fluidity of the social networks through which these realizations are made to operate. While the cultural emphasis upon emotional restraint also fosters the interdependence of band members, it does not, of course, actually relieve the stresses that it represses. One would expect to find, in such a situation, that there are other culturally sanctioned means to express feelings which would permit the discharge of tensions while allowing the community to function at an effective level. Among the people of the band, such opportunities for emotional relief and release take several forms: these include drinking behavior, humor, the beating of dogs, shifts of residence, participation in gossip, and a high level of mobility — patterns of coping which are explored in the next three chapters.

5. IMPLICATIONS

The values that have been focused upon here, along with some of the specific ways in which they are expressed, can not only be found among many northern peoples, but in hunting-and-gathering groups from elsewhere in the world as well. In a landmark symposium devoted to mapping the nature of hunting societies (Lee and DeVore, eds. 1968), fluid modes of social organization, and a flexible approach to residence and group composition, were found to be characteristic of many of the populations considered. Bilaterality, as Murdock (1968) noted, has been especially prevalent among North American hunting groups, a point re-enforced by analyses of the social structure of the Inuit, the Dogribs, and other Dene groups such as the Chipewyan, Bear Lake, and Slavey Indians (cf. Damas 1968; Balikci 1968; Helm 1968a; Rogers and Smith 1981; and sources cited in Chapter 3, note 22) [26]. A cultural stress upon sharing, generosity, and hospitality has similarly been found to have a wide distribution, and the frequent recourse to group fission as a means of resolving conflict also emerges from comparisons with African and other peoples (Lee and DeVore 1968; Turnbull 1968a; cf. also Netting 1977; Service, 1966).

Elsewhere, in a volume summarizing the culture of the Canadian Inuit, Valentine and Vallee (1968) have brought together a number of essays which highlight the inherent flexibility of Inuit life styles and orientations, including approaches to kinship, social organization, and modernization. Works by Chance (1966), Damas (1963), the Hongimanns (1965), and Willmott (1960) have pointed out similar features in specific Inuit communities. Other studies on Northern Indians have brought out some of the same emphases noted here among the people of Colville Lake, viz., the values of egalitarianism, individual autonomy, concensus decisions, economic reciprocity, emotional restraint, and interdependence. Research on the Hare at Fort Good Hope reveals a similar social pattern (Broch 1977/78, 1986; Hara 1980). Athabascan groups demonstrating some or all of these themes include the Gwich'in (Slobodin 1960a; Nelson 1973: 281-282), Kaska (Honigmann 1949), and such Arctic drainage peoples as the

Slavey (Honigmann 1946; Helm 1961; Christian and Gardner 1977), Dogrib (Helm 1965b); Helm and Lurie 1961), Bear Lakers (Osgood 1932; Rushforth 1984), and Chipewyans (VanStone 1965; J.G.E. Smith 1978; Sharp 1988). Northern Algonkian peoples from eastern Canada, including the Cree (Chance 1968; Sindell 1968; Salisbury 1986; Preston 1979, 1991), the Montagnais-Naskapi (Lips 1937; Leacock 1969; Henriksen 1973), and the Ojibwa (Hallowell 1946; Landes 1937a, 1937b; Rogers 1969a, 1969b) have been shown to stress many of the same cultural adaptations.

The general features noted above have been found not only among nomadic groups of the Arctic and sub-Arctic, but also in hunting societies from very different ecologies. Helm (1968a) and Woodburn (1968), for example, point out that the nature of Dogrib socio-territorial groupings — which is quite similar to that found among the Hare — is duplicated in !Kung Bushmen, Mbuti, Ik, and various Australian bands (cf. Turnbull 1961, 1968a; Hiatt 1968). The point being made here, of course, is not that these cultural features are universal traits for hunting groups, for the latter can be found to differ on a great number of parameters, including the nature of band composition and social organization; the type of authority, decision-making and social control that are operative; and the modes of — and motives for — cooperation, hospitality, and food distribution. The frequency of the qualities discussed, however, does indicate their adaptive significance for many hunting peoples, particularly those found in rigorous northern latitudes and other stressful environments.

Although themes such as flexibility, restraint, and reciprocity may not always be explicitly stated in a culture, their indirect and subtle manifestations can often be detected in many areas of life (cf. Opler 1945 on cultural themes and their expression). The people of the Colville band, for example, have no word which corresponds to "flexibility" per se, nor do they voice this concept, in a straightforward manner, as a cultural value. However, they do prize and hold in high esteeem an individual who they feel to be malleable, adjustable, and capable of adapting to diverse ecological and social situations. When they praise a person like Leon Behdzi or Peter Dehdele for being "a good bush man," they mean not only that he possesses all the skills necessary for living off the land, but also that he is alert and innovative enough to meet the challenges of any unusual circumstances that arise. The successful person is thus a flexible one, an individual who can alter materials and rely on inventive procedures when his situation calls for such adaptations. In social contexts, flexibility is often given expression in the way that people boast of and enumerate the various friends and kin who they have, or could have, lived with in the past, and with whom they may yet live or camp with in the future. This is not merely a way of describing the extensiveness of one's *sagot'ine;* it is also an affirmation of how many social possibilities a person has at his disposal, as well as the fluid way in which he can actualize them.

Flexibility, restraint, and generosity are values which also find expression in the affirmation of other cultural themes, some of which can be considered as corollaries of those delineated above (cf. Opler, 1946). One of the most clearly stated values among the Hare is freedom, viz., the freedom to live as one chooses, to move when and where one pleases, and to schedule, order, and arrange one's life as one wishes. The people of the band are continually contrasting the type of existence that they lead with that found at Fort Good Hope, and one of the great advantages with which they characterize the bush and the village is the freedom of life style that it permits them. As they express this idea, it emphasizes the absence — at Colville — of many of the unpleasant features of the more urbanized town, including freedom from overbearing Western time schedules, authoritative whites, discrimination, and high rates of drinking, violence, gossip, and overcrowding. Freedom is also defined positively by the people in terms of the relatively more independent decisions they can make concerning their associations, residence arrangements, physical movements, drinking habits, and the timing of their work and leisure.

Freedom, in this sense, is not only cognate with flexibility, but also with the people's stress upon individualism, equality, anti-authoritarianism, and independence. Their dislike of "bossy" or pushy persons, and their positive evaluation of self-reliance and individual competence, are consistent — though not synonymous — with their emphases on freedom and flexibility. Furthermore, their focus on individuality and autonomy also expresses the themes of emotional restraint and equality: because the people insist that no person is inherently better or more entitled than anyone else, proper behavior includes the norm of restraining one's own feelings and conduct so as not to interfere in the lives of others. Taken together, these attitudes and orientations comprise an independent outlook which resembles the variously individualistic or "atomistic" ethos that Honigmann (1946, 1949, 1968), Hallowell (1946), Landes (1937a), Henriksen (1973), Broch (1977/78), J.G.E. Smith (1978), Preston (1979, 1991) and others have found to be characteristic of specific Northern Athabascan and Northern Algonkian groups. Building on such studies, Honigmann has gone further and described a "pan-Athapaskan social personality" whose traits include "personal independence, present-orientedness, suppression of hostility, dependency strivings, and emotional suppression" (1975: 547, 553). These are qualities found in cultures across the sub-Arctic (Honigmann 1981a: 736-738).

At Colville Lake, while the people can be both flexible and restrained, as well as free and independent, it is evident from the history and current life style of the band that its members are also highly interdependent with one

another. They are bound together by ties of kinship, intermarriage, friendship, generosity, and mutual reliance, a set of conditions and emphases
which constitute counter-themes (Opler 1945: 198) to the autonomous
values described above. Given the nature of the people's existence, both
*in*dependent and *inter*dependent orientations are of prime adaptive significance for them, and a one-sided emphasis on one set of values without the
other would probably be socially and ecologically unfeasible. These existential attitudes are also reflected in the mythology and lore of the people.
Thematic studies that have been done on folktales from Fort Good Hope,
and from the people's regional neighbors the Chipewyans, have revealed a
complementary emphasis upon dependency and self-sufficiency in the
folklore of both these groups; a balance between these value-orientations
was especially evident in the traditional materials collected during earlier
times (Cohen and VanStone 1963; Cohen and Osterreich 1967). At Colville
Lake, where a corresponding balance among traditional needs and motivations is still in force, the people's themes — and their corollaries — help to
bridge the inconsistencies between these two sets of values. The coping
mechanism of physical mobility, and an ethos of emotional restraint and
displacement, help to mediate the ultimately irreconcilable nature of these
"independent" and "interdependent" ethics.

***

In recent years, a number of ethnographic studies in the North have
documented the persistence of the themes we have discussed among
Athabascan, Algonkian and Inuit peoples who live in more urbanized
settings [27]. The cognitive and behavioral problems which confront these
groups are immediate and pervasive, and they hinge not only upon the
inherent complexity of larger and more heterogeneous living situations, but
upon the ambiguity in role and personal expectations which such conditions
generate. The folklore analyses cited above, for example, which compare
traditional and contemporary native persons, have shown that more Westernized or assimilated Indians reveal — in their projective fantasy material
— a level of dependency which significantly exceeds that found among their
ancestors: analysts have argued that this is in part the outcome of the people's
increased involvement in Federal welfare programs [28]. Although the social
and historical materials from Colville Lake concern a people in a "micro-
urban phase" of development (J.G.E. Smith 1978) — and who have therefore
not really experienced the full dimensions of this kind of Westernization —
the band's maintenance of a more traditional life style provides a valuable
picture of the cultural patterns which precede these more urbanized dilemmas. While a detailed analysis of the latter situations is beyond the scope

of this book, some of their dimensions can be delineated here to indicate the directions in which contemporary social change is moving

To begin with, it is imperative to note that generosity emerges as an increasing source of tension in an economy and way of life that are becoming more and more oriented towards aspects of the "Protestant" rather than the "Indian" ethic. When people are taught that they will be esteemed for accumulating and hoarding rather than for distributing their wealth, they will encounter difficulties if others in their society still have strong, traditional expectations of sharing. The stress between these two moral principles is especially felt by the most acculturated indigenous people, who are torn between their old obligations and their new goals. The confusions and frustrations of individuals caught in this cultural limbo can be particularly difficult to bear if they live in a social context that gives them few emotional or physical outlets. Town life severely limits people's mobility, thereby reducing access to the bush and the use of an escape mechanism that traditionally allowed individuals to avoid serious conflict (eg., Welsh 1970: 28; Nelson 1973: 281-282). As long as these tensions persist alongside an emphasis for emotional restraint, one can expect that the few affective releases that the people permit themselves — especially drinking — will continue to be used extensively (Savishinsky 1991b).

A new dimension has also been added to the theme of interdependence. At Colville Lake, for example, in addition to bonds within the band, the presence of permanent white residents in the community has led the people to develop new styles of relationship with these non-native men. In some cases, these ties have taken the form of patron-client roles, a phenomenon of increasing native dependency which Vallee (1967), Paine (ed., 1971), Broch (1983: 168-182), and others have noted in many northern settlements. While the outsiders and the indigenous residents both derive certain benefits from such a system, interdependence is cast in a new form because of the unequal power, prestige, and wealth that the white patrons and their native clients have commanded in recent years. Not only have indigenous people had to adapt to the new and frequently dependent roles that they play vis-à-vis the whites, but interdependent roles within the native population are also affected when people start looking to whites, rather than their own kin, as the main focus of their obligations and expectations. Under such circumstances, kinship relations become more tenuous and difficult to maintain, especially in cases where extended kin networks were not organized to begin with.

With attitudes towards generosity and responsibility undergoing a simultaneous redefinition, the nature of social relations within these increasingly urban communities is being radically transformed. Furthermore, Dene — who have traditionally valued concensus in community decisions — have had to adopt and cope more with Western political forms as they struggle for greater self-determination (D.M. Smith 1992). As changes continue in these directions, people who were once band members and villagers come to think and act more like "townsmen" (cf. Honigmann and Honigmann, 1965; Ervin 1969). If we are to understand the problems that confront these native urban dwellers in the North, we must seek to realize the depth and significance of the older attitudes that they bring into their new environments, as well as the way in which these cultural values have traditionally been integrated with one another in the past. The ethics of kinship, restraint, and responsibility, which are part of this heritage, permeate the new political agendas which northern natives have been articulating in recent decades, especially their concern with cultural survival, self-determination, and respect for the land. The importance, and the integral nature of all these values, constitute one of the most basic lessons that the people of Colville Lake can teach us.

CHAPTER 4

Stress and Mobility

1. INTRODUCTION

There are many circumstances in life which compel people to live together. In his *Notes From A Dead House*, Dostoyevsky wrote of prison life in Siberia as "forced coexistence," and recounted, with wit and compassion, how the men of czarist Russia dealt with the fate of their sentences. Coexistence is not always compulsory, however, not even in the North, for outside of prisons people can choose and create, or at least modulate, the content of their company. There is thus freedom within the conditions of survival, even if — as among the Hare — existence is only possible within the context of kinship.

Although they may be lightly experienced or left unconsidered much of the time, the motives which draw people together are deeply textured, and so are the forces which drive them apart. For the Hare, whether it is habit, family, and obligation, or necessity, desire, and a reluctance to confront life alone, existence apart from one's *sagot'ine* is seen by people as unsatisfying and impossible. In the modern era, social as well as economic factors have contributed to the persistence of the Colville Lake band, reaffirming both a network of affiliations and a style of life. Yet, as the dimensions of kinship reveal, tensions also arise among the very people who make one's life both possible and meaningful.

The psychological and cultural stresses which affect the people derive, in large measure, from the group dynamics of a semi-nomadic existence. The band's necessary alternation between family dispersals in the bush and community reunions at the village creates extremes of isolation and concentration. Each individual's behavior must be malleable enough to preserve the efficacy and satisfactions of these contrasting situations.

Given the interrelatedness and the restraint which characterize the Hare and other Northern Athabascan groups, anger and violence as means of relieving tensions are rarely engaged in. At Colville Lake, verbal or physical aggression is almost entirely restricted to periods of heavy drinking. Even more muted kinds of confrontations are generally avoided as being too compromising to personal codes of conduct and interpersonal ties. Most responses to stress therefore tend to be either repressed or re-channeled. A

111

major consequence of this is the people's resort to mobility as a stress-reducing mechanism. This chapter's discussion of the annual cycle follows this relationship between stress and mobility as it unfolds from season to season, and it relates this pattern to the other coping techniques which form part of Dene culture.

2. DISPERSAL, STRESS AND IDENTITY

The dispersal of the community which occurs with the freeze-up of the lakes and streams each October inaugurates a portion of the year during which the Hare face some of their severest stresses. Environmentally, they now have to contend with the harshest weather, the greatest discomforts, the hardest work, and the most threatening dangers of any season. Accidents may include axe and knife cuts, pulled muscles, smashed fingers, and potentially fatal falls through the lake ice. The possibilities of suffering frost-bite, freezing to death, getting lost in storms, and experiencing extreme hunger are all increased. Deaths from exposure and starvation have occurred within the lifetime of Colville's older adults, and so these hazards are regarded by people as very real threats, not just as vague memories from the "old days," or as events occurring only in myths and folktales.

Since aboriginal times, the food resources of the Hare have been relatively unstable, and while contact with Euro-Canadians has introduced a technology which alleviates some of the resulting hardships, this has not changed the nature of the principal food sources themselves. Thus, trapping, hunting, and fishing activities continue to present their particular frustrations and hazards. The distribution of caribou within the band's game area varies seasonally and annually, and locales that are rich in animals one winter may provide relatively poor hunting in the next. The supply of fish in certain lakes or at specific campsites can also vary over time. Traps and traplines are disturbed by wolves and wolverines throughout the winter, resulting in the loss of valued furs and the need to re-do or redeploy one's sets. Heavy snowfalls cover up both traps and trails, making travelling arduous and trapping tedious.

Despite the difficulty and frustrations of winter life in the bush, the people actively look forward to this dispersal, and they welcome their return to an environment which strikes the outsider as intensely inhospitable. Winter is eagerly anticipated by them for the challenges and the variety it offers. After being gathered together at the village for nearly three months, the people are weary and often tense with one another's company, even somewhat bored with the repetitiveness of summer existence. The busy preparations of the autumn — the sewing of clothes, the repairing of sleds, the training of dogs

— are the more visible signs of an underlying sense of excitement. People are continually in and out of one another's houses, or travelling between the settlement and outlying fish camps, in order to assemble, borrow, exchange and sometimes purchase the equipment they need to complete their winter outfits.

In the weeks before the *K'apamituegot'ine* actually pull out for their trapping areas, the community is already partially dispersed at the fish camps which dot the shores of Colville and Aubry Lakes. There, where they are close to, but no longer in daily contact with one another, clusters of families are scattered among the better fishing spots, laying up supplies of dog food, and experiencing a foretaste of the greater isolation yet to come. At this point in the yearly rhythm, however, such a separation does not carry the burden that it will later bear, for a degree of isolation now presents itself as a release from the strains of village life. Similarly, what will soon become the physical stresses of the bush now appear as renewed challenges, a true change of pace and style, the novelty of which is viewed with anticipation.

When the people finally scatter and move to their base camps, then, pushing their boats up narrow streams in the late fall, or driving their dogs over rough, snow-patched ground in the first weeks of winter, they go to confront a difficult environment with the true spirit of stress-seekers. A world which, in its dangers and life-supporting possibilities, is ambiguous at best, evokes deeply contrasting attitudes from them. The bush is simultaneously threatening and inviting, and the people perceive of and accept it on both these terms. The stress of survival is thus a two-edged sword, cutting out a realm of hazards and uncertainties with one side, and opening up an area of challenge and fulfillment with the other.

The boreal world of the sub-Arctic is not only both dangerous and fulfilling, it is also an intrinsic part of the people's identity. And it is this latter source of meaning which most fully encapsulates the community's perception of the forest. *Dešinta,*"the bush," is the Hare's most visible and immediate link with their past, and involvement in it becomes an act of tradition, a bond with the generations which preceded them. "To be Dene, an Indian," as Yen once declared, "is to live in the forest." To give this up is to lose one's ethnicity, "it is to become like a white man." While some members of the band feel this much more strongly than others, everyone experiences a clear sense of distinctiveness from the Indians who live at the fort, for, as André says,

> they are the people who have given up the old ways. They forget what it is like to be Dene. It is only us who remember.

For all the band members, then, regardless of their degree of involvement with bush life, returning to the forest each year, and seeking one's livelihood from it, is an act of reaffirmation, a participation in a native identity which is a deep part of the people's individual and collective self-image (cf. also Broch 1986: 33, 112). It was in this spirit, in September, that Philip Ratehne spoke with enthusiasm of the winter, and of our forthcoming departure for the bush:

> That's the real Indian time of the year. None of this sitting around like this all summer and just taking out fish. In the bush that's when we really know how to live, and then you'll see how tough we are. Sure it's hard, but when you learn how to take care of yourself then you really learn to love it. That's when you think "this is the real good Indian life. It's hard but it's our own good way." Maybe some white men don't understand it, but that's because they never lived like us.

3. LIFE IN A BUSH CAMP

Philip's vision is a true one, and the contrast with white perceptions is apt. Fur trapping, for example, which has become such a central part of Dene life in recent generations, has meant rather different things to the people and to white outsiders. As already noted, though trapping is built around a commercial relationship established by Euro-Canadians, one of it's most important effects on native communities is that, from a cultural point of view, it has helped keep many indigenous groups on the land. Historically, the fur trade has also fostered the preservation of the natural ecology of the North by holding industrial, extractive, and other economies at bay. In contrast to environmentally destructive pursuits, trapping's premise is to have renewable resources harvested by mobile, thinly dispersed populations that live in the bush.

Dene trappers adhere to values which are consonant with this strategy: they have always respected the animals they harvest, valued the forest in which they live, and prized the freedom of a life in which, as Indians, they could travel and survive without interference. In recent years, when fur trapping has come under attack by animal rights proponents from "outside" (eg., Best 1986, 1989; Klein 1986), native people have been genuinely puzzled by the charges these activists have laid against their traditional lifeway. The assertion that the "fur fashion trade" has destroyed authentic native culture (Best 1989: 140) ignores the way in which trapping has been successfully incorporated into modern Indian life and contributed its vitality (see, for example, Berger 1977i: 85-113; Canada, HC — SCAAND 1986; Herscovici 1986; Keith and Saunders, eds. 1989).

In a second distortion, the Dene have found themselves portrayed as a threat to animal populations and to the ecology of the North itself. The irony in the latter accusations is that, as with other indigenous groups, the

Dene have long felt the land to be their most important heritage; they have taken its resources with restraint; and they have expressed gratitude to its animal species both in ritual and in attitude. They know that the only period in modern times when fur-bearers were seriously threatendd with extinction was when large numbers of white trappers moved into the North to methodically strip the land, often using poisons that killed game indiscrimintately (Fumoleau 1973: 226, 235-250). Indians, by contrast, practice methods of hunting and trapping which conserve animal populations, and informed white northerners — from priests and game officers to Hudson's Bay Company officials — have recognized this merit in native attitudes towards the land. The negative behaviors recently attributed to indigenous people by moralizing anti-fur militants from outside — those of environmental disrespect and destruction — are not qualities the Dene can recognize in themselves. They are features created by other people's political imagination.

Much closer to Indian reality are the daily and the seasonal problems native people do face in maintaining both life and identity in the bush. Accomplishing these two goals requires tolerance and competence as well as enthusiasm, and as I came to realize, some of the people are more abundantly endowed with these qualities than others. Once the villagers achieve the privacy of dispersion, they must then confront its loneliness, and having anticipated the challenges of survival, they must now face its hazards and frustrations. The first few months of the winter, which I spent with Philip's family, showed me how some of the most capable of the Hare dealt with these stresses while preserving themselves and sustaining their unity.

***

The freeze-up of 1967 occurred on the night of October 13th, and within a week of that date the shoreline areas of ice around the Colville Lake were thick enough to allow us to travel. I went out on the ice for the first time with some of the Behdzis a few days later, helping them to set and then check their fish nets. In the meantime, the Ratehnes and I were getting the final items of our outfit together, and we were ready to leave the village about a week before the trapping season officially began. We divided our supplies up among the family's three sleds — Philip's, his father Wilfred's, and his brother Adam's — and we first journeyed to the fish camp of Wilfred's brother George, located about fifteen miles north along the east coast of Colville. Wilfred and his wife Bertha decided to stay there for a few days and then relay their equipment in stages, and so leaving them and Adam behind, Philip and I pushed ahead, carefully picking our way over the still young and dangerously thin crust of ice.

Once we were off the lake, it took us several days to break a trail over the rest of the sixty-five miles of rough ground which separated our intended campsite from the village. The dogs, who were still far from their peak condition after a relatively idle summer, strained under the heavy loads of equipment in the sled. They were also difficult to handle, the younger ones reluctantly pulling in a real team for the first time, and the older ones readjusting to life in harness. On alternate stretches of this northward trip, Philip and I took turns pushing the sled from behind to aid the dogs, and walking ahead with an axe, clearing the path of trees and brush.

At the campsite at *Lugetenetue,* on a high bluff overlooking a large lake, we cleared the snow from a level patch of ground, and pitched our canvas tent. Then we laid a carpet of spruce boughs on the inside floor, and moved in our sleeping bags, sheet-metal stove, cooking utensils, and other gear. While I staked out the dogs and went to cut firewood, Philip began building an *alahfi*

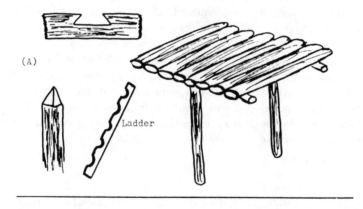

(A)

Ladder

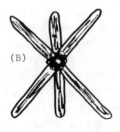

(B)

FIGURE 7   Types of *Alahfi* or Stages

or storage platform where we would keep the fish, caribou meat, and other supplies which could not be stored inside the tent itself (cf. Figure 7).

The second day at *Lugetenetue*, Philip and I set a fish net and cut some brush for the dogs to sleep on. Late the following morning, Adam and his parents arrived, and the dimensions of the camp expanded: saplings were cut down at half-height to one side of the tent for chaining up the new dogs, and two more fish nets were placed beneath the lake ice (Figure 8). There were, in all, five people and twenty canines to be fed now, and there might not be any caribou in the area for several weeks yet. Bertha fixed up the spruce floor and rearranged the tent's contents, pushing the canvas walls out as far as she could, and holding them in place from the inside with vertical sticks stuck into the ground. She piled up more snow and brush around the outside base of the walls, thus sealing the inside off from the wind, and keeping in the warm air created by the stove. Space was at a premium within the tent, and Bertha

(C)

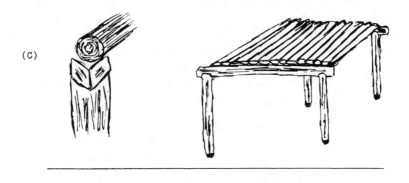

(D)

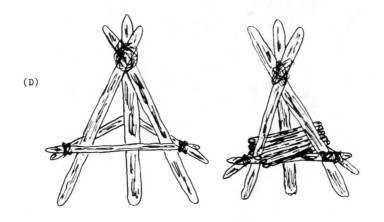

tried to expand its area, not only to accomodate the five of us, but also to make room for the large amount of clothing and equipment we had brought with us (Figure 9). Sleeping bags, cooking gear, sewing materials, spare mukluks, pants and mittens, a radio, candles and a gas lamp for illumination, a water bucket, a large sack of flour to make bannock, cartons of food, salt, tea, tobacco... all of these had to be placed at a safe distance from the stove. Suspended by ropes from the ridge pole of the tent was a wooden bar on which we dried out our clothes at the end of the day; rosaries and calendars hung pinned to the canvas walls. Outside the tent itself were our rifles, extra fish nets, traps, fur stretchers, a five gallon drum of gasoline, axes, and additional tents and stoves for overnight camps on our longer traplines.

The inventory of the camp's contents was long, and it mirrored the people's commitment to Western materials as a standard part of life. What had taken us so long to prepare for the bush had been the collecting of such an array of items, and what had lengthened our final journey had been the necessity of transporting so much in our small sleds: hence the slowness of Philip's progress, and also the need for his parents to relay most of their supplies. Clearly, the people's mobility was affected by the amount of equipment they depended on, and I began to see part of the reason why band members no longer travelled as far, or as extensively, as they did in the old days. Families who relied heavily on Western materials — and the Ratehnes, as it turned out, were neither the most nor the least dependent in this regard

FIGURE 8   Layout of Bush Camp

— had less freedom of movement, not merely because of the quantity of goods they transported, but also because they had to remain within access of the village for purposes of re-supplying themselves. Trapping, then, has not only kept people on the land: it has also re-oriented ecological concerns by expanding people's focus to include different game resources, and it has affected the modes and conditions of mobility by placing life within a larger material context [1].

***

FIGURE 9   Inside of A Bush Tent

Even within the more limited geographic range that some households cover, the people's survival is persistently demanding. A family's full use of the environment's possibilities was revealed in what the Ratehnes did those first few days. Besides the men's work at setting out fish nets and building up *alahfis* and a wood supply, Bertha soon put out snares for ptarmigan and hare to bolster our food supply until fishing and hunting became more productive. With the camp established and the fish nets in place, the men now began their trapping activities. Adam and Wilfred decided to run a joint line to the east of the lake and then split in different directions after having set out "one day's travelling" worth of traps. It was first necessary to break a trail in this direction, however, and I went with the two of them on this arduous, initial trip. We left camp at eight in the morning, and father and son shared the work of taking the lead, one hacking out a path and the other one following behind with the dogs. We gradually moved into an area of high ground where Wilfred

FIGURE 10   Trap Set: Enclosure or "Pen" Set for Marten

said "the marten signs were good," and then he and Adam began to alternate traps just off the trail (Figures 10 and 11). We eventually made a fire to boil tea and have some lunch in the afternoon, and then continued to set traps for another two hours before turning back towards camp.

The next day we returned to extend the trail, putting out more traps, and pitching a tent about twenty miles from our base camp. Wilfred and Adam then set a net in a nearby lake so that they would have dog food whenever they visited this new camp in the future. They laid out some traps within the vicinity of the tent itself, and on the following morning they went off in separate directions — each of them on snowshoes — to lay their own lines. When we travelled back to our main camp the next day, having set out over 170 traps in all, we found two marten in the previously arranged sets, plus three rabbits who had gotten caught trying to reach the bait at some other traps. Whiskeyjacks, a species of small jay (the Canada Jay) who abound in the

FIGURE 11   Trap Set: Leaning Set of "Hung-Bait" for Marten

woods, had also touched off four other traps in attempting to steal the bait. As Adam noted, with a touch of frustration in his voice, a man is helpless against these small animals, for every set that they disturb remains inactive until the trapper comes that way again and re-sets it. In this way, a man can loose his chance at a considerable amount of fur during a winter because marten, fox, and weasel who are attracted by the bait will never be caught in already triggered traps. While a good trapper tries to visit his sets every five or six days, it is difficult to keep to a strict schedule because of weather conditions and the need to hunt and take care of other subsistence needs. As I witnessed many times during the winter, men experience a keen sense of frustration when they see a trail of marten tracks leading up to a trap that already has a worthless whiskeykjack in it. There is a bit of bitter humor in the people's nickname of "the Hudson's Bay Company bird" for the whiskeyjack — for, as Philip put it, "both the bird and the Bay steal our fur."

While Adam and Wilfred had been busy for several days to the east, Philip had travelled on his own to the north, setting out a line of 100 traps. Energetic and resourceful, Philip prided himself on his toughness and trapping ability, and the previous winter, at the age of sixteen, he had taken more fur than most of the older men in the band. Now, back at the main camp, Philip checked the family's nets, and found only eighteen fish. With our stock of *denepere* ("Indian food") low and dogfeed almost gone, Philip went hunting to the northeast the next day, indicating that he had seen some caribou tracks in that direction while he had been laying out his trapline.

By late that evening, however, he had returned empty-handed, even though he had spotted a number of small caribou herds from a distance. Philip tried again the next day with the same result, and Wilfred came up with only a dozen fish from our nets. Only Bertha's snares seemed to be reliable, and so, within those first few weeks, we were already "back to choking rabbits" for our supper. There was some difference of opinion within the family that night over whether or not we should broach our supply of *molapere* (store-bought "white man's food") so early in the winter, and Wilfred and Adam — who took opposite sides on the issue — shot some quick, irritated glances at the floor as they avoided one another's eyes. Philip, somewhat put out by what he felt was his unfair burden of responsibility in the family, took an oblique swipe at Adam by suggesting to his father that they would not have been faced with this dilemma if Adam had spent as much time searching for food as he had done for fur. Before anyone could respond, however, the debate was frozen: Adam reached out for the bucket near his sleeping bag and announced, in restrained, neutral tones, that he was going to get water from the lake so that they could boil some tea. Wilfred silently fingered some spruce needles which lay by his feet, and without any further words, the matter was ended.

The issue was a small but indicative one in the life of the camp: enthusiasm was being tempered by routine, and routine was yielding up its tensions. The deprivations of the winter were making themselves felt, and the family was responding with some muted strains. While the tenseness of the evening had dissipated itself in silence and activity by the time of Adam's return, it was clear that the tenor of existence had changed — however subtly — and that the stresses of the season were upon us (cf. Sharp 1988 for a discussion of tensions in a Chipewyan bush camp).

In the following weeks, the family began to feel the full brunt of winter. Adam and Philip each got a few caribou within the next couple of days, and so our spirits and stomachs improved. But fishing remained poor, and so some of the meat had to be fed to the dogs. Wilfred and Adam gave up a day of trapping to re-set their nets in a different part of the lake, and Philip deferred a visit to his line in order to cut a large supply of firewood for his mother. Bertha, who usually had her adopted daughter Suzanne to help her with camp chores, was alone these first few weeks because Suzanne was off at another camp, helping her natural mother Lena Dehdele care for a new-born baby. With Bertha's arthritic knee paining her, more of the camp work fell to her sons, limiting the time that they could devote to hunting and trapping.

Philip's traps had yielded him a good number of marten in the first three visits that he had made on his line, and his view of the season's prospects was optimistic. But on his fourth trip out he discovered that a wolverine had gotten on one of his trails. The animal had religiously followed the path along much of its fifteen mile route, and in stopping at each set, it had carefully avoided the trap itself and removed the bait. As Philip travelled over the trail he saw — from the leg stumps and bits of fur left in some of the traps — that he had actually caught three marten and one red fox, but that each of these animals had first been found by the wolverine, and that nothing of any value now remained. On his return trip to camp, therefore, Philip made two special sets with very large traps, hoping to catch the wolverine in the event that it continued to raid his line — a pattern which, he explained, the wolverines often followed.

In early December, the cold and snow combined to increase the family's difficulties. A two-day storm deposited enough snow to cover up most of the men's trails, and so the next time we each went out, it was necessary for us to walk ahead of the dogs for most of the route in order to beat down a new path with our snowshoes. Adam had failed to mark many of the places where he had made his sets, and without the tell-tale blazes and cuttings on the trees, he was unable to find a number of his traps. The wind-blown snow had also buried many of the men's other sets, and so the fur yield was disappointingly low. Having harvested their areas for over a month now, each of the men began to pick up some of his traps and branch off into new regions. Fresh trails were broken in different directions, and Philip, deciding to strike off to the west, removed his overnight tent and fishnet from his northern line, and established an entirely new outpost camp on a different lake.

Soon after these new lines had been laid out, however, an intense cold spell put a sudden end to all activity. Wilfred and Adam, trying to reach the main encampment before nightfall, both suffered frost-bitten cheeks on the final leg of their long journey. The next morning, with strong gusts blowing at air already cooled to $-25\,°F$, the wind-chill prevented us from leaving camp. The first day in the tent was a welcome rest, but by the third morning our immobility was becoming its own burden, and people were turning irritable. Furthermore, Wilfred was worried about his lead dog, who had become lame on his last trip out, and Adam, who had shot several caribou a few days previously, was anxious to retrieve the carcasses that he had been unable to haul back before the storm set in. When the weather finally broke on the fourth morning, then, everyone was up early, and with noticeable relief and anticipation, the dogs were quickly harnessed. The men were soon dispersed for the day, and so for the family as a whole, the difficulties of the environment now seemed a welcome alternative to the confined conditions of the camp.

4. STRESS AND RESPONSE PATTERNS

This tension between togetherness and separation, and the people's shifting exposure to social stresses on the one hand and ecological pressures on the other, characterized individuals within the band's larger encampments, just as it affected small groups like the Ratehnes. Later in the winter, when I stayed with three of the Behdzi families, and another time, when I camped first with the Yaweileh households and then with the Dehdeles and Godantos, I found that the rhythm of life continued to fluctuate — for each group — between emotional and social extremes. The parameters remained the same regardless of the size of the encampment: the bush provided a challenging escape from the stresses of what was invariably a closed society, and the camp, in its turn, became a haven of company and comfort from the solitary strains of the forest.

Even in mid-December, when Yen Behdzi's family came to join Wilfred's group, bringing Suzanne along with them from the Dehdele's, the style of life at our camp was not appreciably altered. Yen's move, in fact, itself illustrated the nature of mobility and discontent in a multi-family encampment. The Behdzis had been staying with the Yawilehs, but the younger men from these two families had found it difficult to trap with one another. The good fur areas in the vicinity of their camp had been limited, and so the men were restricted in their trapping range. Each group came to feel that they were being hampered by the other's presence, and — according to Yen's son Yašeh — the Yawilehs kept asking for so much fish that he and his brothers felt they were caring for the dogs of both households. Before matters could deteriorate, however, Yen decided to move his family, and so he, his wife, and his sons gathered up their tents and traps and journeyed — by way of the Dehdele's — to *Lugetentue*.

Socially and psychologically, as the incidents concerning the Ratehnes and Behdzis reveal, the winter dispersal makes the greatest demands on interpersonal relations and individual stress tolerance. This is in large measure a consequence of the fact that, as compared to aboriginal patterns, trapping fragments native communities into smaller and more dispersed groups than a strict subsistence economy would necessitate. To get highly dispersed fur-bearers, people themselves have to disperse in a comparable way. The resulting tensions among small group members who must live, work, and cooperate with one another at close quarters are heightened by their ultimate sense of isolation and periodic boredom. The feeling of isolation can be even more pronounced in other sub-Arctic communities where Indian trappers have taken to leaving their families back at the settlements, reducing bush camps to small, all-male groups (eg., Nelson 1973: 280; Bishop 1974: 31; Jarvenpa 1976, 1977, 1980: 57-60; Salisbury 1986; Sharp 1988). But even for the *K'apamitueg'ot'ine* with their family camps, there are no parties, church services, or daily visits to the store; no parcels or letters arriving from Good Hope; there are no neighbors or kin to drop in or visit [2]. While there is a degree of excitement and stress-seeking in confronting the challenges of the bush, relations within the small, isolated camps can eventually become strained because of the abrasive nature of co-existence under these confined conditions. Minor events or habits overlooked during periods of community reunion may now become highly visible and irritating.

After staying with about two-thirds of the band's households for extended periods during the winter and spring, some stylistic differences emerged in their patterns for coping with stress. It became clear that it was the most assimilated people in the band, i.e., those who had had the most experience in living, working, and going to school in Fort Good Hope and other large settlements, who demonstrated the most pronounced ambivalence about bush life. When I ranked the people according to such criteria as their amount of outside living experience, their ownership and use of commercial foods, commodities and equipment, their participation in such Western-derived forms of leisure as radios and magazines, and their degree of bilingualism and literacy, the villagers formed an acculturative continuum with large clusters of individuals at both the "traditional" and the

"Westernized" poles. As has been found among other Canadian Indians and Inuit in similar situations, many of the people near the "Westernized" extreme exhibited varying amounts of cultural ambivalence. In the Colville band, as elsewhere, this came out in problems of self-identity, feelings of inferiority, involvement in drinking, and ambiguous attitudes towards "bush" versus "fort" styles of living (Chance 1968: 572-573).

It was these acculturated individuals and families who found the winter months of trapping particularly stressful, especially because of their heightened sense of isolation. Whereas they and the other members of the band were equally cut off from one another and the settlement, it was not the people's literal isolation, but rather their *perception* of their isolation, that most affected their behavior and mental state. The more conservative families were comfortable with long periods of bush life: from the way people such as the Behdzis and Ratehnes spoke about where other households were and what their members were probably doing, it was evident that they still sensed a proximity or relationship to those who were not physically there. But relatively Westernized persons wanted a larger and more immediate social presence: a consciousness that others were out there, somewhere, was not sufficient.

This difference in how assimilated and more traditional members of the community were affected by these social and ecological features of life was reflected in their respective mobility patterns. For example, the people of Colville responded to the hardships and dangers of the bush by generally keeping their trapping and hunting camps within a sixty mile radius of the settlement. Besides making travel to and from the village less difficult, this also gave them easier access to the medical aid that the missionary offered and to the supplies that could be bought at the trading post. Traditional families, however, placed less reliance upon Western goods than did more acculturated households, and so it was the men from the latter who made the most frequent trips from the bush to the settlement during the course of the winter. Albert Limertu, for example, made six journeys to Colville from his bush camp during the period between freeze-up and Christmas. His family's shortage of even minor supplies was a sufficient excuse for most of these trips, and between the "shopping" and the drinking that he did at the village, he was away from his traplines for about a third of this time. Assimilated individuals such as Albert consequently spent less time living off the land than did more conservative band members, and their frequent movements were as much a reflection of psychological stress as they were of ecological necessity.

***

TABLE 3

Sexual Division of Labor Among Adults

Men	*Women*
Hunt large game: caribou and moose; haul back game to village and camp	Do some hunting of small game
Hunt smaller game: waterfowl, hares, etc.	Snare ptarmigan and hares
	Assist in the butchering of small and large game
	Treat (i.e., clean, scrape and tan) caribou and moose hides
	Manufacture dried and smoked meat and babiche
Set and check fish nets in the summer and winter	Check nets in the winter
Prepare and fix nets	Help to prepare and fix nets
Construct and repair canoes, scows, and outboard motors	Clean fish
Manufacture ice picks and ice scoops	Manufacture dried and smoked fish; collect firewood for smoking and cooking fish during the summer
	Sew canvas covers for canoes
Do most of travelling, transporting, trail-breaking, and dog driving	Some women drive dogs during the winter
Care for and train dogs; shoot dogs when necessary	Make and prepare sled wrapper (cariole)
Construct and repair sled and braker	
Make trips from bush camp to village for re-supplying	
Cut and haul firewood throughout the year	Help in cutting and hauling firewood throughout the year
Construct saw-horses	
Train sons and help care for children	Do most of caring for children, and train daughters
Construct village houses	Set up bush camps with men
Set up bush camps with women	Care for tent and house, including cutting of spruce boughs
Construct stages, caches, and dog compounds	
Do some cooking and sewing	Cook, sew, make and repair clothes
Make frames for snowshoes	Help put webbing in snowshoes
Do shopping in the village; sell family furs	Do shopping in the village
	Pick berries in the fall
Do most of fur trapping	Do a small amount of trapping
Skin and stretch hides	Help to skin and stretch hides
Do most of wage labor	Do a small amount of wage labor
Manufacture homebrew	Manufacture homebrew

Patterns of travelling reflected not only these subcultural differences, but also distinctive mobility styles for males and females within the band. In all the families, the men engaged in activities which made them considerably more mobile than the women (Table 3). The tasks of adult females usually kept them in and around the family residence both when in the bush and in the village, whereas the men were frequently gone from several hours to several days at a time in connection with their responsibilities for hunting,

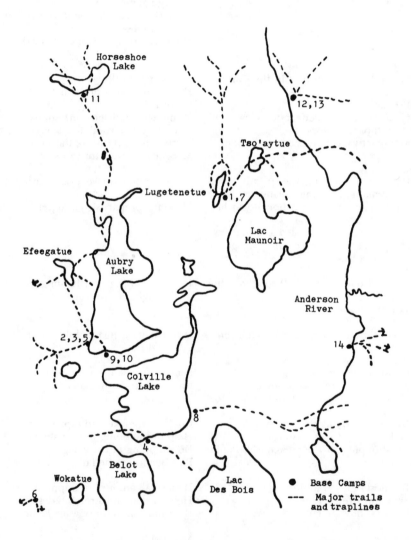

MAP 4   Trapping Camps: Early Winter Dispersal, 1967

fishing, trapping, and transportation. One index of this gender difference in mobility was that only three of the community's thirty-six dogteams were regularly used by women in conjunction with their household tasks and labors. Bertha Ratehne never went further from our camp than her hare snares, and even Albert's wife Paula — who had her own dogteam — rarely travelled further than nearby stands of firewood and her family's fish nets, visiting the village and other camps for only a fraction of the time that her

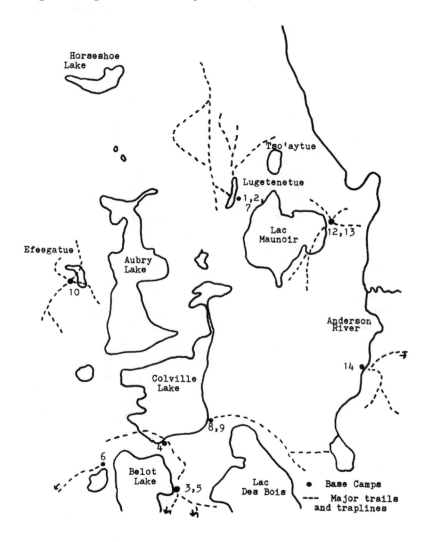

MAP 5   Trapping Camps: Mid-Winter Dispersal, 1967-1968

husband did. Since women are no longer isolated at menstruation in separate
huts, that source of privacy is not available to them either (cf. McClellan
1975b).

By keeping a detailed account of daily movements in all the camps that I
stayed in, I also came to realize that young men did considerably more
travelling than older males: the former made the most frequent hunting and
trapping trips, as well as the most numerous visits to Colville Lake, neighboring camps, and Fort Good Hope. The division of labor in some families, in
which younger men actually specialized in hunting and trapping while their

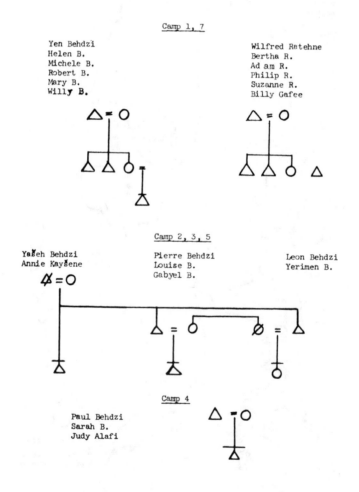

FIGURE 12   Composition of Early Winter Camps

fathers did the more sedentary fishing near their base camp, was another factor in the differentiation of mobility by age as well as by sex. Yen Behdzi, for instance, fished and stayed fairly close to his family's main camp while his three grown sons — Yašeh, Michele, and Robert — travelled after both large and small game over a much larger area. On a more limited scale, similar differences in work and movement distinguished the activities of younger women from those of older females within households. Some of the younger adult women, such as Sarah Behdzi's daughter Judy, and Berona's daughter Monique — both in their twenties — actually set short traplines of their own,

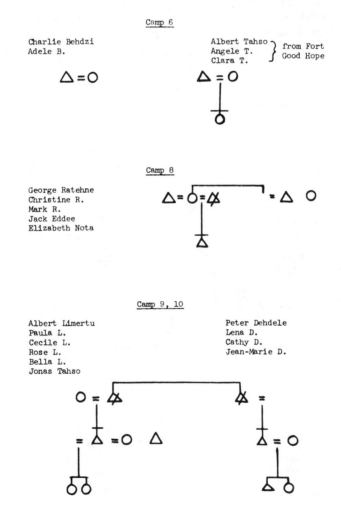

giving them a greater range of activity and mobility than their mothers' [3].

Whole families in the community were also more or less mobile than other households: families differed from one another in how far they went from the settlement to trap, how long they stayed out in the bush, and how much territory they covered during their stays there. Albert's repeated trips to Colville, for example, contrasted with the more persistent trapping efforts of Wilfred's sons, who did considerably more travelling in their subsistence pursuits than did Albert in his attempts to escape from them. This spatial dimension of mobility is illustrated in Maps 4 and 5, which show the distribution of band members among hunting and trapping camps during two parts of the winter of 1967-1968. Figures 12 and 13 (which accompany these maps) show the composition of these various camps, and reflect the kinship and non-kinship bonds influencing these winter alliances [4]. It can

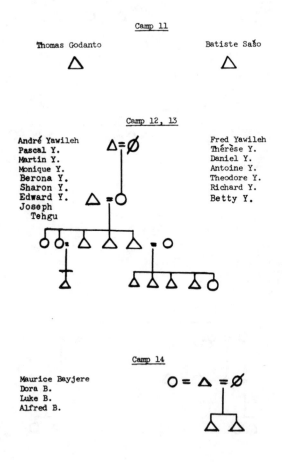

be seen on these maps that only one household in the community (#4, that of Paul and Sarah Behdzi) actually trapped in the area of the village itself, all the other people placing their base camps from fifteen to seventy miles away. Certain individuals and families were thus five times as distant from the settlement as others, and the traplines and hunting trips of the men in these far-flung groups often carried them well beyond a 100 miles radius from Colville. Adult males in these latter families rarely returned to the village between holidays, and with their greater tolerance for the strains and demands of the bush, they supported their families well, and collected a considerable amount of fur.

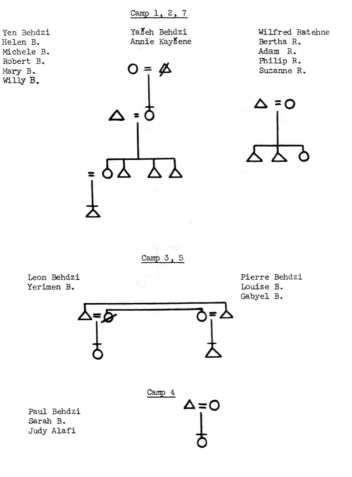

Camp 1, 2, 7

Yen Behdzi
Helen B.
Michele B.
Robert B.
Mary B.
Willy B.

Yašeh Behdzi
Annie Kayšene

Wilfred Ratehne
Bertha R.
Adam R.
Philip R.
Suzanne R.

Camp 3, 5

Leon Behdzi
Yerimen B.

Pierre Behdzi
Louise B.
Gabyel B.

Camp 4

Paul Behdzi
Sarah B.
Judy Alafi

FIGURE 13   Composition of Mid-Winter Camps

Such differences in people's bush style of life produced one ironic economic outcome. While some of the older and more traditional men — such as Yen, Paul, and their brothers Leon and Pierre — trapped less than their sons and other young males, this had little effect on their quality of life. The older men needed less cash income because they used fewer Western goods: they ate more *denepere,* repaired rather than replaced old nets, used home-made canoes instead of skiffs with expensive motors, and were content with well-worn clothing and somewhat outmoded rifles. The only kind of *molapere* that had become a standard part of their diets was bannock and tea. A related feature of their modest need for store goods was that they were less

Camp 6

Charlie Behdzi
Adele B.

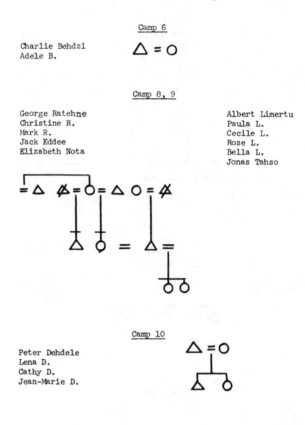

Camp 8, 9

George Ratehne   Albert Limertu
Christine R.   Paula L.
Mark R.   Cecile L.
Jack Eddee   Rose L.
Elizabeth Nota   Bella L.
                         Jonas Tahso

Camp 10

Peter Dehdele
Lena D.
Cathy D.
Jean-Marie D.

Camp 11

Left the Colville Area

affected by fluctuations in fur prices, and were not inclined to trap more just because the value of pelts rose in a given year. This frustrated the trader, but actually resembles a pattern of behavior found among other Canadian Indians in earlier times. In the eighteenth and nineteenth centuries, frontier fur traders often complained about how hard it was for them to induce very traditional natives to trap more, even by increasing the money paid for skins. In modern economic terms, such indigenous people had an "inelastic demand" for Western commodities, and — as was true now for the elder Behdzi brothers — market forces thus had little impact on a way of life geared to old cultural values rather than commercialism (cf. Miller 1991: 122) [5].

5. SPACE, TIME AND TENSION

Although the families of the band differed from one another in their patterns of movement and economic dependency, they also followed some common

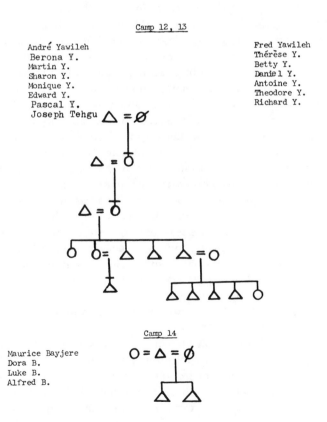

Camp 12, 13

André Yawileh
Berona Y.
Martin Y.
Sharon Y.
Monique Y.
Edward Y.
Pascal Y.
Joseph Tehgu

Fred Yawileh
Thérèse Y.
Betty Y.
Daniel Y.
Antoine Y.
Theodore Y.
Richard Y.

Camp 14

Maurice Bayjere
Dora B.
Luke B.
Alfred B.

strategies in locating themselves in time and space. In choosing their winter
trapping camps each year, the people attempted to enhance their security
and minimize environmental stress by staying in areas well known to them.
While no one owned trapping territories or specific campsites, well-known
patterns of land use by different households lent a degree of predictability
to where people were likely to go. Most families tended to alternate among
a series of favorite camping spots, using them over a cycle of several years, or,
in some cases, occasionally returning to one site for two years in succession.
Their familiarity with the region's topography and its fuel, fish, meat, and fur
resources, thus provided some insurance against the threat of serious
deprivation and hardship.

The very process by which the community as a whole made decisions about
how to distribute its members over the landscape also reflected another
important dimension of Dene culture. In the weeks preceding people's
departure for the bush, adults from different households frequently discussed with one another the trapping partnerships they were contemplating
and the areas they were thinking of going to. As this information was shared
within the community, people were able to modify their own decisions by
taking into account where — and with whom — others were likely to go. The
personnel and locations being planned for the early winter camps shifted and
adjusted themselves several times before people actually moved to the bush.
This process exemplified informal creation of community concensus through
on-going discussion. As with decisions about fishing trips and family adoptions, the outcomes here were the result of dialogue, not formal authority.

Though the selection of winter trapping areas was done with care and
consultation, very few Colville households stayed in just one place during the
long stretch between freeze-up and break-up. The occasional unpredictability
of fish, game and fur from one season or year to the next, and the eventual
depletion of fuel and fur in repeatedly used areas, necessitated that most
families change their camping grounds once or more during the winter and
spring. Furthermore, with the seasonal switch from the winter trapping of
marten and fox to the spring hunting of beaver and muskrat, people also
needed to move into areas better suited for these particular fur animals.
Living off the land thus required constant mobility not only in terms of day-
to-day subsistence and trapping activities, but in the periodic movement of
entire camps because of resource availability and seasonal changes in
economic priorities.

For the people of the Colville band, as well as for the members of other
hunting groups in the world, each annual phase may involve several small or
subsidiary moves by which the trend toward population dispersal or concentration is gradually increased. That is, the extremes of high or low density may
be reached in a series of stages rather than in an abrupt manner. Such a

pattern is approximated in the way that the people of Colville disperse for winter trapping each year. Band members do not like to go too far too fast, and this is due both to the conditions of travelling, and to the social readjustment to conditions of bush living. In effect, community members move away from the village in a series of steps. Several families may leave in a group and then collectively set up a fish camp at the north end of Colville for a period of one to several weeks. Only after such an interval of partial separation from the area of the settlement do the households which have arranged to trap together finally split off from the larger group at the fish camp. Families may also travel out from the community together and, over a period of several days or more, camp with one another at increasingly greater distances from the settlement. After such a succession of moves they eventually separate off as each household or group of families approaches the region in which it is going to trap.

Furthermore, band members tend not to move out en masse: only one or a few families may leave the village at a time, and the departure of the whole population is spread out over a period of about a month. The dispersals that take place in January and at the start of the spring hunt in late April are relatively more abrupt because they involve the movement of a smaller amount of equipment to camps which, in many cases, are already established. They also come after much briefer periods of residence in the settlement. Nevertheless, the general pattern of movement during these seasons nevertheless remains consistent with that of early winter because people continue to travel to their camps in a series of phased moves. The gradualness of all three of these dispersals points up the fact that band concentration and fragmentation is usually in a state of flux. While people are fully together or completely scattered during certain parts of each year, then, these extreme situations are transitory, indicating that there are stresses implicit in them which impel the people periodically either to dilute or concentrate their social milieus. This fluid feature of population density — a kind of community choreography — is a quality which the Hare share with other hunting groups in the world (cf. Birdsell 1968; Deevey 1968; Turnbull 1968b; Jarvenpa 1977).

***

The people's need for and love of movement as a simultaneously ecological, social, and psychological process, has been one of the prime reasons that they have consistently opposed all governments attempts to create fixed and registered traplines in their region. They recognize that what may be an administrative convenience for whites often bears little relationship to Indian reality. While game officers have in fact created large "hunting areas" for most official "bands" in the Mackenzie River drainage area, they have not forced the issue by imposing smaller family trapping areas within these zones. As the Hare and other Dene themselves emphasize, the fixity of a trapline contradicts not only the fluidity of the environment, but also the values of freedom and flexibility in native lifestyles — features whose relevance government officials and consultants often fail to take into account.

Over the years, the connection between ecology, mobility and freedom has been emphasized by the Hare and other Dene in their response to treaty negotiations, game regulations, and proposals to set aside Indian Reserves and Game Preserves. Dene in and outside the Northwest Territories have consistently shown a preference for "group trapping areas" that would allow each band and its members to practice "flexible mobility" (Jarvenpa 1977; Clancy 1991: 198; cf. also Barton 1991). In discussions surrounding Treaties 8 and 11, Indians were emphatic that their hunting, fishing, and trapping rights not be infringed on; later, they objected vehemently both when the government instituted game laws, and when it failed to protect them from the competition of white trappers. Not only did the whites deplete game, but they also restricted native movements by monopolizing the use of valuable resource areas. It was for these reasons that the Dene have periodically supported the idea of Game Preserves within which they would have the exclusive and unrestricted right to hunt and trap. However, their leaders have added the critical caveat that they do not want to have their harvesting of animals *limited* to such preserves. Rather, they still want to be free to travel and hunt throughout their traditional homeland (Fumoleau 1973 : 247-255).

Hare individuals who witnessed the negotiation of Treaty 11 have also recalled equally strong arguments being made *against* the idea of establishing Reserves (i.e., reservations) for Dene groups. In the recollections of Gregory Shae from Good Hope, Indians who spoke during the negotiations stressed the collective nature of their survival:

> The whites asked us if we wanted reserves... But we told them it would be kind of crazy to own little pieces of land. Because if the animals and fur disappear from that little piece of land what would the owner eat. We told them that we would rather hunt and trap all together... (Ibid: 182).

Another man from the fort, Louis Caesar, emphasized the critical need for freedom of movement to enhance Indian survival and avoid conflict:

> If the people were to own small pieces of land and if the animals never come there, they would have to move onto someone else's territory and there would be fighting and arguing. The chief said: No. *The people wanted to go where they wished when they wished*... (Idem; emphasis added) [6].

***

Gregory Shae and Louis Caesar's remarks suggest that opportunities for mobility underlie not only the economic well-being but also the social harmony of the Hare. As I was to learn from experience during the winter and spring, these social motives are quite compelling for the people, often outweighing strictly ecological considerations in the spacing and structuring of their camps. I saw that the cultural values of freedom, sociability, and mobility each affect the way interpersonal and psychological stresses are dealt with when band members live together in the bush. Within the population limits set by the fur and food resources of a particular region, for example, people feel more secure staying in multi-family encampments, especially those which contain at least two or three able-bodied, adult males. In camps of this type, the work and travel loads can be divided up, and companionship is enhanced while isolation is diminished. The importance of this sense of togetherness is also expressed in ritual. On Sundays, for example, people mark both the Lord's day and their own togetherness by gathering in the largest tent to say a rosary with one another.

The rare individual who actively seeks isolation as an end in itself may become a source of worry and concern in the community, and the abnormality of such behavior invites comparison with the fate and dehumanization of *lariyin* or "bush men." Such monstrous figures are used in the socialization of the young. Children are warned not to wander away from the village or camp lest a "bush man" seize them. Youngsters incorporate this belief about the consequences of prolonged separation into their own evaluation of the behavior of older individuals. Several village children commented, for example, about George Ratehne, who found the company of his demanding wife Christine so intolerable that after bringing her to the settlement at the beginning of Christmas, George returned to his bush camp, and stayed on his own there for the next three weeks. This was not the first time that he had voluntarily separated himself from spouse, family, and society, and nine-year-old Cathy Dehdele — reflecting the tenor of community gossip — once said:

> Him, that silly George, he just like to stay alone in the bush all the time. He don't have no one with him. Why soon he's just like a "bush man" [7].

To the Hare, then, co-camping arrangements ease the physical and social hardships of life, and they are viewed as being consistent with both human nature and the nature of the human environment. It is ironic, nevertheless, that they very people in North America who, in a gross ecological sense, have one of the lowest population densities, end up in a social architecture of such confined spaces. Despite the interrelatedness and friendliness of the individuals who come together to form the various camps, then, tensions do arise over such concerns as generosity and work loads, dominance patterns and bossiness, personal habits and interpersonal mistrust. Trapping partners, for example, sometimes become jealous of one another's good fortune, and may occasionally suspect that traplines have been tampered with and robbed of furs. Thomas Godanto confided the following thoughts to me about the behavior of Baptiste Sašo, his partner from Good Hope:

> He was always making up stories. One time I ask him how many traps he set and he say one hundred fifty. The next time Baptiste he say only one hundred. You see? That first time we go visit our lines he say he got sixteen marten but the next chance I ask him he says maybe nine or ten. There's something wrong there with that guy. You can't trust what he says. I got my feelings... That short line I set near our overnight camp was full of good marten signs. So why I never caught anything there? But Baptiste he pass that way when he go to Colville. I'm not saying anything sure, but it looks funny. Those could be my furs sitting at the store right now.

Although feelings such as these rarely result in public accusations, they can generate an atmosphere of mistrust which ultimately threatens the harmony of camp life. The trapping partnership referred to above, for instance, was abruptly dissolved after two months because of the suspicions and antagonisms that had developed between Thomas and Baptiste, and this was not the only such incident that occurred during the winter.

***

Similar tensions may be produced by the presence, in a camp, of an especially "bossy" or overbearing person whose actions conflict with the people's emphasis upon equality and independence. Freedom's ethical corollary of non-interference is a positive one to the Hare, stressing, in their view, a basic respect for other people's individuality, worth, and self-esteem. In concert with these egalitarian attitudes, leadership among the Hare has traditionally been exercised in a highly informal manner, rather than with direct shows of power or force. Whether in the winter bush or, as Broch (1977/78) found, a fire-fighting camp, persons who violate these unwritten norms by acting in authoritative or presumptive ways may provoke either ridicule or rejection: they create the kinds of stresses which can ultimately sabotage relationships. Lena Dehdele once summarized the consequences of such behavior by referring to the conduct of Thomas Godanto, her sister's son:

> Oh, that Thomas just like to tell everybody his own business. He like to be boss and give orders. That's why no one go with him. Last winter that happened when he trapped with my brother Jean from Good Hope. He says Thomas always telling him what to do. So they argue lots and then Jean pick up his traps and pull out.

Generosity, another dimension of proper conduct, can also be a source of provocation if a person's actions are not congruent with the expectations of others. The real or apparent failure of people to contribute or reciprocate in proportion to the largesse and efforts of others in an encampment often leads to strain within the group. To an extent, stresses over generosity stem from two conflicting sets of goals and economic orientations held by the Hare. On the one hand there is the traditional cultural ideology of interrelatedness and sharing, cooperation and hospitality. On the other hand, however, there is the more individualized and familistic economy which develops with a trapping way of life. For much of each winter, it leaves households more on their own than in the past, and while it increases their dependence upon the fur trader, it may decrease their interdependence with other families and *sagot'ine*. The new material conditions of modern life are part of this situation. Household groups now own more supplies and equipment than previously, and the furs and money which they can accumulate with their "capital" and labor are not expected to be shared within the village in the way meat and fish are supposed to be. The fur trade, by emphasizing the socio-economic importance of the family at the expense of the wider community and its kin ties, thus injects a degree of ambiguity into the entire generosity ethic, straining its operation on several fronts.

Two episodes illustrate this kind of tension. The first concerns Peter Dehdele, who had succeeded in putting up a large supply of fish during the fall and early winter at his base camp on Aubry Lake (Map 4, Camp 9,10). Although a fairly assimilated individual in many regards, Peter was one of the best trappers in the band, and he had established his cache of dog food so that he would be relatively free to trap during most of November and December. In these milder winter months, he explained, marten continue to move around freely, thus making them easier to trap than in the later and colder months when they tend to stay underground.

When Peter and his family were joined at Aubry Lake by Albert Limertu and his household, however, Peter's fish supply started to disappear very quickly. Albert needed dog food while he set his own nets, and he often left some of his dogs with Peter when he went on his periodic trips to the village. Without any surplus fish of his own, Albert also turned to Peter's cache whenever his day's fish catch was poor. Peter, who prides himself on his even-temperedness, and who sees himself, above all else, as a generous person — a man "with a good heart," as he expresses it — finally lost patience with Albert, and several tense encounters ensued. When separately visiting neighboring camps, the two men complained about one another's behavior to other people, and they eventually went to trap in different areas following the Christmas reunion.

Albert, in turn, experienced some of Peter's frustration later that same winter in an episode involving one of his own trapping partners, Jonas Tahso. According to Albert:

> He [Jonas] didn't bring much to our camp. Just a box or two of stuff from the store. Then he never shot much caribou either, or cut any wood for us. Me, I'm doing most of the work for everybody. He come and stay with us a long time and that's the way he act. He should know better [than] to treat people that way.

When later recounting these events, Albert added that he finally felt that he "had had enough of that," and let Jonas know that he could either work or get out. Things eventually became so strained in the camp that Jonas — just as Albert himself had done earlier that winter — did indeed pack his gear in his sled, and move away to stay with some of his other kin in a different region.

6. RESIDENCE CHANGES AND DAILY MOBILITY

When personality conflicts, a sense of inequity, or other sources of stress develop within an encampment, a change in residence by one of the individuals or families involved is often the outcome. Many of the residential shifts which occur during periods of bush living can be traced to social causes of this nature rather than to environmental pressures. This pattern of periodic moves and shifting alliances has been observed across the sub-Arctic in other communities of Naskapi, Gwich'in, Cree, Hare and Chipewyan, among whom people also use mobility to reduce or escape the inter-personal stresses of bush life (eg., Henriksen 1973: 44; Nelson 1973: 151-152; J.G.E. Smith 1978: 43; Tanner 1979: 23, 42; Jarvenpa 1980: 128; Broch 1986: 107; Jarvenpa and Brumbach 1988: 607; 126-127; Sharp 1988: 34).

In the Colville band, though *social* tensions may actually precipitate such moves, it is common for people to give instead an *ecological* rationale for their actions: they will explain a change in affiliation or camp site in terms of their need for better fishing or trapping conditions, rather than citing the more pressing social circumstances which really motivated them [8]. It is only later that the true reasons may be brought out. When Albert and Peter first split up at Aubry Lake, for instance, they euphemistically explained to people that they were not getting enough fish there to support themselves. The separation of the Behdzi and Yawileh households cited earlier (Part 4), however, was indeed largely due to a scarcity of fish and fur near their camp, a paucity which became so aggravated that the Yawilehs themselves eventually abandoned the site for a new area.

When families move their trapping camps to a different region, they often

TABLE 4

Camping Affiliations of Colville Lake Families, 1967–1968†

House-holds	1	2	3	4	5	6	7	8	9	10	11	12	13	14
1	--	B,C	C				A,B							
2	B,C	--	A,C		A		B							
3	C	A,C	--		A,B									
4				--										
5		A	A,B		--	C		C						
6					C	--		C						
7	A,B						--			C			C	
8					C	C		--	B					
9								B	--	A				C
10							C		A	--			C	
11											--			
12												--	A,B	
13							C			C		A,B	--	
14									C					--

A........... Camping affiliations during early winter dispersal (1967)
B........... Camping affiliations during mid-winter dispersal (1967-1968)
C .... Camping affiliations during spring dispersal (1968)

† The table omits individuals and families from Fort Good Hope who spent part of the winter and spring with various Colville families. Numbers refer to families discussed in Chapter 3, and in earlier sections of Chapter 4.

take up residence with households they have not been associated with that winter. A comparison of Figures 12 and 13, for example, reveals that the make-up of the band's encampments changed considerably from one part of the winter to the next. Fishing and hunting groups near the settlement, which were formed by families between trapping seasons, also involved residence changes and varying alliances over time. The composition of these latter camps, in fact, often changed from week to week during some periods, and people frequently shifted their residence between these nearby bush sites and the village itself. The same pattern of fluctuation characterized the make-up of certain task groups, including the families collected at the locations of major wage labor projects, such as the logging and construction operations contracted for by the trader. Within the space of five weeks during one spring, there was a turnover of forty percent of the people who made up the band's five major camps during that period: most of these moves were later found to be occasioned by drinking disputes between members of co-resident families at logging sites. As Table 4 makes abundantly clear, when camping alliances at different time horizons in 1967-1968 were compared, I found that not one family in the entire band had maintained a consistent camping arrangement with any other household during that entire year.

Existentially, there is another form of mobility that is even more pervasive than residence changes as a stress-reducing device. Hunting, fishing, trapping, snaring and wood-cutting activities each take family members away from their camps for at least brief periods on almost every day, allowing them to be apart and escape from relatives and neighbors. This other dimension, then, involves the daily movements and temporary separations which stem from the nature of economic activities and the division of labor. The short-term "breaks" that people enjoy in the course of their subsistence and trapping pursuits thus provide "cooling off" periods of several hours to several days during which tempers can be restrained and emotions controlled. When camp members are reunited after such an interval, relations within the group are usually resumed without reference to the previous tense situation: kin and friends can thus continue to live with one another under at least surface equanimity.

The people's ability to anticipate outbursts underlies this system for diffusing conflict before it erupts. The anxiety they experience over the possibility of emotional displays functions to reinforce the whole pattern of restrained behavioral expectations. When the limits on appropriate conduct are overstepped from time to time, temporary or long-term residential shifts are a final resort which explicitly avoids and implicitly denies the social clashes which have developed. As far as public sentiments are concerned, the physical dissolution of an unpleasant situation is tantamount to social amnesia — the mention of such incidents becoming as socially taboo as the kinds of behavior which originally prompted them.

These and similar conditions also characterize the tensions which arise within family units in the bush. The environmental hardships, isolation, and boredom that men and women experience contribute to the amount of friction which develops among them. However, the periodic absence of men in the course of their trapping and hunting activities allows hostilities to be dissipated or repressed by them and their wives, and it gives all family members a respite from the abrasive interaction which often occurs within the cramped quarters of the family tent. Trips are therefore looked forward to by both the mobile and the sedentary members of an encampment. Movement of this sort, in fact, is one of the few ways in which band members can actually obtain a degree of individual privacy from one another. A much calmer atmosphere prevails in the camps following the separations based upon such routine economic pursuits.

When I analyzed the various contexts in which emotional displays took place while people were living off the land, I found that the process of expressing and displacing hostility often occurred along the lines of a pecking order. Men, when they were angry, picked on their wives, their children, and their dogs. When their husbands were gone, the women often yelled at the children. The latter in their turn focused their hostility on one another and on their pups. Among the dogs there was also a hierarchy of aggression based on dominance patterns. Every living thing in the camp was thus involved in an established order of emotional expression and release.

Without mobility and the chances for separation, displacement, and restraint that it provides, it is problematical whether bush life could be maintained within the emotional limits that the Hare permit themselves. The social and psychological value of movement seems to be as significant for them as its ecological utility. Their great emphasis upon freedom and self-sufficiency places particular stress upon mobility as a means to the independence which they so highly prize. Travel, then, becomes something of an end in itself, taking on the dimensions of an expressive activity, besides being an instrumental aspect of survival and subsistence. The flexibile way the people relate to their social and physical reality thus draws much of its strength from the very freedom which mobility allows.

If lack of privacy and personal territory are aggravated by the smallness of the typical family tent, movement permits the unambiguously free use of space by individuals. People on the move are confined only by the narrowness of their trails, but they can break and follow a path in whatever direction they choose. The people's love of mobility, and their respect for the "tough traveller," [9] suggest the trail itself as a metaphor for life: behavior and trails are both bounded, one culturally, the other physically, but the person who can move within these limits enjoys the freedom and

openness which existence provides. People participate in a sense of libera-
tion when they journey, and this is as rewarding for them as the measure of
privacy which it also yields.

7. REUNION, PRIVACY AND PUBLICITY

Ultimately, the stresses of the bush affect everyone to some degree, and the
eventual resolution of hardship and isolation comes with the periodic
reunions of the entire band. While the Christmas, Easter, and summer
ingatherings vary in their length and intensity, they share in the qualities of
release, and in the ultimate re-creation of a sense of community.

People look to their seasonal returns to the settlement with the same spirit
of anticipation with which they approach their moves to the forest. Now,
however, it is an encounter with society rather than with the environment
which excites them, and the days of arrival pulse with the comings and
greetings of each family. Although Colville's residents do not think of their
lives strictly in terms of reunions and dispersals, they do conceptualize the
year in a manner which is congruent with these major phases of movement.
They talk of "hard" and "easy" times, and "bush" and "holiday" periods, and
in conversation they often divide the annual cycle into the harshness of
winter and the ease of summer. Each of the seasonal ingatherings constitutes,
as Bertha explained:

> ...the really good times of the year for us. All the peoples are together and
> then we really happy to see each other. No more being cold and hungry and
> not so much hard work. Everybody just visits lots, have parties and drinks, and
> have a good time.

A large number of persons gathered in one place is seen by the people as
a requisite to a "good time" or holiday. At the beginning of the summer
reunion, Adam Ratehne once said:

> We can't have much of a party with just a few guys here. We should wait till
> more people come in from the bush. Then maybe we'll put up a brew pot or
> drum dance and really start. It's best when the village is full up and there are
> lots of people for visiting.

As Bertha's and Adam's remarks indicate, and as other students of
northern life have noted (eg. Mauss 1904-1905; Welsh 1970; Acheson
1981), the size of groups at different times of the year has its psychological
as well as its ecological significance. The sense of comfort and community
with which ingatherings begin constitutes a dramatic change from the
frequently uncertain and fragmented nature of existence in the bush. Band
members genuinely enjoy seeing one another after the long separations:

encounters at the store stretch out long after furs are sold and purchases made; chance meetings on paths develop into shared cups of tea back at people's cabins; and church services, along with their spiritual satisfactions, are at least as fulfilling in a social way. On occasion, letters even pass between Colville and Good Hope, making the villagers as a whole feel less cut off from kin and the wider world.

As welcome as settlement life is, however, moods imperceptibly shift as the novelty of communal existence gradually gives way to its own tensions and banalities. Reactions to the tenor of daily events in the village vary from person to person. Whereas assimilated individuals generally find bush conditions more stressful than traditional people, the latter, in turn, experience greater anxiety over the drinking behavior which occurs during band reunions. For the community as a whole, the slow-paced tenor of the summer usually proceeds for several weeks before stresses emerge, but the shorter, more intense reunions of the winter holidays — condensed as they are in time and mood — compress these same rhythms into a briefer span.

The mobility that takes place during ingatherings stems more from social than environmental causes, although tensions derived from the latter are not entirely lacking. Each family's possession of fish, caribou meat, and hides varies with luck and effort, and the perceived balance of generosity can be a source of stress within the settlement just as it is in the context of bush camps. The same applies to the sharing of valued and important pieces of equipment — such as boats, outboard motors, gas-powered chain-saws, tools, dogs, and sleds. The heightened social life of reunions increases the rate at which interactions, exchanges, requests, gifts, and loans take place; and it also ensures that people's actions in these areas occur in a highly observable and public manner.

The publicity of life in the community makes the lack of privacy a prime source of concern. The ability of people to conform — or to appear to conform — to social norms rests, in part, on their capacity for impression management: this, in turn, is a function of their control over the information that others have about them [10]. Privacy and secrecy thus affect one's public image, with personal reputations and self-regard weighing in the balance.

The openness of the village area itself (cf. Map 3), and, until recently, the unpartitioned nature of most of the people's own dwellings, are spatial features which limit their access to family and individual privacy. The diagram of the Dehdele's cabin (Figure 14), a representative home, illustrates certain aspects of these information and interaction processes. Because most of the people's houses are single-room structures like the Dehdele's, there is little privacy from observability within each building. People are hidden from one another's views only when it is dark or when they are in their sleeping bags. Except in the case of children at play, no attempts are made to obtain privacy by erecting temporary barriers, by turning one's back and withdrawing into a corner, or by simply ignoring or refusing to acknowledge the presence of others. Aboriginally, women were isolated during their menstrual periods, but there are no longer any such institutionalized forms of seclusion among the Hare. Sulking or withdrawal within a home are prompted only by serious quarrels among household members. Mary Behdzi retreated from her family in this way after she and her mother had argued heatedly over a marriage proposal that the younger woman had received. Marked emotional expression of this kind, however, does not constitute an everyday means of access to privacy, and people in the settlement were struck by the singularity of Mary's reaction.

The stresses of gossip and living together were once expressed by Bella Sinta, a young woman from Fort Good Hope who came to Colville to stay with her relatives, the Yawilehs. One night, in a confessional mood follow-

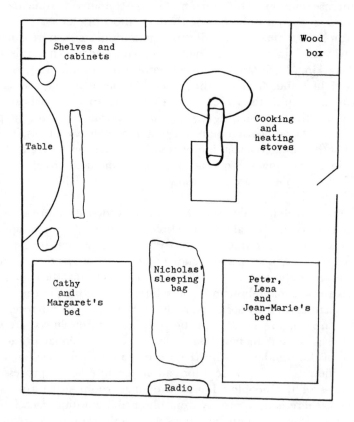

FIGURE 14   The Dehdele Household

ing a brew party, she took my wife and me aside, and complained that although she had been good to the Yawilehs and worked hard for them, the women in that household had nevertheless spread gossip about her sex life, and given her a "bad time." As Bella herself explained:

> Those Yawilehs, they're my cousins. So why do they talk about me like that and tell people stories? Since I came to live with them I thought I got along good with everybody. The old man Andre and his son Martin, we got along fine. But it's that fat old woman and those two girls who start the trouble. Once, that Martin, my cousin, I washed all his clothes for him. Him, he didn't ask me or nothing. I just went ahead and did it on my own. That's the kind of person I am. I took all his clothes and cleaned them for him. Just like that.
>
> But my own cousin, that older one Pascal Yawileh, that Ehja [his nickname], he started a fight with me two days ago I think it was. He's bothering me all the time. Grabbing at me, you know. For no reason. So finally I went after him and hit him with a stick.
>
> Those two girls, that Monique and Sharon, gee they're lazy. They just sleep all day, never do any work. They lie around all the time. It's okay if you're pregnant, then you can sleep two or three hours during the day. But them, they're not pregnant. They're just like that. Them they sleep all the time and don't work. But me, I'm a hard worker. Why are they like that? I haul water and everything. I'm just an Indian. A real Indian woman. I can do everything. That Monique Yawileh, she says she can't make drymeat. How is that? An Indian woman should know that. But her she just doesn't do any of it that Monique.
>
> That fat old woman, she and her daughters just talk about me all the time. When I came here I met that Michele Behdzi and he asks me if I want to get married. But those Yawilehs, that old woman and her girls, they start telling all kinds of stories about me. Why? For no reason. That Berona says that Monique is proud. What that mean "proud"? That Monique is "proud"? It doesn't mean anything to me. But they keep telling stories to people about me. My own cousins, those Yawilehs. Me and that Michele, we were going to get married on July 15th, but now they ruined that. Everything was nice. The people were good and everybody here at Colville was nice. But then those Yawilehs, that fat old woman, started talking and telling those stories. So now it's off. Me, I think I'll go back to Good Hope. I can't live here like this when my own cousins treat me that way and just ruin everything for me.

***

As Bella's account suggests, the settlement's gossip network increases the exposure of individuals to communal awareness. Compared to the "outer space" of the village at large, the "inner space" of the people's cabins would seem to provide residents with at least one private domain inside the public sector. Even here, however, individuals turn out to have a high degree of access to one another. The view of villagers into other families' households is cut off by the walls of the structures, but doors are never locked during the day, and visitors freely enter one another's homes without knocking or asking permission. This behavior is modified only when a brew party is known to be going on inside, in which case people generally do knock first. Community members usually lock their doors and draw their curtains when the whole family retires at night, and the lack of smoke coming from a cabin is also a sign that its residents are asleep. Though drunken individuals may continue to bother a home at very late hours, sober people would not disturb houses showing these outward signs of retirement. In and around each cabin, the only form of total privacy from direct observation is afforded by the use of the family outhouse.

Just as there is little visual privacy among the villagers, auditory privacy is also limited. Within a house, people speaking in the tone of voice normally used by the Hare can be heard anywhere inside the small structure. Gossipers may drop their voices to achieve intimacy, but the lowered sound and the observability of their behavior serve others as clues to what they are doing. The sound of voices that are raised during arguments carries easily beyond the house and attracts the attention of people outside. Where cabins are close to one another, disputes and fights at drinking parties can often be heard in the neighboring residence. Drinking parties themselves usually contain several eye- (and ear-) witnesses to such incidents. These conditions enhance people's awareness of other's conflicts and jealousies, and thereby heighten their own embarrassment when they realize that their neighbors know the same things about them.

In the community's sleeping arrangements, married couples have their own beds, although in some cases, as the Dehdele's, it is shared with an infant. Small households of three or four persons generally have sufficient room on platforms for all the residents, but in larger families, one or more members may have to lie on the floor in their sleeping bags. Night-time sexual activity can be overheard within houses, but it is impossible to say to what extent people intentionally listen for it, or are inhibited by the possibility of others doing so. Children are exposed to and become aware of conjugal relations from a young age, which helps to foster the people's easy acceptance of sexuality among adolescents and adults. When some of the village children were gathered in my cabin one morning, a nine-year-old accused her friend and age-mate of the following behavior:

> Ah, Cecile, you you're always staying up at night to listen to your father and Paula. You try to hear them talking and making love. You told me yourself you just pretend to sleep. You, you're always doing sneaky things like that.

Casual comments by some of the adults also reflect their sense of a lack of sexual privacy in their houses. Cecile's father Albert once took Paula on a summer hunting trip with him to Aubry Lake and, before departing, he jokingly said to me:

> Well, me and my wife we're gonna go and have ourselves a second honeymoon I guess. Just the two of us and the ducks. No one else to say good morning to.

Albert's neighbor Peter Dehdele once commented:

> Me and Lena are going to go by boat to the north end [of Colville Lake] to get the rest of our stuff from there. We'll leave all these kids here with Albert's mother to watch them. It's vacation time, yes sir. Just like when we were young again. My wife will think she's twenty. No worries so long as the boat don't leak.

It is noteworthy that privacy in these cases resulted from the mobility of the persons involved, i.e., a temporary shift of residence and their departure from the village. In a somewhat similar vein, young unmarried adults having a sexual affair often resort to liaisons in the bush near the village, or they take advantage of a house left empty by the absence of one set of parents.

Though privacy from visual and auditory surveillance is minimal within the community's households, there is a certain degree of what could be called "spatial privacy." This concept and the behavior it refers to concern a type of individual territoriality which can be considered an extension of the notion of "personal space" (Sommer 1969; Hall 1969). By "spatial privacy" I refer to the fact that individuals become associated with certain places within their cabins, and these areas are utilized by them much more than by other household residents. A certain degree of exclusiveness and "personalization" characterize these locales. Other family members may in turn have their own small domains which similarly afford them some physical privacy within these highly public environments.

The most prevalent and clear-cut instances of this type relate to the space occupied by a person's sleeping area. People who are in their house during the day or evening usually sit, recline, or work on their own beds. Women sew, men carve, teen-agers listen to the radio, and young children play, each on his own sleeping platform or sleeping bag. Individuals are rarely seen using any other resident's space for such activities. This pattern may be partly due to a scarcity of other household furniture, which in most cabins amounts to one table, a bench, and a few chairs or stools. However, if there were no such pattern of personalized territory, the people's use of household areas would be far more random than it is since the places utilized in this manner are neither economically or socially specialized in any other way.

The concept of spatial privacy gains further support when one considers how people treat the region right around their sleeping platforms (Figure 15). The personal "claim" to this environment extends to the floor area around sleeping bags and to that under bed platforms. Family members usually store individual property there, and no other household resident would disturb this "cache" without permission. Items kept in this way include children's toys, extra clothing, hand tools, sewing materials, pieces of hide, combs, brushes, magazines, cards, letters, and tobacco. Young adults and older people often have small boxes or cardboard suitcases in which such items are kept, and the privacy accorded to these containers turns them into a form of "ego index" (Schwartz 1968: 748). The treatment of personal

Figure 15   Sleeping Area and Personal Space

property stored in this way contrasts with the people's handling of less privatized items, such as their boats, saws, sleds, and dogs, which are items on public view and which can be sold and loaned to other people.

Finally, spatial privacy within households can also include wall space. People who have sleeping platforms often display and store property on the logs above their beds. One can find magazine pictures, photographs, letters, rosaries, fur auction schedules, and calendars pinned up in these regions. If the wall is covered with cardboard or paper, literate adults sometimes write amusing comments or keep count of their fish catch in these spaces. Though some of these articles and notes are clearly less personalized than others, the fact that they have all been placed there by one person — and can only be removed by that person — renders the space a private one. Like the containers noted above, wall areas thus serve as ego indexes and they also constitute a means of individual expression. Sleeping areas, and the adjoining logs and floor space, thus afford the people a type of privacy that visual and auditory conditions would otherwise deny them.

8. DRINKING, STRESS-SEEKING AND MOVEMENT

The sociability of reunions is intrinsically rewarding for the Hare, who value a sense of togetherness and a feeling of community. The pleasure of other peoples' company is most evident in the gatherings which occur at the mission, the store, and movies, as well as at brew parties, drum dances, and the casual visits that take place around the ever-present kettles of tea found atop each family's wood stove. The latter kind of visiting pattern is especially revealing of what people find rewarding in the time they spend with one another. Villagers are free to walk into one another's homes unannounced, help themselves to a cup of tea, and settle in for an hour or an evening. The most striking quality of such casual moments to an outsider is that conversation is optional. People are as comfortable sitting with each other in silence as they are in talking over hunting plans, a child's health, or the feud between the trader and the priest. During my first few months in the community, I found the silent visits unsettling, coming from a culture where a lack of conversation is experienced as either rude or awkward. But the Hare find such times to be a very natural and comfortable form of companionship. In an existential sense, they enjoy the simple act of being together [11].

Reunions have their burdens as well, however, and a surfeit of gossip, and a paucity of privacy, are features that eventually contribute to the stress of community life. Considerable tension in the village also derives from the chronic brewing and drinking which characterize ingatherings. People set up two to five-gallon pots of "homebrew" or *ko^{n}tweh* (literally, "fire-water") to ferment soon after their return to the settlement, and a round of parties is begun which only ceases with the re-dispersal of the community. *Koⁿtweh* is inexpensive and simple to make, requiring sugar, water, yeast, and a fruit or carbohydrate base such as raisins, beans, or currants. All the ingredients are available at the local trading post, and while the mixture should ideally ferment for several days, it can be drunk within twenty-four hours after brewing begins.

Although some adults also make *koⁿtweh* in the bush, the difficulty of transporting large amounts of brew materials to distant campsites limits most of the people's brewing to the village environment. Also, band members generally feel that drinking is incompatible with the rigors of life on the land, which requires discipline and energy in order to carry out bush activities productively and safely. The same attitude characterizes other sub-Arctic communities (eg. Helm 1961; Jarvenpa 1976: 53). At Colville, drinking is therefore largely confined to times spent at the settlement. The amount consumed in the community is also increased by the occasional availability of commercial alcohol brought in from the outside. Heavier drinkers in the band sometimes order expensive, distilled liquor from the government store at Norman Wells, and their bottles of rum and scotch reach the village whenever one of the trader's supply planes comes to the settlement from that town.

While at one level drinking qualifies as a leisure activity along with visiting, card-playing, traditional drum dances, and the occasional movie shown by the priest, it differs from these other pursuits because of the degree of emotional expressiveness which accompanies it. While drum dances are exuberant and hypnotic in their communal and rhythmic movement, drinking is clearly the most cathartic of all the people's activities, and it precipitates much of the latent and otherwise inexpressible tension in their lives. Repressed feelings and jealousies from diverse sources — including stinginess, marital disputes, insults, quarrels, and the events of previous drinking sessions themselves — may all be exposed when alcohol is consumed (cf. also Durgin 1974; Broch 1986: 183-189; Sharp 1988: 47). While the parties at the beginning of each reunion are basically friendly and euphoric, hostility ultimately emerges at these encounters after an ingathering has been in process for a while. During the summer this may not occur for several weeks, but at Christmas and Easter times, with their intensity, condensed time-frame, and high rates of interaction, brew parties may occasion aggression within the first few days of the reunion.

The children of the band get exposed and accustomed to such conduct from an early age, but youngsters who have spent the winter at the residential school in Inuvik find the violence and drinking of the summer the most difficult part of their readjustment to the community. Toddlers and older children are allowed the freedom of the village during all the band's reunions, and no attempt is made to shelter them from brew parties, or from their sexual and aggressive overtones. Young people learn to adjust to drunken behavior with an accomplished air of stoicism and resignation, and they thus become socialized to drinking patterns, hostility, and sexuality at an early age. The place of brew in the ethic of generosity, and the significance of drunken comportment in the community's emotional economy, make it imperative for individuals to accomodate themselves to these features of the culture, just as the ubiquity of these patterns makes it difficult for people to avoid participating in drinking once they have reached adolescence or young adulthood. Violence involving their parents nevertheless visibly distresses and embarrasses young children, who react as nine-year-old Cathy Dehdele did to a fight involving her father:

> Gee, you know I got real scared last night when they were drinking at my house. They was all yelling and me I couldn't sleep. Then my daddy and Albert got real mad and started pushing each other, so everybody starts shouting to them. Then those other guys stopped them and so Albert he left. But after that me I still couldn't sleep the whole night. I get too scared when those things happen.

After a long evening of nearly continuous drinking and episodic violence at another house, Cecile Limertu (aged ten) confided to me her feelings about Albert's treatment of her step-mother Paula:

> When my daddy drinks he always beats up poor Paula. Her she don't do nothin' but he pound her up anyway. Sometime I think what it's for. I sure wish he wouldn't do it. Paula she always cry and later my daddy sometime say he's sorry. It's bad for me in that house when that happen. When we're in the bush it's not so bad 'cause then there's not so much brew.

Children not only learn to cope and put up with drinking situations, but they also learn to interpret them in the same conceptual manner used by adults. Among the people, there is — at a conscious level — a basic attitude of leniency towards drinkers and their behavior: a person is not considered to be responsible for his or her actions when drunk because, as Mary Behdzi explained, "he just don't know what he's doing then." As Cathy Dehdele once observed of an incident:

> Oh look at that Jonas beating his dogs. He's so drunk he can't think what he does. That guy just lose his head when he drink.

The fist fights, shoving, shouting, flirtations, pointed mimicry, and hurried sex which stem from drinking sessions derive less from the lowering of inhibitions by alcohol than they do from the people's cultural appraisal and definition of brew parties as times of excess and expressiveness. Jealous spouses, spiteful neighbors, and angered kin may now respond to the substance of their stresses, seizing on the drinking situation rather than the drinks per se as their excuse. Homebrew in particular is a mild concoction, and because the people rarely let it ferment for more than a day or two, its alcoholic content is generally in the range of four to six percent (Durgin 1974: 59). At parties, however, behavior quickly becomes voluble and animated even before many of the villagers have finished their first drink. Conversely, animated people at a party can quickly become very contained if an unwelcome visitor enters the cabin. Drunken comportment, in essence, can be turned "on" and "off" as circumstances change. *Kontweh* thus serves as a "social lubricant" (Netting 1964: 381), not so much because of its physiological effect, as because of the nature of the situation it defines. Brew is believed to release inhibitions and relieve responsibility, but this is more a product of attitude than chemistry.

***

At a deeper level, however, what is overtly excused by the people may carry covert connotations of responsibility and blame. Just as generosity is an openly applauded but privately monitored pattern, drunken behavior creates its own reputations and rewards. As Luke Bayjere once reflected in a Socratic mood, "I never try to drink so much that I can't remember or know myself." Colville's residents realize the instant publicity that their behavior receives, and they later experience embarrassment — a very painful emotion for the Hare — over the actions of their close kin and themselves. When a brawl breaks out in the village, people call out to one another "free show, free show!", and faces quickly appear in all the community's doorways and windows. Unless serious harm seems imminent, however, the observers rarely interrupt a quarrel: with the full, vicarious pleasure that the role of spectator allows, they instead enjoy the displays of aggression and emotion.

While drinking thus serves as a standardized, sanctioned form of emotional release, it actually operates to inaugurate and perpetuate (rather than simply dissipate) stresses within the community. Though surface relations usually remain quite amiable after a party, the events which occur at drinking incidents are remembered and often resented by the people. What is initially forgiven by the participants is not necessarily forgotten. Grudges and animosities stemming from various sources are often harboured until some future party, at which time their release and expression again raises the level of tension within or between families. A person's generosity with brew is itself a crucial feature of interpersonal relations, and can evoke resentment in the same way that alcohol itself helps to overcome the usual limits on emotional displays. It is when drinking behavior surpasses the boundaries of restraint that culturally sanctioned hostility occurs in its most visible and often its most violent form.

Gabyel Behdzi once observed of brew parties and *kon tweh*:

> There's always trouble around here when people drink. They're always fighting, but I don't know why. Nobody knows why I guess. Just always trouble like that.

Another time, however, Gabyel himself suggested that stress-seeking was part of his own motivation for drinking:

> Me, I should go over to Father [the priest] and buy up some of that liquor from him. Then get drunk again and tie one on and get in trouble once more. One time is not enough. Two times in trouble, that's the way to do it. My stomach's bad, but that don't stop me.

Philip Ratehne perhaps came closer to some of the people's more personalized motives when he discussed the sources of anger among community members:

> Indians are real bad for getting one another angry. They're not like white people, you know. They get onto one another. That's the way they are. Real Indians are "pushy" ... they talk smart and ask for things when they see they want it, so they're always getting each other angry. They talk lots and get pushy and don't know when to stop. Then they get mad and fight and drink or just pull out.

Due to the process of repression, it is not uncommon for witnesses to drinking incidents — and even some of the participants themselves — to lack a full understanding of the causes which underlie drunken conduct. The motivating factors of a quarrel may occasionally be openly expressed by one of the people, but more often the actual sources of the conflict are not immediately evident. They lie buried in the events of the near or distant past. One consequence of this pattern of prior restraint and delayed release is that although a great deal of drinking occurs from the very beginning, for example, of the summer ingathering, it is usually several weeks before tensions build up to the point where people find it necessary to leave the settlement in order to find relief from the conditions of life there. This time lapse — between the beginning of a period of drinking and its culmination in some form of mobility — similarly affects the rhythm of life during each of the year's other reunions.

***

Brew parties are not the only situations in which tensions are produced and reduced in the village context. People seek, experience, and relieve stress in a number of other ways, some of which are direct and obvious, others more muted and vicarious. Drum dancing at the settlement, for example, is a cathartic, communal display of ritualized energies, drawing together the efforts and sentiments of the entire band, and epitomizing the collective force of each reunion. People may sponsor a dance to celebrate a birth, a marriage, a teen-age son's first kill of a caribou. Band members crowd into the cabin of the host family for the evening, and to a chorus of drummers and singers, they dance in shuffling circles for hours on end, enjoying the food and company, and losing themselves in the music and the movement.

Participation in sports and gambling provides other means for seeking or dissipating stress, and allows for physical and personal competition within limits and without violence. Card games and sessions of *udzi*, a native "hand game" played to the accompaniment of fast, rhythmic singing and drumming, generate considerable excitement on the part of participants and observers alike [12]. The very heated and tactile adolescent sport of "boys against girls" — in which the opposing sexes run through the village's plaza, trying to retrieve a rubber ball from one another by means of shoving, tackling, grabbing, and wrestling — affords young adults a sexual and physical outlet for energy and aggression. In addition, the drama and narrative content of both native folkore and Western movies, which the people listen to and watch with great intensity and interest, furnishes them with the opportunity to participate vicariously in the stresses of fictional and mythical characters [13].

Attending movies with band members provided me with an especially striking example of their use of vicarious affect, for the old Hollywood Westerns that the missionary sometimes showed were occasions for true audience participation. These movies displayed a range of emotions and behaviors, such as rage, jealousy, love, kissing, fighting, slapping, and caressing, which the people do not permit themselves to publicly indulge in under normal circumstances. It initially came as something of a shock to me, then, that when scenes portraying these feelings and activities appeared on the screen, my neighbors — in fact the whole audience — responded to them with enthusiastic laughter, cheering, or booing. As in their witnessing of other people's quarrels and drunken disputes, individuals found again in films a setting within which emotions could be vicariously displayed and enjoyed without contradicting the strictures of restraint.

Furthermore, the ubiquitous gossip and humor which punctuate Hare conversations allow many community members to express and redirect their hostility in verbal form. They thereby deal with personal jealousies and antipathies in a non-provoking manner by faulting their neighbors in the company of sympathetic listeners. The people are highly accomplished mimics, as attentive to the nuances of their *sagot'ine* as they are to the features of their ecosystem: subtleties of behavior become the substance of ridicule, and the well-honed, detailed nature of gossip is informed by the limited privacy and openness of village life. Few marital disputes go unnoticed, and it is the rare idiosyncracy of speech which remains unechoed. Both conversation and comedy thus provide important devices for handling and displacing community tensions.

In the full context of all these exchanges, of course, while there are some people who talk, there are others who get talked about. Individuals who are the objects of comment and criticism also experience themselves as the subjects of other people's remarks. One person's comic jabs then become another person's stress, for it is difficult — within the confines of a small community — to avoid becoming the content of other people's discourse. The Hare thus illustrate the kind of anxiety which Heidegger (1962) defines as the sense of "being at issue" (Bakan 1968: 81), for band members do literally experience their own existence as an open question, the outcome of which — both physically and socially — is a source of doubt and uncertainty.

***

People's responses to life in the village as well as the bush indicate that they variously experience either too much or too little of one another at certain seasons of the year. Brewing, drinking, interaction rates, violence, and publicity are stresses directly related to the intensity of band reunions. It is then that mobility becomes an important part of the people's repertoire: it serves as a density and spacing device in the context of the community, just as it does in dealing with the simultaneously compact and dispersed conditions of camp life in the bush.

Movement in the village setting takes several forms. Daily activities, such as checking fish nets, visiting rabbit snares, gathering berries, hauling firewood, and going hunting, all provide a temporary change of social and physical surroundings for band members. As is true during the winter, the men are relatively more mobile than the women in these regards, but the crucial point here is not *who* moves the most as the fact that movement by *any* segment of the population provides separation and relief both for those who depart and those from whom they take leave (Schwartz 1968: 742). One consequence of this gender difference in mobility patterns, however, is that the rare cases of complete withdrawal from interaction within households usually involve women: whereas males can more easily leave the community when tensions and anxieties become oppressive, females — with their lower access to movement — must resort to other coping techniques, among which are immobile retreat and a turning inward.

Also indicative of differential stress response are the distinct mobility patterns of Western-oriented and more traditional families. During the late winter and summer reunions, it is the latter people who seek long-term separations from the village by moving to caribou-hunting and fishing camps in the vicinity of the settlement. Whereas assimilated individuals find the isolation of the bush harder to take, traditional men and women experience the drinking and "information overload" of the village the more stressful of the two situations.

Some highly acculturated individuals also express dissatisfaction with Colville's social life — though in their case it is not because they find the settlement too raucous, but rather because they feel it is too limited. Like conservative families they use mobility as a solution, but for more Western-ized people it is the size and excitement of Fort Good Hope rather than the solitude of the bush which is sought out. There is an additional motive for such trips by some of Colville's young, unmarried men. Individuals such as Adam Ratehne have been unable to find wives in the community, and so they travel to Good Hope during reunions and holidays in order to visit girlfriends and seek out future mates. This continues a traditional male pattern of travel for spouse-seeking found in other Northern Athabascan groups as well. In the Colville band, there is an imbalance in the ratio of marriageable men and women, impelling some of the "surplus" males to travel in search of wives. Several of the village's young adults are too closely related to even consider marriage with one another, further limiting the possible unions within the community. In the late 1960s, for example, of the twenty-nine people in the band between the ages of sixteen and forty-five, only eleven individuals were married (five males and six females), and thirteen out of the eighteen unwed adults were men [14].

Aggravating the stress of this situation was the fact that, in a number of cases, Colville mothers had blocked the marriages of their grown daughters because of their reluctance to lose the labor and services of these young women. In their families' division of labor by gender and age, these adult daughters took on most of the responsibility for female tasks within house-holds, relieving their mothers of the hardest chores. Berona had conse-quently objected to proposals received by both Monique and Sharon Yawileh, and Mary Behdzi who — like the Yawileh sisters — was in her late twenties, had been frustrated several times by the obstructing tactics of her mother Helen. Such situations were at the heart of intergenerational tensions within these families, for the young adults who were seeking to establish their autonomy were simultaneously still trying to respect the roles of their elders and parents. Clashes between mothers and daughters, and the frustrations of single men, consequently added to the stresses and problems of the community.

The diverse motives for travelling to Good Hope during breaks in bush life could thus range from excitement and escape to sex and marriage. I also found it significant, however, that the various individuals and families who journey to the fort usually return to Colville Lake well before the particular holiday they are enjoying has concluded. After a week or two of town-living, they often find that the countervailing stresses of Good Hope — including a somewhat pejorative attitude toward "bush" Indians, the presence of the Royal Canadian Mounted Police, the high cost of living, and a greatly augmented level of drinking and violence — are even more oppressive than the tensions experienced in the small settlement. In retrospect, it often seems, they find it more enjoyable to remember and anticipate the fort than to experience it. As Henriksen has observed of the Naskapi, people alternately tend to idealize either the bush or the town when they are in the other place (1973: 17).

Back at the settlement at Colville, a similar rhythm plays itself out. Just as people welcome a return to the village after a prolonged period in the bush, the members of the band are equally anxious to disperse once more to trapping, hunting, and fishing camps following an extended reunion. During their time together at the village, they have learned from their neighbors about the areas that are especially rich or poor in meat, fish and fur that year, and they take that knowledge into account when deciding where — and with whom — to camp the next season. Reunions thus serve not only as an opportunity to renew supplies and social ties, but also as "an information-dissemination mechanism" (Jarvenpa 1976: 56; Jarvenpa and Brumbach 1988: 612; cf. also Heffley 1981: 138-140 and Riches 1982: 52-53). The motives and feelings for returning to the bush are nevertheless mixed. As they do in accounting for their moves from camp to camp, the people can again provide ready-made ecological explanations for leaving the settlement. But as André Yawileh once remarked from the peace and solitude of his family's bush camp:

> When we are out here alone you know it is hard for us. But sometimes I think it is even harder for us to live like that together. We just bother each other too much. That brew does it sometime I think. People shouldn't argue and be jealous but they do. Here in the bush things can be tough, but you're not troubled so much as back in Colville. So the winter is good for something too.

9. CONCLUSIONS AND IMPLICATIONS

Social and ecological sources of stress and mobility are dimensions of life in all human societies. Every human community, however, exhibits distinctive patterns in the types of movement and the content of the tensions which affect its members. The life style of the Hare Indians of Colville Lake combines features of traditional sub-Arctic hunting bands with adaptations to the conditions of Western contact. The villagers are therefore involved in a series of challenges derived from two different cultural traditions. Within the framework of a highly mobile existence, band members respond to a wide variety of stresses with a number of different coping techniques. The primary aspects of their mobility are ecological, being a function of the people's dependence upon migratory and sparsely distributed faunal resources. The size and nature of the human groups created by the movements of the band are in turn productive of a series of social and psychological tensions which are partially relieved by additional mobility.

Movement is not always the primary device resorted to for the relief of stress. For instance, drinking and aggression towards dogs are two alternative modes of release. A great deal of hostility is also displayed in the high level of gossip maintained by community members. Vicarious emotional participation — channeled through gambling, sports, folklore, mimicry, movies, and other people's quarrels — is also an important part of the band's psychic economy [15]. In addition, tensions stemming from the village feud between the fur trader and the priest, which are considered in detail in the following chapter, are dealt with by the people through such mechanisms as patron-client relations with these men, rather than by movement into or out of the settlement. Nevertheless, the level of mobility maintained by band members during all periods of the year, including both reunions and dispersals, is much greater than that required for successful exploitation of the environment. Mobility is therefore serving more than ecological needs, a point made by several other observers of sub-Arctic communities [16].

In the North I was initially unaware of the relationship between mobility and stress until I myself began to experience some of the same tensions which affected the people. The hardship and insularity of the bush often stretched my tolerance and patience to the breaking point, and on occasion I had deep feelings of hostility towards both my hosts and myself. I wondered, in the moments of intensest anxiety, why I had ever gone North in the first place and subjected myself to this way of life. The repetitiveness of existence, the monotony of conversations, and the compactness and privations of the camp all came to oppress me in their turn.

At first I was too doubt and guilt-ridden to express these feelings openly. But while I consciously supressed them, I unwittingly turned to my field diary as a convenient outlet for venting my anguish and frustration. When I re-read my journal while I was still in the bush, I began to recognize the process of emotional restraint and displacement which I had been engaging in. I noted that not only was I using the diary as a confessional, but that I had come to value the trapping and hunting trips, and even the daily chores of net-checking and wood-cutting, as opportunities for escaping the confinement of camp. This led me to consider what stresses the people themselves were experiencing, as well as the techniques that they were using to cope with them. Without the aid of literacy, how did the people handle their tensions?

At this point my concern shifted from a focus on the material aspects of survival to the nature of human relationships within the camp. Sensitized by my own experiences and reactions, I became a much more attentive observer of individual behavior and interaction. Fluctuations in mood, petty annoyances, the treatment of dogs, and the sources of worry and satisfaction now became increasingly evident. The people's own evaluation of mobility was openly expressed in the excitement and relief that they experienced in travelling. The most striking feature about these events was the rhythmic nature of the changes in camp life and mood, and it was in trying to understand this process that the importance of restraint, displacement, and mobility began to emerge. At the village I had also been struck by the people's frequency of movement and residence shifts, and I had begun to keep a detailed, daily record of the trips, travels, and outings made by individuals and families. Now, when I combined the data on moods, stress sources, and mobility rates into a chronological document, the crucial role of movement in the stress coping process became manifest. Careful observation during the remainder of the year confirmed and amplified what had initially been a very tentative hypothesis based on my own experiences.

Living with the people also revealed stress-seeking as an existential feature of their adaptations. In the context of the bush, the encounter with challenge became a fundamental part of band identity, and at the village, the actively sought stresses of gambling, sports, and drinking were intrinsic to an emotional economy of well-defined release mechanisms. Taking stress and mobility in their widest senses, one could argue that a balance betwen stress-seeking and stress-avoidance, as well as one between interdependence and independence, were necessary for an optimum level of individual and group coping. As an operative mode of this system, mobility was an inherent part of the flexibility which characterized so many of the people's adaptive procedures.

***

Students of other sub-Arctic groups have shown that anxiety and stress can function both as centrifugal and centripetal forces in society. Latent hostility, insecurity, and fears of witchcraft, for example, contribute to the atomism of the Ojibwa and Kaska; anxiety over isolation and "bush men" operates as a cohesive force among the Kutchin (Hallowell 1941; Landes 1937a; Barnouw 1950; Honigmann 1947, 1949; Slobodin 1960a). An important point not emphasized by previous writers is that *both* major aspects of population mobility — ingathering *and* dispersal — can each serve as a source of stress as well as a means of resolving it. At Colville Lake, each of the six periods in the band's annual cycle has its characteristic environmental and social tensions. The successive periods of population re-distribution relieve many stresses which have been generated in previous phases. Each new phase in its turn creates other stresses which find release in the next part of the cycle. Mobility thus serves both to generate and relieve stress within a social and ecological framework. Furthermore, within each part of the cycle, day-to-day mobility and other coping techniques offer temporary respite from pressures and anxieties. The entire year is therefore characterized by a continual, dialectical alternation between periods of high and low stress: major shifts in the rhythm coincide with large-scale population movements, while changes of a lower magnitude generate mobility among smaller groups of people.

Individual and family participation in this rhythm is affected by such factors as age, gender, degree of assimilation, and the division of labor. These variables lead to differential exposure, susceptibility and responses to stress on the part of community members. Reactions which overcome the people's efforts at emotional restraint are channeled and displaced so that they usually come out in predictable and socially acceptable ways. Even drinking situations, as volatile as they can be, follow a rhythm and format with which band members are familiar. These arrangements and patterns permit the maintenance of social relationships in spite of both stressful situations and the expressive, and potentially disruptive acts, which some-times accompany them. The cultural emphasis on emotional containment leads people to supress, displace, or delay their reactions to provocative situations, and the vehemence and directness of their responses are there-fore not as extreme as might otherwise be the case.

Given the universality of stress and mobility in human groups, it is possible that the type of relationship found between them among the *K'apamituegot'ine* may also characterize behavior in other social systems. In order for this functional relationship to be operative, the specific tensions and movements which occur in other groups need not be identical to those which affect the Colville band. The model presented here, which differentiates social from ecological sources of stress, and seasonal from daily types of mobility, is broad enough to accomodate a wide range of threats, coping techniques, and patterns of movement. In applying this scheme to different human groups, it would nevertheless be necessary to separate the general from the particular in order to see if the underlying pattern is, in fact, the same as the one that has been outlined. To this end, three hypotheses are proposed here as a means of testing the wider applicability of the model.

First, the interrelationship between stress and mobility that has been found at Colville Lake suggests that when high mobility is a basic feature of a society's ecology, then movement will also be utilized by people as a way to relieve social sources of stress. Mobility in such cases will therefore be greater than is strictly necessary from an ecological point of view. Such movements can involve either individuals or groups, and they can encompass temporary or long-term separations or reunions of people. Mobility which is basically ecological in significance may be used simultaneously as a stress-reducing device, although the persons involved may commonly explain their moves as a purely environmental necessity.

A second implication is that if the ecological situation of a group involves prolonged conditions of extreme dispersal or concentration, then these will both constitute major sources of tension for the members of the society. The stresses resulting from these extreme conditions will be coped with, in part, by forms of mobility which allow the people either (a) to escape isolation by coming together in larger groups, or (b) to find relief from the abrasive social interaction which such large groups generate. Interactions within small groups will also be abrasive over time, and mobility will then function as a stress-reducer by allowing members temporary separations from one another. The stress and mobility dimensions of existence will therefore constitute a dialectical process.

Finally, the situation among the Hare suggests that if the people in a community are socially differentiated on the basis of gender, age, status, degree of acculturation, or some other criterion, then this will be reflected in (a) their varied exposure, susceptibility, and responses to stress, and (b) their varied modes and levels of mobility, including recourse to movement as a stress-reducing technique.

Each of these features of the situation at Colville Lake could be tested as a hypothesis on the mobility and stress patterns characterizing other human groups. Since the conditions of life among the people at Colville do not occur universally, modifications of the above model, or the proposal of alternate schemes, are developments to be expected from such work. The presence of stress also serves important social functions in human societies, and the necessity of considering this positive aspect of the problem as part of any cultural analysis has already been demonstrated by Hallowell (1941), Selye (1956), Slobodin (1960a), and others. For the people of Colville Lake a degree of stress-seeking is itself an implicit part of social ecology. Furthermore, the tensions experienced over generosity and emotional restraint help to reinforce the basic patterns of behavior which underlie the coherency of community social life. Child-rearing techniques also include the induction of anxiety in youngsters, as seen in the concerns children develop about drinking and "bush men": these experiences serve as a way of socializing the young to the expectations and conduct of others. Among adults, the anxiety of being the subject of other people's gossip and ridicule similarly underlies the effectiveness of discourse and humor as informal modes of social control.

Since the problems and issues which have been raised here constitute a basic dimension of the human condition, I would suggest that fieldworkers should devote more attention to them than they have in the past. The process of stress production and reduction offers a context within which a large number of social phenomena — ranging from kinship relations and politics to physical mobility and economic behavior — could all be fruitfully reconsidered. Studies of tension and movement among foragers and horticulturalists reveal how important seasonal group fission can be as a technique for the peaceful resolution of conflict (eg., Turnbull 1968a; Gregor 1977) [17]. The situation presented here indicates how the people of one human group are affected by a similar process, and it is hoped that future research will broaden our knowledge in this area by developing comparable models for other societies.

CHAPTER 5

The Missionary and the Fur Trader

1. INTRODUCTION

The perception of direction and dimension is one of the most deceptive experiences of life in the North. Distance and depth in the environment can be judged only after one has learned to appreciate texture and sound as well as sight, for in some seasons, gauging spatial relationships requires sensory awareness of great subtlety. As the people's methods for coping with a "white-out" reveal, they orient themselves by such features as the sound of the wind and the feel of the snow, and the crucial sensations of movement are more often kinaesthetic than visual in nature.

The deceptiveness of physical space is consonant with some parallel problems in judging the scale of social relationships. In the North, numbers are not necessarily equatable with power, and in certain circles, a few white men may wield more influence than a dozen Dene. Depending on the context, people can be perceived, grouped, and experienced in a variety of ways. For native individuals, the kin, friends, strangers, and whites in their world each evoke distinct responses, and people frequently adjust their behavior to the qualities and statuses of their companions. Beneath the surface of small scale communities like Colville, then, there also lies a subtle fabric of bonds and divisions, woven from the nature of Dene and whites alike.

A frequent condition of fieldwork situations which often produces both practical and methodological problems for an anthropologist is the presence of other "non-native" persons in the community under study. Among the most frequently encountered individuals are representatives of government, religious and commercial institutions who, in many cases, have a longer history of involvement with the local population than the ethnographer can himself claim. It is not unusual for the fieldworker to find that these non-native residents are often engaged in conflicts with one another, and that, as a researcher and an individual, it is difficult for him to avoid being drawn into their disputes, regardless of his personal wishes or professional poses. The influences that such outside personnel have upon local conditions, and the relations that they maintain with indigenous people, with the ethnographer, and with one another, thus constitute both legitimate areas of inquiry for the anthropologist, as well as basic conditions which affect the nature of his work.

Feud situations of this type, developing initially as personal quarrels between white "outsiders," are common throughout the settlements of the Canadian North, and Colville Lake provided a poignant case for study (cf. Dunning 1959; Henriksen 1973; Brody 1975; and Broch 1983 for other examples). The conflict at Colville involved the community's only permanent, non-native residents, a white missionary and a fur trader, whose increasing mutual enmity over the years had crystallized certain stress patterns and identity processes among the villagers. Specifically, the whites' feud constitutesd an important source of tension for native people, who were periodically pressured by these men to take sides and display allegiances in a conflict that was not of their own making. By becoming involved in this feud, however, the Hare were not only subject to manipulation by the whites, but they also learned to capitalize on their own situation by playing the priest and trader off against one another in order to derive certain material benefits from these men. Beyond this, the people had gradually come to define the feud and its protagonists as prime sources of many of their other problems, and hence the whites had unwittingly provided the community with a means of displacing anger and blame from some unrelated, but equally stressful areas of life. Finally, rather than promoting the rise of village factionalism, the feud actually tended to foster a sense of native unity and identity by creating, within the settlement, a community of interest which centered around the people's shared dilemma of coping with these powerful local figures.

The poignancy of the village feud stemmed, in large measure, from the disproportionate amount of influence and power which these two white men had over the members of the band. When the people were gathered at the settlement, the relatively unscheduled and subsistence-oriented life of the bush gave way to a more structured existence, the primary dimensions of which were set by the community's trader and priest. At the settlement, where they remained during all seasons of the year, these two men controlled many of the economic and religious aspects of the people's lives, including the distribution of government assistance checks, and the provision of wage employment opportunities. Beyond their traditional commercial and spiritual roles, these two men also served as the settlement's primary link with the outside. They handled the local disbursement of mail, medicine, and money, in addition to controlling much of the flow of information and supplies into and out of the community via their access to chartered airplanes and a short-wave radio. Although the local people continued to live off the land, therefore, their well-being was inextricably bound up with the goods and services, as well as the attitudes and aspirations, of the priest and trader, white men who had come to dominate their small, circumscribed world in an effective though not always conscious manner.

2. THE FEUD

The quality of life at Colville Lake was a function of many factors, embracing not only how humans interacted with nature, and how Dene and whites related to one another, but also with how the whites themselves have adapted to each other's presence. Given the influence of the community's white residents upon the entire village, it is relevant to relate, however briefly, the short but dramatic saga of the relationship between the fur trader and priest. Without such a summary, the bitter feud that these men developed with one another, and the repercussions of this conflict, could not be fully appreciated.

As detailed in Chapter 3, the village of Colville Lake is a relatively new settlement in the Canadian Northwest, and in large part, it owes its existence as a permanent community to the two white men who came to dominate so much of its life. In the winter of 1959-1960, after several decades of disease, starvation, and migration had severely reduced the size of the Colville band, Dave Heathson — an independent fur trader from Fort Good Hope — opened up an outpost store on the southeastern shore of the lake. This store was first run by the Godanto family, which worked in the employ of the trader. In the years after its inauguration, a substantial community began to develop around the trading post as families from the original band were attracted to re-settle there. Then, in 1962, a Catholic missionary order — which had been active in this area of the North for over a century — sent Father Claude Valois to Colville for the purpose of establishing a church and mission in the village. The settlement continued to grow, and approximately a year and a half after the mission was built, the fur trader from Good Hope closed down his business at the fort and moved to Colville Lake with his family in order to run the store there himself.

Initially, the trader and the missionary got along well with one another, both feeling that their common interest lay in working towards building up the community and making it more attractive to people. This would have personally benefited both of them: one man would have a successful business, the other a flourishing parish. And so, while living in separate houses, Father Claude and Dave Heathson began a congenial joint residence in the village by sharing one another's company, equipment, supplies, and hospitality.

Being both strong-willed, independent, and authoritarian individuals, however, the incompatability of their personalities — which was magnified by their focal roles in the settlement — eventually led to a rupture in their relationship. The attitudes which underlay this split are evident in the tone of an informal "gentleman's agreement" that the two men made with one another shortly after they found themselves sharing the spotlight in the community. The priest, for his part in the arrangement, promised to encourage the Hare to sell all their furs at the trading post rather than ship them out or take them to the Hudson's Bay Company Store in Fort Good Hope. The trader, in turn, being a prominent figure in the village, was to set an example for the people by regularly attending Church services, and by holding down the supply of liquor and materials for making homebrew [1].

This *modus vivendi* was effective and operative for a period of about one year. There are numerous reasons given by each white man to explain his eventual disillusionment with the way things were working out. Each of them accuses the other of a number of unfair or abusive tactics to gain advantages and pre-eminence on the local scene. Currying favor with visiting government officials and the local people, broken promises, vindictive actions, behind-the-scenes moves, and abuses of privileges, good-will, and generosity — plus more personal accusations which need not be chronicled here — are all cited as leading up to their open conflict. Understandably, each man interprets the course of events quite differently. At the same time, however, there is a curious agreement in their respective accounts of the one event that finally touched off the feud. According to both men, it happened one Sunday afternoon when a pilot was visiting the village. He was at the mission with Father Claude when the trader, who had not attended Mass that morning, stopped in to say hello. The priest asked Dave why he had not been to services that morning. According to Father Claude, this was a legitimate question since he felt that the trader was reneging on their agreement. To Dave, however, the implication that he was responsible to the priest for his actions, especially with the question being presented in front of another white man, was a grave insult. The trader angrily left the mission, and he and the priest have not spoken to one another since then.

This event brought feelings which had been building up for over a year to a head. Since the split, the animosity between the two men has increased, as has the number of actions they have employed to dislodge one another from the community. To cite some recent examples, Dave began circulate a petition among the people, asking the regional bishop to remove the priest from the community for his purportedly irreligious behavior. Father Claude, in turn, opened up a small store of his own in the settlement, as well as made plans for the start of a fur-marketing cooperative, in order to divert fur pelts and profits from the trader, and ultimately to drive him out of business. Both men agree that at one point a reconciliation may have been possible between them, but now they feel that things have gone too far to warrant this. What was originally a clash of personalities has since been transformed into an ideological series of moral and economic arguments: Dave accuses the missionary of unchristian and unpriestly conduct, and Father Claude, in turn, argues that the trader is exploitative and abusive in his pursuit of power and profit. Nevertheless, the initial agreement that these men made between themselves, i.e., to support one another in their institutionalized roles, indicates that neither economic or religious motives were really at the root of their differences.

The native people of the village subsequently became involved in the actions and stratagems of the feud, and they were exposed to continual pressure from both the trader and the priest to support their respective sides in the conflict. The members of the band were thus placed in the undesired role of pawns in a power struggle, a set of circumstances over whose genesis they had little influence. They found that their business, their furs, their assistance checks, their credit and debt, their friendships and associations, and their symbolic acts of support, were all coveted prizes for which the whites constantly competed.

The missionary and trader, in their turn, each felt that as a result of the feud, the other white man was seriously holding back the growth of the village. Each claimed that the other benefited most from their original agreement, and that he therefore lost the most by breaking it. Furthermore, Dave and Father Claude each maintained that he himself was mainly responsible for the revival and development of the settlement. Each man also claimed that if he left, the village would ultimately collapse, and that the people would move back to Fort Good Hope. They both gave as reasons for this that: (a) no one would come to replace him, and (b) the people would not be able "to put up with that other man." To a considerable degree, therefore, each man's participation in the feud was bound up with his sense of mission or profit, as well as with a commitment to power, autonomy, and the maintenance of a distinct self-image.

3. INITIATION

When I arrived at the settlement in 1967, five years after the missionary had come, three and a half years following the trader's arrival, and two and a half years after the feud's inauguration, I was only dimly aware of what the local situation was like. I was quickly baptized into village politics by the pilot who flew me into the community. As we hovered over the settlement and the bay on whose shores it is located, he asked me whose dock I wanted to land at: the missionary's or the trader's. Showing a reluctance to make any kind of a decision, I said that I really did not care. Besides, I offered, what difference would it make? Shocked at my naiveté, the pilot just stared at me silently for a moment. And then, in about two minutes of torpid flying and torrid prose, he quickly filled me in on the entire history of the feud — a feud whose story was apparently well known throughout this part of the North.

Moments later, sitting in the cockpit a sadder, more apprehensive, but wiser person, I realized that some sort of decision was necessary, and so I asked the pilot to circle the village one more time. Acting on an impulse

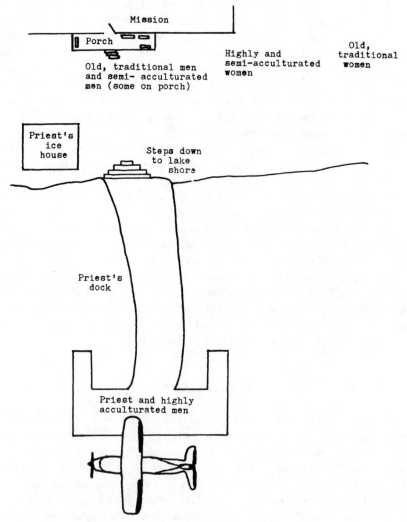

FIGURE 16   Positioning of Villagers at Plane Arrival

whose rationale still escapes me, I felt that I had better determine who had the larger dock, the trader or the priest. And, satisfying myself that it was the latter, I asked the pilot to land there.

Almost the entire community turned out to greet the plane — the trader and his family being notable exceptions — and in a short period of time I had made a nodding acquaintance with the village's population. Later in the year I came to appreciate how standardized was the way in which people grouped themselves at a plane's arrival (Figure 16), but on that day I was more interested in making a good, first impression. I soon found myself alone

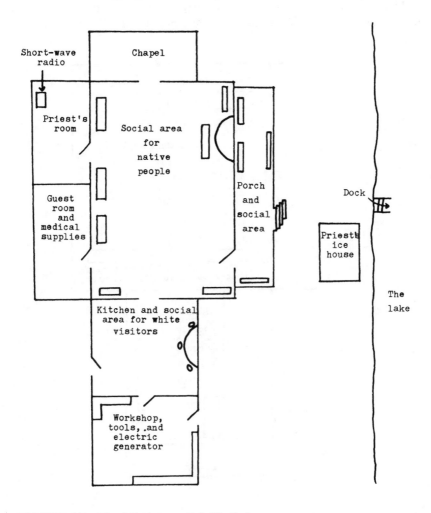

FIGURE 17   The Mission at Colville Lake

inside the mission, however, and while talking to Father Claude, I became aware of how distant and deferential most of the people were towards him, as well as how hesitant they were to intrude into his presence when he had company. Meanwhile, the missionary explained that the small cabin that had been set aside for me in the native part of the settlement was not quite ready yet, and that I could stay with him for a few days while it was being cleaned out. Before long, his conversation got around to the trader and the feud, and I found myself in the midst of my first indoctrination session, one that was to be followed by many others during my year's stay in the community.

Living at the mission those first few days was an educational experience in several regards. Besides learning the priest's side of the story, I soon

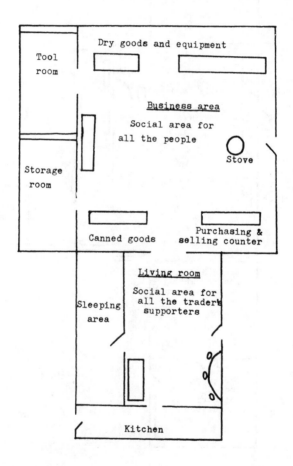

FIGURE 18   The Trading Post at Colville Lake

realized how difficult it would be for me to establish rapport with the people if I became too closely identified with either white man. From observing village patterns of interaction and avoidance, I came to appreciate the caste-like nature of social relations between Indians and whites, and its reflection in the physical and social distances that these people maintained between one another [2]. Not only did Dave and Father Claude segregate themselves from the people spatially (Map 3), but they carefully regulated which parts of their homes the people could enter: certain rooms and areas of the mission were out-of-bounds to all but a select few of the Indians, whereas the whites, as a prerogative of their status and power, could freely penetrate the living quarters of all the native people if they so wished (cf. Figures 17 and 18) [3]. As soon as it was feasible for me to do so, therefore, I left the mission to pay an initial social call upon the trader, and then, at the earliest convenience, I moved into my own cabin, and started trying to mix with the Dene on a much more informal basis. My first priority was to avoid being type-cast into the same "white man's" role that the priest and trader had assumed, and in order to do that, I needed the freedom of movement that would allow me to establish a unique identity.

Within a day of changing my residence from the mission to my cabin, I began receiving a stream of young visitors who were curious about my presence and my person. It took a bit of explanation to make clear my motives for coming to Colville, and primarily to settle the matter of why I had chosen to live in the Indian part of the settlement rather than isolate myself from the Dene as the missionary and trader had done. After a few days had passed, and I began to cut my own wood, draw my own water, hunt for my own supper, and "go native" in many other small ways, the villagers began to appreciate the fact that I did not intend to live in the "colonial" style of the other white men they had had contact with, and that I was indeed serious about learning and emulating their life style. Unlike the priest and trader, I did not set my residence apart from theirs, nor did I expect band members to perform essential services for me on a voluntary or cash basis. Furthermore, given the way in which I was conducting myself — including my physical separation from the whites, my residence in the Dene part of the village, and my early friendships with the children — the people came to accept my publicized position of neutrality in the local feud. They thus began to feel comfortable in my presence, and — with the help of Mehna and the other children — soon lost the reluctance to speak with me that they had exhibited while I was still living in the mission.

The feud between Father Claude and Dave Heathson thus worked to my advantage during my initial weeks in the settlement: people came to look upon me as a sympathetic, neutral outsider with whom they could register their complaints, sentiments, hopes, and grudges without any fear of reprisal or recrimination. Within a surprisingly brief period of residence among them, their conversations with me covered a great variety of topics, ranging from the psychology and economics of the local conflict to sex and marital problems. I thus found myself the recipient of a great deal of personal information and gossip within a few weeks of my arrival — and much of the information that I received was of such an intimate nature, that it provided me with the kinds of insights that one feels fortunate and privileged to discover after months of careful and patient fieldwork.

It took longer to establish my position of neutrality in the eyes of the priest and trader, and, in a very real sense, this was a struggle that I had to keep up throughout my stay in the community. Visits or favors to one man always had to be balanced by a comparable gesture towards the other one, and I found myself spending an inordinate amount of time placating, pleasing, and patronizing each of them so as not to jeopardize my position in the village. As a result of the layout of the community, I soon discovered — as had the people long ago — that it was almost impossible to hide from either man the fact that one had visited the other. Dave and the priest, from their respective front windows, could each see who was paying a call upon the other man: both the winter and summer trails to the mission and store, whether the people walked on the land or took a short-cut across the bay by boat or snowshoe, were within the purview of each of the whites. And if bad weather or heavy winter clothing obscured a person's identity, both Father Claude and the trader kept a pair of binoculars close at hand to aid in the process of identification. Furthermore, because the mission was raised up off the ground on wooden supports, it was even possible for the priest to see down into the shopping bags of individuals who passed below his window on their way back from the trader's store. He thus knew who was selling furs and buying commodities, as well as which people had been given large amounts of credit or were planning to make homebrew.

Similar to what had happened to many of the other community residents, I also found that my earnest statements to the whites that I did not wish to become involved in their struggle was accepted by both of these men but that, nevertheless, neither of them ever really ceased to court my favor or to try to use me as a source of information and leverage. This put me in a position to enjoy from them some of the same confidences that I received from the people, but in my dealings with both whites and Dene, I was placed in a position where my trustworthiness as a confidant was continually being tested by all the interested parties. And at Colville Lake, *everyone* was an interested party.

The Indians' role and interest in the feud was closely bound up with the control that the whites exercised over important goods and services in the community. Wage labor, assistance checks, medicine, loans of money and equipment, credit, movies, the provision of liquor and brew materials, and access to the primary means of communication with the outside, were all in the hands of the whites. The Dene, in their turn, had the souls and the furs, and the support and the public opinion, that the whites needed to bolster their egos, their pocketbooks, and their power plays. The situation thus echoed the ties between Indians and whites that one would have found in eastern Canada during the seventeenth century, when the early French missionaries and traders were vying to establish themselves among the Huron and Iroquois (Miller 1991: 23-40). At Colville Lake in the twentieth century, however, the feud was still central to existence and survival in the village, and one could not hope to ignore it and still grasp the essence of community life.

Though it was a hard lesson to learn and follow through with, I soon realized that the distinctive features of the local situation made naiveté a pose rather than a real possibility. All the villagers, natives and whites — myself included — needed to receive and give information on a regular basis lest we lose touch with the realities of life and thereby impair our ability to adapt to them. People not only required such knowledge in order to survive, but the participation in gossip was also a pursuit which had its own intrinsic rewards. In the small world of Colville Lake, just as Gluckman (1963) notes in a variety of other settings, information and gossip were among the basic fuels of life, providing a kind of social energy which had no direct counterpart in the more material realms of food and nutrients. And to the extent that social relations were instrumental means to survival as well as expressive outlets, the useful knowledge conveyed in gossip was a *sine qua non* of life itself.

I eventually realized that, at one and the same time, I had become many things to many people: communication channel, information filter, high-status friend, local resource, experimental subject, object of trust, source of suspicion, a link in the network, an outlet for stress [4]. Perhaps the most difficult part of the entire northern experience, therefore, was not adjusting to the physical conditions of life, but rather learning to juggle and play all of these roles simultaneously [5]. I was never really offstage, and I continually had to confront one or another personage in the local drama and perform in accordance with his or her expectations. This was, however, the kind of position that everyone in the settlement occupied to some degree, for we were all in this together. And, perhaps unwittingly taking my cue from Hamlet, I realized that the drama was an opportunity rather than an inconvenience, being a performance which could reveal much of the inner workings of the people who were caught up in it. Without expecting it to be so, then, the village play became the thing wherein I hoped to catch the conscience of the community.

4. ALLEGIANCE, ALLIANCE AND ATTITUDE

A key aspect of community conscience in the feud was the depth and variety of individual commitments to the main protagonists. The peoples' leanings in the conflict tended to be heavily influenced by their perception of the roles of missionary and trader, perceptions which were colored by their previous experiences with other incumbents of these positions. Historically, concepts of the roles of fur trader and priest have been rooted in the accumulated experiences of band members since the early and mid-nineteenth century. Nowadays, for example, the people do not differentiate between the roles of "missionary" and "priest," referring to all clergymen, in fact, as "priests" or "Fathers." This is because the conversion of all the Hare in the region to Catholicism was begun in the 1860s, and so the real missionizing phase of activity has long since past. Similarly, fur trading activities in the area began in the early nineteenth century, and have continued with varying degrees of intensity up to the present day. Involvement in commercial exchange as a dimension of the native economy, then, is also an established part of Dene existence. Based upon their past and their recently intensified exposure to storekeepers and clerics, therefore, band members are well aware of the types of behavior that these roles entail. Without, of course, using the word "role," the people have — and express — definite ideas on what they expect a fur trader and priest to be like. Consequently, it was only the role *incumbents*, and not the roles per se, who were new to members of the settlement.

The people therefore evaluated Father Claude and Dave Heathson in comparison to other traders and priests they have known. Dave, for example, was unfavorably contrasted with a Hudson's Bay Company manager from a generation ago at Good Hope — a long enough time interval to permit what might have been a process of "retrospective sanctification" for this man [6]. Father Claude was similarly found wanting in comparison to a parish priest who had recently served at a nearby fort. Invariably, however, Colville's whites came off better than some of their peers, and worse than others. It was striking, nevertheless, that even the harshest judgments of Father Claude did not diminish the religious sensibilities of his sharpest critics. In fact, most community members found various aspects of their Catholicism very fulfilling: their belief in God was sincere; and they enjoyed Mass and other rituals both for the spiritual and the social experiences they provided. Most of the families I stayed with in the bush, for instance, said a rosary together each week even in the absence of Father and church. Their religion was well insulated against the personality and the frailties of any one priest.

Despite, or perhaps because of people's awareness of what a "good" Father or trader should be like, another factor in the feud was the discrepancy local residents felt between the ideal and actual behavior of the two white men. "He doesn't act like a *real* priest," complained some of the villagers, while others protested that "the trader doesn't treat us the way he *should.*" The concepts that the people held of these Western roles, and the disparities that most of them saw in the behavior of Colville's two white men, varied with the backgrounds of community residents. People with different degrees of outside experience and white contact showed distinct attitudes towards Father Claude and Dave. More acculturated individuals generally sided with the trader, while traditional band members tended to be among the most consistent supporters of the priest. To express the matter somewhat differently, a small number of the most conservative people did not find Father Claude's behavior incongruent with his role, and the most Westernized Dene felt largely the same way — though not quite as consistently — about Dave Heathson. More pronounced and open support of the trader was connected with drinking and the wage labor situation in the community since Dave's provision of brew materials, liquor, and employment, were prime sources of his power and influence in the feud [7]. Furthermore, the trader spoke only English, and his close contacts with the people were therefore limited to the bilingual individuals.

The most conservative members of the community, who the more acculturated people sometimes referred to as "the *real* Indians" or "those old bush Indians," were primarily monolingual, bush-oriented non-drinkers, who had relatively little experience outside the village. Their more pronounced and open support of Father Claude related again, in part, to the provision of wage labor within the community: the priest (like the trader) offered more work to his supporters than he did to other individuals. Father Claude also had a good command of the native language, and so the more traditional individuals of the community had more frequent interaction with him than they did with the trader.

Although Dave and the priest each had a small core of supporters, the majority of the villagers had no clear set of allegiances in the feud, and, correspondingly, only a small number of them could be characterized as being highly acculturated or traditional. The band's population actually formed a continuum in the areas of assimilation and allegiance, with most individuals falling somewhere between the two extremes on each of these issues. Since my own status in the community made me an intimate of both band members and whites alike, I could follow their respective motives, strategies, and responses on a day-to-day and issue-to-issue basis. I saw that from time to time the Dene changed their leanings in the conflict in accordance with their perception of what actions and alliances would do them the most good. For the most part, however, the bulk of the residents tried to maintain a conscientious neutrality in the conflict, desiring to enjoy the good will, the services, and the goods of both white men.

The corollary of this strategem in the realm of attitudes was the fact that most band members felt that trader and priest each had their faults as well as their virtues. In most cases, as a result, native opinions about these individuals tended to be more balanced than one-sided. In Lena Dehdele's estimation:

> Father's okay and he does a lot for the people, but he shouldn't go around getting mixed up in everybody else's business.

Lena's husband Peter once complained:

> Dave, he been good to us the last few years, but now he's trying to cut our fur prices too much. How're we going to pay up our debts with him? If he and Father stopped fighting, things would be better for the people.

***

To the limited extent that feud alliances consistently followed acculturative levels in the band, this presented an incipient, divisive factor in the settlement. There were few cases of permanent feud leanings, however, and these allegiances took the form of patron-client relationships, i.e., in return for support, information, furs, gifts, meat, fish, and other considerations, the trader and the priest each reserved for particular families most of their wage labor positions, the use of their equipment and supplies, and access to liquor, credit, or other resources and services. But such a strategy of commitment in the feud was followed by only a small number of families, and most of the people tried to play the game both ways.

All of the Hare, regardless of their leanings in the feud, felt that it was in their own best interests to maintain good relations with both white protagonists because, in their view, neither of these men — by himself — could have insured the continuance of current services and the level of living in the community. That is, the goods, services, and benefits that they offered were complementary. Dave provided liquor, Father Claude showed movies and provided medicines; the trader chartered most of the airplanes, the missionary sent messages on his short-wave radio; both men offered wage labor, but not enough — individually — to employ all the men of the village each summer. The people, therefore, for these and related reasons, recognized the need to court the good will of both men.

Even the trader and missionary's most open supporters generally attempted to remain on good terms with the feud's other protagonist, hoping to realize some of the benfits of the "neutralist" position. Consequently, the people rarely criticized either Dave or Father Claude to his face, and instead used various material and expressive means to please the whites. In several cases, some of these actions were motivated by genuine friendship for these men. In most instances, however, achnowledged supporters of both whites, as well as relatively "neutral" individuals, were observed to participate in these activities in order to please either one or both individuals.

The missionary and fur trader realized that most of the community's residents leaned both ways when it was beneficial for them to do so, and each man accepted this as one of the features of the conflict. They realized, in fact, that this type of behavior was often necessary for the people's own well-being. "I know," said Father Claude,

> that everyone had to sign the trader's petition [against me] or else they would have lost their credit. I guess I really can't blame them for doing it.

The trader, for his part, once commented:

> I know that lots of them are giving caribou meat to the priest. They'd sure be in Dutch with the Father if they didn't make some presents like that during the winter.

While it may appear to an outside oberver that it was the whites who controlled the local drama, to the participants it was equally evident that the local people themselves were often in a position to manipulate and exploit the situation. That is, natives also used their role in the feud to their own advantage, and there were several ways in which the dynamics of the conflict accorded benefits and stress-releasing mechanisms for the people (cf. Dunning 1959: 118). In return for their good will and support, for example, they could secure from the whites such things as larger amounts of credit, liquor, more wage work, or the loan of some piece of equipment. They were also allowed to use the mission and store facilities for informal social gatherings, and such events were a major part of the people's leisure life.

Dave and Father Claude accepted these and similar facets of their relations with the villagers as part of the dynamics of the feud. The whites were thus as much concerned with accomodating themselves to local conditions as were the Hare. At the same time, nevertheless, these two men continued to exert pressures for allegiance upon the people, resulting in the need for this type of dualistic behavior. In indirect and sometimes less subtle ways, the trader and priest each interrogated many of the people who visited them about the activities of the other man, a form of questioning to which I was also subjected. Everyone at Colville was an interested party to the dispute, and knowledge was a precious commodity. Whites and natives avidly sought out and used information on a number of issues, including current policies at the village's two stores, the status of the petition and the planned cooperative, the fur and food prices being offered locally, the level of wages, and the amount of employment being made available. Dave and Father Claude, for example, both pressed band members to sign over their government assistance and family allowance checks to them: "cashing" a check actually meant giving the recipient credit and, therefore, getting that person's business either at the trading post or the mission store. Many pressures and tensions consequently stemmed from the whites' behavior in these regards, and these stresses were the source of the people's most commonly expressed complaints about the feud. In the view of my "father" Wilfred Ratehne:

> These guys are always after us to do this or do that. They both want our fur, they want us to sign things, they're always asking us questions. They can't leave each other in peace and so the same thing happens to us.

Most of the people in the community had mixed feelings about the trader and the priest, which could vary from season to season and even week to week. Poor fur prices, for example, brought criticism of Dave from Piere Behdzi, but two weeks later he praised the trader's generosity when the latter gave him a contract for cutting logs. Albert Limertu, who usually thought of himself as an ally of Dave's, had kind words for Father Claude one winter because the latter had lent him the tools he needed to fix his sled and harness. At different points in time, therefore, contradictory statements could be (and were) heard from the people, depending upon how the course of the feud and the behavior of the two white men had most recently affected them. When villagers had complaints to express about the whites, they did it to one another, to the man whom they supported at the moment (that is, if they had strong leanings in the conflict), and to uninvolved outsiders such as myself, but never to the missionary or trader if that particular man was not a patron of theirs. Such a move would have been seen by the people as a provocation or an invitation to trouble. As Philip Ratehne, a relatively "neutral" young man expressed it:

> It is bad to get mixed up with this whole thing. You try to please everyone but it's not easy. These white guys are always fighting and getting us into it even if we don't want to. It always means trouble for us Indians.

5. "TRUTH" AND CONSEQUENCES

To Father Claude and Dave Heathson, the feud was primarily a personal concern. They each viewed it as a series of attempts by the other man to have his antagonist removed from the community. Each man saw his own actions as countermeasures to insure his self-preservation, as well as to preserve what he regarded as his unique and essential contribution to the life of the community.

Given the considerable degree to which the feud affected the lives of the people, the villagers also viewed their own actions in terms of their personal welfare. Hence, feud involvements constituted a series of pressures and stresses for them which touched upon most areas of their lives. After a hard winter spent trapping in the bush, the people returned to the settlement to find the whites competing for profits and pelts by raising and lowering fur prices (Table 5), by extending or witholding credit, and by offering or denying services, jobs, check-cashing privileges, homebrew materials, and liquor. Furthermore, during economically slack periods between trapping seasons, band members discovered that wage labor positions were variously given or withheld from them as a reward or punishment for past gestures of support and friendship. Such gestures were themselves the result of other pressures and strategems, such as "volunteering" to sign a petition, join a cooperative, or offer "gifts" of meat, fish, firewood, or hides to the whites.

TABLE 5

Fur Income by Household, Winter of 1967–1968

Household	Number of Active Trappers	Value of Fur Catch *
1	2	$ 447.20
2	1	341.00
3	1	151.20
4	1	538.80
5	2	651.40
6	1	91.00
7	3	1,705.40
8	2	1,079.00
9	2	499.00
10	1	853.00
11	1	127.00
12	3	497.30
13	1	412.25
14	3	1,655.20
Men from Good Hope who camped for part of the winter with Colville families and traded some of their furs at the village		1,422.50
		10,471.25

*Includes the value of furs that were directly shipped out by Colville trappers to fur auctions.

With two stores operating in the village as a result of the competition between Dave and the priest, the people found that they could get more credit by utilizing both of these outlets. The trader and the priest were each reluctant to deny a man's request for more debt lest they lose his business and his furs. This strategy of playing competing storekeepers off against one another has been used effectively by other Indian trappers in Canada throughout the history of the fur trade (Bishop 1974: 211, 242-243; Miller 1991: 36-37; Blain 1991). Another consequence of this situation, however, was that community members found themselves taking on more and more credit over the years, and accumulating considerably greater debts than they had been able to handle in the past. This provoked resentment on their part because they felt it was the whites' responsibility to control the amount of their debts so that they would never lose all their credit, or owe more than they could expect to pay back (cf. Adams 1963, for a comparable situation). Caught between the demands and blandishments of trader and priest, many villagers felt that they were being unjustifiably victimized. The general decline in fur prices since the 1950s, coupled with occasional sharp profit-taking by Dave, the feeling that the missionary was deceptive in the handling of payments for shipped-out furs, and the people's lack of understanding about the "outside" fur market system, all added to the level of tension and rancor. André's son Fred once said:

> To hell with both of them. Those guys are cheating me and everybody. You work hard and then they fight for your fur. The trader's marten prices go down and you're left with nothing. If you ship them out then the priest won't show you your fur slips. What's a guy supposed to do?

Many trappers emphasized that it was difficult for them to pay up their debts with the low fur prices they were being paid. Although most villagers were concerned with keeping the size of their debts down, one consequence of the feud over the years was that, as debts mounted, some people came to look upon wage labor and assistance checks, rather than trapping, as the surest means of achieving the payment of what they owed (cf. Balikci and Cohen 1963: 40; VanStone 1963; Sharp 1975). Whereas wage labor underwrote the costs of bush life for traditional families by supplying the cash they needed for their outfits, for others wage employment was beginning to supercede life on the land. Hence, trapping activities, and the incentive to trap, were slowly declining in some households as people looked more and more to other sources of income for their livelihood.

In such a situation, the individuals who controlled these other sources of income came to play an increasingly decisive role in orienting community life styles. Wage employment was such a valued reward on the local scene that the whites — especially Father Claude — had come to use it more and more over the years to cement patron-client relationships and to win people's support [8]. Not only did the amount of wage work grow in the community over time, but some local construction projects, such as the priest's store, were inaugurated as a direct result of feud strategies. In some years, periods of wage employment were being extended into seasons which had been previously devoted exclusively to trapping (Salisbury 1986: 25 also notes this trend among the Cree). Occasionally, Dave and the priest even "invented" jobs so as to be able to give one of their favorites a special reward.

In a similar way, liquor and brew materials were made available to the people on a selective basis in order to reinforce particular allegiances. The trader recognized that increased drinking over the years was connected with the fact that the people had been catching less fur each winter, and that they had gradually been going deeper into debt. He nevertheless derived a good deal of control in the community from the fact that he was the only one who sold brew materials in his store, and that it was he — not Father Claude — who allowed liquor to be brought in from the outside on his chartered supply planes. The fact that the Indians' drinking also upset the missionary reinforced Dave in his stand on this issue. At the same time, most local people rejected Father Claude's criticism of their drinking, pointing out that it was whites who had taught their ancestors what and how to drink in the first place (cf. also Durgin 1974; Broch 1986: 206-207). Since the people's participation in drinking and wage labor cut down on the amount of time and energy that they devoted to trapping, fishing, and hunting, the feud therefore had some indirect, but significant effects, upon the ecological patterns exhibited by band members [9].

The increase in ambivalence towards trapping and bush living was particularly evident among the more acculturated individuals, especially the younger adult males. Adam Ratehne's opinion was that:

> We work all winter and don't get anything out of it. I've been trying to get out of debt since last fall but I still can't do it. Both the trader and Father are out to make so much money they won't leave us anything. Maybe I should give it up and try to get work in town like I did a few years ago. At least I wouldn't have to worry that way.

It should be emphasized that the feud was really only one of several factors underlying the doubts and uncertainties of these young adults. Their acculturative experiences, along with the difficulties that many of them had encountered in finding spouses and achieving an enhanced social life, were also at the root of their ambivalence. It is more accurate to say, therefore, that the feud operated to accentuate and reinforce, rather than initiate, their feelings of dissatisfaction with the village and bush life. The conflict and its protagonists thus served as an opportunity for them to gossip and express their complaints about the community. Even older, less acculturated adults were frequently found to verbally redirect a good deal of their personal tensions and hostilities by displacing them towards the feud's main figures and the situation of stress and conflict they had created.

***

The phenomenon of whites feuding with one another is a common feature in isolated northern settlements, and the ubiquitousness of such conflicts outside of Colville Lake has been discussed by Dunning (1959), Vallee (1967), Henriksen (1973), Brody (1975), and others. According to Dunning, whereas the period before World War II was one in which these small settlements characteristically had a single, dominant white person, the postwar growth of the North has brought with it an influx of outside personnel. Subsequent conflicts have been the result of attempts by these traditionally high status whites to dominate their local scenes. The previous monoploy of power by the one non-native resident has been lost, and there is no defined order of rank among the outsiders (Dunning 1959: 117-119).

Although Colville Lake's history has differed in several regards from the model outlined by Dunning, developments in the community during its first decade of existence have yielded strikingly parallel results. The genesis of the feud has had similar roots, particularly in the authoritarian personalities of its main figures. They various ways in which it has been fought out are also largely the same as those described for other communities [10]. Furthermore, students of "contact" situations have emphasized the fact that feuds among whites stem, in part, from the isolation, boredom, frustration, and monotony of their life styles. Their patterns of interaction with one another are often intense and emotionally laden because they have no one else to turn to for company because of their variously ethnocentric, "racist," or "colonialist" rejection of native people as proper companions (cf. Hongimann 1952: 520-521; Dunning 1959: 118-122; Saum 1965: 61-68; Brody 1975: 56-102). Such attitudes color and affect relations among the whites themselves by defining the range and content of appropriate friendships for them. These factors heighten the potential for conflict that Dunning, Vallee, Henriksen and others have noted, based upon the personalities of these "marginal" white outsiders in the North, and the general lack of a commonly accepted hierarchy of status and power among them. When ambiguity is thus combined with authoritarianism under conditions of isolation, frustration, boredom, and intensified interaction, stress and conflict are a common outcome.

The people of Colville Lake were well aware of the ubiquity of feud situations in the North, and many of them consequently claimed not to be surprised by the behavior of the whites. As Peter Dehdele once observed,

> In most places I been in, Indians get along and stick together and it's
> the whites who fight and cause trouble.

Despite their level of awareness, community residents were nevertheless resentful of many of the local consequences of the feud, especially the air of tension and pressure that it had created. The stresses which resulted from this situation did not easily find release in everyday life. Expressions of hostility were strongly repressed among the Hare, and they considered it foolhardy to directly confront the whites. Their tensions found some release in drinking, physical activities, and mobility patterns, but the feud left a residue of discontent about life as a whole in the village.

On the other hand, the feud and its protagonists also served to channel and release some stresses. Tensions resulting from the feud, as well as discontents derived from personal problems, acculturative disorientations, and other sources, found direct or indirect expression in gossip and verbal attacks on Dave and Father Claude. Band members frequently used me as an outlet or sounding-board for their negative sentiments about the whites [11], and after living with the people for a full year — both in the village and in the bush — I found that the gossip and complaints about these two men were so central and ubiquitous in the villagers' conversation that one could regard their discontent about these whites as a cohesive element in their lives. That is, the community, in part, was held together and defined by the gossip, the scandals, and the concerns which its members shared and exchanged (Gluckman 1963: 311-315). As the pioneer sociologist Georg Simmel noted long ago (1908), conflict situations such as this can be a powerful course of unity and identity among people who have a shared sense of being threatened or victimized (Simmel 1964: 13-56). At the same time, the fact that strong antagonism and hostility between Indians and whites was generally expressed in an indirect manner permitted relations between these two ethnic groups to be maintained under a peaceful facade (Honigmann 1952: 521).

The presence of these two white men also involved, as we have seen, a number of services which they provided for the people. The positive and negative aspects of the roles of these outsiders underlay the range of reactions to them that the people displayed. Dunning noted that in the settlements he had studied, indigenous residents had to learn to adjust and accomodate to "the often unreasonable behavior" of the whites because of their dependency upon them (Dunning 1959: 122). At Colville, the whites also had to learn to accomodate to the behavior and expectations of the Dene as well, for the trader and priest — in their own way — were as dependent upon the Indians as the latter were upon them [12].

Given several factors, including the strong pressures for taking sides in the conflict, the selected allegiances that were consequently formed, and the varying acculturative backgrounds of the people, the question arises as to why the feud did not lead to the creation of clear-cut factions in the settlement. Taking the whole social situation of the community into consideration, there were several countervailing forces in the village which mitigated against this potential for factionalism. To begin with, the majority of the Dene were basically "neutral" in the feud, and so their attitudes thus overlapped with those of the less numerous people at the two extremes of the conflict. In this way, they helped to hold the village together by the expression of sentiments to which everyone could subscribe, at least in part. Furthermore, except for the few cases of close, patron-client ties, leanings in the feud changed from time to time, and alliances were thus tenuous and loosely structured. When the people's expressions of sentiments were compared with their actual participation in the conflict, it was found that community members changed their sides much more frequently than they could later recall. Statements indicating fairly stable allegiances were often not confirmed, or were flatly contradicted, by people's actions: their need for wage work, and their desire to placate and enjoy the services of both white men, induced them to periodically alter their behavior and revise their attitudes.

***

The fragile nature of affiliations within the community, and the way in which the drama of the feud was played out by residents, thus reflected some of the influences working against factionalism. In addition to the people's dependence upon *both* of the whites, the village lacked any large corporate groups or institutionalized authority patterns around which factions could have been formed. As already noted, decisions were commonly the outcome of informal concensus-building, rather than the formal exercise of authority. The lack of any cohesive groups held together by jointly owned property or political leadership was evidenced in the loose ties that obtained among the networks of bilaterally-linked families. Formal leadership among the people was almost non-existent beyond the nuclear household, and the Hare regarded the exercise of authority as an attribute of "white" status. The village's "chief," for example — a position created as an administrative convenience by the government — had no power or authority among the Indians. Most influential, informal leaders operated mainly in the role of spokesmen for the villagers in their dealings with white outsiders, rather than actually organizing the people or exercising authority over them. As an extension of this attitude, therefore, individuals were reluctant to take any steps which would have been interpretted as authoritative by their fellow band members. Such themes did not conflict with the formation of ad hoc feud alliances and patron-client relations, but they did predispose people against the formation of more organized and visible groups on the basis of such leanings.

Another factor that militated against factions was the people's emphasis on interdependence, generosity, and reciprocity. The uncertainty of environmental conditions, and the fluctuations in each family's success in gaining a living from the land, made all the band members interdependent with one another for their well-being. The successful hunter or fishermen helped out his less fortunate fellow villagers because next week, next month, or perhaps next year, their respective positions may be reversed. The expectations, obligations, and ties that were built up in this way — especially in a community with such a small and closely interrelated population — would have made formal factions difficult to form and tenuous to maintain.

Kinship bonds were strongly emphasized among the people, and the complex network of cross-cutting bilateral and marital ties would have had to have been superceded, destroyed, or radically modified in content if factional groups were to emerge. The band's size was also a limiting factor: it is questionable whether an interdependent, interrelated community with only sixty to sixty-five people could have maintained itself under factional conditions. Furthermore, there was a sense of solidarity among the villagers as a whole which stemmed not only from their interrelatedness, but also from their status as Indians. There was a feeling, as André Yawileh said, that

> We Indians have to stick together in this white man's world because these white men are just out to steal everything from us.

In one frame of reference, therefore, the people — as Indians — categorically set themselves off from the white missionary and trader. In this context, the Hare viewed the feud as a set of conditions which resulted in their exploitation by whites. The conflict was thus, in the sociologist Georg Simmel's words, "a way of achieving some kind of unity" (1964: 13), and these feelings of exploitation and ethnicity were given expression in the anti-white gossip which bound the community together. In this regard also, therefore, the feud and its stresses had a unifying effect. In the face of their tensions and divisive pressures, the villagers responded by emphasizing their Indianness, their kinship ties, their distinct way of life, and their common problems — including their hardships living off the land, and their difficulties in living with whites.

CHAPTER 6

The Hare and the Dog

1. INTRODUCTION

Anthropologists often feel a call to play the role of tribal historian to the groups among whom they have done their fieldwork. In the case of peoples without written records and a strict historical consciousness, the methods of archaeology and ethnohistory often yield novel and provocative results. While scholars concerned with Dene communities in Canada and Alaska are currently working hard to reconstruct their past, another, more current way of life is quickly passing away in the modern generation, and the next few years might provide us with a final opportunity to study and understand it. Specifically, I refer to the semi-nomadic "bush" culture whose economy of hunting, fishing, and trapping has been the primary mode of existence for most Athabascan peoples since at least the early nineteenth century. It is a form of livelihood that is rapidly disappearing from the Indian realm of experience in many areas of the North, and some day it may be as irretrievably lost as are the aboriginal patterns which anthropologists devote so much energy to re-creating. While the opportunities still exist to study and comprehend what it is like to live off the land and survive in the forest, we should make the most of our possibilities. Not only the traditional economy of the Athabascans, but their social structure, their patterns of family life and socialization, and their personalities and philosophies, all stem, in part, from their long-standing involvement with *dešínta*, the bush. The more we can learn about the nature of this relationship, the richer will be our insights in all areas.

It is a relevant fact that when the Dene speak of their past, they often talk of "the old days" — but by this phrase they refer not to aboriginal times, but rather to the period from the mid-nineteenth century up to World War Two. When the Hare at Fort Good Hope and Colville Lake speak admiringly of "the real old-timers," they are talking primarily about Indians who lived in the last century, not individuals who existed two hundred or more years ago. The people's interest in their own history, although not exclusively defined in this way, does tend to focus on the post-contact, fur-trapping, and fort-trading period, the era that they know best from the oral traditions

190

of their own elders.

In this chapter I would like to focus on an aspect of bush life which has points of continuity with both the aboriginal and the post-contact culture of the Dene, but which has received little attention in spite of its continued significance in modern times. Specifically, I would like to explore the relationships between the Hare and their only domesticated animal, the dog, and try to delineate certain areas of canine experience which can provide us with useful insights into Indian life styles. At first glance, a study of the cultural significance of the dog would seem to need little justification because of the ubiquity and economic importance of the animal. Perhaps it is the obvious nature of this situation which has led to its ethnographic neglect. Yet the issue is more complex and subtle than may be realized, and a few introductory comments are in order concerning the role and importance of dogs in Athabascan existence.

One outstanding fact that emerges from the literature, and from the recollections of informants from many areas of the North, is the scarcity of dogs in aboriginal and early post-contact times. There would seem to have been a paucity of canines for hunting, packing, and traction purposes not only among the Athabascans, but among other northern Indians and Inuit as well. Several studies provide evidence indicating that prior to the modern era, native groups had very few dogs, rarely enough for more than a few well-off families or bands to muster full teams of six or seven animals. The literature on the North covering the early periods of contact show us groups of native people who are usually pulling or pushing their own sleds, or dragging and carrying their own loads. In general, dog traction and dog packing seem to be of limited occurrence and limited significance because people could not afford to maintain many animals. As the early and oft-quoted descriptions of Hearne (1795), Franklin (1824), and Richardson (1851) make evident, women — rather than dogs — would appear to have been the traditional beasts of burden among most northern groups (cf. also Jenness 1967: 55, 104).

Evidence from several regions of the North further indicates that dogs became a major factor in transportation and traction only after native people became deeply involved in fur trapping and the use of Western technology (eg., McClellan 1975b: 161-162; 1981a: 485; 1981b: 498; 1981c: 390; 1981d: 473-474; Lantis 1980: 9; de Laguna and McClellan 1981: 649). Serious fur trapping requires a type of mobility which is radically different from the style of movement which characterized aboriginal life. People who are living off the land move in conjunction with seasonal animal migrations and patterns of resource depletion. There is no special premium on speed, nor is there an economic commitment to non-food producing faunal resources.

Trapping as a way of life introduces new considerations, primary among which is the need to travel quickly and repeatedly over specific routes in pursuit of animals that contribute little to immediate family subsistence. The effective harvesting of fur resources is enhanced by a person's capacity to visit his traplines frequently and speedily, setting up new lines and extending old ones when the opportunities to do so are propitious. Furthermore, trapping constitutes a commitment, albeit a temporary one, to a fixed area. Since a region may not contain all the resources needed for the maintenance of one's family, a trapper may have to transport many more materials and equipment than was true aboriginally — including tents, steel traps, stoves, rifles, and foodstuffs — and he may find it necessary periodically to undertake long trips from his base camp for purposes of hunting or replenishing supplies. Along with these new patterns, the acquisition of more dogs during the fur era may, ironically, have also lessened certain types of movement: successful hunters could now use their sleds to bring game from a kill site to their families, instead of moving their entire camp unit to where the animal was slain (Asch 1977; Rushforth 1984: 24, 42-43).

In sum, fur trapping, and higher numbers of dogs, both increased general mobility while diminishing people's level of nomadism (J.G.E. Smith 1978: 40). The modern result is that the life of a "bush" family now centers on its capacity for certain kinds of movement, with dogsled travel providing the main means to meet this need. Not only do native groups need and use many more dogs than was the case aboriginally, but they also need the special kinds of equipment that are appropriate for rapid travel with a team of canines. Thus Indian trappers eventually learn from whites and other Indian groups to use toboggan-style wooden sleds, harnesses, carioles, backboards, brakers, and all the other specialized items that are associated with the use of a dogteam.

The changed cultural significance of dogs is also related to yet other aspects of Western technology, especially rifles and nets, for it was the Indians' access to these latter items which enabled them to get enough meat and fish to support a larger number of animals (cf. Jenness 1967: 104; Birket-Smith 1929i: 170; Nelson 1973: 175-176; J.G.E. Smith 1975: 396) [1]. The economic and technological innovations accompanying trapping and dogsled travel thus have to be looked upon as an interrelated complex: trapping necessitates the use of more dogs, but it is the availability of rifles and commercial netting which enables indigenous peoples to maintain an increased number of animals. This is particularly relevant in view of the fact that a high proportion of hunting and fishing activities in many communities is devoted to securing food for the dogs rather than people, underlining the focal role of these animals in the lives of Indians.

While dogs are among the oldest of domesticated animals known to man, then, and while tame canine species undoubtedly accompanied Asiatic people on some of their later migrations to the New World, we must keep before us the realization that the development of different economies, including post-contact ones, has given the dog a new cultural significance in North America. In more recent years, especially in the post-World War II era, there has once again been a series of major cultural and economic transformations among northern peoples. This has included the disappearance of most "bush" communities as native groups have been drawn more and more into towns and urban centers. Under these conditions, the introduction of snowmobiles and similar types of automated land transport has hastened the decline of dogs as important economic resources. Just as dogsleds made traditional hunting and trapping more productive by increasing speed and efficiency, the snowmobile has had a similar effect in those northern communities where it has successfully replaced canines as a means of transport for traditional bush life (see, for example, Usher 1971, 1972; and Salisbury 1986, on the Inuit and Cree). Ecologically, however, the significance of trapping has been appreciably reduced throughout much of the North in the last few decades, and there has also been a decline in the reliance upon hunting and fishing as subsistence activities. Since trapping utilizes dogs for transportation, and since hunting and fishing were carried out, in part, for the purpose of providing food for these animals, such changes indicate the diminished importance of dogs in Indian life in recent years.

However, this process of culture change has not occurred uniformly throughout the North, and some communities and bands continue to utilize and appreciate their dogs in terms of traditional bush activities. The people of Colville Lake have perpetuated just such a pattern. I would like to focus here upon certain social and psychological aspects of their relationship with their dogs because of the historical interest of such a situation, as well as for the enlightenment that this can provide us with about other aspects of Dene culture. In particular, I will describe how the people's treatment of their dogs reveals some basic features of Hare values, socialization processes, sensory modalities, patterns of emotional expression, and modes of social exchange.

It is appropriate that these features be viewed within the context of how the people use their dogs to further their own survival. Since the bulk of the *K'apamituegot'ine's* subsistence and income is derived from winter activities, winter transportation becomes basic to the entire livelihood of the band. Travel between the village and their bush camps; the process of setting, checking, and extending traplines; the hauling of wood, fish, meat, and equipment; the movement to caribou areas; and the periodic trips to the settlement to trade furs and replenish supplies, are among the essential tasks that require the use of a dogteam. Furthermore, in transporting wood and supplies in the late spring, summer, and fall — even though the snow cover on the ground is poor or absent — the people nevertheless continue to use their dogs as pack and traction animals. During the course of a single winter, a conscientious hunter and trapper may cover 2,500 miles with his dogs, and spend literally hundreds of hours getting the necessary meat and fish to feed them. It is not surprising, then, that the condition, the training, and the food supply of their teams constitute some of the most ubiquitous concerns of the Hare throughout the annual cycle.

One index of the Colville band's commitment to a semi-nomadic life style, and a good reflecton of its members' dependence upon their dogs, is the number of domesticated animals supported by the community (cf. Table 6). In a dog "census" conducted in the winter of 1967-1968, the residents of the settlement were found to be keeping approximately 224 canines. This

TABLE 6

Distribution of Dogs Among the Village's Population

Household	Number of Dogs	Number of Teams
1	21	4
2	5	1
3	8	2
4	7	1
5	17	3
6	8	1
7	20	3
8	12	2
9	20	3
10	7	1
11	9	1
12	22	4
13	8	2
14	18	3
Missionary	7	1
Trader's son	12	1
Three men from Fort Good Hope	23	3
	224	36

Average number of dogs per team = 6.22

The census includes three men from Fort Good Hope who were trapping in the Colville area and were living with families from the band at the time the survey was taken.

was a ratio of three dogs for every man, woman, and child in the village, and a figure of one team for every two persons. The teams averaged out to 6.2 animals apiece, and this corresponds to the number of dogs (i.e., six) which the people consider to be sufficient for adequate travelling. Four dogs are generally thought to be the minimum number required for a usable team. While the men of the community take most of the trips made by dogsled, the women of the band are also adept at handling the animals, and several of the younger adult females regularly drive their own teams, set their own traps, and do some of their family's hunting and transporting.

2. EMOTIONAL EXPRESSION AND SOCIALIZATION

While the economic significance of dogs is evident from the community's ecology, there are several other respects in which dogs play an equally significant, if more subtle role, in the people's lives. In a community where canines outnumber people by three to one, one would expect them to have some pervasive influences. Forms of emotional expression among band members constitute one area of life in which the animals play an intrinsic and important part. There are a limited number of circumstances under which direct emotional displays are culturally permissible, and a significant proportion of these situations involve canines and young children in focal roles.

People show a great deal of concern over their dogs, and the animals are one of their most frequent topics of conversation. The role of canines as expressive outlets is especially evident in the people's relationship with young pups. The latter are spoiled, indulged, played with, given choice food and scraps, and sheltered from harsh weather (cf. also Hara 1980: 188-192). Fondling and handling pups occurs often, and these animals are rarely scolded or punished before they are several months old. They are also sources and objects of pride which people talk about and display with great frequency. Members of the community constantly compare and comment on the care, condition, and growth of one another's dogs, noting special qualities of size, strength, color, speed, and alertness. This affectionate and concerned treatment of young animals is participated in by people of all ages, and the nature of the relationship bears a striking resemblance to the way in which the Hare treat young children. Pups and infants are, in essence, the only recipients of unreserved positive affect in the band's social life, with all other relationships being tinged with varying degrees of restraint.

In every generation, however, both dogs and children must eventually be domesticated, and it is significant how much the Hare employ children and dogs to socialize one another, and how much consistency there is in the way the young of both species are brought up [2]. The raising of pups plays an important and early part in the training of children, and given the value of dogs in the people's way of life, these animals are an appropriate medium for this purpose. Underlying the efficacy of this technique is the fact that the psychosocial development of domesticated canines and humans show many remarkable parallels in both sequence and process (Scott 1963). Among the Hare, all dogs end up pulling in an adult team when they are grown, but as pups they are usually raised by young children. A child of four or five years of age will be made responsible for the care and feeding of a pup, and youngsters from two years on will hold, play with, and treat young dogs as pets. Since pups and infants are often both placed in the care of slightly older children, they are frequently exposed to the same socializers.

Young children learn to handle dogs by observing the way in which their peers, older children, and adults deal with the animals. From infancy, they have travelled by dogsled with their parents, and these experiences enhance their familiarity with canines. Two or three-year-old children, for example, will tie up three and four-month-old pups to large paper boxes or fragments of wooden sleds, and then have the dogs pull them around the village or camp. In such play situations, the children will yell at and beat the pups who disobey or frustrate them, imitating their elders in sudden displays of mock or real anger at the animals (cf. Sue 1965: 36-37). Along with their familiarity, ease, and lack of fear of dogs, children also develop a respect for their potential ferocity. They learn which dogs are habitually vicious, and, from experience, they can tell when an animal is angry, as well as what kind of behavior will provoke a dog. They are also taught never to walk or run through an area where another family's canines are chained up, for their presence may excite the dogs to the point where one may break loose and attack them or another animal. A more experienced child or an adult will sometimes point out to a youngster that what he is doing will anger a dog and cause him to bite. Among the few instances where parents feel that spanking or smacking a child is warranted is when one of their offspring repeatedly provokes dogs or exposes himself to danger in this way.

Children who are five years of age and older are given more responsible experince in handling the animals. They are often asked by their parents or older siblings to go along and help feed dogs: by the age of eight or nine years, this task will become an expected part of their household duties. During this same age period, children will often be given their own sled and harness to play with in conjunction with their pups, or they will be allowed to use their parents' spare equipment. A mother may sew a special harness or sled wrapper (cariole) for her child's "outfit," and a father will either make or adapt a backboard for it, as well as shorten the length of the old sled itself in order to make it easier to handle. Children between the ages of five and ten thus often have a completely miniaturized dogsled outfit to play and experiment with while gaining experience in handling the dogs themselves. Mary Behdzi's six year old son Willy was actually allowed to travel with his own sled when his family moved from camp to camp during the winter. He stood behind the small sled while two nearly-grown pups pulled it directly behind his mother's team.

Having the use of their own sled and dogs is a matter of pride to young children, which in turn is reflected in their parents' pride in them. By the age of five or six, not only is a child's play with dogs a close approximation of adult practice, but verbal behavior is also a close (if not perfect) imitation of what adults say and do. Children use the proper signals for "left" and "right," and they employ the same curse words and phrases (both in English and Atha-bascan) that their elders use in yelling at their dogs. People in the village or a camp encourage the children in their handling of dogteams, shouting to them as they ride by, and commenting to one another on both a youngster's ability, and on the strength and appearance of his dogs. Despite the high level of adult interest, however, there is little formal instruction given to children in the driving of sleds, and most of what they learn is gotten from direct experience or by observation around camps and while travelling [3].

As children grow older, they take on increased responsibilities in regard to the care and use of dogs. Nine-year-old Daniel Yawileh, Fred and Therese's son, had the responsibility of supplying a good portion of his family's wood. He would harness up four of his father's dogs to a full-length sled, drive about a mile and a half to a good stand of timber, cut the wood, haul it back with the dogs, and then unharness them. He did this several times a week during the coldest part of the winter. Fourteen-year-old Suzanne Ratehne, who had two older and fully able brothers, was still expected to regularly drive dogs and bring in two or three loads of wood for her family every week. All young female adults were expected to be able to drive and handle a dogteam, and only the very old or young of either sex were exempted from this. Most of the women in the band between the ages of twenty and thirty-five cared for and periodically drove their own teams, and young men and women in their mid-teens were usually outfitted with a team, sled, and harness by their families. By their thirteenth or fourteenth year, most young people were fully contributing, economically productive members of their households, making dogsled travel an integral part of their everyday lives.

***

At the same time that young males and females get socialized to the care, handling and use of dogs, the latter are, in turn, being domesticated to their tasks and roles by the children and young adolescents who train and raise them. By the age of six or seven months, a dog is strong enough to pull its own weight in a team of adult animals, and it is at that age that a pup will be harnessed up for the first time in a full team. While a dog has been prepared and partially trained for this eventuality by its exeriences with children in the preceding months, this new role nevertheless marks an abrupt and radical transformation in its life. As in the education of a child, a young animal receives almost no directed help or assistance from either driver or fellow dogs in learning its new tasks, and its adjustment can thus be a long, hazardous, and painful process. The affection and relative ease with which the dog has been treated are suddenly withdrawn and they are now replaced with new levels of discipline, authority, strenuous work, and dominance competition within the adult team.

The parallels to the socialization experiences of young children are striking and suggestive, for the relatively undisciplined, indulgent, and affection-laden early life of the child undergoes similar changes during an individual's fifth and sixth years. It is at this age that important tasks and responsibilities are first given to a youngster, including the hauling of wood and water, the feeding of dogs, and the time-consuming care of younger siblings. While parental shows of affection are by no means abruptly terminated, they are gradually reduced in frequency and warmth, slowly giving way to an increase in discipline, commands, and reprimands. Loss of parental attention may be aggravated by the birth of another sibling at this time, which also introduces factors of rivalry and dominance for both younger and older offspring. These experiences constitute a difficult period of adjustment for children, and the sharp discontinuities in this phase of socialization have been described and commented upon in other Athabascan communities (cf. Hongimann 1947: 236; 1949: 306-315; Helm 1961: 76-77; VanStone 1965: 51, 57; Broch 1986: 132-133). This stage of life is marked by an undertone of rebellion and stubbornness; and the somewhat traumatic treatment that children experience in being "put in harness" resembles the difficulties faced by dogs in the corresponding phase of their own lives.

Adult responses to aggression among people and dogs extend the parallel still further. Mature, sober adults are never supposed to display hostility towards one another, and although dogs are not constrained by such cultural considerations, their owners are disturbed when canines also become aggressive. This is because dog fights frequently lead to the injury of at least one of the combatants, reducing the size of the working team, and making travelling that much more difficult. If such fights cannot be broken up swiftly — and this is a dangerous enterprise, since the peacemaker may get bitten in the process, just as drunken brawlers turn on neutral interlopers — a dog may be so severely hurt that it will have to be destroyed. The people say it is very difficult to control dogs "that have tasted blood in a fight." As Luke Bayjere explained:

they go on to tear one another to pieces and you can't stop them. Sometimes they rip open the neck or practically pull one another's guts out. Then there's nothing to do but get someone to shoot it.

In contrast to the distress which aggression among adult canines provokes, the people find amusement and enjoyment in the fighting, snapping, and barking of young pups. These animals are often set off against one another intentionally, in fact: people will take pups by the scruff of the neck, rub their heads in one another's faces, and set them to biting and wrestling with each other. Observers respond with laughter and shouts of encouragement, often re-engaging the pups repeatedly, even after the animals have lost interest or stopped fighting of their own accord.

The vicarious, aggressive pleasure that people experience with dogs in this manner finds its parallel in the way that individuals react to the fighting of young boys. Youngsters who begin to quarrel and wrestle quickly attract an adult audience in the village, and bystanders respond with advice and amusement, commonly encouraging first one fighter and then the other. As with pups, people comment on the strength and wiliness of the youngsters, showing their greatest approval for qualities of toughness and persistence, regardless of who the actual winner is. Young boys who are playing peacefully with one another may even be urged to fight by idle adults who enjoy watching them in combat. Older people thus manipulate both youngsters and pups to display emotional responses which they themselves are not permitted to indulge in: adults thereby enjoy vicarious affect and the stress-seeking of violence by recruiting the young of both species to perform as expressive actors for them. Both the canines and the children thus bear the burden of other people's adult repression, just as they themselves will later undergo, in their own adulthood, the stress of having to restrain the very aggressiveness which they have previously been encouraged to exhibit.

There are, therefore, a number of shared experiences in the domestication of children and dogs, and the parallels are further accentuated by the fact that socialization is itself a mutual and reciprocal process in which youngsters and pups educate each other for their ultimate confrontations with adults and adulthood. The upbringing of dogs can be viewed in its context, content and style as an extension of the education of children, just as children and their young dogs may be viewed collectively as constituting a single peer group. Their respective socialization processes are so intertwined and interrelated that one would be incomplete and inadequate without the other. Both children and dogs depend upon reciprocal feedback and information from one another in order to learn and complete their respective roles [4].

Another factor which is also relevant to Hare socialization processes has been expressed in an argument made by William Laughlin, viz., that a crucial element in developing effecive hunters in a society is "the ethological training of children to be skilled observers of animal behavior, including (that of) other humans" (1968: 304). Laughlin explains that:

> Three indispensable parts of the hunting system are programmed into the child beginning early in life. These are the habits of observation, a systematic knowledge of animal behavior, and the interpretation and appropriate action for living with animals and for utilizing them for food and fabricational purposes... Appropriate behavior towards animals is prominently based upom familiarity with animal behavior and includes ways of living peacefully with animals, of maintaining a discourse with them, as well as the appropriate behaviors, the highly coordinated movements of the hunter proceeding toward a kill, and appropriate social behavior where other hunters are involved (1968: 305).

One can suggest that, in the case of the Hare, childhood experience with dogs is an important first step in people's ethological training, being a type of programming which later pays off not only in their ability to handle dogs, but also in the hunter's capacity to understand, track, and relate to his prey. Sharp (1978) has shown several striking parallels in the ethnology of wolves and caribou-hunting Chipewyans, which suggests that the Hare — who are also an edge-of-the-woods, caribou-hunting people — may be part of a comparable relationship, albeit with domestic canines descended from wolves. Here again, dogs would be the masters and teachers, people the pupils.

***

The distinct way in which adults treat children of different genders bears additional resemblance to the upbringing and utilization of dogs. One basic distinction made in how children are reared hinges on the sex of the child, and the same criterion applies to the treatment of canines. While all infants are ideally loved and indulged regardless of their gender, some perceptible differences in the treatment of boys and girls emerge at around the age of five or six. Males tend to be spoiled more and shown greater affection for a longer period of time than females, and their introduction to responsibilities is often deferred for a year or two beyond the age at which such tasks begin for girls (cf. VanStone 1965: 57-58; Honigmann 1949: 185; Broch 1986: 132-133). Furthermore, in the limited number of cases observed in the field, it appeared that, among other things, boys received somewhat better treatment than girls in the quality and quantity of food and clothing given to the two sexes. Hurlbert (1962: 39) recorded two cases among the Hare, occurring between 1959 and 1961, of female infants being neglected to the point where one child required hospitalization and the second one died.

These observations may indicate the persistence, in modified form, of some aboriginal attitudes towards selective infanticide and the relative desirability and economic worth of males and females. The available evidence, however, is too scant to warrant any conclusions [5]. It is worthwhile noting, however, that there are, once again, some suggestive parallels between the treatment of children and the fate of dogs. Female pups are often killed at birth because they are potentially less valuable than males: they grow up to be smaller and weaker, and are thus less desirable as sled animals (cf. also Hara 1980: 190-191). Bitches will occasionally be kept for breeding purposes, but according to informants, their presence in a team — especially when they are in heat — is so disruptive that they are of limited utility as draft animals. A taboo which is still adhered to by some of the more traditional families in the band forbids adult women to step over a dog harness lest the family's bitch have all female pups. In some respects, therefore, female canines and humans appear to be evaluated and treated in similar ways [6].

***

The correspondences between human and canine sex roles and attitudes are admittedly tenuous and incomplete, but they derive some indirect support from the strength of the other parallels we have noted. There are, in addition, some other facets of people's relationship with their animals which further reinforce the image of dogs as members and extensions of the social system. As they do with humans, people recognize distinctive identities and personalities among their dogs. This individuality is acknowledged and symbolized by extending to canines the human process of naming, and if, as Hara noted,

> one of the owner's favorite dogs has recently died, the deceased dog's name may be given to a newborn one which resembles the former (1980: 191; see also Birket-Smith and de Laguna 1938: 57).

Athabascan concepts of reincarnation (Slobodin 1970; Sue 1965: 12-13; Hultkrantz 1973: 129-130; McClellan 1975b; 1981a: 487; 1981b: 501), which often involve naming a child after a recently deceased person whom it resembles, or about whom the pregnant mother or child has dreamed, thus apply to the canine as well as the human realm, underlining the bonds and continuities between the two species. Dogs are even included within human names themselves for, in accordance with the Athabascan system of teknonymy, a childless adult, or one whose children are fully grown, may be referred to teknonymously by the name of his favorite or pet dog [7].

Some people also stress the significance of what they regard as "kinship" bonds among dogs. Several young men, for example, claim that they prefer to keep together sets of "brothers" in their teams because "they get along so well and work good together." They note with marked approval how, in a given dog fight, the canine brothers "stick together against the other dogs" and never turn on one another. In the words of Philip Ratehne, "that's the way brothers should be with one another." The Chipewyan apply the same concept of fraternity to their sled animals (Sharp 1988: 121). Among the Hare, while these observations may not be totally accurate for the dogs in question, the model of social relations that they project is a clear reflection of how people themselves (i.e., siblings of the same sex) are ideally expected to behave towards one another (cf. Hara 1980: 178; Honigmann 1949: 126). Hare perceptions and attitudes thus extend human kinship into the canine realm, incorporating the relations among dogs into familial and familiar patterns. Just as pups become the children's children, so that the child is father to the dog, man's best friend becomes his brother.

***

That dogs become members of the family through an extension of the corporate social bonds of the household is also evidenced by some deep-seated anxieties that people experience over the well-being of their animals. A lame or sick dog becomes a source of concern and worry for all family members, occupying their attention and efforts for many days. The members of a household or camp may spend hours discussing the conditions and treatment of their animals, and other people will often be consulted in the search for an effective cure. Special brush will be cut for the dog to rest on, its sleeping place and hair will be covered with ashes from the stove (which is "real Indian medicine" according to many of the people) [8], its sore limbs or paws will be rubbed with liniment, and its diet will be varied and improved, including an increase in its portion of meat and the serving of a warm caribou or fish broth to it. People's solicitousness is also evident in the hide booties they make for their sled animals in the spring. At that season, the *golu* ("crust") cuts the dogs' feet, just as the slushy snow packs and lumps up between their toes: these conditions can cause considerable pain and discomfort, which the booties help alleviate.

The health of their animals is a matter of concern to the people which goes beyond the economic value of the dogs. This deeper concern becomes especially evident when an animal becomes so sick or aged that it must be destroyed. People show an extreme reluctance to shoot their own dogs, and they will resort to numerous rationalizations, strategies, and subterfuges in order either to postpone the inevitable or to induce someone else to perform the act for them (cf. Nelson 1973: 172-173 for a contrary case). The dilemma becomes especially pronounced at the beginning of the summer period, for this is the only season of the year during which the dogs are relatively inactive, and band members do not care to feed any more non-working animals than they have to over this three month span. The anxiety over killing one's own dogs nevertheless persists. People may try to sell or give away canines that they consider too old or too sick to be worth keeping for the following winter, but few are willing to take on new animals at this time of year. If this strategy fails, a person will usually try to get another individual to destroy the dog for him, but this is one of the few favors that people may refuse to do, even for a close friend. As Peter Dehdele once explained:

> Me, I just can't look at that dog and shoot it. It sure feels bad when you have to shoot a dog, especially when it's your own.

Statements like this, coming from people who hunt, trap, and even kill animals with their bare hands during the course of every year, clearly indicate an attitude toward dogs which places them in a category apart from other animals. The Hare share with other Athabascan Indians a deeply-felt set of traditional proscriptions on both the killing and eating of dogs, and they also surround their animals with a series of taboos, including a prohibition on allowing dogs to gnaw the bones or parts of certain animals lest the dog's owner incur bad luck in future hunting and trapping. It has been suggested by some observers (eg., Franklin, cited by Birket-Smith 1930: 40, 106; Osgood 1932: 82-83) that the reverence, respect, and fear associated with canines in some Athabascan groups (eg., the Chipewyan, Satudene, and Dogrib) is related to the dog's role as one of the mythological ancestors of these people. Although all of the northern tribes do not share this specific belief, the basically supernatural attitude towards canines which can be derived from it is ubiquitous among them. The idea that dogs have spirits, and are themselves ancestral beings, fits with the basic animistic concept that the Hare hold about animal souls (*supra*, Chapter 2). If, indeed, the dog is reciprocally "father to the child" in the context of socialization, then perhaps there is more than meets the ear in the northern origin myths which give the Athabascans a canine forebear [9].

As sub-human members of the human family, dogs provoke a pronounced ambivalence on the part of individuals who must dispose of them, and the problem of what to do with an animal may become a great source of stress. In their preoccupation with their canines, the Hare alternately curse and commiserate with them. They complain of an animal's worthlessness and the trouble it has given them, and they then recall what a good worker it has been and how sick it must feel. The hostility and aggression which are usually displayed toward adult dogs are thus balanced with other "human" feelings at these moments. In the existential terms of Martin Buber (1968), dogs are neither an "It" nor a "Thou" to the people, they are beings of another order, perhaps somewhere in-between.

Due to the people's ambivalence in the matter of unwanted dogs, an interval of several days or even weeks may elapse before action is finally taken on an ailing or elderly animal. If the dog gets loose during this period, only half-hearted attempts will be made to catch it in the hope that some other person will eventually shoot it because of its troublesomeness. In some cases, rather than face up to the necessity of destroying their own animals, band members have actually abandoned undesired dogs at their bush camps when returning to the community at the end of the spring [10].Such an action was disapproved of by many of the villagers, however, who considered it harsh and cruel. Nevertheless, at this end point in the dog's life cycle, his fate again resembles one feature of people's treatment of fellow humans, recalling the occasional neglect — and aboriginal aban- donment — of the infirm and aged by many northern groups.

There are a few remaining strategies which people employ to dispose of an unwanted animal. If the RCMP are expected to visit the settlement soon, a dog may be intentionally turned loose so that the police, in fulfilling their responsibilities, will shoot it as a stray animal. A person may even offer to pay someone else to destroy the dog. This is a rare instance of direct payment being preferred for a service because Colville Lake, being a kin-based community, is a village in which goods and services are generally exchanged on the basis of generosity and reciprocity rather than money. The offer of a direct cash payment underlines the exceptional and traumatic nature of the task, and it is only as a last resort that a man will kill his own animal.

***

The complex involvement of dogs in the people's emotional and social life also includes their use as a means of escape and their role as outlets for aggressive and negative feelings. As social and psychological extensions of the human group, dogs are important as an instrumental as well as an expressive medium for people. Consistent with the Indians' emphasis upon emotional containment, the Hare — as we have seen — rely heavily upon physical mobility as a way of avoiding socially disruptive encounters. This mode of coping with stress may help to explain the great love of travel, and the dislike for, and difficulty in coping with, prolonged periods of sedentariness, which are traits manifested by many Athabascan peoples (Honigmann 1949:102, 156; Hara 1980: 252; Helm 1961:88, 111, 176; Welsh 1970). Dogs, as a major means of movement, thus become an intrinsic part of this process.

During the winter, adult dogs are also prime objects of verbal and physical abuse from their drivers. Although much of this treatment is the direct outcome of the animals' misbehavior and disobedience, a good deal of what they experience is also the result of aggressive feelings which people have re-directed from other areas of life. Men and women who set out from a bush camp in an angry mood are more prone to beat and yell at their dogs than a person who leaves in a tranquil frame of mind. Individuals who usually react mildly to the frustrations and stresses of dogsled travel tend to respond much more violently to the identical provocations when they have just left a tense social situation in the village or bush.

Drinking events, as already noted, are also culturally permissible occasions for emotional release, and drunken individuals occasionally direct some of their hostility towards their dogs — either when the animals are pulling in a team or are chained up at a camp. There is considerable variation in the extent to which dogs are treated in this way, but most people indulge in such acts, at least when they are sober, from time to time. The inclusion of dogs within the human social and psychological order emerges dramatically in the development of the emotional "pecking order" which characterizes most bush camps. Patterns of emotional restraint among the Hare are thus made viable, in part, because the people can rechannel their aggression towards the dogs in a variety of ways. As described above, children learn to relate to their animals in this manner at an early age, establishing an emotional precedent which will be followed throughout their adult lives [11]. Dogs are thus as crucial to these social processes as they are basic to economic tasks, and family life would be incomplete — and perhaps unbearable — without them.

The occasionally rough treatment accorded to dogs raises an interesting cross-cultural question about concepts of "abuse." Some Western people who keep pets would regard Hare patterns of canine discipline and displacement to be brutal. But the Hare perceive of their behavior in a different way. Their canines are, foremost, working animals, and they feel that periodically beating dogs is a necessary part of the dominance and discipline required for reliable sled travel. Canines, as just noted, also provide an outlet for personal tensions generated by the Hare's close living quarters. Yet people in the community are strongly critical of individuals who neglect their dogs or fail to feed them properly. Furthermore, canines are absolutely tabooed as food, and individuals usually refuse to kill their own animals. The dogs have names and identities, they save travellers' lives during winter storms, they are mythically connected with the ancestral canine from whom several northern groups trace their descent, and they even substitute for the offspring of childless couples in the Hare's system of teknonymy. The ambivalence of intimacy, then, is once again apparent here in an animal that can be beaten but not eaten, named but not killed (Savishinsky 1990a: 222-3).

The Hare, I think, would vehemently object to the idea that their harsh treatment of domesticated animals is abusive — just as they reject the argument that their hunting and trapping of wild animals is in any way disrespectful of other species. To the contrary, their everyday acts of reverence and gratitude towards creatures of the bush express a system of economic interdependence and spiritual regard (Chapters 2 and 4). Dogs, who descend from wolves and who are, in turn, ancestral to people, are a living bridge between nature and society. Community members feel that they treat them in both required and respectful ways. The Hare might well turn the tables on their would-be critics and note the widespread neglect and abuse of pets in Western culture, and the wholesale abandonment and slaughter of animals left in pounds and shelters. For Westerners to gratuitously treat in these ways animals with whom they claim no special kinship would puzzle and appall the Hare far more than any of their actions would shock us.

3. DOGS AND THE PRESENTATION AND EXTENSION OF SELF

If dogs are social and emotional members of the Indian family, each with an identity, a name, and a set of roles and functions, then it is possible that dogs, like people, have public images. In addition, if canines and people both derive and maintain their roles, in part, on the basis of their interaction with one another, then it is also possible that their public images are similiarly a product of their mutual relationship. And furthermore, if dogs are physical, economic, social and psychological extensions of the human group, then it follows that their public image would be an extension of the individual and collective image of their extended family.

There are several respects in which family and individual identity among the Hare includes and incorporates the kind of public image projected by one's dogs [12]. Families and individuals are known, to an extent, by the quality, condition, and number of dogs that they keep, as well as by their ability to handle, train, and drive their teams. As noted previously, a minimal number of dogs is needed for adequate travel. People with very few dogs, just like individuals with very few kin, are considered to be poor and hard-pressed (cf. Osgood 1932: 54). When community members tell hard-luck stories about others, or when they want to portray situations of distress and hardship that others have experienced, one of the first details seized upon is the number and condition of the victim's dogs: it will be related that they had few dogs to begin with, that some went lame, or that some got lost, sick, or injured in a fight. The drastic outcome is a portrait of a family which did not have enough animals to pull their sled effectively. As a consequence, they could not trap, or haul wood or caribou meat, and they may have had to walk all the way back to the settlement, pulling their own sled. There may then follow an account of the somewhat embarrassing act of having to borrow dogs, or the economic hardship of having to buy animals.

The ultimately destitute man, according to Baptiste Sašo, is the one "who is so poor he had to sell all his dogs, his sled, and even his harness." Such a person's reputation and image suffer considerably, and most people become very *self*-conscious when the low number and poor condition of their dogs invite public comment and thinly-veiled mockery and derision. It is noteworthy that in the many tales and pieces of folklore that were collected among the Hare, most of which dealt with aboriginal hardships and dangers confronting the people, none of the stories made the paucity or abundance of dogs a crucial element of well-being during that period.

People are very aware of the movement of others by dogsled, and every trip into or out of the village receives at least perfunctory notice within the community. Large teams invite admiration and respect, and they may be the subject of comment for several days after their appearance. Villagers will stand at the edge of the settlement, overlooking the large lake which borders the community, and they will be able to identify individuals and families at great distances simply by the size and appearance of their teams. People are very proud and self-conscious when setting off with a large number of animals, and from travelling with such persons on numerous occasions, I have seen how their enhanced self-image becomes evident in their comments, their bearing, their posturing, and their close attention to details of appearance. Since a large dogteam — one with nine or more animals — is often unwieldy, a strain on one's fish supply, and rarely an improvement to one's speed, the motive for travelling with so many canines clearly has more to do with self-image than with logistics.

The relationship between dogs and extended images of self also involves people's participation in cultural patterns of generosity, reciprocity, and economic exchange. At various times of the year, band members find themselves in the position of either having to request or give fish and meat in order to feed, respectively, their own or someone else's dogs. Travellers who visit one's bush camp should be warmly received, and they and their dogs well fed. At the village, kin and friends who, from either ill-fortune or inaction, are temporarily without fish, should similarly be assisted in feeding their animals. Economic exchanges, involving the sale or trade of dogs, sleds, harnesses, and related pieces of equipment, also provide opportunities for the display of largesse, and young men sometimes give away good dogs to their girlfriends in the hope of gaining their family's approval for marriage. The loan of a dog to a needy friend or relative is an especially praiseworthy act. In a community where the good person is the generous person, the unending series of goods and services which people supply and reciprocate with are central to an individual's public and self-image. In-deed, in a band whose life style revolves around dogs, one's responses to human needs are often a response to those of people's animals; and since the welfare of humans and canines are so inextricably bound up with one another, it is, in essence, often impossible and unnecessary to separate one source of action from the other. Among the Hare, as in Western society, anyone who is kind to children and dogs cannot be all bad.

A more direct presentation of one's self, as personal as your reputation for generosity but even more expressive than the number of dogs you possess, is the quality and appearance of your animals. A well-fed, good-looking team is an advertisement of one's concern, care, and industrious-ness. People are very attentive to the size, weight, coat, color, and over-all condition of dogs, and the collective image projected by a team is very much an extension of an individual's ego. Although the members of the band exercise little control over the breeding patterns of their animals, once a litter has been born they do attempt to weed out the weak and sickly pups, and several families have made a concerted effort to raise only dogs of a certain color. They state that they like the appearance of a uniformly-colored team, and they trade and exchange animals with other households just to get the kind of dogs they want.

Public awareness and personal sensitivity to the appearance of dogs is reflected not only in conversations which center on the animals, but also in the content of some popular jokes and phrases which have had currency in the band. One family was notorious for the large number of scrawny, pathetic-looking dogs that it kept: not only were this group's teams the object of invidious comparisons by other community members, but when-ever a person encountered an underfed animal wandering around the village, the usual comment was: "Well, there goes another Yawileh dog looking for something to eat." Another family's dogs were so slow and out-of-condition that people used to joke about giving them "a three-hour headstart for a two-hour trip."

This concern with canine appearance and performance was widespread both at Colville Lake and at the Hare community of Fort Good Hope (cf. also Sharp 1988: 138-139). It became especially manifest when individuals were approaching the town or village with their team after having spent a long period in the bush. When there was only a mile or two left to the journey, a man would often stop his team so that his animals could rest for a while, and thus appear "fresh and strong" upon entering the community. People took advantage of this stop to tidy up their sleds by readjusting and retying the load, and some men, who had painted the front and backboard of their toboggans, would wipe these areas clean of snow and mud so that they would show up better. A few individuals had fancy dog "blankets," i.e., specially hand-embroidered collars and harnesses, some fixed with pom-poms and bells, which would be put on their dogs in place of their regular trail harnesses at this time. Finally, before starting off again, a person might take off the everyday parka and mukluks that he had been wearing in the bush, and replace them with elegant, flower-embroidered garments reserved just for occasions like this. When such a person entered a community then, he did it not only in the company of his dogs, but — visually and aesthetically — in concert and in costume with them as well.

***

The unitary image projected by driver, sled and dogs is not merely a static pose, it is also an image created by performance. The ability to train, drive and handle animals well are prestigeful skills instrinsic to the social psychology of people's relationship with their dogs. Among the highest compliments that a man or woman can earn is to be considered a good hunter and "good with dogs." Capable children can earn such reputations by the time they reach their pre-adolescent years, and one of the most desirable qualities in a prospective husband or wife is that person's renown as a "good bush man" or "good bush woman." Young adult men frequently race their teams against one another, either in formally arranged competitions or, less directly, by comparing their travel times over standard bush routes. Status and respect go not only to the fastest but also the toughest man-and-dog team. People take pride not merely in the speed of their animals, but the colder the weather, the longer the trip, the rougher the trail, and the fewer the number of stops and rests taken during the journey — these all attest to the strength and toughness of driver and dogs. Travelling is thus a form of stress-seeking which offers rewards of pride as well as privacy.

These are not the only facts of canine culture which receive publicity and affect a person's image, however, for dogs are potentially a source of embarrassment as well as prestige. The breaking-in of new animals into a team, and the toughening-up of dogs after a long summer of inactivity, provide situations in which a person's patience and abilities are put to an acid test. The recalcitrance, rawness, and inexperience of dogs at such times make it difficult to control a team, and a person's efforts and level of success in handling his animals are publicly displayed when he leaves and enters the village. Even a well-seasoned team can give a driver trouble, and it occasionally happens that a man or woman is thrown from the back of a sled by a balky or irritable group of dogs who then proceed to run away. When such an event is witnessed by other villagers, the driver's self-esteem suffers a sharp, though temporary, decline. The chagrin experienced by an individual at such times is manifested in the severe beatings usually administered to dogs following such an incident (cf. McClellan 1975b: 147, 164–65 for the use of magic or medicine by Yukon Indians to control dogs).

The best insurance against the occurence of such incidents, and a key element in the successful presentation of self by means of one's team, lies in the quality and ability of one's lead dog. By late adolescence, most people have become experts in the area of canine psychology and behavior, and an individual can judge the worth of an animal, and pick out the hard workers and the potentially good leader. Qualities of strength, dominance, intelligence, sensitivity, and tractability are what make for a good lead animal, but these traits must first be recognized and then developed if a dog's potential is to be realized. Good lead dogs make for good teams, as the people say. Such canines are objects of intense pride, and they may acquire village-wide reputations for their outstanding abilities. The drivers, who put so much of themselves into the training of these animals, share in the prestige and become part of the collective image, for the owner's name is always linked to that of the dog when the latter is being discussed.

Some of the most frequently and excitedly told stories in the band center on the exploits which people have shared with their animals. These tales usually relate dangerous adventures in which a person's dogs have been instrumental in avoiding tragedy and disaster. Several men tell stories about getting lost in a severe winter storm while crossing a large, frozen lake, and having to turn to their lead dog to rediscover the trail and guide them to shelter in the forest. While Indians share with Inuit a high degree of environmental and spatial sensitivity, in both groups, as Carpenter (1959) points out for the Inuit,

> a good lead dog is apparently indoctrinated with some of this knowledge, or at least possessed of a remarkable ability of spatial orientation.

A number of other men at Colville have come within a few feet of possible death, only to be saved by their animals. Luke Bayjere, whose story is similar to those related by others, was travelling across a frozen lake on a windy, winter night. The swirling snows and lack of moonlight made for poor visibility, and he could barely make out his lead dog running some thirty feet ahead of him. Suddenly his dogs stopped, and he yelled at them to continue. When they failed to respond to a second and third command, Luke angrily grabbed his whip and ran up to where his lead dog stood. He raised the whip over his head, and was just about to bring it down on the animal's back, when he saw the huge, wide opening in the lake ice which had brought his team to a halt. The gaping hole lay some ten feet in front of his lead dog, and the animal had stopped just in time to prevent the team, the sled, and the driver all from plunging into the icy water.

Stories such as this illustrate an added dimension to the role of dogs in

Hare culture. These animals are not simply economic, social, and psychological extensions of individuals and families, they are also, in McLuhan's (1966) terms, sensory extensions of the human central nervous system. Dogs can smell, see, hear, and feel under conditions where the corresponding human senses are inadequate to the situation. In some cases, canine sensory acuity is clearly superior to that of humans: dogs can smell or feel out a trail, and can sense the proximity of caribou and hear the approach of other dogteams, much more rapidly and accurately than their drivers. At other times, dogs are simply in a better physical position to acquire sensory data than are the people whom they serve: a dogteam is linear in form, and lead dogs are literally ten to thirteen yeards ahead of their drivers. Their sensory apparatus spatially extends the human eye, ear, and nose, just as their legs and paws are extensions of the human foot.

***

It is especially significant that in a hunting style of life, such as the one led by the Hare, dogs play only a marginal role in the actual stalking and killing of game. This may have some important implications for interpretting the aboriginal significance of dogs in Athabascan cultures. Ecological factors and the type of game being hunted are key variables which have to be considered here. For example, while the men in more southerly Hare bands, such as the ones at Fort Good Hope, occasionally employ dogs to chase moose, the people of Colville Lake, for whom caribou supercede moose as the major meat source, do not utilize dogs in this way. While dogs are more sensitive to the proximity of game than people are, they become extremely noisy and difficult to control when they come within sight, for example, of a herd of caribou. Their loud barking alerts the animals, and they generally scare the game away before a hunter can get close enough to get off a shot. When a herd of caribou inadvertently crosses a lake and approaches a bush camp, the greatest difficulty that the people have is to keep their dogs quiet enough so that a hunter can successfully stalk the animals without their being alarmed. Men who set off on a hunting trip by dogsled usually tie their teams up in the woods once they have reached an area where caribou signs are good, and they then proceed on snowshoes so that the noise and excitability of their dogs will not ruin their chances of a kill.

One implication of the way in which the *K'apamituegot'ine* use and refrain from using their animals, then, is that their dogs are good sensors but bad hunters. The people do not even utilize canines to run down wounded game: if two caribou out of a herd of ten are shot, a hunter wants to get at the remaining eight animals, and a bunch of loose dogs may only serve to scare them off. The wounded caribou can always be recovered later by following their spoor, and, if they are initially left unpursued, they will travel a shorter distance than they would if immediately followed. During the interval they get progressively weaker and stiffer as they rest, making their ultimate capture easier (cf. Carpenter 1961: 148-149).

While the dogs at Colville do not play much of a role in hunting, the fact that people do appreciate and value the sensory capacities of their animals is evident from the stories related above. By extending human senses, dogs enhance human survival. With the exception of the sense of taste, the whole repertoire of human sensory abilities is amplified, intensified, and spatially magnified by the people's special relationship with their one domestic animal. If dogs can be kept quiet and at a safe distance, they can also serve to locate and point out game to hunters. The alert traveller is always aware of the direction in which his dogs' eyes, ears, and noses are pointed, for a sudden shift in their orientation often indicates the presence of other animals nearby. At a bush camp, dogs will suddenly stand up when they sense dogteams or caribou approaching, and here again the direction of their sensory organs points to the stimulus for their response. In the words of one man, Thomas Godanto, the ears of the people's dogs constitute their "personal radar" and "warning system" [13]. As in our own culture, then, the Hare enjoy the varied sensory services of "pointers," "watch dogs" and "seeing-eye dogs" who "see" with several senses.

4. DISCUSSION AND CONCLUSION

There is the possibility that if dogs can warn people of the approach of game and kin, then aboriginally they could have also alerted the Dene to the approach of enemies. On the other hand, by their noisy reactions, they could just as easily have tipped off the enemies to the presence of the people themselves. Since the Hare often made their traditional summer camps in isolated locations, their emphasis upon hiding from enemies during this season of warfare and raiding would indicate a strategy of inaccessibility and quietude which noisy dogs could have jeopardized. The aboriginal value of dogs for either hunting or defense among the Hare is thus ambiguous and inconclusive, and the animals would appear to be, at best, a mixed blessing in both regards. In the nineteenth century, Richardson and Wentzel (cited by Hara 1980: 110) reported that the Hare used small dogs to run down moose on the hardened, crusty spring snow, but no other mention of the Hare's use of dogs in connection with hunting is made in the post-contact literature. Their possible utility for taking caribou and other game does not materialize as a cultural technique. Currently, the use of dogs for direct stalking, tracking or chasing of either small or large game is rarely exploited in the Colville area. A more exhaustive analysis of folklore and post-contact documents may ultimately help to resolve these historical issues, but at present they remain unclear. The extent to which the current utilization of dogs by the Hare reflects the aboriginal (and modern) significance of these animals among other Athabascan groups is also an open question, but this is a problem to which I think we can attempt at least a partial answer.

If the Hare and some other Athabascan peoples did make only limited use of their dogs in the areas of hunting and defense, then observations which have been made on the role of canines in other hunting societies would indicate that the northwestern Indians were not alone in these respects. M.J. Meggitt, for example, after reviewing the literature on Australian Aboriginal use of tame dingoes, offered the following conclusion:

> The available evidence, limited and uneven as it is, suggests that over wide areas of Australia the tame dingo was by no means an effective hunting dog and that it contributed relatively little to the Aborigines' larder. It seems that only in ecologically specialized regions where particular kinds of game were abundant (as in the tropical rain forest) was the dingo a significant economic adjunct to the family hunting unit (1965: 24).

Edmund Carpenter has made observations that are even closer to home for consideration of the Athabascans:

> Canadian Indians, in my experience, prefer not to hunt with dogs. Could it be that their attitudes stem from an ancient hunting tradition? We know that dogs were fairly common in many prehistoric camps in the Northeast, yet we know little of their role. Historic records refer more frequently to them as a source of food, or in connnection with ceremonies, than as aides in hunting, and it may be that their hunting duties were slight.
>
> Hunting with a bow is quiet work. The hunter must get in close to game and here a dog could prove more troublesome than helpful. The Eskimo use dogs to locate seal-holes in the ice; Australian and Kalahari Bushmen dogs harrass and keep at bay large game; Iban dogs tree game in the Borneo rain-forest. In the woodlands of the Northeast, however, where deer are the principal game, dogs can prove far less helpful.
>
> One advantage the bow has over the rifle is silence. If the first arrow misses, the animal may fail to bolt and simply stand there, thus offering the bowman a second chance. A dog, however, would probably set the animal to flight.
>
> Similarly, a wounded animal, if not pursued by dogs, often flees but a short distance, rests and stiffens up. Modern Indian hunters know this and generally, after wounding a deer, instead of racing after it, brew tea. Then they track down the animal which probably is but a short distance away (1961: 148-149).

I do not mean to imply by the above quotations that dogs are everywhere of marginal utility to hunters: as Meggitt, Carpenter, and many others have noted, certain groups do make considerable use of canines in taking game.

In the North, the Inuit employed dogs for hunting polar bear, seal, walrus, and musk-oxen, and the Tanaina used well-trained canines for pursuing or scenting several different kinds of animals, including porcupine, bear, caribou, sheep, and beaver. Dogs were also commonly used for hunting among the Great Bear Lake Indians, and the Gwich'in in Alaska and the Yukon employed them to run down moose and caribou on the hard spring snow (or "crust"), as well as to chase wounded game. The Upper Tanana similarly used dogs for pursuing moose and bear, as well as for treeing lynx and wolverine. Elsewhere, the Tahltan raised a special breed of small dogs for driving bears out of their dens, and the Eyak of coastal Alaska employed canines to chase mountain goats and scent out bears and porcupine. Other Northern Athabascan groups among whom the use of dogs for hunting is reported include the Han, Ahtena, Tutchone, Tagish, Kaska, Koyukon, Nahane, and Slave [14].

In contrast to the above cases, the Ingalik of interior Alaska only began to utilize dogs for pursuing game in historic times, and, with the exception of Richardson's account (1851ii: 26, 30), the Chipewyans to the east of the Mackenzie are generally reported not to have used dogs for hunting moose or any other game. To the south and west, the Kaska, while utilizing dogs to take porcupine, rarely employed them for pursuing moose, and their hunting dogs were actually purchased from the Tahltan. Furthermore, while some of the Tanaina in Alaska did use dogs for chasing caribou, different bands in the area captured them in surrounds without the aid of dogs, much like other Athabascan groups did [15].

***

It should be evident from the foregoing that tribal and ecological variations have to be taken into account in order to evaluate the importance of dogs in specific Athabascan cultures. Domesticated canines play a large role in the hunting techniques of some groups, while in others their significance is minimal, marginal, or non-existent. Even in regions where the role of dogs is evident, the specific animals that they are used to pursue, and the type of pursuit for which they are employed, also show variation from area to area. To cite just one non-northern instance of this kind of phenomenon, Meggitt makes an observation for Australia that may be indicative of comparable situations in many parts of the world:

> ... there may have been significant differences among tribes or from region to region in the efficiency of the training and use of dingoes, or in the kinds, number and habits of the animals available for hunting (1965: 18).

The Athabascan evidence would seem to bear out, in a general way, a similar observation made by Harold Driver in his discussion of the use of dogs for hunting in North America:

> In general, it appears that dogs were of limited utility for large animals running in herds, which were easy for man to locate, but were of greater utility in hunting animals which were solitary or lived in small social groups and were, therefore, more difficult to find (1961: 60).

This argument is especially pertinent for the Hare because of the contrasting dependence of different regional bands upon either migratory caribou herds, which are found mainly in the northeast of the Hare's range, or more sedentary and solitary moose, which are concentrated primarily in the south and west. The argument concerning dogs and the type of game to be hunted is relevant historically as well as ecologically because, in Richardson's (1851ii: 26) estimation, the Hare were not successful in hunting moose, and according to modern informants,

> ...in the old days, there were mainly caribou in the area, and the moose were concentrated in the Rockies (Hara 1980: 107).

It was only recently (i.e., in the mid-nineteenth century), that "the moose started to come downhill and move all over the Fort Good Hope Game Area" (Idem). A similar northward movement of moose has also occurred in parts of Chipewyan territory, as well as in other regions of the sub-Arctic (cf. McKennan 1965: 18; Rogers 1969a: 28-29; Peterson 1955: 36-45). There is, in fact, convincing evidence for the absence of moose as part of the aboriginal economy of specific Chipewyan bands, whose subsistence was focused mainly upon the taking of caribou (cf. the name "Caribou-Eaters"). In the case of certain northern Hare and Chipewyan groups, therefore, their traditionally greater dependence upon caribou herds rather than solitary moose as a major food source might have been a key factor in the limited role of dogs in their respective hunting techniques.

A major problem that we face in trying to determine the total cultural significance of dogs for the whole northern Athabascan area is that our historical sources are often silent or contradictory on certain aspects of the matter, while our contemporary material frequently neglects the wider dimensions of the issue. Comparisons and generalizations are thus difficult to come by. I have tried to show in this chapter that the modern role of dogs in Athabascan culture, especially as extensions of human senses, emotionality, and social structure, can provide a key to what the aboriginal importance of these animals may have been. The basic economic functions that we usually associate with dogs, particularly traction and hunting, would appear to be primarily either of recent vintage (traction) or of debatable or only regional validity (hunting). Perhaps there is an incompatability between the use of dogs for traction and their employment as serious hunting aides. It may be that animals which have been trained and used in one capacity may be of limited utility in the other. If aboriginal Athabascans could not support enough dogs to make them significant as draft animals, it may have been more worthwhile for them to train the limited number of canines as stalkers and game chasers. This aspect of canine culture would perhaps have been superseded in some areas by the introduction of modern dogsled travel, with its focus upon different patterns of canine training and utilization.

Domestic canines were probably resorted to for food and clothing only in extreme situations in the North. This is supported by the strong and pervasive taboos on killing and eating dogs which continue to exist among almost all the Athabascans [16]. The potential significance of canines for packing and dragging, while undeniable, was probably limited by the small number of animals that the people were able to maintain in the past. That dogs may have also been used as a source of direct, bodily warmth during night-time sleep is also a possibility, but one for which I can find no substantial proof. It seems more likely that dogs, as extensions of human senses, were more valuable as receptors, integrators, and conveyors of information for many groups rather than as executors of economically important tasks. Furthermore, by giving children and adults experience in relating to a non-human species, the presence of domesticated canines may have been an important aspect of sensitizing hunters to the ethological patterns of animals in general and their prey in particular, thereby making people more effective stalkers. The fact that some Athabascan groups aboriginally maintained other types of animals as "pets" (including bear cubs, foxes, rabbits, wolf pups, minks, an several species of birds) may indicate a similar extension of human social bonds: temporarily adopting wild creatures as pets provided relationships that allowed people to take advantage of these other species as teaching aides in the area of animal behavior [17].

***

In the contemporary case of the Hare and their dogs, the process of sensory and social extension is ultimately an act of mutual incorporation and learning. People, in a sense, identify with and *become* their dogs while their dogs become members of society. Artists, photographers, and psychotherapists in Western cultures have poignantly (and therapeutically) shown how much people and their pet animals actually come to physically, psychologically, and behaviorally resemble one another over time (Szasz, 1969), and the same may be true within the cultural aesthetic and self-image of the Hare. People not only "become what they behold," as Carpenter (1970) and McLuhan (1966) have shown, but they are also domesticated by their domestic animals (Savishinsky 1983). In such cultural traditions, psychological processes of projection, displacement, dominance, aggression, identification, nurturance, succorance, and incorporation accompany, or supersede, the more utilitarian aspects of dog ownership (cf. Fox 1965; Beck and Katcher 1983; Serpell 1986). When thus viewed as "domesticated" members and extensions of the human social system, the dog's cultural significance takes on the added dimensions of sociability and companionship. The social and psychological integration of the Athabascan band would then have to be viewed from this wider perspective: dogs serve as sources of emotional interest and anxiety, as well as outlets for affective displays of both a positive and negative kind.

It is a short step, in the case of the Hare, from identifying people *by* their teams to identifying people *with* them. If one can do this for others, one can also do it for one's self, and people's animals thus become an inherent part of their identity. Dogs are thus a social, sensory, and psychological, as well as an economic resource, and they are a self-producing resource at that. If one considers the various ways in which dogs are extensions of Hare social groups, then one must expand one's concept and definition of the band. At Colville Lake, for example, in a social, emotional, and economic sense, the band is no longer composed of just seventy-five people, but rather it consists of some 300 social beings, 224 of whom happen to be dogs.

I do not wish to stand Alexander Pope's dictum on its head (or tail) by suggesting that the proper study of mankind is the dog, but I think we can learn a great deal about certain groups of human beings by observing how they relate to domesticated canines. In recent decades, as snowmobiles have gradually come to replace dogs throughout much of the North, native people have often been ambivalent about this change, citing the reliability, adaptability, low cost, greater safety, and sensory value of canines as compared to machines (eg., L. Smith 1972; Nelson 1973: 178-182; Jarvenpa 1980: 120-126; Broch 1986: 36-38). I think their cultural reluctance to abandon their dogs can also be traced to the social, spiritual, and emotional bonds they would be losing in the process.

Such ties can be found in many societies. In an excellent essay on the role amd position of dogs in Polynesian culture, for example, Katherine Luomala (1960) has pointed out many of the same social and psychological factors which have been summarized here, including processes of mutual identification and domestication between canines and humans. Similar insights have emerged from the work of Lorenz (1954), Szasz (1969), Scott (1963), Fox (1965), Levinson (1972), Fogle (1983), Bustad (1980), Arkow (1984), and other scholars, all of whom have looked at the the social psychology of pet-keeping in Western societies. Evans-Pritchard's classic study of the Nuer (1940) long ago demonstrated how central domesticated cattle could be in the thoughts and social relations of pastoralists, and so by now we should be sensitive to the possibility of analogous situations in societies with different economies and ecologies.

My own observations on the Hare, while directed to just such an analysis, have two obvious limits to them. First, by arguing from the present to the past, there is the problem of their validity as historical arguments. Hopefully, future work in archaeology and ethnographic reconstruction will enable us to verify or reformulate our ideas on this and related problems. Second, my arguments are limited by the fact that they are derived primarily from the study of one community — a representative and crucial community, I would argue, but a single case nevertheless. Thus, it is difficult to judge the degree to which contemporary and historical statements about the Hare are applicable to other Athabascan groups. The paucity of comparative data on this problem makes generalization a tenuous proposition [18]. There has evidently been a great deal of regional diversity in the training, breeding, significance and use of dogs in the North, and this variety has undoubtedly had its social and psychological concomitants. Regional differences in modern trapping patterns and techniques may also be reflected in these ways. The Hare indicate how complex and subtle a people's relationship with their dogs can be, and if the ideas presented here have a wider apllicability, then there are some important areas of Athabascan culture which demand a searching reappraisal.

CHAPTER 7

Conclusions

1. "THE EXALTED MELANCHOLY OF OUR FATE"

The paradoxes of existence are often it deepest sources of pain and revelation. Living with ambiguity can be enriching as well as stressful, however, if one can appreciate the multiple meanings of life's experiences. To the Dene of Colville Lake, existence is ambiguous in a multitude of ways, and this has been seen in their involvement with their environment, their kin, their identity, their dogs, and their white neighbors. Each of these relationships shares in a basic paradox, namely, that the people are ambivalent about the very sources of their survival and being. The bush is variously bountiful or empty. Whites provide goods and services, but can also be authoritarian and exploitative. Your own kin are sometimes generous, other times withholding. Parents are warm and permissive in one's youth, then more distant and demanding as one grows older. Dogs are economically essential and emotionally valuable, but they are also vicious and frustrating. And to be an Indian is a source of pride, but when it is also the touchstone for discrimination, it then becomes a cause for self-doubt.

If, as Martin Buber (1958: 11) declares, "all real living is meeting," then the case of Colville Lake reminds us that it is separation which makes relation possible. It is only by periodically leaving the people and the contexts of ambiguity that reunion with them becomes feasible and desirable. This dialectical rhythm underlies the villagers' mobility, and makes intelligible the stresses which they alternately seek to experience and escape. Perhaps it is in this way that the Hare encounter what Buber (1958: 16) has called "the exalted melancholy of our fate, "the paradox that every *Thou* in our world must become an *It*.

As relations with the trader and priest revealed, stress could contribute as much to the band's unity and identity as it did to people's disunity and uncertainty. The feud — like dogs and inanimate objects — was a means for redirecting energies and aggression from within the group to outside sources. Trying to manipulate the whites was a clear instance of stress-seeking by village residents, just as their participation in the conflict helped to define them as a people and clarify their distinctiveness. Identity, however, was not

219

a matter of simple "Indian" ethnicity for them, even though their relations
with the whites often defined them in just these terms. Rather, there was a
great deal more subtlety and substance involved in being Dene than could
be conveyed by skin color, language, or segregation. The people's involvement with their *sagot'ine* and their land, their sense of continuity with
tradition, their celebration of self-sufficiency, and their emphasis on the
value of freedom — these were all at the core of how they saw themselves.

Encountering the people again in 1971, several years after my first visit, I
was reminded of how complex and vulnerable their lives could be. My wife
and I flew into the village from Norman Wells, landing on a small airstrip
which had been completed at the community shortly after my departure in
1968. We were flown in by Father Claude, who had recently purchased a
small, single-engine plane. At Norman Wells, where he met us, the stark
airport had seemed absorbed by the helicopters, cargo planes and ubiquitous crew men of the oil and mineral companies, who were staging one of
the most concerted invasion that the North had ever seen. As we flew the
124 miles to the village, Father Claude pointed out the naked seismic lines
and abandoned camps of the geologists, whose survey parties had spent the
last few summers stripping and probing the land near the settlement with
their unique economy of style. For all the miles of water-soaked, sun-
drenched, and uninhabited taiga we had just crossed, that landing strip,
those seismic scars stretching to the earth's horizon, and our own small
aircraft, suddenly made Colville seem less cut off and more exposed to the
outside world than ever before.

In several ways, the "outside" had penetrated the community in some very
visible forms during those three years. Andre Yawileh's family, and Yašeh
Behdzi and his grandmother Annie, were now living in new log cabins, the
first buildings ever to be erected in the village as part of a government
housing program. Luke Bayjere had become the first native person in the
settlement to purchase a snowmobile, and several people who had spent their
whole lives cutting wood with axes were now the owners of chain-saws. A
number of households had also supplemented their transistor radios with
battery-operated record players and cassette tape-recorders. Even the size, if
not the number, of outboard motors had increased, for many of the young
men were now visiting their fish nets with the aid of *klason* that were several
horsepower stronger than the ones they had been using before.

The people of the villlage had also built their own boat dock at the foot
of the embankment behind Wilfrid Ratehne's house. There was even a new
body of water just to the southeast of the settlement: the sluggish stream
which had once indifferently drained the swamp behind the community
had been dammed up, the year before, by the game officer from Good
Hope. His plan was to stock this artificial lake with muskrats. However, he

failed to trap any of them alive his first few attempts, and since — characteristically enough for the government — he had been transferred to another region before muskrats could be introduced, the village now had a new lake without anything to harvest from it.

The changes which had occurred among the people themselves were more noteworthy, if less immediately visible. There had been a number of marriages, births, and deaths which had altered the composition and life of the band. Old Joseph Tehgu had died at the age of ninety-one, breaking the strongest and most substantial link with the community's folklore and oral history. A remarkably dramatic and energetic raconteur, Joseph had had no equal among his contemporaries for either knowledge or style, and two and a half years after his death, no one had replaced him as a source or a focus for narrative culture.

***

Marriage had also removed some people from the village. Suzanne Rahtene and her brother Adam had both found spouses from other settlements, and Suzanne was now living in Fort Good Hope with her husband's family. Adam, after having tried unsuccessfully for several years first to marry Mary Behdzi and then Monique Yawileh, had finally gone all the way to Fort Franklin on Great Bear Lake to find a wife. He and his spouse had alternated living between Colville and Franklin for the last few years, and they were now back at the village to spend the summer months with his kin.

Mary Behdzi had also finally married, but only after overcoming her mother's opposition with a good deal of help from community opinion and public pressure. Unlike Suzanne and Adam, however, she had been able to marry within Colville itself: her husband was Maurice Bayjere's eldest son Luke. Many of the people had sympathized with Mary in her attempts to realize two previous proposals of marriage, but it was only in this third and most recent instance that she had felt confident enough to contravene her parents' wishes. Being an adult, the priest had explained to her, she could marry without parental consent: torn between her personal wishes and a sense of filial respect — but bolstered by the concensus of the band — Mary had finally gone ahead with her decision.

Her father Yen and mother Helen had nevertheless felt so strongly about the matter that, as a public but silent protest, they pulled out of the village on the eve of their daughter's wedding, and spent the next few days at a fish camp some ten miles away. The symbolism of the move behind them, however, Yen and Helen eventually returned to the settlement, and gradually became reconciled to both Mary and her marriage. No small factor in the rapprochement was their close bond to Mary's son Willy who, born out-of-wedlock to her six years previously, was himself very attached to his grandparents. During the next two years, Luke and Mary had two more children, and these infants further helped to cement their ties with Yen and Helen. The elder Behdzis also wanted the help and company of the younger couple during their winter stays in the bush, something which could only be realized by resolving their differences.

The Behdzi's prolonged opposition to Mary's marriage, and their ultimate readjustment to it, highlighted one of the most stressful but infrequently discussed aspects of life among the people. At stake here — as well as in other cases of resistance to the marriage of sons and daughters — was not simply the issue of parental authority, but the ultimate dilemmas of security and aging. As people like Helen and Yen grow old, the vigor and resourcefulness which have earned them their survival and reputation over the years suffer a decline. Now, with age, they must look more and more to their adult children to aid and support them, a form of dependence which induces many parents to try to control their children's lives so as to be assured of their assistance. Marriage, which involves young adults in a wider range of family and kinship obligations, is often seen by parents as a threat to their influence over their grown children.

Even in their early years, youngsters are told, only half-jokingly by their parents, that when they grow up, they should remember how well their mother and father treated them, and that they should reciprocate by caring for their elders in later years. A child will be given a piece of candy by his father and laughingly admonished to "remember how good I was to you when I'm an old man." Reflecting this indoctrination, adolescents often express their commitment "to take care of [their] parents when they are old, and not," as Philip Rahtene once said, "ignore them like other people do." To reinforce these feelings, villagers also try to publicize — both to their offspring and others — how good and generous they are to their children: they thereby prove not only their worthiness as parents, but also their right to receive respect and good treatment from their progeny in late life. Food, clothing, and affection are publicly bestowed on youngsters, and since children roam the settlement freely — being literally raised and socialized by the entire community — people can advertise their care and concern by their treatment of an entire generation, not just that of their own offspring.

The relationship between children and adults, by affecting the latter's public image, thus influences their fate as elders. Despite attempts by parents to ingrain a sense of obligation in their children, however, the same adolescents who profess commitment are often the very individuals who later turn from their elders in proclaiming their own freedom. Three years after Philip had pledged his filial concern, his parents were actively blocking his intended marriage to a girl from Good Hope, and now, at the age of nineteen, he was talking about

> leaving them, because all they care about is themselves. I'll go to town if I want and marry Dora, and when I bring her back here I'll build my own house. I'll show them that I don't need them and that they can't boss me.

The ambivalence surrounding the obligations at issue here draws its force from the people's emphasis on self-sufficiency and strength. In a culture where energy, resourcefulness, and competence are highly regarded attributes, growing old is a stressful experience, mitigated only by the support that one can count on from others. The traditional Dene ethic of honoring the elders — a point that Philip and other Hare maintain (cf. Broch 1986: 167-169) — is sometimes hard for people to put into practice. The "old-age pensions" which are now given by the Canadian government make the elderly an important economic asset to a household, but individuals who are not productive in a direct physical or subsistence sense are more often tolerated than respected. The aged no longer face the abandonment which might have been their fate in aboriginal times, but the poor food, tattered clothing, and general neglect which is meted out to some of them makes their later years an anxious experience. People in the process of growing old, aware of how they often treated their own parents, and reminded of this by the state of some of their village peers, react possessively to the possible loss of their children's presence. In their concern for their own security, they thus draw the next generation into the circle of their own stresses.

***

While some people in the settlement were growing old, others were growing up. The community's contingent of infants and youngsters, commanding — as always — the attention and center of the village, was larger than before. Besides Mary's two youngest children, Fred Yawileh's wife Thérèse had given birth once in each of the last three years, and Judy Alahfi had also had a little girl, purportedly fathered by a white government official who had spent several months in the village one winter writing a native dictionary. The youthfulness of the band, over fifty percent of whose members were under thirty years of age when I had last lived there, was thus being sustained. The pace of maturation was also a steady one. The young children whom I had known three years ago as expressive, uninhibited, and assertive individuals, free with both their laughter and their anger, were now shyer, more reserved, and emotionally less demonstrative as they entered adolescence. And it was their younger siblings, whom they now often had to care for, who exhibited the openness which had once been theirs.

A number of the children had also been to school for the first time, which had opened up both new opportunities and some old anxieties for them and their parents. Adults at Colville have always been ambivalent about the value of formal education for their children because of the nature and content of schooling in the North. Because the community is too small to warrant its own facility, youngsters have had to go to the large residential schools in the Mackenzie Delta, most recently the one at Inuvik. This has involved a lengthy, ten-month separation for them and their parents during each year of schooling, which has compounded the children's anxiety over having to face a new life style in a strange environment. The stresses of living away are manifold, including the barracks-like quality of the hostels in Inuvik; their lack of privacy, which exceeds even that of the people's own houses and tents; the uncustomary discipline and corporal punishment administered by school officials and the nuns who supervise the residence halls; and the compulsory and sudden switch from a monolingual to a bilingual existence. These are among the most commonly lamented features cited by the people.

While parents recognize the value of their sons and daughters receiving some education, they regret the circumstances under which this must occur. The last week in August, just before the plane comes to the village to take the school children away, is consequently a trying one for many families. Parents must sign a release form if they want their youngsters to go, for without their signatures, no child can be compelled to attend school and leave the settlement. Parents are dealing here not only with their own ambivalence, but also with the demands and pleas of their children, some of whom vehemently oppose a return to the scene of their former distress. In many cases adults yield to the wishes of their offspring, and I have seen parents — who have signed the release forms several days previously — change their minds on the morning of the plane's arrival, and keep their children home for the year.

The ambiguous nature of schooling also derives from the content of the curriculum. Almost all the people want to see their youngsters learn some English, attain a degree of literacy, and achieve some competency in dealing with whites. Beyond this, however, the value of education is debatable, and adults question the relevance of protracted schooling. They feel, essentially, that courses of study taken from the urbanized schools of southern Canada bear little relevance for the life of small Arctic communities [1]. They know from experience that education rarely prepares their children for secure, wage labor positions: most of which have inevitably gone to the better trained whites who are not only given job reference, but who are often especially recruited from the "outside" [2]. A child who has had several years of schooling, therefore, cannot easily enter the "white" job market, which has a limited number of openings to begin with, and which has expanded very little over the years in proportion to a burgeoning native population. Most of the people continue to feel that much of their children's future still lay in living off the land, and, as they argue, this requires the skills provided by experience rather than schooling. In Peter Dehdele's words,

> Someone who's been to school so long can't even take care of himself in the bush, maybe he's never even lived one winter there. But that same guy can't even get a white man's job either. So him he's good for nothing. Too much school is no good. It's like those kids at Good Hope — they're spoiled and soft for the bush, and they can't do anything else. They just hang around and take rations from the government.

In recent years, the people have consequently solved the dilemma of education by using the schools in moderation. Children are most often sent away for two or three winters — not necessarily in succession — and are then kept home so that they can develop basic bush skills. They can thus deal with the *mola* ("white") world when they have to, and can cope with survival and the forest as they must. The families of the band have never tried to get a school built at Colville itself, for many of them are aware of what such a step has meant for other communities, including Good Hope. Whereas the people at small settlements without schools can remain mobile during the year and live off the land, native populations at the larger forts become more settled since parents stay in town to look after and be with their offspring (cf. Hurlbert 1962; VanStone 1965; Welsh 1970; Hara 1980). Even the construction of local hostels, or the placement of school children in other native homes, has not reversed this trend towards sedentariness and dependency, and it has usually spelled the end of a bush way of life for the people affected. The families of Colville, however, by keeping schooling at both a distance and a minimum, have so far managed to adapt to the modern culture of the North without losing their heritage or their ties to the land.

***

When I returned to Colville in 1971, I found that the Western presence in the village itself had changed considerably. In the fall of 1968, the community's fur trader suddenly died, and with his passing, and the departure of his family, the long-standing feud with the priest had finally been laid to rest. The settlement's trading post was initially taken over by the government, but had since been turned into a publicly sponsored co-operative, managed and operated by a young and very capable native couple from Good Hope. The missionary, with his rival removed from the scene, had closed down his own small store, and so the people once again had a single commercial outlet available to them.

The villagers were pleased with the new situation, not only because the feud's termination had reduced the level of tension within the community, but also because Baptiste Sašo, the new store manager, was holding down the level of their debts. Furthermore, Baptiste drew his salary from the government rather than from the trading post's profits, thus giving people a larger percentage of the auction value of their furs: since Baptiste was technically a Territorial employee, an expensive middleman in the fur marketing process had been eliminated [3]. Furthermore, in its reincarnation as a co-operative, the former trading post had also created some new economic opportunities for villagers. Band members were being encouraged to produce and sell handicrafts through the region's co-op system, and so their bone knives, model dogsleds, fish-skin boats, and finely-sewn mukluks were bringing them in some additional income.

Relationships with Father Claude had also been redefined, not only as a result of changes in personnel at the store, but because of some actions by the priest himself. His acquisition of an aircraft had made travel more convenient and reliable for people who wanted to visit other settlements, but the villagers remained ambivalent about the man and his motives. Since Father Claude did not have a commercial flying license, he was not allowed to charge people for his services — except for the cost of fuel. Yet some residents claimed he had been requiring them to pay a mileage fee for the trips he was taking them on. Although the priest's cost was still lower than that of most commercial pilots in the area, this policy provoked the same kind of resentment as the people had experienced over the financial strategies of the old feud.

Also reminiscent of that earlier conflict were some of the recent transactions between the missionary and the new co-op manager. In the beginning, the priest welcomed the idea of a village co-operative, and praised Baptiste and his wife for their efforts at the store. In what now seems a spirit of *déjà vu*, however, he eventually took to criticizing some of their policies, using a vocabulary of "inefficiency" and "exploitation" which he once reserved for the trader. According to band members, the priest had also used his influence in government circles to get co-op funds diverted to projects from which he himself had personally benefited. For example, a large percentage of the profits from the store's first year of operation were used to repair the village's caterpillar tractor so that the air-strip could be cleaned of snow... and made usable to the priest for his own aircraft. Father Claude countered these innuendoes by arguing that both the strip and the aircraft were really there for the benefit of all the people, and so the project was in actuality a community one. Wherever truth may lie in this matter, and regardless of the persons involved, one could feel a sense of repetition about it, a reminder that in the village, as in the world outside, *plus ça change, plus c'est la même chose.*

***

Finally, identities as well as relationships had been revised in the community. The single most dramatic development was that the missionary had literally ceased to be a priest. Several years after my initial fieldwork, and after gaining a release from his vows, Father Claude resigned from his position within the Church. Though the people continued to call him "Father," he no longer performed any priestly offices, and the villagers instead conducted their own rosaries each week, using either the community church, or one of their own homes. The ex-priest had also announced his intention to marry a woman from outside the settlement, making his new role a radical one indeed, and giving rise to a good deal of community gossip. While on the one hand the people remained puzzled by these sudden changes in Father Claude's status — he gave them no explanation or advance warning of his decisions — they continued nevertheless in their sincere commitment to

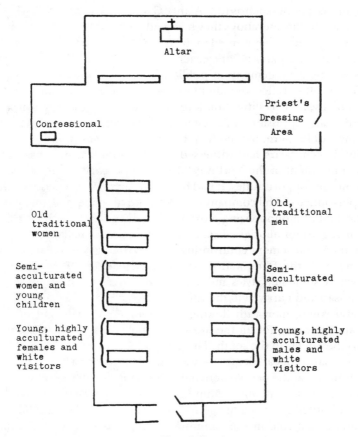

Figure 19   Seating Arrangement at Church Services

Catholic belief. As in the past, they derived a deep sense of peace and satisfaction — both as individuals and as a community — from a collective and ritualized relationship with God, and their communal ceremonies thus persisted as a meaningful and cohesive element in their lives. In a world-view that comfortably accomodated both Christian dogma and aboriginal taboos, the frailties of white men were no barrier to Dene belief.

Among the people themselves, the nature of identity had undergone some subtler changes. In the summer of 1971, the area administrator from Good Hope gave the members of the band a supply of building materials to repair and improve their homes. Doors were replaced, roofs re-shingled, and floors were re-laid. But most striking of all were the new partitions that went up in many of the houses. In a privacy-sparse village where all but two families were living in single-room structures in 1968, there were six multi-room dwellings by the start of August 1971. The instigators of these changes were primarily young adults, people such as Judy Alahfi, Gabyel Behdzi and Philip Ratehne, who explained the alterations they had made in their houses quite explicitly in terms of privacy. They wanted their "own rooms," they did not want to "be bothered by their parents," they each wanted to create their "own place." Just as seating arrangements at public occasions — such as Church services (Figure 19) — reflect the voluntary segregation of the community by sex, age, ethnicity, and acculturation level, internal living space was now being divi-ded as an expression of the needs and self-image of a new generation.

Young adults were also both redefining and re-affirming their ethnic identity. Recent years had witnessed the development of a nascent "red power" movement in the Northwest, focusing primarily upon native rights and economic opportunities. It had begun in response to a massive influx of white personnel and oil company capital whose ultimate goal, many Indians felt, was that of monopolizing most Territorial resources without consideration or regard for aboriginal claims and interests in the land.

The native movement confronting these challenges (see Part 2, below), involving both the Dene and the Inuit, had made itself even in Colville Lake, where some new styles and painful questions were much in evidence. When Susan and I arrived in the village, we were greeted by the novel sight of several young men with flowing, shoulder-length hair and bright red headbands, looking for all the world like their distant, Athabascan-speaking Apache kin far to the south. This pan-Indian appearance — so clearly a borrowed part of local identity — was a mask as well as a display, however, for we found that the people were harboring some deep resentments about their fate and their situation. Administrators, the police, the game department, and other government agencies were constantly being criticized for their ineffectual role in the community, and many felt that Colville was being ignored both administratively and financially in preference to larger settlements. Despite the construction of a still-unstaffed nursing station in the village, for example, the ex-priest continued to be responsible for the community's only medical supplies. And local residents said that rather than interrupt his painting or his chess games, the "Father" often kept them waiting for over an hour before giving them the medication they had come to him for. People also catalogued the variously condescending, impatient, and paternalistic attitudes shown towards them by the wealthy white fishermen who came to stay at the Father's lakefront tourist cabins each summer. It was not uncommon for these visitors to command, correct, and criticize their native guides and cooks, oblivious to their own lack of tact and competency. Their behavior was the latest injection of life's ambiguities, for the people both ridiculed and felt debased by it at the same time.

Since working for these tourists was often degrading as well as remunerative, a number of the band's young men — including Philip Ratehne and some of his friends — had begun to seek employment outside the community. While working as firefighters, as camp crew for seismic survey parties, and as manual laborers for oil and exploration companies, their intensified contact with whites had heightened their ethnic self-consciousness. One result was that these men externalized their Indianness in dress and hair styles. Yet they also betrayed some deep confusions about their image and their own worth. Since whites were simultaneously admired as well as disliked by these young people, being "put down" by them was having its cumulative effect in the form of ethnic and self-denigration (cf. Nelson 1973: 285-288). Alternatively troubled and amused by their experiences, some individuals expressed their feelings by scrawling their doubts on the new plywood partitions in their homes. As Philip declared through the graffiti in the Ratehne's house:

What am I, nothing
but a crazy Indian

I'm nothing but
a dark Indian

I'm too much
of a crazy Indian

These people here
are all stupid
just like old Indians

If these young adults were becoming ambivalent about their identity, they were also threatening parts of their culture with obsolescence by means of electricity. Within a brief span of years, native music had become a sometimes substitute for the radio and the phonograph, and traditional gambling was turning into an almost forgotten pasttime. Whereas the summer — even just a few years ago — had been a season for renewal and performance, the power of batteries now seemed stronger than the motives of tradition. People were capturing their parties on cassette tape-recorders, and preserving the rare drum dance or game of *udzi* in the same way. One evening of drinking, dancing, and gambling thus furnished the substance for hours of listening, so that — in three years' time — recreation had almost given way to re-creation. It often seemed that certain people would rather re-play than perform their culture, and remember rather than participate in it. For a group which had always been concerned with its identity, content suddenly seemed a very disposable commodity for some of its younger members.

2. TIMES OF CHANGE AND CHOICE

Things change, and even in the North, where seasons and ecosystems succeed one another with a very measured pace, perhaps nothing has altered as much in recent years as the rate of change itself. The sense of identity, which had seemed so tenuous for some of the Hare in the early 1970s, has turned out to be a central concern for them and other Dene in the decades since then (see, for example, Asch 1982 and D.M. Smith 1992). In recent years the Hare have joined and helped form activist organizations, they have spoken out against oil pipelines at public hearings, they have helped elect Dene to the Territorial Council, and they have even established their own historical archive at Fort Good Hope. The people's pre-occupation with their identity and their rights has been connected to several profound issues affecting the political economy of all northern natives, Inuit as well as Indians: these have included indigenous struggles over land, resources, legislation, and the power of self-determination. In their recent advocacy, the Dene have been joined by the Metis — people of mixed Indian and white ancestry in the Territories — whose legal status and claims have often been ignored in previous government programs and treaty negotiations. Current Dene, Metis and Inuit efforts in pursuit of their rights has involved native communities in confrontations with governmental, industrial and judicial systems, and in processes that could shape the people's future for generations to come.

The most compelling crises of modern times have come from the land itself. As noted earlier, the treaties which the Hare and other Dene groups in the Territories signed with Canada — Treaty 8 in 1899, and Treaty 11 in 1921 — have been interpretted quite differently by the federal government and contemporary Indian people. Canada's official position for many years — that these agreements extinguished native title to the land — has been challenged by both historical research and the legal claims of Dene organizations. James Wah-Shee, writing as President of the Indian Brotherhood of the Northwest Territories, has argued that "the treaties did not involve cession of Indian land, but were friendship or peace treaties, implying a mutual respect for the rights and way of life of both parties involved" (Wah-Shee 1973: 11). Documentary evidence, and the recollections of elderly Dene who participated in the treaty negotiations, support Wah-Shee's view of how Indian people understood the meaning of the documents they were subscribing to (Fumoleau 1973). In 1973, 16 Dene chiefs took the dramatic step of filing a claim to 400,000 square miles of the Northwest Territories, arguing that their ancestors had never relinquished this domain as their homeland (Ibid.: 13). The Metis added their voice to that of the Dene in 1974, and the joint Dene/Metis claim was applied to an area of 450,000 square miles (Canada, DIAND 1990) [4]. The Supreme Court of the Territories found that this case was strong enough to have legal standing and consideration under Canada's Land Titles Act, and the basic issue — as we shall see — is only now approaching final resolution.

A major impetus for the land claim by Dene leaders came from oil — the same natural resource that lay behind the government's earlier efforts to secure Treaty 11 [5]. In the 1970s, however, the stimulus took the form of a proposal by Canadian petroleum companies to construct an enormous pipeline down the length of the Mackenzie River valley — a route that would cut right through the heart of the Dene's traditional territory. Native peoples responded to this threat to their environment in several ways. One was the filing of the 1973 lands claim. A second was the issuance of the Dene Declaration of 1975 — a manifesto of Indian rights issued on behalf of aboriginal peoples throughout the Northwest Territories. And a third was native testimony before the Berger Commission, which was a government inquiry charged with surveying northern opinion on the pipeline proposal.

The Dene Declaration was a powerfully worded assertion of native claims to land and self-determination. It was unanimously adopted by the Dene chiefs at the 2nd Joint General Assembly of the Indian Brotherhood of the Northwest Territories and the Metis Association of the Northwest Territories, held at Fort Simpson in July 1975. It opened with the words: "We the Dene of the Northwest Territories insist on the right to be regarded by ourselves and the world as a nation." The Declaration cited as its model the successful struggles of African and Asian people of the Third World, who "have fought for and won the right to self-determination, the right to recognition as distinct people and the recognition of themselves as nations." Affirming Dene solidarity with other native groups who live as oppressed "Fourth World" peoples within modern nations, the chiefs went on to argue that "the Government of Canada is not the government of the

Dene," and that the colonial experience had deprived the Dene of their aboriginal lands. The chiefs' Declaration concluded with the assertion that "What we seek then is independence and self-determination within the country of Canada. This is what we mean when we call for a just land settlement for the Dene nation" (Cf. Watkins, ed. 1977 and Asch 1984 for the full text, and analyses, of the Declaration).

The Dene's demand for a "just land settlement" came, as noted, in the midst of the emerging controversy over oil and pipeline development in the North. The controversy had begun with a 1970 government proposition to transport natural gas and oil from the Arctic Ocean to Alberta. Detailed proposals for construction of such a pipeline were subsequently developed by two consortia of energy companies. One group wanted to bring natural gas from Alaska across the northern Yukon to the Mackenzie Delta and then down the Mackenzie River Valley. The second and somewhat more modest scheme would have originated the pipeline in the Delta and then followed the river's course southward. If constructed, the Mackenzie Valley pipeline would have been the longest in the world "and the greatest construction enterprise ever undertaken" (Marsh 1985: 1061). The proposals also represented a radical departure from the kind of economic system that had traditionally characterized native life throughout the region. Whereas the fur trade had made indigenous people important because they were the harvesters of animals, the switch to non-renewable resources made the North's energy reserves, rather than its people, the true source of value.

A direct response to the public debate generated by the pipeline proposals was the appointment, in 1974, of a Royal Commission headed by Justice Thomas Berger. Generally known now as the Berger Commission, this body conducted a widely publicized set of hearings throughout the Northwest Territories, the Yukon, and southern Canada, during which environmental and native viewpoints were extensively and articulately expressed (Canada, DIAND 1976; Berger 1977i and ii). Dene, Metis and Inuit leaders, and community members from virtually every northern settlement, spoke eloquently about the dangers of the project to their land, their livelihood, and their way of life. Trappers at Colville Lake testified from experience about how "seismic cut lines... can disturb the land" so that "the fur is not the same, and the wildlife is not the same" (Berger 1977i: 80). Explained one Colville trapper: "If just the seismic trail can cause trouble like this, just think what would happen if the pipeline goes through" (Canada, DIAND 1976: 230). One of the Colville band's elders reflected: "This land fed us all even before the time the white people ever came to the North. To us it is just like a mother that brought her children up. That's how we feel about this country. It is just like a mother to us. That's how serious it is that we think about the land around here" (Berger 1977i: 94).

A point repeatedly emphasized at the hearings was that still-unresolved native land claims cases applied to most of the region to be traversed by the 2,200 mile long pipeline and the "energy transportation corridor" that would accompany it. Writings and testimony by anthropologists and geographers who had worked with the Inuit, Dene and Metis — including Michael Asch, Hugh Brody, Peter Gardner, June Helm, Scott Rushforth, Peter Usher, George Wenzel, and myself — were cited in the Commission's Final Report to support indigenous people's arguments about the continued importance of the natural environment in the native economy and value system (eg., Berger 1977i: 96, 98, 101-111; 1977ii: 256-268; cf. also Asch 1977, 1982; and Rushforth 1977). The Commission's conclusions vindicated the concerns of aboriginal people in the region that the pipeline would bring "an influx of construction workers, more alcoholism, tearing of the social fabric, injury to the land, and the loss of their identity as a people" (Berger 1977i: xxi). The Commission specifically opposed construction across the fragile environment of the northern Yukon. And while it found that a corridor from the Delta to Alberta was feasible, it recommended that its construction be delayed for at least ten years so that native claims could be settled first, and new institutions and programs established to foster self-determination among the North's indigenous people (Ibid.: xiii, xvi-xvii, 83). In the end, the combined effect of community opposition, and the increasing uncertainty about the economy and the energy demands of the times, contributed to the suspension of all plans to build the pipeline (Marsh 1985: 1062; Miller 1991: 255).

***

The pipeline controversy demonstrated how even the most remote communities in the North could be affected by the world's industrial markets. Another threat of a different kind came from an upheaval in an unexpected quarter —this one in the world's fur markets. Beginning in the 1970s, animal rights activists started a campaign to oppose Arctic seal hunting, and they subsequently moved on to efforts directed against fur garments in general and Northern fur trapping in particular. While the initial agitation for a seal ban impacted mostly on coastal Inuit hunters, the broader anti-fur movement has since targetted Indian communities. Here, unlike the conflicts over oil and land, it was groups hostile to native interests who have taken the moral high ground, while indigenous people have had recourse to economic and cultural arguments in their own defense [Barton 1991]. As shown in Chapters 2 and 4, Dene and other Indian groups have pointed out how central the fur trade has been to native life for centuries; how effective trapping has been in keeping people on the land and nature itself in balance; and how Indian attitudes towards all game — whether taken for meat, hides, or fur — have remained rooted in a spiritual ethic of respect and gratitude. It has been difficult, however, for these social and ecological arguments by native groups to attract the public attention they deserve. In a world where debates of this sort have been played out in media more attuned to popular sentiment than cultural sensitivity, it has been a struggle for aboriginal peoples to get a fair hearing for their views (Herscovici 1985; Canada, HC - SCAAND 1986: 3, 43-44; Brody 1987; Keith and Saunders, ed. 1989; Wenzel 1991).

In all these major developments — the assertion of a Dene lands claim, the Dene Declaration, the Berger Commission inquiry, and the controversy over fur trapping — Indians in the Northwest Territories have drawn on their own revitalized political organizations, as well as on lessons they have learned from the experiences of other native populations in Canada and Alaska. In recent years, groups such as the Indian Brotherhood of the Northwest Territories, the Dene Nation, the Metis Association, and the Assembly of First Nations, have begun to weld together the scattered voices and demands of Dene dispersed over dozens of communities and thousands of miles. In formulating policies and programs, these organizations have taken into account the struggles of the North's other indigenous peoples. To the east and north of the Dene, in the high Arctic and eastern Canada, they have witnessed Inuit economic interests undermined by inflammatory publicity and media manipulation over seal hunting. To the West, in the wake of Alaskan oil discoveries and pipeline plans, they have seen that state's Indians, Inuit, and Aleuts form an effective political lobby to block pipeline construction in the courts, and press for a lands claim settlement in the United States Congress. By linking these last two issues — making pipeline approval contingent upon an acceptable resolution of native resource and territorial claims — Alaska's indigenous peoples were able to secure the largest land and financial settlement in history. The Alaska Native Claims Settlement Act, passed in 1971, extinguished all native claims to land, water, and aboriginal hunting and fishing rights, but transferred title to 40 million acres of land and their mineral rights to the state's indigenous people; it also gave the latter close to $1 billion as part of an Alaska Native Fund. The Fund is to be derived from Federal appropriations and a 2% share in revenues from both State and Federal mineral leases. Control over the capital assets of money and land is being vested in 12 Regional and 220 Village Corporations, with each native person having shareholder membership and a voice in Corporations at both of these levels [cf. French (1972) for details of the Act's provisions; Hall (1988: 153-154) for a summary of the Act's subsequent, negative consequences; and Dickason (1992) for a discussion of what Canadian natives have learned from these experiences].

In re-thinking and asserting their own claims to land and sovereignty, the Dene and Metis in the Northwest have been aware not only of what has been happening in Alaska and the high Arctic, but also of developments among indigenous and minority peoples in other parts of Canada and elsewhere in the world. In the United States, for example, the federal government's Indian Lands Claim Commission has been negotiating tribal claims to aboriginal lands and monetary compensation for decades. Since the early 1970s, the Canadian government has been involved in a comparable process with native groups from its various provinces and territories, and a number of major settlements have resulted in recent years. The most dramatic and widely publicized of these has been the 1975 James Bay and Northern Quebec Agreement negotiated by the Cree Indians. Finalized in the same year as the Dene Declaration, it recognized Canadian sovereignty over Cree land but yielded these Indian people a considerable amount of financial and political control over their social and economic future. Other Canadian groups that have made comprehensive agreements with federal and provincial governments to settle land, resource, and financial claims include the Naskapi and Inuit of Quebec (1978) and the Inuvialuit (Inuit) of the Western Arctic (1984). Taken together, these Cree, Naskapi, and Inuit peoples number about 19,500 individuals. Most of these developments, as well as the recent establishment of Nunavut (*infra*) and the settlement of smaller claims, have actually been the outcome of long-term efforts and struggle by many Indian and Inuit organizations in Canada, several of which have been lobbying for indigenous rights since the dawn of the twentieth century. Some of the first and most effective political groups of this kind began in the early 1900s in British Columbia (Miller 1991: 211-229) — a province that includes Mackenzie drainage Dene in its northeast section. The very fact that the terms "Dene" and "Inuit" have now superceded "Indian" and "Eskimo" in common discourse about the North is itself a powerful comment on how much has changed not only in the politics of language, but also in the language of politics.

***

Besides examples such as the Alaskan and Cree cases, there are other influences which have also been felt in the Northwest. Political activism by African-Americans and Native Americans in the United States — especially the civil rights movement of the 1950s and 60s, and the subsequent red power movement — have also provided recent models for Canada's "first peoples" in their efforts at organizing, agitating, and legislating. In addition, there have been precedents from the larger sphere of global politics. Of particular importance has been the process of decolonization that has taken place in much of the Third World during the second half of this century:

as the Dene Declaration itself proclaims, this development has inspired members of the "Fourth World" — the indigenous minorities living within large nation-states — to seek their own forms of self-determination. As a result, aboriginal peoples from throughout the Americas, Africa, Northern Europe, the Pacific, and Asia have begun to work together on issues of mutual concern, thereby fostering enhanced levels of political power and visibility for native communities in Canada and other countries (Hall 1988).

Collectively, the combined impact of decolonization, the civil rights movements, successful land claims negotiations, old and new indigenous organizations, and Fourth World solidarity, have contributed to a political atmosphere in Canada in which native groups in the Northwest now have their most promising opportunity to secure their rights to land, resources, and self-government. The development of a new Canadian constitution during the 1980s and 1990s, with its clear recognition of the "aboriginal and treaty rights" of native peoples, has lent further weight to the cause of indigenous groups. The fact that these "rights" have yet to be defined, however, remains a source of considerable concern among Indians and Inuit.

The most tangible expression of this struggle in the North are the three comprehensive land claims which have been under negotiation in recent years in the Yukon and Northwest Territories — one claim put forth by the Inuit, a second by the Council for Yukon Indians, and the third by the Dene and Metis. Each of these claims has included a call for political self-determination by the people concerned.

A. *Nunavut: The Inuit Agreement.* The largest comprehensive land claim in Canada is that being negotiated with the 17,500 eastern and central Inuit represented by the Tungavik Federation of Nunavut (TNF). A Final Agreement, initialled in January 1992, provides 136,000 square miles of land; $1.14 billion dollars in financial compensation over 14 years; a share of resource royalties; and a guarantee of Inuit rights to harvest wildlife and participate in decisions on land and environmental management. Furthermore, a political accord has also been reached to divide the Northwest Territories into two sections and establish one of these divisions as Nunavut ("Land of the People"), a new territory with its own government and an Inuit majority (Canada, DIAND 1992a: 1, 5; 1992b: 6; Farnsworth 1992). A vote in favor of such a split was held in the Northwest Territories in May 1992, with a 54% majority approving the western boundary for the division [6]. The next step needed for the creation of Nunavut took place in November 1992, when the Inuit voted to ratify the land claims settlement upon which the new territory would be based. Formal signing of the Nunavut Agreement by TNF, Territorial and Federal leaders is expected in 1993 (Lawrence 1993).

B. *The Yukon Indian Agreement.* The Council for Yukon Indians ratified a Final Agreement with Canada's federal government in December 1991. Its terms granted 7,000 Indians some 16,000 square miles of land, which is equivalent to approximately 8.6% of the Yukon. It also gave them $248 million (in 1990 dollars) in financial compensation and a share in the Yukon Government's future resource revenues; and guaranteed native participation in the management of lands, resources, fish, and wildlife. A second stage of this agreement process remains to be completed, however. It will involve negotiating individual land and financial settlements with each of the 14 Yukon Bands (or First Nations) represented by the Council. These Bands will also be entitled to negotiate self-government arrangements with federal and territorial authorities. By early 1992, five of these individual settlements had been successfilly concluded (Canada, DIAND 1992b: 4-5).

C. *Denendeh and The Dene/Metis Agreement in Principle.* The Dene and Metis struggle for land and self-determination has had a long and complex history, and the basic issues are yet to be resolved. The lands claim advanced by Indian leaders in 1974 was reiterated in principle by the Dene Declaration of 1975. The federal government of Canada formally accepted claims for negotiation from the Dene in 1976 and the Metis in 1977. However, as the process of resolving these issues dragged on, a radically different proposal was developed in 1982 by the Dene Nation and the Metis Association of the Northwest Territories. Representing approximately 12,000 people of Indian ancestry in the Mackenzie Valley, these organizations proposed the creation of *Denendeh* ("The People's Land"), which would be a new territorial entity formed out of the western portion of the Northwest Territories (Dene Nation and Metis Association 1982). Like Nunavut, it would not have "an ethnic government," but would "entrench the rights of the aboriginal peoples of the region... because [the Dene and Metis would] hold majority or near-majority status in the jurisdiction" (Asch 1984: 94). Among the specific provisions indicated for *Denendeh* were: the recognition of native languages as official languages; the creation of a territorial Senate with exclusive Dene membership and veto powers; and the conduct of governmental decision-making on a consensus model using community assemblies and referendums (Dene Nation and Metis Association 1982; Asch 1984: 96-99).

While the *Denendeh* proposal never achieved fulfillment, its existence was a spur to continued efforts to negotiate Dene and Metis claims. Thirteen years after the Dene Declaration of 1975, the people of Indian ancestry in the Northwest Territories did reach a tentative accord with the governments of Canada and the Territories to resolve native claims to aboriginal and treaty rights. In the accord, the Dene/Metis sought to preserve features which they felt the Alaska natives and Cree had compromised too much on in their settlements, viz., the retention of hunting-fishing-trapping rights, and special status for indigenous people and their heritage (cf. Berger 1977i: 176-179,

196). In 1988, Canada signed an Agreement-in-Principle (AiP) with the Dene/Metis which addressed the issues of land title and ownership, game regulation and harvesting, financial compensation, and indigenous self-government. The major features of the Dene/Metis AiP were similar in nature to those found in earlier settlements reached with the Inuit and Yukon Indians, and had the following, specific provisions.

1. *Land.* The Dene/Metis will cede aboriginal claims to lands and waters within Canada, but will receive title to up to 70,000 square miles of territory. They will also own the subsurface resources on 3,900 square miles of this land. Selection of the tracts will be negotiated with Dene/Metis organizations, which will hold formal title to the parcels agreed upon.

2. *Compensation.* A capital transfer payment of $500 million (in 1990 dollars) will be paid to the Dene/Metis over a period of 20 years. $75 million of this will be in compensation for the Norman Wells oil field. In addition, the Dene/Metis will receive a portion of the government's royalties from non-renewable resources in the settlement area: they will receive 50% of the first $2 million, and 10% of the balance of the royalties. The capital transfer payments and the first $20 million of royalty shares will be exempt from taxation.

3. *Renewable Resources.* The Dene/Metis "will have the right to harvest all species and populations of wildlife at all seasons of the year subject to conservation and certain other limitations. The Dene/Metis will have the exclusive right to harvest furbearing animals" (Canada, DIAND 1989i: 2). In addition, the harvesting of trees and plants for personal purposes is also guaranteed. Furthermore, the Dene/Metis will be given "the right of first refusal" concerning new economic opportunities related to wildlife, such as licenses for commercial harvesting; for the operation of commercial guiding, hunting, fishing and naturalist enterprises; and for the commercial cultivation or husbandry of wildlife species indigenous to the area (Ibid.: 2). The Dene/Metis will also "be compensated if losses in relation to wildlife harvesting are suffered as a result of commercial, industrial or governmental undertakings" (Ibid.: 3).

4. *Self-Government and Administration.* The Dene/Metis will establish wholly owned and controlled organizations, such as corporations or trusts, "which will receive and manage financial compensation, benefits, and titles to lands" (Canada, DIAND 1989i: 1), and which will carry out Dene/Metis obligations under the agreement. The corporations may use their assets to promote health, housing, educational, economic, and cultural programs, and income used for these purposes will be non-taxable (Ibid.: 2). Government economic development programs in the region "will take into account the objectives of maintaining and strengthening the Dene/Metis traditional economy and the objective that the Dene/Metis should be economically self-

sufficient" (Idem.). Finally, three boards will be established to administer land and resources in the region: a Land Use Planning Board, an Environmental Impact Review Board, and a Land and Water Management Board. The Dene/Metis will have equal membership with the government on each of these bodies. The Dene/Metis will also be "actively involved in the conservation and management of heritage resources... [and] have preference in employment at public sites, museums and similar facilities..." (Canada, DIAND 1989i: 4).

***

The Agreement-in-Principle, like all such settlements, was a compromise. It would have extinguished aboriginal title to the land, and given natives far less power than the *Denendeh* proposal incorporated. Though the AiP was tentatively accepted by the Dene and Metis in 1988, and then initialled by negotiators in April 1990, the Dene/Metis General Assembly finally rejected the accord in July 1990 because of the reluctance of native leaders to relinquish their aboriginal rights to the lands covered by the settlement. The Dene/Metis Assembly was bolstered in this action by recent Canadian Supreme Court decisions which indicated a judicial willingness to shore up treaty and aboriginal rights (Miller 1991: 299). As explained by Bill Erasmus, the Dene president of the Assembly of First Nations: "Our rights are entrenched with the Canadian Constitution; Supreme Court cases are beginning to define those rights and we as Dene are not prepared to give up any of those treaty or aboriginal rights" (Idem).

The General Assembly's decision meant the suspension of government efforts to achieve a comprehensive claim settlement with all of the Dene/Metis. It did not, however, preclude other attempts to resolve the issues on a more localized, regional basis. Using the April 1990 Agreement-in-Principle as a foundation, the federal government subsequently offered to negotiate more limited settlements with five groups of Dene/Metis from different regions within the Northwest Territories (cf. Canada, DIAND 1990a; and Map 6: Dene/Metis Land Claims Regions). Following the Dene/Metis General Assembly's rejection of the AiP, two of these regional groups withdrew their authorization for the General Assembly to represent them, and they then expressed a willingness to negotiate with the federal government on their own. The first of these groups, the 2,200 Gwich'in (the Dene/Metis of the Mackenzie Delta), ratified an agreement with the Canadian government in 1991: it gave them a proportional share of the land, subsurface interests, moneys, and royalties spelled out in the original AiP; and guarantees of wildlife harvesting rights, and participation in economic and environmental decision-making. The 1,800 Dene/Metis of the Sahtu (Bear

Lake) region, which includes Colville Lake and Fort Good Hope, were the
second group to ask the government to settle their claim on a regional basis.
Negotiations with the Sahtu Tribal Council are currently under way (Canada,
DIAND 1992b: 5). If the latter negotiations are successfully concluded, and
if they incorporate the basic provisions of the AiP, then the gains for the Hare
and the region's other Dene and Metis could be substantial. In exchange for
recognizing Canadian sovereignty over their settlement area, the Dene and
Metis of the Sahtu region could acquire title to specific lands and subsurface
resources; short and long-term financial compensation; access to game and
other renewable resources; exclusive rights to fur-bearers; opportunities to
participate in future employment and economic development programs;
and enhanced organizational ability for self-determination [7].

The major features of the regional Dene/Metis settlements would be
similar in nature to those won by the Cree, the Inuit, the Yukon Indians, and
the native peoples of Alaska. Each of these Northern groups will have
achieved, through these agreements, substantially more control over their
territory, their economy, and their culture than previous treaties — or their

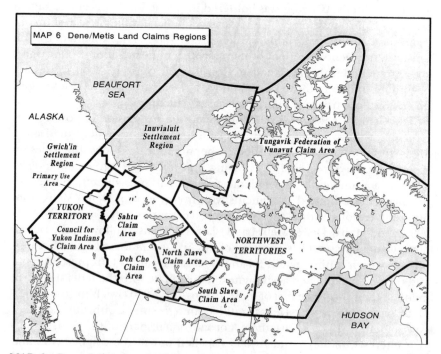

MAP 6   Dene/Metis Land Claims Regions, *reproduced with the permission of the
Minister of Supply and Services Canada, 1992*

recent circumstances — would have allowed. Controversy nevertheless persists within native communities over how much oil and resource extraction to allow in the future. While the proposed settlements would not give the Dene/Metis as much as some of their leaders have claimed or felt entitled to, these accords could place in Dene hands more land, resources, and power than many other North American native peoples now enjoy. Most importantly, the agreements would create a framework for the future within which key Dene values would hold a central place: namely, they would uphold the importance of the land; the viability of hunting, fishing and trapping; the freedom of the people to live without unwarranted outside regulation or interference; and the opportunity for indigenous communities to develop meaningful political structures that would enhance their heritage and their collective well-being. Having won these gains through the political process, the native peoples of the Northwest would then have to see if the rights and resources they control would be sufficient to preserve their cultural integrity and promote their self-sufficiency into the next century.

3. MODELS AND METAPHORS

In close to two centuries of contact with Western society, the Hare have seen the technological, economic, and political context of their lives change in profound ways. From a mobile life without permanent settlements, they have moved to a semi-nomadic existence oriented towards communities built around Euro-Canadian institutions. Arrows have given way to rifles, canoes to skiffs, axes to chainsaws. Populations have grown, children go to school, and death by starvation is only a memory. The Hare have used their language in inventive ways to create new *deneké* words for what whites have introduced to them: *thledaffo*, from "grease" and "yellow," becomes butter; *sasunehbe-sheneh* combines "sled" and "stove" to mean caterpillar tractor; and *k'apason*, from "ptarmigan" and "excrement" is the very expressive description for cheese doodles and similar confections. Beyond language and utilitarian technology, people also cash checks, make homebrew, take antibiotics, and listen to radios. They still pray to the spirits of animals, but also attend Mass. A purely subsistence economy has been re-constructed to include the commerce of fur trapping and the advent of wage labor. And bands that once lacked formal leadership now know how to cooperate with other native groups in the pursuit of shared political goals.

Throughout all these changes, the Hare have also held onto a core set of values and adaptations that continue to define them as a people and serve them in the modern world. Some of the central themes in their lives have been considered here, including their cultural emphases on kinship, concensus, equality, interdependence, generosity, individual autonomy, non-interference in the lives of others, and the moral meaning of the land itself. They continue to take great joy in the bush, they value its aesthetics and age-old meaning, and they take pride in their own competency in dealing with its challenges. The people also prize flexibility and adaptability, along with the virtues of emotional restraint, sensory awareness, and physical toughness. The Hare cope with and seek stress in a number of ways, and their patterns of mobility, drinking, and displacement figure prominently in this repertoire. These behaviors constitute important, culturally sanctioned techniques for dealing with environmental, social, and psychological threats to the people's well-being. A more extensive inventory of the stresses and coping methods found among band members is presented in Tables 7 and 8.

TABLE 7

Stress Sources

Scarcity of environmental resources: this includes cyclical and seasonal features of meat, fish, and fur sources; there is an unstable income from fur trapping.

Harshness of bush life and working conditions: these include cold, wetness, hard physical labor, dangers, and the difficulties posed by weather and animals.

Isolation during bush living: this generates interpersonal stresses from relations within families, and from those between partners and co-workers; isolation is itself a serious form of deprivation.

Dogs and travelling: the sources of concern include the behavior, health, and appearance of dogs, the supply of dog food, and the hardships and dangers of winter and spring dogsled travel (e.g., snowblindness). For some people, travelling under dangerous or challenging conditions is a form of stress-seeking.

Interdependence, cooperation, and helpfulness; and generosity, hospitality, and reciprocity: these themes involve the provision of goods, food resources, and services; jealousies arise over hunting, trapping, and fishing luck, as well as over invitations to brew parties. There is strong consciousness of the balance of generosity in conjunction with kinship and friendship obligations; this is accentuated by the diffuseness of expectations and the lack of specificity in relations among extended kin; interdependence is thus stressful in conjunction with interrelatedness. People show anxiety over owing things to others. These types of behavior relate to an individual's status and reputation in the village.

Population concentration: there are interpersonal, aggregate, and psychological stresses during village reunions and visits to Fort Good Hope.

Drinking behavior and aggression: disruptive and abusive drinking behavior generates conflicts and tensions. Gossip, and sexual and other jealousies:

these occasion, or are occasioned by, extra-marital affairs and illegitimate children, rumors, criticisms, accusations, relative generosity, and feud tensions and allegiances.

Limited privacy: village and bush living conditions have few readily available "back" regions; interaction and observability are often at a high level. People become conscious of and irritated by the surveillance of others; this heightens the extreme distress felt by individuals when they are in embarrassing situations.

Old-age insecurity: there is a loss of respect, authority, and economic usefulness that comes with advanced age; there is consequently poor treatment of the elderly which is related to their inability to live up to the themes of generosity and self-reliance.

Generational and acculturative differences in outlook and orientation: acculturation levels affect attitudes and participation in most areas of life; there is ambivalence shown by some people over Colville Lake versus Fort Good Hope as places of residence, and trapping versus wage labor as a way of life; some individuals show cultural disorientation, and acculturative differences have been aggravated by feud allegiances. There are conflicts and/or misunderstandings between some parents and their grown children because of subcultural differences in life style.

Sex and age composition of the village: these accentuate the generational split, and aggravate frustrations over blocked marriages and the level of village social life. The interrelatedness of band members also restricts sexual and marital possibilities.

Family authority structure: this involves some parental controls over the mobility and activities of younger family members; there are several cases of parents blocking the marriages of younger adults.

Socialization processes: there is a shift around five or six years of age from indulgent and affectionate treatment of children to increased responsibilities for them and a lessened show of warmth; favoritism is shown towards boys. Young children often receive rough treatment in their play and peer groups, and they learn to respond in kind; later, however, they must adjust to the more emotionally restrained behavior of adult life.

Emphases on individualism, individual competence, self-reliance, and non-interference with others: these contrast with the generosity ethic and its implications; people feel a loss of pride in having to ask others for help.

Emotional restraint: it masks, defers, redirects, and intensifies reactions to stresses from various sources; people continually strive to inhibit both their own hostile outbreaks, as well as actions which would provoke such displays in others; a basic underlying factor is the knowledge of, and need for, one's interdependence with others.

The feud between the missionary and the fur trader: it involves various pressures for alliance and compliance which capitalize on the people's reliance upon the goods and services of these men. Major pressures and strategies focus on the people's fur catch, their government assistance checks, and their symbolic acts of support.

High debts and loss of credit at the trading post: these involve severely limited access to the Western foods and items upon which the people depend.

Number of children in the household: a large number can create economic difficulties and great hardship for the mother. In very small family units, adults may be lonely for children, and they may also lack sufficient help in the division of labor. Lack of children can also mean lack of security in one's old age. Illegitimate children are a serious cause of tension among married couples.

Schooling: the prolonged periods of separation between children and their families, necessitated by the educational situation in the area, is a source of psychological stress for both students and parents.

Health and disease: tuberculosis has largely been brought under control, but cases occasionally become reactivated; minor injuries and illnesses persist, several of which are derived from bush activities. People must often depend upon the local priest and the village's limited supply of medicine for medical aid. For operations, major types of treatment and births, band members are flown to a hospital or nursing station.

Belief in ghosts, medicine men, magicians, "bad medicine," magic and predictive or manipulative superstitions: there is little evidence for active belief in these ideas, and there are no accusations or hostilities derived from them; they are not of great consequence in the current context, although certain taboos are observed in hunting, fishing, and trapping.

Belief in "bush men" and fear of isolation in the bush: "bush man" ideas are not taken too seriously by most adults, but they are used as a scaring technique in socialization. People dislike the idea of themselves or others being isolated for protracted periods because of the personal and psychological dangers involved. People generally do not like to trap far from the village or in unknown areas.

TABLE 8

Coping Techniques

Caching and storage of meat and fish for times of shortages: this is done for both human and dog food.

Native and Western-derived technologies for coping with conditions of bush life: these include the use of moss and snow for insulation, snowshoes, bone hide-scrapers, steel axes, rifles, nets, canvas tents, etc.

Isolation during bush living: this affords privacy and relieves stresses from population concentration.

Treatment of dogs: this involves beating, kicking, whipping and cursing when people are both drunk and sober; it is a sanctioned and frequently used outlet for aggression, and it is also participated in by children. Travelling by dogsled is also a major form of stress-seeking in the band, especially among young adult males; in addition, dogs are a source of pride, a part of individual self-image, a mode of self-presentation, and an emotional and sensory extension of people.

Population concentrations: these relieve isolation tensions and include reunions at Colville and Good Hope, trips from the bush to the village and the town, and visits between different bush camps; in the village, a few houses, and the mission and trading post, serve as primary social centers.

Friendships, warm ties, the formation of partnerships, and camping and work alliances: warm ties are found between parents and young children, grandparents and grandchildren, some husbands and wives, and some siblings. Partnerships and alliances make work easier, and they relieve the loneliness and the fear of bush isolation and its dangers; these arrangements stem from kinship ties and friendships.

Camping in familiar areas that are not far from the village: this relieves anxieties about the hazards of bush life, lessens feelings of isolation, and eases travelling hardships.

Listening to radios, and sending and receiving letters and parcels: these relieve feelings of isolation and help maintain contacts with physically distant kin and friends; economic interchanges also provide the people with certain scarce and needed materials, such as moose hide.

Preference of some people for seasonal wage labor over trapping: the former provides greater security of income and permits one to avoid some of the hardships of bush life.

Governmental family allowances and old-age pensions: these provide steady income for families, permit the coverage of debts, and provide economic and social security for the elderly.

Generosity, hospitality, and reciprocity; and interdependence, cooperation, and helpfulness: these expectations and obligations between kin and friends provide security and help in times of need and shortages.

Emphases on individualism, individual competence, self-reliance, and non-interference with others: these afford people pride in their work and accomplishments in the face of hardships with which they must contend. The focus on non-interference provides some insulation against bothersome, "bossy" and nosy concern by others in one's personal affairs.

Limited privacy: a few opportunities for relative privacy exist, including family and personal property and caches, "personal territory" within houses and tents, the use of outhouses, the locking of doors at certain times, limited withdrawal from interaction, travelling, and periods of bush life. On the other hand, access to information about others is facilitated by the limited availability of means to privacy.

Drinking: this overcomes restraints on emotional expression due to the cultural definition of the drinking situation and drinking behavior. Drunken comportment permits release of stress in verbal, aggressive, and confrontative modes of interaction.

Gossiping, sexual adventures, gambling, and other forms of leisure: these provide both relaxation and opportunities for retaliation and indirect hostility against people. Along with drinking, they constitute both direct and vicarious means of stress-seeking.

Humor and joking: these are prevalent modes of tension release, and they are often thinly veiled expressions of hostility, jealousy, and similar emotions.

High mobility: this occurs in various forms on an individual, household, and village level. Tensions from isolation, population concentration, drinking encounters, family arguments, feud pressures, bush hardships, ambivalent and acculturative orientations, and other sources, all find release in this way.

Emotional restraint: this restricts and channels outbursts to expected and culturally sanctioned times and places.

Conciliatory actions to please the missionary and fur trader in their feud: the people's interactions with these men relieve tensions surrounding the conflict. Their use of the mission and store as social centers also provides people with opportunities for relaxing and releasing other stresses of life: included in this is the projection by the people of some of their non-feud stresses and dissatisfactions onto the feud and its principal characters. In addition to the sale of their fur, the people sell resources (meat, fish, wood), engage in wage labor, and sign over their government assistance checks to the whites, in order to prevent the loss of their credit and to cover their debts. Resentment over the feuding of whites also serves as a source of identity for the band as a whole.

Giving or taking children for adoption or for care for a period of time: these relieve stresses for families with too many children or too few children. Illegitimate children produced by a member of a married couple are usually given away to lessen tensions within the family.

Schooling: the values and the dilemmas presented by the current educational system in the North are balanced by the people through their limited use of schooling opportunities; they thereby insure their children a modicum of education, as well as appropriate types of experience in learning more traditional skills and life styles.

Medical aid and assistance: they are provided both by the village's missionary and by government personnel and facilities from outside the community.

Participation in Catholic beliefs and services: religious involvement provides psychological and social release from a variety of stresses in the people's lives, and affords the members of the band an opportunity to enjoy a sense of communality and communion with God.

While an inventory such as this is a useful device, it has three limitations. First, as a catalogue, it presents life as a static picture, whereas the preceding chapters have brought out the dynamics of stress-and-coping as an ongoing process.

Second, the tables are also highly redundant, for many of the same cultural features appear on both inventories: this redundancy derives from the fact that numerous for dealing with tension and anxiety become, in their turn, sources of further stress.

Third, the tables do not try to indicate how specific stresses and coping methods are connected to one another. This is because such simple, one-to-one relations are usually not found in real life. A given stress may simultaneously or sequentially be responded to in a variety of ways, just as a specific response pattern may simultaneously operate as a way for handling a number of tensions. A man releases hostility, for example, by beating a dog that misbehaves, but the tension created by the dog's conduct is only part (and usually only a small part) of the total motivation for the man's aggression. When a family leaves a campsite it has been sharing with other households, the real stress of a fur or food shortage may also serve as the reason for escaping from the irritating habits and untrustworthiness of others. Emotional restraint and repression can, in such cases, obscure the links between stresses and their specific releases. The stress process is thus often subtle and dialectic in nature, and it affects social life and individual existence on a number of levels.

***

Every human community combines qualities that are culturally unique with those that are universally human. The Hare face an sub-Arctic environment whose extremities are rare in most other societies, but they also have certain experiences that other people do share. All groups develop values, utilize sensory abilities, orchestrate their emotions, define their identities, adapt to an ecosystem, and contend with stress. While the content of a people's adaptations may be particular for their own culture, then, one can also discern certain general features of their life style which may be relevant to the existence of other human groups. I would therefore propose that the following characteristics of the situation at Colville be considered as possible elements in the stress patterns of any society.

1) *Environment* The context of living must be broadly construed to include the physical, social, and psychological environments. Stress should be viewd as an organism-environment transaction (McGrath 1970: 14). Natural elements and processes, wild and domesticated species, social and ethnic groups, ambience and architecture, and supernatural beings, are all significant ecological features that affect the creation, experience, and handling of stress. Just as witchcraft beliefs have been shown by anthropologists to be both a symptom and a cause of tension (Naroll 1962: 65-66), ancestral cults, Christianity, "bush man" beliefs, and related spiritual concepts may constitute a projection and a personificiation of cultural anxi-

eties. The Hare alo show how fulfilling engagement with the physical world can be, providing a source of meaning, identity, and personal accomplishment. Other "environmental" relationships may involve similar ambiguities, and reveal the subtler contours of the coping process. Affective displacement among the Hare, for example, involving physical aggression towards dogs, trees, and inanimate objects, and the expression of verbal hostility towards neighbors and whites through gossip and humor, helps clarify the dimensions of the people's total ecology.

2) *Process*   One can only understand the stresses of existence if one looks at them dynamically, not just in terms of their basic sources and the kinds of responses they typically evoke. Rather, one must seek to understand stress and coping as a process involving perception, emotion, action, redundancy, and pattern, as well as the individual nuances of the people concerned.

3) *Specificity*   The experience of the Colville band indicates that there is rarely a one-to-one relationship between specific stresses and particular coping techniques. Each stress may be met with a diverse repertoire of responses, and one coping style may be operative in dealing with a range of problems. Furthermore, specific aspects of the coping process may not be equally relevant for dealing with all situations. In the case of the Hare, for example, mobility is used for dealing with ecological scarcity and population densities, but it is less germane for coping with white men. Some native individuals have been able to minimize their dependence on outsiders by living off the land as much as possible, but there are certain goods and services — ranging from matches to medical care — which have remained in the hands of whites. Hence, the people ultimately have to confront and deal with these outsiders, and so strategies that are more "political" than mobility must eventually be brought into play.

4) *Sensory Context*   The dynamic aspects of the stress process become meaningful only when they are considered within their full cultural context. Relevant variables include not only people's definitions of what constitute stressful circumstances and appropriate modes of response, but also their patterns of perception and cognition. The latter involve both the interpretation of environmental stimuli and situations, and one's appraisal of how to cope with them [8]. Cognitive adaptations in various cultures may place different kinds of emphasis on how the senses are employed. Dene ways for coping with a white-out reveal how touch and sound — as well as sight — can be utilized in spatial orientation. Senses may also be extended through the use of electronic media or, as at Colville, through a relationship with domesticated animals. The over-all level of sensitivity to the

environment should be considered in assessing a society's response to physical threats, as well as the ways in which its members' memories are trained and utilized. In essence, all major psychological parameters should be exmained for their role in the coping process: one dividend of such an approach would be a fuller appreciation of the acquisition, use, storage, and retrieval of knowledge in the group being studied.

5) *Emotional Context*   The types of emotional expressiveness which people are allowed, and the cultural definition of the appropriate contexts in which feelings can be displayed, channel both the experience of stress and its creation. In acquiring a culture, individuals learn the range of emotions that are socially acceptable, the situations in which they can be expressed, and the use of enhancers and inhibitors such as alcohol, drugs, and meditation. The rhythms of constraint and release among the members of the Colville band also suggest that comparable cycles may be found in other groups. It is possible that these periodicities may be related to the pervasive biological rhythms which govern the human organism [9]. Furthermore, the fact that young people in the community must change and constrict their emotional repertoire as they grow older highlights both the stresses of socialization itself, and the process by which response patterns are learned — and restructured — during an individual's life cycle.

6) *History*   The cognitive and emotional roots of a society's stress patterns can often be illuminated by an examination of their history. Previous circumstances may have been conducive not only to the formation of types of social structure, but to the establishment of behavioral and coping styles as well. Among the Hare and neighboring peoples, for example, chronic environmental threats during aboriginal and post-contact times would appear to be related to the bilaterality, individual autonomy, self-reliance, emotional restraint, and kinds of cognitive sensitivity which characterize these groups. The continued presence of historically relevant coping patterns may, of course, simply be a cultural artifact; on the other hand, it may indicate the persistence of earlier stresses into contemporary times, and/or the applicability of established behavior to more recent problems. Each of these possibilities deserves investigation.

7) *Socialization*   It is necessary to translate "historical" time into "life"-time in order to grasp the existential quality of a culture. The patterning of an individual's experience of stress, as part of the process of socialization, includes his training in the treatment and perception of threat, challenge, anxiety and tension. Furthermore, the acquisition of a broad spectrum of social and technological skills is essential for coping with interpersonal and

survival problems. Competence and success thus constitute the outcome of one's ability to mobilize effort, expertise, support, and the appropriate materials to confront a specific challenge (cf. Pepitone 1967: 201-202). Training and experience may also involve exposure to, and acquired tolerance for, certain levels of stress (Naroll 1962: 72), whether these be — as in the case of Colville — the tensions of drinking, or the deprivations of isolation. Socialization often includes the patterned induction of anxiety as well (such as the fear of "bush men"), plus the learning of an emotional repertoire, as illustrated by the band's inculcation of restraint and displacement techniques in young children.

8) *Identity* Stressful experiences may promote unity and identity among a people by defining their corporate boundaries and their ethnicity (Klausner 1968). Confrontations with the bush and with white men have affected the Hare in these ways, although the former involvement has recently also divided the community in terms of life style, just as the latter involvement has, on occasion, led to a questioning of ethnicity itself.

9) *Population* The distribution of people in time and space is one parameter of their subsistence needs, but population densities also influence their styles and rates of interaction. Certain contexts may involve social and sensory deprivation or information overload as stressful circumstances [10]. There may be group and individual limits to how long extremes of isolation and concentration can be endured by the members of a community. Architecture, and the social uses of living space, may reflect these thresholds, as well as contribute to the very conditions which eventually violate the tolerance levels possessed by a people. Cultural and situational limits on privacy, and on the control which individuals have over the flow of information about themselves, can aggravate stresses pertaining to public and self-image. Broad statements about the desired nature of social groups and interaction, such as the enthusiastic way in which the people of Colville speak of the bush and the village, should be compared with the actual behavior of individuals under these same conditions.

10) *Mobility* Physical movement can be a way of simultaneously readjusting a population both to the distribution of ecological resources and to the limits and demands of sociability. Either one of these functions may take precedence over the other as the prime cause of a given move, although the actual motives for mobility may be consciously unrecognized or publicly unackowledged by the participants. In groups where patterned movement is of adaptive significance, it will usually be part of a larger coping repertoire: technological procedures and materials will be relevant

for dealing with economic problems, communications media may temper the rigors of isolation, and institutionalized forms of separation — such as seclusion or the use of veils — may augment privacy (Murphy 1964; Gregor 1977: 224-244). It is therefore not sufficient merely to describe how people choreograph their movements, for their mobility must be related to the other techniques which complement it.

11) *Values* Social orientations include values which bear upon the experience of stress. Cultural themes may prescribe the seeking or avoidance of stressful circumstances, such as the way in which the people of Colville anticipate the challenges of bush life but avoid confrontations with whites. Values may also embody generic response patterns to tension and anxiety, as in the Hare ethos which emphasizes self-reliance, affective containment, individual autonomy, and personal competence. Themes which relate to the handling of stress may, however, be a source of stress themselves if — as in "interdependence" and "independence" — they are contradictory, or if the behavior and role conflicts they promote cannot be realized or resolved much of the time. The latter situations may be a pre-condition for anomie, and would, at the least, be productive of frustration [11]. This can sometimes be seen in members of economically disadvantaged groups who struggle to help their kin economically while also accumulating enough capital to move themselves out of poverty (eg., Stack 1975; Fitchen 1981).

12) *Individuality* Different segments of a population may have distinctive susceptibilities to types of stress, and these may be accompanied by characteristic coping styles. Culturally defined patterns for age and sex groups, for example, including their participation in the division of labor, may crystallize some of these key variations in the experience of stress. Acculturative differences in the Colville band had similar consequences. Other societies may have correspondingly distinctive stress patterns for ethnic, racial, religious, and socio-economic sub-groups [12]. Furthermore, beyond these cultural and subcultural differences, individuals in a population will also have idiosyncratic tolerance levels and response patterns, a feature which complicates but enriches the dynamics of the coping process.

13) *Ambiguity* Relationships and processes often incorporate ambiguities which promote stress. Certain involvements may be simultaneously disparaged and esteemed by people, or sequentially reacted to by them in contrasting ways. The Hare, for example, are drawn to and then withdraw from the bush; their closeness to their grown children is compromised by conflicts over marriage; their sled dogs are both beaten and nurtured; and the whites they interact with are alternately praised and condemned. Thus,

environmental, inter-generational, inter-specific, and inter-ethnic ties at Colville each illustrate the quality of ambiguity. Cultural and social changes over time may also create or intensify contradictions in value orientations, as well as prompt the redefinition of individual and group identity. The recent rise of political activism among the Hare and neighboring groups, for instance, can be seen as a resolution of people's former uncertainty about the worth of Dene identity.

14) *Dialectics* A basic feature of the coping process is that solutions or responses to a given stress usually create other stresses in their turn. As one anthropologist has expressed this:

> man's physical, social and cultural environments are so clearly interwoven that stresses which accompany them should be viewed as interdependent. The resolution of stress in one sphere not infrequently promotes additional stress in another (Chance 1968: 572).

It is therefore a measure of completeness rather than redundancy that most of the factors presented in Tables 7 and 8 appear as both producers *and* reducers of stress. The duality of these elements contributes to the ambiguous and dynamic aspects of existence: the alternation between involvement and disengagement, as part of the coping process, imparts a dialectical quality to life as people experience its rhythms in time and space.

15) *Creativity* The degree to which stress-seeking is emphasized in a culture may affect the amount of innovation and individuality which people participate in (Selye 1956: 269, 277). The pursuit of challenge, and the experience of stimulation, may also enhance competence, as well as the satisfactions which can be derived from it. Furthermore, direct and vicarious stress-seeking, such as in sports, exploration, gambling, humor, intoxication, and narrative drama, may rechannel energies from more destructive outlets (Bernard 1968: 17), and heighten a people's sense of their own creative capacities. Life on the land, for example, possesses such creative meanings for the people of Colville, who find in their experiences there the materials and opportunities to sustain their sense of identity, capability, and community. The importance of story-telling and sewing among the Hare, both as emotional and expressive outlets, also underlines the power of artistic experience as a fulfilling part of life and coping.

***

Anthropology, as a pursuit, is a form of stress-seeking in its own right, as are most attempts to "get close to strangers" (Marshall 1968: 64). The satisfactions of fieldwork derive from the experience of uncertainty, and from the sense of understanding that one ultimately hopes to achieve. Part of the challenge for the anthropologist, and for the reader of ethnography, is that the encounter with other peoples forces us to confront our own strengths and frailties. In the case of the community of Colville Lake, the experience has also suggested to us a dynamic and multi-dimensional approach to stress as a quality of life. In addition, the holistic model of coping that has been proposed here exposes the inadequacy of some of Western culture's metaphors for existence. The engineeer's notion of "stress and strain" may be appropriate for solid materials of limited plasticity, but it scarcely encompasses the subtlety and flexibility of human behavior. An hydraulic metaphor may be more germane, for at least fluids adapt readily to the forces of stress and the contours of their environment, and then return to their previous state after a period of "release" and "relaxation" (Blum 1972).

All equilibrium models of stress, however — whether derived from solid or liquid metaphors — are also deficient in one other important regard: by emphasizing homeostasis, i.e., the continual return of a system to a prior and undisturbed condition, they either overlook or minimize the dynamic and dialectical quality of human existence. Stabilizing mechanisms are, of course, operative in all social systems, and one could, for example, interpret techniques for the handling of stressful emotions at Colville as attempts to restore order in people's relationships. A purely static perspective, however, not only misses the entire dimenion of stress-seeking, but the nature of growth, change and maturation as well. Individual and cultural development are processes rooted in the experience of stress, and they should be appreciated for their sources as well as their outcomes.

If metaphors from physics are not always as useful as models from real societies, then the latter are only as good as the descriptions upon which they are based. Besides the data presented in the preceding chapters, this book's arguments concerning the people of Colville Lake derive support from the nature of other hunting, fishing, and gathering groups: many of them, as shown in Chapters 3 and 4, share with the Hare emphases on flexibility, restraint, equality, generosity, mobility, and bilaterality. These cross-cultural similarities — which can be found in both sub-Arctic and many non-northern societies — do not constitute a case for the universality of any of these coping techniques, but they do highlight the wide ecological utility of a spectrum of adaptive procedures.

Even when different societies have similar coping styles, their cultures may vary in the amount and types of stress that they impose upon people (Honigmann 1967: 86). While some scholars have tried to characterize entire systems as being either "tough" or "easy" on their members (Arsenian and Arsenian 1948), there are no well-established indicators that one can use to measure the over-all level of stress in a given society. Some anthropologists (Nadel 1952; Naroll 1962) have tried to compare cultures by using such stress symptoms as homicide, suicide, witchcraft accusations, and drunken assault, but such analyses are necessarily limited to those groups in which these reaction patterns are already institutionalized. Of the four variables just cited, for example, only the last one would be applicable to the people of Colville Lake.

It is also difficult to measure or determine whether the general level of stress within a social system is more than the members of that society can bear, or whether the stress level is more than the social system as a whole can deal with. One gross index of generalized stress is the incidence and nature of mental illness in a population, with a high incidence of psychopathology (as defined by the members of that society) being indicative of severe strain. In one Western culture, for example, the pioneering Midtown Manhattan Study in New York showed an extremely high rate of neurotic and psychotic disturbance among urban dwellers, a situation which the study's inter-disciplinary research team attributed to a wide variety of stress sources (Langner and Michael 1963). Since we have also been dealing with stress, tension, and anxiety in the case of Colville Lake, it is noteworthy that only one individual in the entire band has been defined as mentally unbalanced by the people themselves; and this particular woman has only periodically exhibited symptoms severe enough to warrant that community members intercede and request her hospitalization. Even the village's level of alcohol consumption must be interpretted with caution. Though certain people in the band drink a great deal at some seasons of the year, no one in the community is — clinically speaking — an alcoholic. Even the most dedicated drinkers can go for months in the winter without a drop of homebrew. Though the community has its problems, then, mental illness and addiction are not among them.

***

The experience at Colville Lake also highlights some misconceptions and stereotypes about Athabascan Indians, especially their undeserved reputation as aloof, cold, taciturn individuals. People who have spoken of them in these terms have failed to appreciate the social ecology of their lives, and its impact upon their emotional repertoire. The people clearly possess outlets for their feelings... though some are more understated than those which Westerners are wont to experience in their everyday lives. The reticence that the Hare exhibit to outsiders is quite different from the affectionate child-rearing, adult humor, and enthusiasm for the bush which they share among themselves. These qualities should sensitize us to a basic problem in intercultural relations, viz., the need to discover and appreciate the unique emotional styles which people employ in a society, be they direct, manifest, subtle, or vicarious in nature. We would then be in a better position to realize the dimensions of other people's feelings, and could improve upon the pioneering but simplistic culture-and-personality labels that have been suggested in the past, such as the concepts of "Dionysian," "Apollonian," "tough," "easy," and "shame" and "guilt" cultures (Benedict 1934; Arsenian and Arsenian 1948; Piers and Singer 1953).

If the above request for cross-cultural understanding sounds painfully contemporary, then perhaps it is because it reminds us of how pressing and similar some of Western society's own problems are. The fact that we experience a totally different environment from the people of Colville Lake may be a deceptive screen which masks the common features of our respective fates. In what one critic (Canby 1971) has called our "see-through civilization," there are few places left for us to hide, either from ourselves or from the outside. We have abdicated our privacy for the sake of efficiency, and display our neuroses like red badges of urban courage. With the partial (and sometimes total) collapse of extended families in urban settings, people who want to escape personal stresses often have no one to turn to. Friends may replace kin as a means of support, but unless friendship has attained a level of commitment comparable to deep family ties, its bonds may prove to be just as fragile. A communal home away from "hell" may eventually become a "hell" away from home, destroying these non-kinship ties, and leaving a person with few other alternatives.

All too often, nomadism, drugs, avarice, religion, or psychoanalysis fill an existential vacuum by defining a life style for people who can no longer define themselves. For many people, modern sects and crisis cults have now come to play as large a part in the Western stress experience as revitalization and nativistic movements do in the rest of the world (cf. LaBarre 1971: 22ff.). One urban scholar (Doxiadis 1963: 38-39) has even suggested that Westerners travel so much in order to escape the horrid architecture that their cities envelop them with. We are certainly more mobile, as a society, than ever before, but it is a moot question whether movement alone will be sufficient to relieve the anxieties of crowding, deprivatization, and depersonalization we are exposed to.

The fact that some ethnic and economic segments of Western societies are financially better off and less visibly stressed than others should not obscure the fact that we all pay the costs of inequity in terms of the insecurity and the lowered quality of the environment in which we must live. If some people can afford a richer coping repertoire than others, and if some groups appear to enjoy a disproportionate share of the more satisfying stresses of life, then we are all still impoverished either by the seductions of style, or by the narrowness of our envy. While many people find the distractions and the density of modern life difficult to bear, it is not a paradox that their cities and towns are simultaneously among the most *stressful* and the most *creative* of settings: the latter two qualities are really complementary. In most cases, however, we have yet to realize the full dimensions of our human potential, for we have not learned to control our stresses or cope with their possibilities. Until we confront that reality, both as individuals and as a society, we will not achieve the kinds of freedom, commitment, and creativity that a deeper level of awareness would allow.

Notes

PREFACE

1. Northern Athabascans cannot be neatly divided into distinct cultural or political entities because of the fluidity of their social organization and the overlap of shared traits among neighboring peoples (cf. Osgood 1936a; VanStone 1974; Helm ed., 1981; and Chapter 2, Note 2).

CHAPTER 1: INTRODUCTION

1. Although I have used pseudonyms in the text, the names employed reflect the kind of naming patterns actually followed by the people. In real life, family names — which are a Western introduction — are in most cases derived from a native word for an object or animal species, or they are taken from a European family name. Hence, among the pseudonyms, one finds such names as Limertu ("hammer"), Tahso ("crow"), Behdzi ("owl"), Godanto ("door"), Nota ("lynx"), Bayjere ("navel"), Ratehne ("storm"), Alahfi ("canoe head"), Yawileh ("duck"), Dehdele ("pike"), Tehgu ("hawk"), and Sašo ("grizzly bear"). Surnames are most often of European origin, with the actual range of choice being influenced by the French-speaking priests of the area. This is reflected in the use of such names as Leon, Michele, André, Monique, and Thérèse. Among themselves, the people also use nicknames, as well as their own unique pronunciation of certain European names: thus, Joshua becomes Yašeh, Germaine becomes Yerimen, John appears as Yen, and Bernadette is transformed into Berona.
2. These themes in Hare Indian life, and similar emphases in the cultures of other Arctic and sub-Arctic peoples, are discussed in Chapters 3 and 4.
3. The issue of ethnic and tribal names for the Hare and other Dene groups is considered more fully in Chapters 2 and 3. See especially Chapter 2, Note 14, and the linguistic evidence summarized in Savishinsky and Hara (1981: 324-325).

CHAPTER 2: ECOLOGY AND COMMUNITY

1. Archaeological work, summarized by Noble (1981: 97), indicates aboriginal occupation in the central District of Mackenzie dating back at least 5,000 years.
2. It is difficult to specify with accuracy the territorial range of any of the Northern Athabascan groups. There were no corporate tribes or boundaries in aboriginal and early contact times, and all of the regional bands were highly nomadic.

Historical sources, however, delineate the general area which the people's ancestors occuppied. In the nineteenth century, the missionary and explorer Emile Petitot placed the Hare along the lower Mackenzie River from Fort Norman to the Arctic Coast, extending eastward to the area of Great Bear Lake and down northward along the route of the Anderson River (1876: xx; 1891: 362). Other early accounts of the Hare largely agree with this description. Osgood, writing in 1936, described their traditional range in the following terms: "Northwest of Great Bear Lake, a section of the Lower Mackenzie River and its drainage, Northwest Territories" (1936a: 11).

3.   Descriptions of Fort Good Hope can be found in the works of Hurlbert (1962), Cohen (1962), Balikci and Cohen (1963), Sue (1964, 1965), Durgin (1974), Hara (1980), and Broch (1986). The figure of 360 reflects Good Hope's size in the late 1960s and early 1970s, which is the "ethnographic present" that much of this book is set in (Savishinsky and Hara 1981: 324). It is significant that Good Hope had approximately the same population some 50 years before when the Hare signed their first treaty with the Canadian government in 1921 (Fumoleau 1973: 160). By 1990, there were 438 registered Indians at Good and 98 at Colville Lake (Canada, DIAND 1990b: 167).

4.   Work on a landing strip for the community was finished in the autumn of 1968, allowing wheeled aircraft to land there for the first time. By 1971, there had been a small but noticeable increase in the amount of air traffic into the village.

5.   In 1970 the village's missionary purchased a single-engine aircraft, and this, like the presence of the air-strip, somewhat reduced the settlement's isolation and relative inaccesibility. The control over air traffic was still a "white" monopoly, however, and this was so direct and more manifest than before, that the people's resentment was intensified. It also echoes the feeling that other northern Indians have expressed over the control of air transport by whites (eg., Salisbury 1986: 48, on the Cree).

6.   See the estimates and percentages cited by Symington (1965: 21, 66) and Kelsall (1968: 47, 56).

7.   The scientific names for the species of fish most frequently mentioned in this and subsequent chapters are: lake trout (*Cristivomer namaycush*); pike (*Esox lucius*); white-fish (*Coregonus clupea formis*); loche (*Lota leptura*); grayling (*Thymallus signifer*); and sucker (*Castosmus catomus*) (see Hara 1980: 122-123; Gillespie 1981a: 17).

8.   This is elaborated on in Chapter 4, "Stress and Mobility."

9.   See Osgood (1975) for an ethnography of Indian place-names around Great Bear Lake. The Yukon Native Language Center and the Alaska Native Language Program have sponsored a rich body of work in recent years on the importance of place-names in Athabascan thought. For a summary, see McClellan (In Press).

10.   Descriptions of traditional clothing styles among the Northern Athabascans can be found in early historical sources and more recent ethnographies, including Hearne (1795), Mackenzie (1801), Richardson (1851ii: 8-11), Jenness (1967: 67-76), Oswalt (1966: 25-26), Hatt (1969), Osgood (1936b, 1937, 1940, 1971), Honigmann (1946, 1954), Clark (1974: 120-138), and Rogers and Smith (1981: 138-141).

11.   Symington (1965: 39) and Kelsall (1968: 269-274) provide both pictures and

detailed accounts of warble fly infestation on caribou.

12. Cf. Symington (1965: 52) and Kelsall (1968: 276). Native band names for many of these groups reflected their geographic and ecological position. Helm (1965a), for example, mentions "edge-of-the-woods" Dogrib bands, and the people of Colville Lake are descended, in part, from a nineteenth century Hare group called the *Nne-lla-gottine* (Petitot 1875, 1876, 1891), *Ne la go t'ine* (Osgood 1932), or the "end of the earth people" (cf. Hara 1980: 22-25). The taiga-tundra ecology of the Chipewyans is summarized by Oswalt (1966: 30-32) and J.G.E. Smith (1975, 1976).

13. Indians and Inuit who utilized caribou for clothing preferred different types and parts of hides for different items of apparel. Symington (1965: 53) notes that: "Calf skins were favoured for undergarments, and summer or autumn skins for outer parkas. Leg skins [which the people of Colville stress as being especially tough and long-lasting] were used for mittens, for mukluk legs, and for the soles in the absence of the superior moose or seal skin" (cf. Kelsall 1968: 211, and Hatt 1969, for further descriptive material).

14. Kelsall (1968) contains excellent maps showing the limits of the winter migrations by caribou herds. Fort Good Hope is clearly beyond the western border of the Barren Ground caribou's winter range, but it is in the midst of a forest ecosystem (a willow, poplar, and birch succession area) favored by the moose. As noted, the caribou generally restrict their movements to the climax spruce-lichen forest, which typifies the ecology of the Colville area (cf. Kelsall 1968: 53, which draws upon the forest region classification given in Rowe 1959).

15. Excellent descriptive material on human-animal ties can be found in Henriksen (1973: 33-39) for the Naskapi, Tanner (1979) for the Cree, D. Smith (1973, 1985, 1990) and Sharp (1988) for the Chipewyan, Clark (1970) for the Koyukon, and Ridington (1988) for the Beaver. Information on the Hare from some 19th century sources is summarized in Hultkrantz (1973: 126-127). A controversial book that presents an antagonistic portrait of Indian-animal relations in the sub-Arctic is Martin (1978); critical responses to this portrayal are collected in Krech (ed., 1981).

16. Some of the names which have been applied to regional groups, either individually or collectively, are Hare Indians, Hareskins, Harefoot Indians, Rabbitskins, *Peaux-de-Lièvres, Dene Peaux-de-Lièvre, Ka-cho-'dtinne, Kah-cho-tinne* ('Arctic hare people'), *Kat'a-gottine, Kha-t'a-ottine, K'a-t'a-gottine* ('People among the hares'), *Kawchodinneh* ('People of the great hares'), *Khatp-Gottine* ('People among the rabbits'), and *Kawchogottine* ('Dwellers among the large hares') (cf. Bureau of American Ethnology 1907: 667-668, which gives an extensive listing of names which have been used and recognized). Savishinsky and Hara (1981) reconsider the problem of Hare identity and nomenclature.

17. Additional data on the population cycle of the snowshoe hare and other rabbit species is provided by Chitty (1971).

18. Statements of these positions (eg., Best 1986, 1989; Klein 1986) are presented and critiqued in Herscovici (1985), Keith and Saunders (eds., 1989), Wenzel (1991), Barton (1991), and the report on "The Fur Issue" prepared by Canada's House of Commons' Standing Committee on Aboriginal Affairs and Northern Development (1986; hereafter referred to as Canada, HC-SCAAND 1986).

19. A daily temperature chart was kept from August 1967 to August 1968 by means

of an indoor-outdoor thermometer. While this was not a precision instrument, I believe that the readings I obtained were accurate to within a few degrees. I periodically checked my data against the readings on the thermometers kept by the priest and fur trader.

20. "Windchill is a measure of dry atmospheric cooling, or heat loss, in terms of temperature and wind... The higher the wind and the lower the temperature, the greater the loss of heat. Although a temperature of -30°F with no wind may not be uncomfortable, the same temperature in conjunction with a 32-mile-per-hour wind will freeze exposed human flesh within one-half minute" (Kelsall 1968: 49).

21. Other examples of Athabascan lunar calendars can be found in the monographs by Osgood (1932, 1936b, 1937, 1959), Honigmann (1946, 1954), McKennan (1959), McClellan (1975b: 81-82), Hara (1980), and de Laguna and McClellan (1981).

22. In aboriginal times the Hare also ate the contents of caribou stomachs as a source of vegetable food, as did other regional groups such as the Chipewyans (Oswalt 1966: 28, 33).

23. The unpredictable nature of certain caribou movements is documented by Symington (1965: 35-36, 45) and Kelsall (1968: 106ff, 231).

24. Kelsall (1968), Fumoleau (1973), and Chapter 3 ("Kinship and History") summarize much of the evidence on the sporadic availability of caribou to many northern Indian groups, including the Hare. For example:

> Fort Franklin, populated largely by Hare Indians, probably did not have caribou even in early times. It is on the northwestern range extremities for the species. Anthropological evidence suggests that rabbits, moose, and fish supplied the basic necessities of life...
>
> The large fluctuation in number of caribou taken at Fort Rae (affecting the Dogribs on the north arm of Great Slave Lake) appears common to virtually all points on the caribou range. Nor were such fluctuations uncommon when the caribou population was high. Russell documented the near absence of caribou in the Fort Rae area in 1893-94 and preceding winters, and Anderson recorded such scarcity that Eskimos starved at Padlei in 1926-27, continued scarcity in 1927-28, and abundance in the following 2 years (Kelsall 1968: 231; references omitted).

25. Estimates of the number of caribou needed by families living off the land are based upon data cited by Kelsall (1968: 207).

CHAPTER 3: KINSHIP AND HISTORY

1. Representative studies and summaries of social organization from these areas can be found in the writings of Osgood (1936b, 1937, 1958, 1959, 1971),Birket-Smith and deLaguna (1938), Whitaker (1955), McKennan (1959, 1965), Slobodin (1962), Forde (1963), Pehrson (1964), Graburn and Strong (1973), Bishop (1974), Clark (1975), McClellan (1975b, 1987), deLaguna (1975), Krech (1978a, 1983), and Riches (1982).

2. Cf. Jenness (1967: 385-399), Helm and Leacock (1971), and Cohen and Osterreich (1967: 4-5) for brief summaries of seasonal patterns among the

aboriginal Hare and other Northern Athabascans. Helm (1965a, 1968a) discusses the demographic and ecological factors which would have promoted regional ties among bands.

3. The maps and descriptions in Osgood (1936a) and Jenness (1967) place the Hare in relation to these neighboring peoples. Jenness (1967: 392-396) provides a brief summary of aboriginal Hare culture, stressing its basic similarity to that of other Mackenzie drainage groups.

4. This pattern of Indian intermediaries characterized the expansion of the fur trade into most areas of North America. In eastern Canada, for example, it had been the Algonkian tribes and the Iroquois who had acquired and fought over this highly profitable, monopolistic position (Innis 1962; Rich 1967: 1-23; Bishop 1974: 308ff.; Miller 1991: 37, 121). The situations in the sub-Arctic Shield and Cordillera are discussed by Gillespie (1975, 1981b) and McClellan (1975a, 1981a, 1981b, 1981c, 1981d).

5. There is evidence that the Hare and other lower Mackenzie groups had already felt the impact of white men and the fur trade prior to Mackenzie's trip. European goods had been spreading westward from the trading forts on Hudson's Bay since the early eighteenth century (Rich 1967: 102-103), and Hearne (1795) reports trading activity by the Dogribs and Copper Indians (Yellowknives) at Fort Prince of Wales on Hudson's Bay in the 1760s and 1770s. Mackenzie states in his journal that he interviewed Copper Indians and Slaveys along his northern route, and that these people attested to their being plundered by the Cree and Chipewyans for furs (1801: 3, 18, 20). The fact that all the groups in the vicinity of the Hare were already involved in the fur trade by 1789 implies that the Hare were probably trading furs with people to the south and east of them by that time as well. Mackenzie urged the Hare to trade their pelts to the Dogribs, a group which was already being supplied with iron and goods by the men of his company (1801: 83). McClellan (1981c) discusses inter-cultural relations and trade goods among groups to the west of the Hare.

6. In the Yukon and Alaska, some Athabascan peoples to the west and southwest of the Hare were more organized for purposes of trade and warfare. See, for example, McClellan (1975a) on the Northwestern Athabascans; de Laguna and McClellan (1981) on the Ahtna; Honigmann (1981ab) on the Kaska; and McClellan (1981a, 1981b) on the Tagish and Tutchone.

7. Mackenzie noted the contempt in which the Kutchin held the Hare (1801: 50), and cited instances of hostility between the Hare and the Eskimo (1801: 83). In the nineteenth century, Richardson emphasized the Hare's great fear of the Eskimo, even though the former had possession of firearms by the time he wrote (1851i: 212, 352-353). Richardson also dwelt upon the Hare's reputation for timidity and cowardice, stating that: "unless... they are assembled in large numbers, as we found them at the Ramparts (on the Mackenzie River), they seldom pitch a tent on the banks of the river, but skulk under the branches of a tree cut down so as to appear to have fallen naturally from the brow of a cliff; they do not venture to make a smoke, or rear any object that can be seen from a distance. On the first appearance of a canoe or boat, they hide themselves with their wives and children, in the woods, until they have reconnoitered, and ascertained the character of the object of their fears" (1851i: 212).

8. As MacNeish has described this situation: "The following set of conditions are

all that investigators have to work with when staking out tribes or other major divisions of the Northeastern Athabascans...: a set of peoples living in physical contiguity (but not together), speaking a mutually intelligible tongue (though often with regional dialectical variations), sharing a common culture (though not necessarily one distinct in essentials from neighboring tribes), and having at least a vague sense of common identity which may be based in whole or in part on the foregoing conditions" (1956: 133).

9.　Helm (1968a) makes a related point in her discussion of the three major types of socioterritorial groups found among the Dogribs. She distinguishes between regional bands, local bands, and task groups, and goes on to point out that: "Membership in these three kinds of socioterritorial entities is in no wise mutually exclusive. An individual may at the same time have social identity as a member of a regional band and of a local band, and, by the simple fact of his presence, also be a member of a task group" (1968a: 118).

10.　Rogers (1969a: 36) documents the fact that the confusion in band names for the Cree and Ojibwa of the eastern sub-Arctic stems from a similar set of ecological, historical, and cultural features.

11.　The most comprehensive account of the history and negotiations surrounding Treaties 8 and 11 is provided by Fumoleau (1973), who stresses the major differences in how government and Indian representatives understood the meaning of these compacts. The actual language of Treaty 11, which the Hare were signatories to, addresses the issues of land and resource use in the following words: "The said Indians do hereby cede, release, surrender and yield to the Government of the Dominion of Canada, for His Majesty the King and His Successors forever, all their rights, titles, and privileges whatsoever to the lands included... [T]he said Indians... shall have the right to pursue their usual vocations of hunting, trapping and fishing throughout the tract surrendered... subject to such regulations as may from time to time be made by the Government of the Country... and saving and excepting such tracts as may be required or taken up from time to time for settlement, mining, lumbering, trading or other purposes" (Fumoleau 1973: 166-167). Of the native people covered by the treat, Fumoleau writes, "Very few could read it then; most have not read it yet" (Ibid: 165). For more recent discussions of treaty issues for Canada as a whole, see Miller (1991) and Dickason (1992).

12.　McKennan has documented the fact that the Chandalar Kutchin owe their name to a similar derivation: "From the time of the first white trader-explorers, the least known of the various Kutchin groups trading at Fort Yukon were the people inhabiting the mountain fastness to the north. The voyageurs of the Hudson's Bay Company called them *gens du large*, a name that stressed their highly nomadic existence in the wide expanses between Fort Yukon and the Arctic Ocean... This term was easily corrupted into Chandalar, and came to be applied to both the natives and the principle river that flows through their territory..." (1965: 14).

13.　The latter estimate is based upon Helm's kinship chart of the band for the period 1956-1957 (Helm 1965a: 365).

14.　The complex history of post-marital residence choices among Colville Lake's married couples has been summarized in another work (Savishinsky 1970a: 57-65), which shows a trend towards the solidarity of sibling sets, and a slightly higher incidence of virilocal over uxorilocal unions (cf. also Helm 1965a, 1969b).

15. Cf. J.G.E. Smith (1976: 21) and Lanoue (1981) on the importance of Dene sibling bonds.

In earlier times, young husbands among the Northern Athabascans lived for a period with the family of their new spouse (i.e., uxorilocal residence), providing a year of "bride service" for these people. As Helm states, this "makes possible a flexibility in residence. A man thus makes a contact in his wife's area and then returns to his own band where he is already acquainted with the people and the locales. Manoeuverability is possible between the two regions" (1969d: 238). McClellan carries the implications of this one step further: "I had thought that I found a functional correlate in this as well. Although the Southern Tutchone and Atna [Athabascan groups to the south-west of the Hare] did not know what they were doing, their initial uxorilocality really insured that in times of starvation and famine they could quickly mobilize their forces, for the adult males would be familiar with two hunting territories" (1969: 238).

16. Some of the key features of the social system can be delineated as follows. Six of the community's fourteen native households (numbers 1 through 6 in Figure 6) are composed of families with the same surname, i.e., Behdzi. Four of these six units (numbers 1, 3, 4, and 5) are headed, respectively, by Leon, Yen, Pierre and Paul Behdzi, a set of four brothers. Charlie Behdzi, the married stepson of Pierre, heads a separate household (number 6), and Yašeh, the son of Yen, maintains his own residence (number 2) with his maternal grandmother, Annie Kayšene. Furthermore, two of the four Behdzi brothers, Leon and Pierre, are married to a pair of sisters, and Yen's wife Helen is a parallel cousin to two other married adults in the community.

Two other brothers, Wilfred and George Ratehne, head households 7 and 8, and they have established marital ties with several band families. Another set of family units (numbers 12 and 13) are headed, respectively, by André Yawileh and his married son Fred. The male heads of ten of the fourteen native households, therefore, are connected by a series of primary linkages through men. Historically, it was the cluster of Behdzi households, along with the elder Yawileh family, which formed the nucleus of the band in the 1950s. This core population thus centered around a set of male siblings and the elderly, patriarchal Joseph Tehgu, André's father-in-law, who was a dominant or focusing figure for the Yawilehs. It was on the basis of the kinship links extending outward from this nodal group of older people that the Colville community was ultimately re-formed. [Writing about the Chipewyans, J.G.E. Smith makes a similar observation: "the smallest groups are essentially nodal kindreds based primarily on the principle of sibling solidarity" (1976: 21).]

Beyond the linkages already noted at Colville, ties within the settlement can be — and are — traced bilaterally and affinally as well as patrilaterally. Of the four households not considered above (numbers 9, 10, 11, and 14), two (numbers 9 and 14) include wives from one of the aforementioned patrilaterally-linked families: Albert Limertu's wife Paula (number 9) is a Ratehne, and Maurice Bayjere's wife Dora (number 14) is the daughter of André and Berona Yawileh. A former marriage of Dora's husband Maurice involved a case of sister-exchange with a man from a different family in the band, Wilfred Ratehne. Nora Godanto and Lena Dehdele, the wives of the men who head the remaining two households in the village (numbers 10 and 11), are sisters. Lena's husband Peter is a parallel cousin of the male head of another community household, Albert Limertu. Through his deceased brothers, Peter is also related to the wives in two of the settlement's other families. Adoptions, out-of-wedlock children, ties through additional ascending and lateral kin, and the previous marriages of some of the community's older men and women, further expand the picture of band interrelatedness. Sister-exchange unions, and pairs of brothers marrying pairs of sisters, are some of the traditional marriage arrangements still illustrated by the current community, and they constitute marital forms which would have intensified ties within and between bands in earlier times as well.

The possibility that cross-cousin marriages were once a significant practice among the Hare was raised by MacNeish (1960) and Sue (1964), but a subsequent statistical study of Hare marriages by Helm (1968b) has not borne this out. MacNeish (1960: 288-289) cites evidence for polygamy, polyandry, sister-exchange, wife-exchange, and sororate and levirate unions among the Mackenzie Dene in the past.

17. Slobodin points out (1969: 75) that the ambivalence surrounding the brother-in-law relationship among the Kutchin, which combines elements of closeness with distrust and hostility, is reflected in the variable way in which people use and extend the term for "brother-in-law."
18. Cf. Hara (1980: 250-252) for a full explanation of these kinship norms.
19. Cf. the accounts of Hearne (1795: 33-34, 74, 294-295, 331), Back (1836: 209), King (1836: 170-171, quoted in Helm 1965a), Richardson (1851i: 211), Hooper (1853: 268-282, 303-305), Petitot (1889: 39-44), Wentzel (1889: 106-107), Keith (1890: 118-119), Bureau of American Ethnology (1907: 667), McLean (1932: 343), Osgood, 1932: 37, 42), Hurlbert (1962: 11-12), Jenness (1967: 394), Fumoleau (1973: 31, 36, 55, 111, 130-131, 135, 138), Krech (1978a, 1980b, 1983), and Hara (1980: 14, 35, 106, 144). A cautionary essay on the various meanings of "starvation" in ethnohistoric sources on the sub-Arctic is provided by Black-Rogers (1986).
20. Descriptions of shamanistic curing in the nineteenth century are given by Keith (1890: 118, 127). Curing of ghost sickness or illness entailed singing over the afflicted person, with blowing, sucking, and the laying on of hands onto the ailing part of the body being involved in cases of disease. The curer extracted a small piece of wood, a sliver of bone, or some other tiny object, and then displayed this as the cause of the sickness.
21. In terms of the actual number of people who are still living off the land in the Colville-Good Hope-Bear Lake region (i.e., excluding the sedentary individuals living permanently in fort towns), the present population density of this area is probably comparable to what it was in earlier periods (see Chapter 2, note 3).
22. The nature of aboriginal and post-contact social organization among the Northern Athabascans has been a matter of some controversy. Data and arguments in favor of fluid bands with a flexible, bilateral kinship system, have been put forward by a significant number of anthropologists, some of whom would extend their interpretations to sub-Arctic Algonkians and other hunter-gatherers. See Osgood (1958), Helm (1965a, 1968a; Helm et. al. 1975),

Savishinsky (1970b, 1974), Hultkrantz (1973), J.G.E. Smith (1975, 1976, 1978, 1979), Sharp (1977, 1978, 1988), Rogers and Smith (1981), Lanoue (1981), Rushforth (1984), Broch (1986), and Jarvenpa and Brumbach (1988). These scholars see this pattern of social organization as a fundamental adaptation to an uncertain and fluctuating ecosystem, rather than a response to "the shocks and dislocations of European intrusion" (J.G.E. Smith 1976: 22). However, other anthropologists have argued for different models of aboriginal sub-Arctic social organization (Krech 1980a: 84-88; Riches 1982: 18-19, 56-106). Service (1962: 59-107; 1971: 76-78) has made a case for patrilineal and patrilocal bands, whereas a matrilineal and matrilocal basis for Northern Athabascan groups has been posited by, among others, McKennan (1959), McClellan (1964), Dyen and Aberle (1974: 352-423), Clark (1975), deLaguna (1975), Krech and Bishop (Krech 1978a; Bishop and Krech 1980; cf. also Bishop 1974: 349), and Hosley (1980). Krech (1978a, 1978b, 1979, 1980b, 1983) has argued that the depopulating effect of epidemic diseases among Northern Athabascans, rather than environmental hazards, underlay a post-contact shift to bilocal and bilateral social patterns from an aboriginal system of matriorganization. Helm (1980) has presented evidence for female infanticide, rather than disease, as the main limiting factor on the size of Mackenzie Dene groups; she therefore rejects depopulation as an explanation for bilateral social organization, and reasserts the likelihood that bilaterality was the aboriginal pattern.

23. For an analysis of how stress is produced and coped with by the people of the Colville band, see Savishinsky (1971a) and the detailed material in the following three chapters.

24. Cf. the discussion of envy by Foster (1972), and the comment on Foster's analysis by Savishinsky (1972b). Slobodin (1969) describes a similar pattern of distributing a moose-kill among the Kutchin.

25. Helm (1965b) notes the same procedure among the Dogrib, and describes the patterns of allocation which operate among these people. Writing of the Chipewyan, Sharp (1988: 31-33) has observed how patterns of reciprocity and food sharing are built around the ties among women within a camp — a feature which makes economic exchanges less formal, and embeds them in the daily flow of bush life.

26. Bilaterality, however, is not found among the Northwestern Athabascans (cf. McClellan 1964, 1975b; de Laguna 1975).

27. Some of the contemporary studies which deal with the advantages and problems derived from the persistence of these values include those of Chance (1966, 1968), Ervin (1969), Lubart (1969), Sindell (1968), D.G. Smith (1968), Vallee (1967), VanStone (1965), J.G.E. Smith (1970, 1978), Welsh (1970) Henriksen (1973, 1981), Bishop (1974: 24), McClellan (1975b, 1987), Sharp (1975, 1988), Koolage (1976), D.M. Smith (1976, 1992), Berger (1977i), Jarvenpa (1980), Acheson (1981), Barger (1981), Rushforth (1984), and Ridington (1988).

28. In one study the authors compared early twentieth century Chipewyan tales with stories told by contemporary Chipewyan children (Cohen and VanStone 1962). In a subsequent study, a group of tales recorded by a Loucheux (Gwich'in) man, Paul Voudrach, who has lived most of his life among the Hare at Fort Good Hope, were similarly analyzed for themes of dependency and self-sufficiency (Cohen and Osterreich 1967). In comparing the results of these two studies, Cohen and Osterreich concluded:

In both the children's stories and in the contemporary adult's material there is a substantial rise in the percentage of scores devoted to dependency. Although dependency is somewhat higher than self-sufficiency for early twentieth century Chipewyan tales, it is on balance more nearly equal to self-sufficiency than in the contemporary material. We have therefore obtained further substantiation for the hypothesis that the contact period, especially that part that includes government welfare programs, tends to stimulate the dependency motivations at the expense of desires for self-sufficiency (1967: 50).

CHAPTER 4: STRESS AND MOBILITY

1. The inhibiting influence of Western materials upon native mobility has been documented in several areas of the North: see, for example, VanStone (1965), Helm (1965b), and Graburn (1969).

2. In the 1960s and 1970s, the Hare had not been introduced to the two-way radios which — by the 1980s — were helping to reduce the sense of isolation in the camps of other sub-Arctic trappers (eg., Salisbury 1986: 82). In his summary of modern bush life among the Cree, Salisbury (Ibid: 78-82) also notes other features of the growing mechanization of Indian camps: snowmobiles, chainsaws, large caches of gasoline and supplies, and increasing reliance on airplanes to transport families and equipment, all contributed to making winter sites more sedentary and permanent than in the past.

3. The way in which individual, family, and acculturative differences in the band affected people's use of environmental resources is discussed more fully in Savishinsky (1978).

4. The numbers identifying the camps in the maps and figures refer to households discussed in Chapter 3. Several of the early and mid-winter encampments included men from Fort Good Hope, who spent part of the winter trapping with Colville families: these include, in Figure 12, Billy Gafee (Camp 1, 7), Antoine Tahso and his family (Camp 6), Jack Eddee (Camp 8), Jonas Tahso (Camp 9, 10), and Baptiste Saso (Camp 11). Jack Eddee and Jonas Tahso were also members of Camp 8, 9 (Figure 13) during the mid-winter dispersal. Thomas Godanto (Camp 11, Figure 12), whose parents left Colville just before the trapping season in order to take government wage jobs, spent the first part of the winter with Baptiste Saso. After these two men quarreled and split up during the Christmas ingathering, Baptiste returned to Good Hope, and Thomas left to rejoin his parents. Hence there is no Camp 11 on Figure 13.

5. Jarvenpa (1976, 1977, 1980; also Jarvenpa and Brumbach 1988) and Rushforth (1984) document how differences in age, gender, and degree of assimilation contribute to distinct mobility, trapping, and bush life patterns among English River Chipewyans and Bear Lake Indians. Jarvenpa (1977) provides quantitative data for the Chipewyan showing how trapping productivity varies in a linear fashion with the size of trapping areas and their distance from settlements

6. Indians have resisted the establishment of family trapping areas in most parts of the Northwest Territories. Several groups of Chipewyans, for example, have opposed it, "saying that it would limit their mobility" (Oswalt 1966: 48; cf. also

J.G.E. Smith 1975: 446; 1976: 20; Jarvenpa 1980: 43, 129).

7. More extensive discussions of Athabascan "bush man" beliefs can be found in Basso (1978) and Sharp (1988). Basso (1978), who summarizes material found in monographs on various groups, emphasizes the importance of "bush man" tales as an expression of cultural ideas about morality. Whereas Hare adults use anxiety about "bush men" to control children, Sharp observes that Chipewyan men promote fear about them to control women (1988: 102-103).

8. Turnbull (1968a, 1968b) and Woodburn (1968) cite instances of African hunting groups, the Mbuti and the Hadza, who also employ ecological arguments to explain socially motivated separations.

9. This set of values and attitudes concerning travelling has been noted by Slobodin (1969: 84) for the Kutchin; and by Brody (1987) and Ridington (1988) for the Beaver. See also McClellan (In Press) for a comparative analysis.

10. The relationship between impression management, privacy, and public and self-image is discussed by Goffman (1959), Schwartz (1968), and Gregor (1977).

11. Christian and Gardner (1977) and Christian (1989) have some very perceptive comments on the meaning of silence in Dene culture, and the difficulty outsiders can face in understanding it. The same dilemma confronts people in Western societies who try to relate to individuals from their own culture who cannot talk. This is true, for example, in the case of nursing home staff and family members dealing with persons suffering from stroke, Alzheimer's, or other forms of dementia. The act of simply being together in silence requires a suspension of the cultural rules of everyday etiquette (cf. Savishinsky 1991c: 124-142).

12. Helm and Lurie (1966) provide an excellent description of how *udzi* is played among the Athabascans.

13. Bernard (1968) points out the stress-seeking qualities of gambling, sports, and such dramatic forms as folk and fairy tales, novels, and theatre. As Bernard notes, intoxication is also a form of stress-seeking.

14. VanStone (1965) documents a similar problem, with comparable statistics, in a contemporary Chipewyan community. McClellan (1975a: 241-53) discusses the same gender imbalance in the historical demographics of several Alaskan and Yukon groups. Some of the major demographic features of Colville Lake, besides the preponderance of unmarried males, can be summarized as follows:

Composition of Population by Sex and Age

Age Range	Number of Males	Percentage of Males	Number of Females	Percentage of Females
0-15	12	29.2%	9	30.0%
16-30	9	22.0	6	20.0
31-45	9	22.0	5	16.6 2/3
46-60	5	12.2	2	6.6 2/3
61-75	5	12.2	6	20.0
76-90	1	2.4	2	6.6 2/3
Totals	41	100.0%	30	100.0%

15. The significance of vicarious experiences in the community's emotional life is analyzed in Savishinsky (1982).
16. See Henriksen (1973: 17) on the Naskapi; Tanner (1979: 23) on the Cree; Jarvenpa (1976: 68; 1980: 3,171; Jarvenpa and Brumbach 1988: 616) on the Chipewyan; and Broch (1986: 79) on the Hare.
17. Data on mobility as a tension-reducing device for other hunter-gatherers and foragers are presented in Lee and DeVore (eds., 1968). The way in which residence arrangements reflect stress patterns has been noted by anthropologists in many groups from diverse ecologies: see, for example, Mead's description of the Samoans (1968: 22, 42-43, 158, 198), Gluckman's comments on the Zulu (1967: 99-100), Gregor's observations on the Mehinacu (1977: 217), and Riches' analyses of seasonal fluctuations in Inuit camp size (1982: 21-55).

CHAPTER 5: THE MISSIONARY AND THE FUR TRADER

1. It should be noted that although the settlement's priest belongs to a missionary order, the Indian people of the region had been fully converted to Catholicism by the early years of the twentieth century. Hence, the local feud and its strategies did not directly stem from religious or "missionizing" activities per se.
2. Honigmann (1952), Welsh (1970), Koolage (1976), Acheson (1981) and Barger (1981) provide analyses of how patterns of ethnic segregation have developed in larger northern communities.
3. In the dramaturgical framework suggested by Goffman (1959), the living quarters of the store and mission were "backstage" areas in which the trader and priest could meet with native allies and white visitors. The ability to penetrate these private spaces was thus a mark of status for people (cf. also Schwartz 1968: 743; Sommer 1969:18-19). Broch (1983: 168-182) applies these concepts in his analysis of Indian-white relations at the Dene community of "Fort Sunset."
4. In structural terms, I occupied the position of "high-status friend" that Morris Freilich denotes in his discussion of the "natural triad" (1964). A high-status friend is someone who, "though superior in status to ego, frequently plays the role of intimate friend, adviser and helper... In many field work situations anthropologists (and at times sociologists) are the (high-status friend) to their informants (the low-status subordinates), whose activities are directed by various people (i.e., high-status authority figures)" (1964: 530- 531).

   As Balikci (1960-61), Paine (1971, ed., 1971), Henriksen (1973), Koolage (1976), Broch (1983) and others have shown, native populations in small northern settlements are really not completely undifferentiated, and problems of social structure should be approached with these subtleties, and patron-client ties to whites, in mind. The number of triads or triangles (natural or otherwise) which could be delineated within the community would thus depend upon how many distinctions one wanted to make within the village's population. Furthermore, additional geometric models could be utilized if the triads were combined in various ways. As Homans notes in his discussion of triangular situations, a rule applicable to one triad "can be extended to any number of persons, and thus a matrix or system of relationships is formed" (1950: 248).

5. I.C. Jarvie, in discussing the problems confronting fieldworkers, has observed that "... it is his lack of a fixed and defined role, or his shifting about among the various roles, that enables him to get at information which would otherwise be inaccessible" (1969: 508). Jarvie also notes that: "... to some extent the success of the method of participant observation *derives from* exploiting the role clashes insider/outsider, stranger/friend, pupil/teacher" (1969: 505). Brody (1975) provides rich, insightful material on his experiences as a social researcher in communities of Inuit and Whites in the eastern Arctic.

6. Lopata (1979) uses this phrase to describe how some widows remember their deceased husbands in a distortedly positive way.

7. In describing a conflict between a storekeeper and missionary in a Naskapi community, Henriksen (1973: 71, 91-100) also observed how non-drinkers supported the priest, while drinkers sided with the trader.

8. Since the priest's strongest supporters came from among the village's most traditional and religious families, Kluckhohn and Leighton's observations on the Navaho are suggestive of the type of situation which developed at Colville:

> Of those who practice the Christian religion, it is merely factual to point out that a higher proportion are directly or indirectly dependent on the missionaries for their livelihood (1962: 133).

9. The effect of the feud upon the people's ecological involvement was really quite complex. Some of the more traditional men actually increased their fishing in the spring and summer, selling their surplus fish to the trader in order to clear up part of their debt. Most of this fish was later resold by the trader to more acculturated, heavy-drinking families for use as dog food during the following winter. Caribou hunting was also increased by some people in the village and the surplus meat was similarly sold by them to the trader to pay off their debts. In general, however, if one considers the activities of all band members, their subsistence pursuits have declined over the years as people have come to rely more and more upon Western commodities and new techniques for obtaining them. VanStone (1963) has documented the fact that increased wage labor opportunities and sedentariness, unpredictable and sometimes incomprehensible fluctuations in fur prices, and related social, economic, and ecological factors, have reduced and restricted Indian trapping throughout the eastern and western sub-Arctic (cf. also Usher 1971).

10. Dunning (1959: 119-121), for example, in discussing the strategies used by whites to win favor and power among native persons, notes the following features in the communities he considers: the spatial segregation of ethnic groups and the carefully controlled access of natives to "white" areas; the manipulation of wage labor, store prices, and assistance funds by whites; and the white monopoly over communication channels. Honigmann, in describing the situation at the northern settlement of Great Whale River, also points out the position of power enjoyed by the trader there because of his control over radio contact with the outside (1952: 515-516). Other useful studies of how outsiders and natives in the Arctic wield power and influence in their relations with one another are contained in Paine (ed., 1971).

11. Freilich notes that the high-status friend often functions as a major tension-reducer within the triadic social situation by providing people with a safe outlet for the expression of their feelings (1964: 532-533).

12. Cf. Honigmann (1952) for a discussion of symbiotic interdependence between ethnic groups in the North.

CHAPTER 6: THE HARE AND THE DOG

1. Weyer (1969: 100-101), Graburn (1969: 44), Birket-Smith (1929i: 170), Hara 1980: 190-191), and others have commented on the periodic, epidemic diseases which have wiped out large numbers of dogs in the North, and this may have also been a factor in keeping down the size of the aboriginal canine population among sub-Arctic Indians. Lantis (1980) examines the relationship between canine and human disease among the Alaskan Eskimo. Franklin described a unique occurrence among the Chipewyans in the early nineteenth century which adds a religious dimension to the scarcity and limited utility of dogs: "The Northern Indians suppose that they originally sprang from a dog; and, about five years ago, a superstitious fanatic so strongly pressed upon their minds the impropriety of employing these animals, to which they were related, for purposes of labour, that they universally resolved against using them any more, and, strange as it may seem, destroyed them. They now have to drag everything themselves on sledges. This laborious task falls most heavily on the women..." (1824: 160-161). The relevance of Athabascan mythology and religion to their treatment of dogs, as indicated here in the case of the Chipewyans, is more fully considered later in this chapter.

2. Cf. the same parallel described among the Kaska by Honigmann (1949: 55, 185).

3. Cf. also Honigmann (1949: 185), Nelson (1973: 9), Christian and Gardner (1977: 24-26), and Hara (1980: 279-281) for observations on the unstructured nature of childhood learning in Athabascan culture.

4. The raising of young dogs as pets by children is a common feature in other Athabascan groups (eg., see McClellan 1975b). The same process is noted by Driver among the Eskimo: "Puppies were even turned over to children who harnessed them to toy sleds: both the pups and the children were supposed to learn something of value from this experience" (1961: 466-467). Robert Flaherty captures just such a relationship on film in one of the segments of "Nanook of the North."

5. Demographic evidence for the widespread occurrence of female infanticide among the Hare and other Mackenzie Dene is presented by Helm (1980). A nineteenth century observer of the Hare, Bernard Ross, wrote that: "Male children are invariably more cherished and cared for than females. The latter are mere drudges, and obliged on all occasions to concede to their brother; and though female infanticide, formerly so prevalent, is now unknwon, still in seasons of starvation or times of danger, girls invariably fall the first sacrifices to the exigencies of these cases" (this 1866 source is quoted in Hara 1980: 266). Hara gives population figures for the Hare in the Fort Good Hope-Colville Lake area which show "that today [c. 1963] more males of age 10 to 30 have survived than females. The same reasons as mentioned by Ross may be partly responsible for this fact" (1980: 266). Osgood (1932: 76) supplies additional historical documentation concerning the prevalence of female infanticide in

the region. See also the demographic material for Alaskan and Yukon groups in McClellan (1975a).

6. Sharp (1976) offers an intriguing analysis of Chipewyan beliefs about men, wolves, women, and dogs, in which a number of positive symbolic links are made between man and wolf, and a parallel number of negative equivalents drawn between woman and dog. Among the Hare, as indicated, the negative meanings apply to female humans and female dogs; I am not aware of an extension of these ideas to wolves. However, Sharp does note several aspects of Chipewyan culture which parallel Hare patterns, including concepts of rein- carnation applied to canids, a canine origin myth for humans, and forms of brutality and child training that involve dogs.

7. Names are given by the Hare in both English and Athabascan: examples of the former are Gray, Buck, Aces, Horse, and Blacky. The English equivalents of some of the dog names in *deneké* are Butter, Skinny One, and Sharp Ears. The practice of naming dogs is, of course, not unique with the Hare: see for example Osgood on the Tanaina (1937: 161) and the Ingalik (1959: 28); McKennan on the Kutchin (1965: 58); Honigmann on the Kaska (1949: 56); and McClellan (1975b) on Yukon groups.Lantis.....As part of the Tanaina system of teknonymy, Osgood notes that: "Before a man marries, people call him by his own name and if he marries and has no children, they substitute the name of his dog" (1937: 161). McKennan points out a parallel process among the Chandalar Kutchin, among whom a childless man "might be known as the father of his dog" (1965: 58). Teknonymy involving dogs and children or childless adults is described among the Southern Tutchone, Tagish, Inland Tlingit, Atna and Dogribs by McClellan (1975b: 166).

8. Ashes are used especially for treating a dog who has lice, a practice which Honigmann also describes among the Kaska (1949: 56). Osgood (1940: 187; 1958: 230) notes that the Ingalik used charcoal and ashes to treat themselves: they employ these substances both internally, in the form of a drink, for stomach aches, and externally for wounds, but he does not refer to their use for treating dogs. McClellan (1975b: 164-165) also notes remedies for dog illnesses among the Yukon Indians.

9. Birket-Smith and de Laguna, in their monograph on the Eyak (1938: 57, 427- 429, 492), and McKennan, in his work on the Upper Tanana (1959: 92, 162- 163), have summarized much of the relevant literature on Athabascan atti- tudes towards dogs. McKennan's states: "The Upper Tanana hold the dog in peculiar reverence, and they will neither kill nor eat it although they have no rationalized explanation for this taboo.

"Such a regard for the dog is widespread among the Northern Athapaskans. The Hare, Dog-rib, and other Mackenize groups will not kill this animal, and the Chipewyan explain a similar taboo by claiming descent from the dog. This belief in canine descent is not found among the Alaskan Athapaskans, but the Han, Kutchin, Eyak, and Tanaina all hold the dog in such reverence that they will neither kill nor eat one. Many of these groups extend this taboo to forbid the eating of wolves also, but among the Upper Tanana the latter animal is occasionally eaten in times of famine" (1959: 162-163; the references cited by McKennan are omitted here).

Birket-Smith and deLaguna provide additional information on related beliefs among other Athabascan and Inuit groups, suggesting that: "It is probable that this attitude (of reverence) towards both dogs and wolf should be seen in a far wider connection, i.e., the typical circum-Pacific mythology to which Koppers has called attention" (1938, p.492). Other pertinent data relating to native beliefs and attitudes concerning dogs among the sub-Arctic Indians are given in Savishinsky (1974, 1975, 1990a, 1990b) and Sharp (1976).

10. An observer of the Tanaina (cited by Osgood 1937: 37) has written of their recourse to a similar strategy.

11. Helm writes as follows concerning the Slavey utilization of dogs as an emotional outlet: "The fact that any display of anger is so severely checked in the interpersonal situation gives special interest to the observations on the treatment of dogs. Toward dogs, all, but the men especially, give free vent to angry actions, shouting, swearing, and belabouring them. More than one man spoke, almost with pride, of a flaring rage toward a loafing sled-dog that was released by sending a bullet or an axe into the animal's skull. The excited, angry actions of the men towards their dogs are startling to the observer accustomed to their usual quiet, controlled behaviour. By the age of two, children begin practicing the raging and beating techniques of their fathers on any amenable dog" (1961: 89-90).

12. Many of the points in this section have benefited from the writings of Szasz (1969) and Goffman (1959).

13. The imagery resembles a point made by McLuhan, who speaks of art as a "radar environment" and the arts as "radar feedback" (1966: xi).

14. Cf. Birket-Smith (1929i: 112, 119); Birket-Smith and deLaguna (1938: 241, 427-429); Osgood (1932: 40; 1936b: 27; 1937: 32-33); McKennan (1959: 49; 1965: 32, 42); Weyer (1969: 100); Nelson (1973: 103); McClellan (1975b: 162-163); and the tribal ethnographies in Helm (ed., 1981).

15. Cf. Osgood (1937: 33; 1940: 451); Richardson (1851ii: 26, 30); Birket-Smith (1930: 19-26); Hearne (1795: 284); and Honigmann (1949: 54, 56, 64).

16. See the summary of Athabascan evidence given in note 8 (*supra*). Jenness states that dogs were "of little value for either food or clothing" among Canadian Indians (1967: 29). Brief summaries of the use of dogs for food by Native Americans are provided by Wissler (1957: 36) and Driver (1961: 34), who stress its rarity outside of certain geographic regions, and its general restriction to ceremonial and religious occasions.

17. Cf. Osgood (1940: 185-186; 1958: 259-260); Honigmann (1949: 187-188); Hara (1980: 190-192); Helm (1961: 74); and de Laguna (1969/1970: 26), who notes a taboo on non-canine pets among the Atna.

   Laughlin, in his analysis of hunting as a process, mentions "pets" (i.e., captured wild animals) as a source of feedback for hunters: they provide people with information about the nature of the game that they pursue. He adds that these "pets" are also a useful means for instructing children about animal behavior (1968: 310, 320). Although Laughlin does not discuss domesticated dogs from the cybernetic-feedback viewpoint suggested here, his analysis could be extended to include this aspect of their use.

18. Additional materials related to the points raised in this chapter are provided in Savishinsky (1975), where documentation is given concerning the scarcity and limited use of dogs in aboriginal northern cultures.

CHAPTER 7: CONCLUSIONS

1. Sindell (1968) has written of a comparable situation among the Cree at around the same period of time. Broch (1986: 148-151), describing schooling at Good Hope in the 1970s, observed how the white emphasis on competitiveness that was being taught there conflicted with the Dene ethic of not excelling or embarrassing others. Critical views of schooling in the Northwest, offered by a Dene from Good Hope and a Metis, can be found in Kakfwi and Overold (1977: 142-148). Remarks by others, who raise related questions about the appropriateness of Indian education, can be found in Berger (1977i: 90-93, 181-184) and Hodgkinson (1970). It should also be noted that serious attempts have been underway in the Northwest Territories, and elsewhere in northern Canada, to reform school curricula and bring them into line with the needs and backgrounds of the region's native populations. See, for example, Salisbury's account of recent changes in Cree education (1986: 117-131).

2. One recent attempt to make education programs more valuable to native people in the Territories has been the introduction of vocational training in such areas as nursing, mechanics, and heavy-duty equipment operation.

3. When the store was under private ownership, the people sold their pelts to the local trader, who then shipped them out to one of the large fur auction centers in the southern Canadian provinces. Except for a small percentage retained by the auction company, the trader earned close to the full auction value of the furs, which was anywhere from ten to one hundred percent more than what the trappers at the village received for the same skins.

4. Details given below of the negotiations and governmental agreements subsequently made by the Dene/Metis, Inuit, and Yukon Indians are largely taken from summaries and documents published by Canada's Department of Indian Affairs and Northern Development. Unless otherwise indicated, information and quotes from these publications are cited in abbreviated form in the text as Canada, DIAND.

5. Previous changes in the North's political economy had also been occasioned by outside exploitation of non-renewable resources: major developments involved gold in the Klondike in the 1890s, petroleum near Fort Norman in the 1920s, and prospecting and mining in the Northwest Territories in the 1920s and 1930s, including uranium mining at the eastern edge of Great Brear Lake (Fumoleau 1973: 263).

6. Dene in the Northwest Territories opposed the political accord because the proposed western boundary of Nunavut cuts across traditional Dene hunting and trapping lands.

7. Since completing the text, a third group — the Dogrib Nation — has also begun negitiating a regional settlement with the federal government (Canada, DIAND 1992c). A Sahtu Agreement was initialled in March 1993.

8. On perceptual and cognitive aspects of stress, see Opler (1967a), Lazarus (1966, 1967), and Klausner (1968).

9. The relation of biological and social rhythms to stress and release is discussed by Aginsky (1939), Chapple (1970), and Wallace (1970: 236).

10. Cf. the summary of the literature on stress resulting from "underload" and "overload" in McGrath (ed., 1970).

11. These points have been elaborated by Merton (1957), Honigmann (1967: 351ff), and Wallace (1970: 230-232).
12. Cultural data from a number of settings which illustrate this point may be found in the works of Langner and Michael (1963), Opler (1967a, 1967b), Honigmann (1967), Torrance (1968), and Kleinman (1991: 18-52).

References

Abel, Kerry and Jean Friesen (eds.). 1991. *Aboriginal Resource Use in Canada: Historical and Legal Aspects.* Winnipeg: University of Manitoba Press.

Acheson, Ann Welsh. 1981. "Old Crow, Yukon Territory." In Helm (ed., 1981).

Adams, William Y. 1963. *Shonto: A Study of the Role of the Trader in a Modern Navaho Community.* Washington, DC: Smithsonian Institution, Bureau of American Ethnology, Bulletin 188.

Aginsky, B. W. 1939. "Psychopathic trends in culture." *Culture and Personality* 7: 331-343.

Appley, Mortimer H. and Richard Trumbull (eds.). 1967. *Psychological Stress: Issues in Research.* New York: Appleton-Century-Crofts.

_____ 1967. "On the concept of psychological stress." In Appley and Trumbull (eds., 1967).

Arkow, Phil (ed.). 1984. *Dynamic Relationships in Practice: Animals in the Helping Professions.* Alameda, CA: The Latham Foundation.

Arsenian, John and Jean M. Arsenian. 1948. "Tough and easy cultures." *Psychiatry* 11: 377-385.

Asch, Michael. 1977. "The Dene economy." In Watkins (ed., 1977).

_____ 1982. "Dene self-determination and the study of hunter-gatherers in the modern world." In Eleanor Leacock and Richard Lee (eds.), *Politics and History in Band Societies.* Cambridge: Cambridge University Press.

_____ 1984. *Home and Native Land: Aboriginal Rights and the Canadian Constitution.* Toronto: Methuen.

Back, George. 1836. *Narrative of the Arctic Land Expedition... in the Years 1833, 1834, and 1835.* London: John Murray.

Bakan, David. 1971. *Disease, Pain and Sacrifice.* Boston: Beacon Press.

Balikci, Asen. 1960-1961. "Ethnic relations and the marginal man in Canada: a comment." *Human Organization* 19: 170-171.

_____ 1968. "The Netsilik Eskimo." In Lee and DeVore (eds., 1968).

Balikci, Asen and Ronald Cohen. 1963. "Community patterning in two northern trading posts." *Anthropologica* 5: 33-45.

Barger, W.K. 1981. "Great Whale River, Quebec." In Helm (ed., 1981).

Barnouw, Victor. 1950. "Acculturation and personality among the Wisconsin Chippewa." *American Anthropologist* 52: 19-27.

Barton, Barry. 1991. "Defending world markets for furs: aboriginal trapping, the anti-harvest movement and international trade law." In Abel and Friesen (eds., 1991).

Basso, Ellen. 1978. "The enemy of every tribe: 'bushman' images in northern Athapaskan narratives." *American Ethnologist* 5: 690-709.

Beck, Alan and Aaron Katcher. 1983. *Between People and Pets.* New York: Putnam.

Benedict, Ruth. 1934. *Patterns of Culture.* Boston: Houghton Mifflin.

Berger, Thomas. 1977. *Northern Frontier, Northern Homeland: The Report of the Mackenzie Valley Pipeline Inquiry: Volumes 1 and 2.* Toronto: Minister of Supply and Services Canada.

Bernard, Jessie. 1968. "The eudaemonists." In Klausner (ed., 1968).

Best, Steven. 1986. "The animal rights viewpoint." In J. Green and J. Smith (eds.), *Native Peoples and Renewable Resource Management.* Edmonton: Alberta Society of Professional Biologists.

_____ 1989. "Roundtable discussion on 'Aboriginal societies and the animal protection movement: rights, issues, and implications." In Keith and Saunders (eds., 1989).

Birket-Smith, Kaj. 1929. "The Caribou Eskimos." *Report of the Fifth Thule Expedition 1921-1924, Vol. 5.* 2 volumes. Copenhagen: Gyldendalske Boghandel, Nordiske Forlag.

_____ 1930. "Contributions to Chipewyan Ethnology." *Report of the Fifth Thule Expedition 1921-1924, Vol. 6, No. 3.* Copenhagen: Gyldendalske Boghandel, Nordisk Forlag.

Birket-Smith, Kaj and Frederica de Laguna. 1938. *The Eyak Indians of the Copper River Delta, Alaska.* Kobenhavn: Levin and Munksgaard.

Bishop, Charles. 1974. *The Northern Ojibwa and the Fur Trade: An Historical and Ecological Study.* Toronto: Holt, Rinehart and Winston of Canada.

Bishop, Charles and Shepard Krech III. 1980. "Matriorganization: the basis of aboriginal subarctic social organization." *Arctic Anthropology* 17: 34-45.

Black-Rogers, Mary. 1986. "Varieties of "starving": semantics and survival in the subarctic fur trade, 1750-1850." *Ethnohistory* 33: 353-383.

Blain, Eleanor M. 1991. "Dependency: Charles Bishop and the Northern Ojibwa." In Abel and Friesen (eds., 1991).

Blum, David. 1972. *Axial Pressure Profiles in Non-Newtonian Flow.* Unpublished doctoral dissertation. The City University of New York.

Broch, Harald Beyer. 1977/78. "Forest fire fighting — a light on Hare Indian social organization." *Folk* 19-20: 103-112.

_____ 1983. "The Bluefish River incident." In Adrian Tanner (ed.), *The Politics of Indianness: Case Studies of Native Ethnopolitics.* Social and Economic Papers No. 12. St. John's, Newfoundland: Memorial University of Newfoundland.

_____ 1986. *Woodland Trappers: Hare Indians of Northwestern Canada.* Bergen Studies in Social Anthropology No. 35. Bergin: University of Bergin.

Brody, Hugh. 1975. *The People's Land: Eskimos and Whites in the Eastern Arctic.* New York: Penguin.

_____ 1983. *Maps and Dreams.* New York: Pantheon.

_____ 1987. *Living Arctic: Hunters of the Canadian North.* London: Faber.

Buber, Martin. 1958. *I and Thou.* 2nd edition. Ronald Gregor Smith, translator. New York: Charles Scribner's Sons.

Bureau of American Ethnology. 1907. "Kawchodinne" (anonymous). In Frederick Webb Hodge (ed.), *Handbook of American Indians North of Mexico,* Vol. 1. Washington, DC: Bureau of American Ethnology, Bulletin 30, Part 1.

Burt, William H. and Richard P. Grossenheider. 1952. *A Field Guide to the Mammals.* 2nd revised edition. Boston: Houghton Mifflin.

Bustad, Leo. 1980. *Animals, Aging, and the Aged.* Minneapolis: University of Minnesota Press.

Canada, Department of Indian Affairs and Northern Development. 1976. *Mackenzie Valley Pipeline Inquiry, Summaries of Proceedings. Volume 4: Community Hearings.* Ottawa: Department of Indian Affairs and Northern Development.

_____ 1989. *The Dene/Metis Land Claim, Information Sheets Nos. 1, 2, 3, 4 and 5.* Ottawa: Department of Indian Affairs and Northern Development.

_____ 1990a. *Canada Agrees to a Request for Regional Negotiations on the Dene/Metis Claim: Backgrounder.* Ottawa: Department of Indian Affairs and Northern Development.

_____ 1990b. *Schedule of Indian Bands, Reserves and Settlements.* Ottawa: Department of Indian Affairs and Northern Development.

_____ 1992a. "Final Agreement reached on Tungavik Federation of Nunavut Claim." *Transition (1): 1, 5.* Ottawa: Department of Indian Affairs and Northern Development.

_____ 1992b. *Comprehensive Claims (February 1992).* Ottawa: Department of Indian Affairs and Northern Development.

_____ 1992c. "Dogrib Nation to pursue land claim." *Native Agenda: News (August 1992).* Ottawa: Department of Indian Affairs and Northern Development.

_____ Canada, House of Commons Standing Committee on Aboriginal Affairs and Northern Development [HC-SCAAND]. 1986. *The Fur Issue: Cultural Continuity, Economic Opportunity.* Ottawa: House of Commons.

Canby, Vincent. 1971. "Film: two parallel love stories with one object (review of 'Sunday Bloody Sunday)." *The New York Times,* September 22, 1971: 56.

Carpenter, Edmund S. 1959. *Eskimo.* With Frederick Varley and Robert Flaherty. Toronto: University of Toronto Press.

_____ 1961. "Ethnological clues for the interpretation of certain northeastern archaeological data." *Pennsylvania Archaeologist* 31: 148-150.

_____ 1970. *They Became What They Beheld.* New York: Outerbridge and Dienstfrey.

Chance, Norman A. 1966. *The Eskimo of North Alaska.* New York: Holt, Rinehart and Winston.

_____ 1968. "Implications of environmental stress: strategies of developmental change in the North." *Archives of Environmental Health 17:* 571-577.

Chapple, Eliot D. 1970. *Culture and Biological Man.* New York: Holt, Rinehart and Winston.

Chitty, Dennis. 1971. "The natural selection of self-regulatory behavior in animal populations." In Ian A. McLaren (ed.), *Natural Regulation of Animal Populations.* New York: Atherton Press.

Christian, Jane. 1989. "The northern Dene." *The World and I 4:* 648-659.

Christian, Jane and Peter Gardner. 1977. *The Individual in Northern Dene Thought and Communication: A Study in Sharing and Diversity.* Ottawa: National Museum of Man, National Museums of Canada, Mercury Series, Canadian Ethnology Service Paper No. 35.

Clancy, Peter. 1991. "State policy and the native trapper: post-war policy toward fur in the Northwest Territories." In Abel and Friesen (eds., 1991).

Clark, Annette M. 1970. "Koyukon Athabascan ceremonialism." *Western Canadian Journal of Anthropology* 2: 80-89.

_____ 1974. *The Athapaskans: Strangers of the North.* Ottawa: National Museum of Man, National Museums of Canada.

_____ 1975. "Upper Koyukon social culture: an overview." In Clark (ed., 1975).

278   The Trail of the Hare

_____ (ed). 1975. *Proceedings of the Northern Athapaskan Conference, 1971, 2 Volumes.*
    Ottawa: National Museum of Man, National Museums of Canada, Canadian
    Ethnology Service Paper No. 27.

Coates, Ken and W.R. Morrison. 1992. *The Alaska Highway in World War II: The U.S.
    Army of Occupation in Canada's Northwest.* Norman: University of Oklahoma Press.

Cofer, C.N. and M.H. Appley. 1964. *Motivation: Theory and Research.* New York: John
    Wiley and Sons.

Cohen, Ronald. 1962. *An Anthropological Survey of Communities in the Mackenzie-Slave
    Lake Region of Canada.* Ottawa: Northern Co-ordination and Research Centre,
    Department of Northern Affairs and National Resources.

Cohen, Ronald and Helgi Osterreich. 1967. "Analysis of 'Good Hope Tales' by Paul
    Voudrach." In *Contributions to Ethnology 5.* Ottawa: National Museum of Canada,
    Bulletin No. 228.

Cohen, Ronald and James W. VanStone. 1963. "Dependency and self-sufficiency in
    Chipewyan stories." In *Contributions to Anthropology 1961-1962, Part II.* Ottawa:
    National Museum of Canada, Bulletin No. 194.

Damas, David. 1963. *Igluligmiut Kinship and Local Groupings: A Structural Approach.*
    Ottawa: National Museum of Canada, Bulletin No. 196.

_____ 1968. "The diversity of Eskimo societies." In Lee and DeVore (eds., 1968).

_____ 1969a. (ed.). *Contributions to Anthropology: Band Societies. Proceedings of the 1965
    Conference on Band Organization.* Ottawa: National Museum of Canada, Bulletin
    No. 228.

_____ 1969b. (ed.). *Contributions to Anthropology: Ecological Essays. Proceedings of the
    1966 Conference on Cultural Ecology.* Ottawa: National Museum of Canada, Bulletin
    No. 230.

de Laguna, Frederica. 1969/70. "The Atna of the Copper River, Alaska: the world of
    men and animals." *Folk* 11/12: 17-26.

_____ 1975. "Matrilineal kin groups in northwestern North America." In Clark
    (ed., 1975).

de Laguna, Frederica and Catharine McClellan. 1981. "Ahtna." In Helm (ed., 1981).

Dene Nation and the Metis Association of the Northwest Territories. 1982. *Public
    Government for the People of the North.* Yellowknife: The Dene Nation and the Metis
    Association of the Northwest Territories.

Dice, Lee. 1943. *The Biotic Provinces of North America.* Ann Arbor: University of
    Michigan Press.

Dickason, Olive. 1992. *Canada's First Nations: A History of Founding Peoples from the
    Earliest Times.* Norman: University of Oklahoma Press.

Dostoyevsky, Fyodor. (no date). *Notes from a Dead House.* Moscow: Foreign Languages
    Publishing House.

Doxiadis, Constantinos. 1963. *Architecture in Transition.* London: Hutchinson and
    Co.

Driver, Harold. 1961. *Indians of North America.* Chicago: University of Chicago Press.

Dunning, R.W. 1959. "Ethnic relations and the marginal man in Canada." *Human
    Organization* 19: 117-122.

Durgin, Edward. 1974. *Brewing and Boozing: A Study of Drinking Patterns among the Hare
    Indians.* Unpublished doctoral dissertation, University of Oregon.

Dyen, Isidore and David Aberle. 1974. *Lexical Reconstruction: The Care of the Proto-
    Athapaskan Kinship System.* London: Cambridge University Press.

Ervin. A.M. 1969. "Conflicting styles of life in a northern Canadian town." *Arctic* 22: 90-105.

Evans-Pritchard, E.E. 1940. *The Nuer*. Oxford: The Clarendon Press.

Farnsworth, Clyde. 1992. "Canada to divide its northern land." *The New York Times* May 6, 1992: A17.

Fitchen, Janet. 1981. *Poverty in Rural America: A Case Study*. Boulder, CO: Westview Press.

Fogle, Bruce. 1983. *Pets and Their People*. New York: Viking.

Forde, C. Daryll. 1963. *Habitat, Economy, and Society*. New York: E.P. Dutton.

Foster, George. 1972. "The anatomy of envy: a study in symbolic behavior." *Current Anthropology* 13: 165-202.

Fox, M.W. 1965. *Canine Behavior*. Springfield, IL: Charles C. Thomas.

Franklin, John. 1824. *Narrative of a Journey to the Shores of the Polar Sea in the Years 1819-20-21-22*. 2nd ed. 2 volumes. London: John Murray.

Freeman, J.D. 1961. "On the concept of the kindred." *Journal of the Royal Anthropological Institute* 91: 192-220.

Freilich, Morris. 1964. "The natural triad in kinship and complex systems." *American Sociological Review* 29: 529-540.

French, Stewart. 1972. *Alaska Native Claims Settlement Act*. Montreal: Arctic Institute of North America.

Fumoleau, Rene. 1973. *As Long as This Land Shall Last: A History of Treaty 8 and Treaty 11, 1870-1939*. Toronto: McClelland and Stewart.

Gillespie, Beryl. 1975. "Territorial expansion of the Chipewyan in the 18th century." In Annette M. Clark (ed., 1975).

_____ 1981a. "Major fauna in the traditional economy." In Helm (ed., 1981).

_____ 1981b. "Territorial groups before 1821: Athapaskans of the Shield and the Mackenzie Drainage." In Helm (ed., 1981).

Gluckman, Max. 1963. "Gossip and scandal." *Current Anthropology* 4: 307-316.

_____ 1967. *Custom and Conflict in Africa*. New York: Barnes and Noble.

Goffman, Erving. 1959. *The Presentation of Self in Everyday Life*. Garden City, NY: Doubleday.

Goodenough, Ward. 1962. "Kindred and hamlet in Lakalai, New Britain." *Ethnology* 1: 5-12.

Graburn, Nelson H.H. 1969. *Eskimos Without Igloos*. Boston: Little, Brown and Co.

Graburn, Nelson and B. Stephen Strong. 1973. *Circumpolar Peoples: An Anthropological Perspective*. Pacific Palisades, CA: Goodyear Publishing Co.

Gregor, Thomas. 1977. *Mehinaku: The Drama of Daily Life in a Brazilian Indian Village*. Chicago: University of Chicago Press.

Hall, Edward T. 1969. *The Hidden Dimension*. Garden City, NY: Doubleday.

Hall, Sam. 1988. *The Fourth World: The Heritage of the Arctic and Its Destruction*. New York: Vintage Books.

Hallowell, A. Irving. 1941. "The social function of anxiety in a primitive society." *American Sociological Review* 7: 869-881.

_____ 1946. "Some psychological characteristics of the northeastern Indians." In Frederick Johnson (ed.), *Man in Northeastern North America*. Andover: Papers of the Robert S. Peabody Foundation for Archaeology, No. III.

Hara, Hiroko Sue. 1980. *The Hare Indians and Their World*. Ottawa: National Museums of Canada, Canadian Ethnology Service Paper No. 63.

Hatt, Gudmund. 1969. "Arctic skin clothing in Eurasia and America: an ethnographic study." *Arctic Anthropology* 5: 3-132.

Hearne, Samuel. 1795. *A Journey from Prince of Wales's Fort in Hudson's Bay, to the Northern Ocean... In the Years 1769, 1770, 1771, and 1772.* London: A Strahan and T. Cadell.

Heffley, Sheri. 1981. "The relationship between northern Athapaskan settlement patterns and resource distribution: an application of Horn's model." In Bruce Winterhalder and Eric Alden Smith (eds.), *Hunter-Gatherer Foraging Strategies: Ethnographic and Archaeological Analyses.* Chicago: University of Chicago Press.

Heidegger, Martin. 1962. *Being and Time.* John Macquarrie and Edward Robinson, translators. New York: Harper and Brothers.

Helm, June. 1961. *The Lynx Point People: The Dynamics of a Northern Athapaskan Band.* Ottawa: National Museum of Canada, Bulletin No. 176.

———— 1965a. "Bilaterality in the socioterritorial organization of the Arctic drainage Dene." *Ethnology* 4: 361-385.

———— 1965b. "Patterns of allocation among the Arctic drainage Dene." In June Helm (ed.), *Essays in Economic Anthropology: Proceedings of the 1965 Annual Spring Meeting of the American Ethnological Society.* Seattle: University of Washington Press.

———— 1968a. "The nature of Dogrib socioterritorial groups." In Lee and DeVore (eds., 1968).

———— 1968b. "The statistics of kin marriage: a non Australian example." In Lee and DeVore (eds., 1968).

———— 1969a. "Remarks on the methodology of band composition analysis." In Damas (ed., 1969a).

———— 1969b. "A method of statistical analysis of primary relative bonds in community composition." In Damas (ed., 1969a).

———— 1969c. "Relationship between settlement pattern and community pattern." in Damas (ed., 1969b).

———— 1969d. "Discussion." In Damas (ed., 1969a).

———— 1980. "Female infanticide, European diseases, and population levels among the Mackenzie Dene." *American Ethnologist* 7: 259-285.

———— (ed.). 1981. *The Subarctic. Handbook of North American Indians, Vol. 6.* Washington, DC: Smithsonian Institution.

Helm, June and David Damas. 1963. "The contact-traditional all-native community of the Canadian North: the Upper Mackenzie 'bush' Athapaskans and the Igluligmiut." *Anthropologica* 5: 9-21.

Helm, June and Eleanor Burke Leacock. 1971. "The hunting tribes of Subarctic Canada." In Eleanor Burke Leacock and June Helm (eds.), *North American Indians in Historical Perspective.* New York: Random House.

Helm, June and Nancy O. Lurie. 1961. *The Subsistence Economy of the Dogrib Indians of Lac la Martre in the Mackenzie District of the Northwest Territories.* Ottawa: Northern Co-ordination and Research Centre, Department of Northern Affairs and National Resources.

———— 1966. *The Dogrib Handgame.* Ottawa: National Museum of Canada, Bulletin No. 205.

Helm, June, Edward S. Rogers, and James G. E. Smith. 1981. "Intercultural relations and cultural change in the shield and Mackenzie borderlands." In Helm (ed., 1981).

Helm, June et. al. 1975. "The contact history of the subarctic Athapaskans: an overview." In Clark (ed., 1975).

Henriksen, Georg. 1973. *Hunters in the Barrens: The Naskapi on the Edge of the White Man's World*. St. John's, Newfoundland: Newfoundland Social and Economic Studies, Institute of Social and Economic Research, Memorial University of Newfoundland.

_____ 1981. "Davis Inlet, Labrador." In Helm (ed., 1981).

Herscovici, Alan. 1985. *Second Nature: The Animal Rights Controversy*. Montreal: CBC Enterprises.

Hiatt, L.R. 1968. "Ownership and use of land among the Australian Aborigines." In Lee and DeVore (eds., 1968).

Hodgkinson, Jean. 1970. "Is northern education meaningful?" *Western Canadian Journal of Anthropology* 2: 156-163.

Hoijer, Harry. 1966. "Hare phonology: an historical study." *Language* 42: 499-507.

Homans, George. 1950. *The Human Group*. New York: Harcourt, Brace and Co.

Honigmann, John J. 1946. *Ethnography and Acculturation of the Fort Nelson Slave*. New Haven: Yale University Publications in Anthropology No. 33.

_____ 1947. "Witch-fear in post-contact Kaska society." *American Anthropologist* 49: 222-243.

_____ 1949. *Culture and Ethos of Kaska Society*. New Haven: Yale University Publications in Anthropology No. 40.

_____ 1952. "Intercultural relations at Great Whale River." *American Anthropologist* 54: 510-522.

_____ 1954. *The Kaska Indians: An Ethnographic Reconstruction*. New Haven: Yale University Publications in Anthropology No. 51.

_____ 1967. *Personality in Culture*. New York: Harper and Row.

_____ 1968. "Interpersonal relations in atomistic societies." *Human Organization* 27: 220-229.

_____ 1975. "Psychological traits in northern Athapaskan culture." In Clark (ed., 1975).

_____ 1981a. "Expressive aspects of subarctic Indian culture." In Helm (ed., 1981).

_____ 1981b. "Kaska." In Helm (ed., 1981).

Honigmann, John J. and Irma Honigmann. 1965. *Eskimo Townsmen*. Ottawa: Canadian Research Centre for Anthropology, University of Ottawa.

Hooper, W.H. 1853. *Ten Months among the Tents of the Tuski*. London: John Murray.

Hosley, Edward. 1980. "The aboriginal social organization of the Pacific drainage Dene: the matrilineal basis." *Arctic Anthropology* 17: 12-16.

Hultkrantz, Ake. 1973. "The Hare Indians: notes on their traditional culture and religion, past and present." *Ethnos* 38: 113-152.

Hurlbert, Janice. 1962. *Age as a Factor in the Social Organization of the Hare Indians of Fort Good Hope*. N.W.T. Ottawa: Northern Co-ordination and Research Centre, Department of Northern Affairs and National Resources.

Innis, Harold A. 1962. *The Fur Trade in Canada*. Revised edition. New Haven: Yale University Press.

James, Preston. 1957. *A Geography of Man*. Boston: Ginn and Company.

Jarvenpa, Robert. 1976. "Spatial and ecological factors in the annual economic cycle of the English River Band of Chipewyan. *Arctic Anthropology* 13: 43-69.

_____ 1977. "Subarctic Indian trappers and band society: the economics of male mobility." *Human Ecology* 5: 223-259.

———— 1980. *The Trappers of Patunak: Toward a Spatial Ecology of Modern Hunters.* Ottawa: National Museum of Man, National Museums of Canada, Canadian Ethnology Service, Mercury Series Paper No. 67.

Jarvenpa, Robert and Hetty Jo Brumbach. 1988. "Socio-spatial organization and decision-making processes: observations from the Chipewyan." *American Anthropologist* 90: 598-618.

Jarvie, I.C. 1969. "The problem of ethical integrity in participant observation." *Current Anthropology* 10: 505-508.

Jenness, Diamond. 1967. *The Indians of Canada.* 6th edition. Ottawa: National Museum of Canada, Bulletin No. 65.

Kakfwi, Steven and Bob Overold. 1977. "The schools." In Watkins (ed., 1977).

Keats, John. 1817. "To George and Thomas Keats." In John Keats, *Selected Poems and Letters* (1959). Douglas Bush, ed. Boston: Houghton Mifflin Co.

Keith, George. 1890. "Letters to the Hon. Roderic McKenzie, 1807-1817." In L.R. Masson (ed.), *Les Bourgeois de la Compagnie du Nord-ouest.* Deuxième Série. Quebec: A Coté.

Keith, Robert and Alan Saunders (eds.). 1988. *A Question of Rights: Northern Wildlife Management and the Anti-harvest Movement.* Ottawa: Canadian Arctic Resources Committee.

Kelsall, John P. 1968. *The Migratory Barren-ground Caribou of Canada.* Ottawa: Canadian Wildlife Service, Department of Indian Affairs and Northern Development.

Kelsall, John P., Vernon D. Hawley and Donald C. Thomas. 1971. "Distribution and abundace of muskoxen north of Great Bear Lake." *Arctic* 24: 157-161.

King, Richard. 1836. *Narrative of a Journey to the Shores of the Arctic Ocean in 1833, 1834, and 1835.* 2 volumes. London: R. Bentley.

Klein, Esther. 1986. "Remarks." In Canada, House of Commons Standing Committee on Aboriginal Affairs and Northern Development, *The Fur Issue: Cultural Continuity, Economic Opportunity.* Ottawa: Queen's Printer.

Klausner, Samuel Z. (ed.). 1968. *Why Man Takes Chances: Studies in Stress-seeking.* Garden City, NY: Doubleday.

———— 1968. "The intermingling of pain and pleasure: the stress-seeking personality in its social context." In Klausner (ed., 1968).

Kleinman, Arthur. 1991. *Rethinking Psychiatry: From Cultural Category to Personal Experience.* New York: The Free Press.

Kluckhohn, Clyde and Dorothea Leighton. 1962. *The Navaho.* Revised edition. Garden City, NY: Doubleday.

Koolage, William. 1976. "Differential adaptations of Athapaskans and other native ethnic groups to a Canadian northern town." *Arctic Anthropology* 13: 70-83.

Krech, Shepard III. 1978a. "Disease, starvation and northern Athapaskan social organization." *American Ethnologist* 5: 710-732.

———— 1978b. "On the aboriginal population of the Kutchin." *Arctic Anthropology* 15: 89-104.

———— 1979. "Interethnic relations in the lower Mackenzie River region." *Arctic Anthropology* 16: 102-122.

———— 1980a. "Northern Athapaskan ethnology in the 1970s." *Annual Review of Anthropology* 9: 83-100.

———— 1980b. "Introduction. "Reconsiderations" and Ethnohistorical research."

Arctic Anthropology 17: 1-11.

_____ (ed.). 1981. *Indians, Animals, and the Fur Trade: A Critique of Keepers of the Game*. Athens, GA: University of Georgia Press.

_____ 1983. "The influence of disease and the fur trade on Arctic drainage lowlands Dene, 1800-1850." *Journal of Anthropological Research* 39: 123-146.

Kroeber, A.L. 1939. "Cultural and natural areas of native North America." *University of California Publications in American Archaeology and Ethnology* 38. Berkeley, CA: University of California Press.

LaBarre, Weston. 1971. "Materials for a history of studies of crisis cults: a bibliographic essay." *Current Anthropology* 12: 3-44.

Landes, Ruth. 1937a. "The Ojibwa of Canada." In Margaret Mead (ed.), *Cooperation and Competition among Primitive Peoples*. New York: McGraw-Hill.

_____ 1937b. "The personality of the Ojibwa." *Character and Personality* 6: 51-60.

Langner, Thomas S. and Stanley T. Michael. 1963. *Life Stress and Mental Health: The Midtown Manhattan Study, Volume II*. New York: The Free Press.

Lanoue, Guy. 1981. "Flexibility in Hare social organization." *Canadian Journal of Native Studies* 1: 259-276.

Lantis, Margaret. 1980. "Changes in the Aalaskan Eskimo relation of man to dog and their effect on two human diseases." *Arctic Anthropology* 17 (1): 1-25.

Laughlin, William. 1968. "Hunting: an integrating biobehavior system and its evolutionary importance." In Lee and DeVore (eds., 1968).

Lawrence, Raymond. 1993. "Our land: Inuit dream of Nunavut now a reality." *Transition* 6 (6): 1, 6, 8.

Lazarus, Richard S. 1966. *Psychological Stress and the Coping Process*. New York: McGraw-Hill.

_____ 1967. "Cognitive and personality factors underlying threat and coping." in Appley and Trumbull (eds., 1967).

Leacock, Eleanor. 1954. *The Montagnais 'Hunting Territory' and the Fur Trade*. American Anthropological Association Memoir No. 78, 56, No 5, Part 2.

_____ 1969. "The Montagnais-Naskapi band." In Damas (ed., 1969a).

Lee, Richard B. 1968 "What hunters do for a living, or how to make out on scarce resources." In Lee and DeVore (eds., 1968).

_____ 1969. "Kung Bushman subsistence: an input-output analysis." In Damas (ed., 1969b).

Lee, Richard B. and Irven DeVore (eds.). 1968. *Man the Hunter*. Chicago: Aldine Publishing Co.

_____ 1968. "Problems in the study of hunters and gatherers." In Lee and DeVore (eds., 1968).

Lefroy, John Henry. 1938. "Sir Henry Lefroy's journey to the North-West in 1843-44." W.S. Wallace, editor. *Transactions of the Royal Society of Canada, Section II*.

Levinson, Boris. 1972. *Pets and Human Development*. Springfield, IL: Charles C. Thomas.

Lips, Julius. 1937. "Public opinion and mutual assistance among the Montagnais-Naskapi." *American Anthropologist* 39: 222-228.

Lopata, Helen. 1979. *Women as Widows*. New York: Elsevier.

Lorenz, Konrad. 1954. *Man Meets Dog*. London: Methuen.

Lubart, J.M. 1969."Psychodynamic problems of adaptation — Mackenzie Delta Eskimos." *Mackenzie Delta Research Project, Report No. 7*. Ottawa: Northern Science

Research Group, Department of Indian Affairs and Northern Development.

Luomala, Katherine. 1960. "The native dog in the Polynesian system of values." In Stanley Diamond (ed.), *Culture in History: Essays in Honor of Paul Radin*. New York: Columbia University Press.

Mackenzie, Alexander. 1801. *Voyages from Montreal on the River St. Laurence, Through the Continent of North America, to the Frozen and Pacific oceans; in the Years 1789 and 1793*. London: R. Noble.

MacNeish, June Helm. 1956. "Leadership among the northeastern Athabascans." *Anthropologica* 2: 131-164.

———— 1960. "Kin terms of the Arctic drainage Dene: Hare, Slavey, Chipewyan." *American Anthropologist* 62: 279-295.

Marsh, James. 1985. "Mackenzie Valley pipeline." *The Canadian Encyclopedia Vol. II: 1061-1062*. Edmonton: Hurtig Publishers.

Marshall, S.L.A. 1968. "The better part of man's nature." In Klausner (ed., 1968).

Martin, Calvin. 1978. *Keepers of the Game: Indian-animal Relationships and the Fur Trade*. Berkeley: University of California Press.

Mauss, Marcel. 1905-05. "Essai sur les variations saisonnières des sociétés eskimos. Essai de morphologie sociale." *L'année Sociologique* 9: 39-132.

May, Rollo. 1967. *Existential Psychotherapy*. Toronto: Canadian Broadcasting Corporation, CBC Publications.

McClellan, Catharine. 1964. "Culture contacts in the early historic period in northwestern North America." *Arctic Anthropology* 2: 3-15.

———— 1969. "Discussion." In Damas (ed., 1969a).

———— 1975a."Feuding and warfare among Northwestern Athapaskans." In Annette M. Clark (ed., 1975).

———— 1975b. *My Old People Say: An Ethnographic Survey of Southern Yukon Territory*. 2 Parts. Ottawa: National Museum of Man, Publications in Ethnology 6.

———— 1981a."Tagish." In Helm (ed., 1981).

———— 1981b."Tutchone." In Helm (ed., 1981).

———— 1981c."Intercultural relations and cultural change in the Cordillera." In Helm (ed., 1981).

———— 1981d."Inland Tlingit." In Helm (ed., 1981).

———— 1987. *Part of the Land, Part of the Water: A History of the Yukon Indians*. Vancouver: Douglas and McIntyre.

———— In Press. "Travel." In David Yesner (ed.), volume to appear in the Aurora Series, Alaska Anthropological Association.

McGrath, Joseph E. (ed.). 1970. *Social and Psychological Factors in Stress*. New York: Holt, Rinehart and Winston.

———— 1970b. "A conceptual formulation for research on stress." In McGrath (ed., 1970).

McKennan, Robert. 1959. *The Upper Tanana Indians*. New Haven: Yale University Publications in Anthropology No. 55.

———— 1965. *The Chandalar Kutchin*. Montreal: Arctic Institute of North America, Technical Paper No 17.

McLean, John. 1932. *Notes of a Twenty-five Years' Service in the Hudson's Bay Territory*. W.S. Wallace, ed. Toronto: The Champlain Society.

McLuhan, Marshall. 1966. *Understanding Media: The Extensions of Man*. New York: New American Library.

Mead, Margaret. 1968. *Coming of Age in Samoa*. New York: William Morrow.
Meggitt, M.J. 1965. "The association between Australian Aborigines and dingoes." In Anthony Leeds and Andrew P. Vayda (eds.), *Man, Culture, and Animals*. Washington, DC: American Association for the Advancement of Science, Publication No. 78.
Merton, Robert K. 1957. *Social Theory and Social Structure*. Revised edition. Glencoe, IL: The Free Press.
Miller, J.R. 1991. *Skyscrapers Hide the Heavens: A History of Indian-white Relations in Canada*. Revised edition. Toronto: University of Toronto Press.
Mooney, James. 1928. "The aboriginal population of America north of Mexico." *Smithsonian Miscellaneous Collections* 80, No. 7. Washington, DC: Smithsonian Institution.
Murdock, George Peter. 1949. *Social Structure*. New York: Macmillan.
_____ 1968. "The current status of the world's hunting and gathering peoples." In Lee and DeVore (eds., 1968).
Murphy, Robert F. 1964. "Social distance and the veil." *American Anthropologist* 66: 1257-1274.
Murphy, Robert F. and Julian H. Steward. 1956. "Tappers and trappers: parallel process in acculturation." *Economic Development and Cultural Change* 4: 335-355.
Nadel, S.F. 1954. "Witchcraft in four African societies." *American Anthropologist* 54: 18-29.
Narroll, Raoul. 1962. *Data Quality Control — A New Research Technique: Prolegomena to a Cross-cultural Study of Culture Stress*. New York: The Free Press of Glencoe.
Nelson, Richard. 1973. *Hunters of the Northern Forest: Designs for Survival among the Alaskan Kutchin*. Chicago: University of Chicago Press.
Netting, Robert McC. 1964. "Beer as a locus of value among the West African Kofyar." *American Anthropologist* 66: 375-384.
_____ 1977. *Cultural Eecology*. Menlo Park, CA: Benjamin/Cummings Publishing Co.
Noble, William C. 1981. "Prehistory of the Great Slave Lake and Great Bear Lake Region." In Helm (ed., 1981).
Opler, Marvin. 1967a. *Culture and Social Psychiatry*. New York: Atherton.
_____ 1967b. "Cultural induction of stress." In Appley and Trumbull (eds., 1967).
Opler, Morris. 1945. "Themes as dynamic forces in culture." *American Journal of Sociology* 51: 198-206.
_____ 1946. "An application of the theory of themes in culture." *Journal of the Washington Academy of Sciences* 36: 136-166.
_____ 1965. *An Apache Life-way*. New York: Cooper Square Publishers.
Osgood, Cornelius. 1932. *The Ethnography of the Geat Bear Lake Indians*. Ottawa: National Museum of Canada.
_____ 1936a. *The Distribution of the Northern Athapaskan Indians*. New Haven: Yale University Publications in Anthropology No. 7.
_____ 1936b. *Contributions to the Ethnography of the Kutchin*. New Haven: Yale University Publications in Anthropology No. 14.
_____ 1937. *The Ethnography of the Tanaina*. New Haven: Yale University Publications in Anthropology No. 16.
_____ 1940. *Ingalik Material Culture*. New Haven: Yale University Publications in Anthropology No. 22.

_____ 1958. *Ingalik Social Culture*. New Haven: Yale University Publications in Anthropology No. 53.

_____ 1959. *Ingalik Mental Culture*. New Haven: Yale University Publications in Anthropology No. 56.

_____ 1971. *The Han Indians*. New Haven: Yale University Publications in Anthropology No. 74.

_____ 1975."An ethnographical map of Great Bear Lake." In Annette M. Clark (ed., 1975).

Oswalt, Wendell H. 1966. *This Land Was Theirs*. New York: John Wiley and Sons.

Paine, Robert. 1971. "A theory of patronage and brokerage." In Paine (ed., 1971).

_____ (ed.). 1971. *Patrons and Brokers in the East Arctic*. St. John's, Newfoundland: Newfoundland Social and Economic Papers No. 2, Institute of Social and Economic Research, Memorial University of Newfoundland.

Pascal, Gerald R. 1951. "Psychological deficit as a function of stress and constitution." *Journal of Personality* 20: 175-187.

Pehrson, Robert N. 1964. *The Bilateral Network of Social Relations in Konkama Lapp District*. Oslo: Samiske Samlinger, Bind VII, Utgitt av Norsk Folkemuseum, Universitetsforlaget.

Pepitone, Albert. 1967. "Self, social environment and stress." In Appley and Trumbull (eds., 1967).

Peterson, R. 1955. *North American Moose*. Toronto: University of Toronto Press.

Petitot, Emile. 1875. "Geographie de l'Athabaskaw-Mackenzie et des grands lacs du basin arctique." *Sociètè de Geographie, 6me Serie* 10: 5-42, 126-183, 242-290.

_____ 1876. *Dictionnaire de le Langue Dene-dindjie... Precedé d'une Monographie de Dene-dindjie*. Paris: Ernest Leroux.

_____ 1889. *Quinze ans Sous le Cercle Polaire*. Paris: E. Dentu.

_____ 1891. *Autour du Grand Lac des Esclaves*. Paris: Albert Savine.

Philips, R.A.J. 1967. *Canada's north*. Toronto: Macmillan Company of Canada.

Piers, Gerhart and Milton B. Singer. 1953. *Shame and Guilt: A Psychoanalytic and a Cultural Study*. Springfield, IL: Charles C. Thomas.

Preston, Richard J. III. 1979. "The development of self-control in the eastern Cree life cycle." In K. Ishwaran (ed.), *Childhood and Adolescence in Canada*. Toronto: McGraw-Hill Ryerson.

_____ 1991. "Interference and its consequences: an east Cree variant of deviance?" *Anthropologica* 33: 69-80.

Rand. A.L. 1945. *Mammals of Yukon, Canada*. Ottawa: National Museum of Canada, Bulletin No. 100.

Rich. E.E. 1967. *The Fur Trade and the Northwest to 1857*. Toronto: McClelland and Stewart.

Richardson, John. 1851. *Arctic Searching Expedition*. 2 volumes. London: Longman, Brown, Green, and Longmans.

Riches, David. 1982. *Northern Nomadic Hunter-gatherers: A Humanistic Approach*. New York: Academic Press.

Ridington, Robin. 1988. *Trail to Heaven: Knowledge and Narrative in a Northern Native Community*. Iowa City, IO: University of Iowa Press.

Rogers, Edward S. 1969a. "Band organization among the Indians of eastern Subarctic Canada." In Damas (ed., 1969a).

_____ 1969b. "Natural environment — social organization — witchcraft: Cree versus Ojibwa — a test case." In Damas (ed., 1969b).

Rogers, Edward and J.G.E. Smith. 1981. "Environment and culture in the shield and Mackenzie borderlands." In Helm (ed., 1981).

Rowe, J.S. 1959. *Forest Regions of Canada.* Ottawa: Forestry Branch, Department of Northern Affairs and Natural Resources, Bulletin No. 123.

Rushforth, Scott. 1977. "Country food." In Watkins (ed., 1977).

_____ 1984. *Bear Lake Athapaskan Kinship and Task Group Formation.* Ottawa: National Museum of Man, National Museums of Canada, Mercury Series, Canadian Ethnology Service Paper No. 96.

Sahlins, Marshall. 1968. "Notes on the original affluent society." In Lee and DeVore (eds., 1968).

Salisbury, Richard. 1986. *A Homeland for the Cree: Regional Development in James Bay 1971-1981.* Montreal: McGill-Queen's University Press.

Saum, Lewis O. 1965. *The Fur Trader and the Indian.* Seattle: University of Washington Press.

Savishinsky, Joel S. 1970a. *Stress and Mobility in an Arctic Community: The Hare Indians of Colville Lake, Northwest Territories.* Unpublished doctoral dissertation. Cornell University.

_____ 1970b "Kinship and the expression of values in an Athabascan bush community." *Western Canadian Journal of Anthropology* 2: 31-59.

_____ 1971. "Mobility as an aspect of stress in an arctic community." *American Anthropologist* 73: 604-618.

_____ 1972a. "Coping with feuding: the missionary, the fur trader, and the ethnographer." *Human Organization* 31: 281-290.

_____ 1972b. "Comment on 'The anatomy of envy' by George Foster." *Current Anthropology* 13: 195.

_____ 1974. "The child is father to the dog: canines and personality processes in an Arctic community." *Human Development* 17: 460-466.

_____ 1975. "The dog and the Hare: canine culture in an Athapaskan band." In Annette M. Clark (ed., 1975).

_____ 1976. "On getting married and staying connected: family, kinship and history in a Hare Indian community." In K. Ishwaran (ed.), *The Canadian Family,* revised edition. Toronto: Holt, Rinehart and Winston of Canada.

_____ 1977. "A thematic analysis of drinking behavior in a Hare Indian community." *Papers in Anthropology* 18: 43-60.

_____ 1978. "Trapping, survival strategies, and environmental involvement: a case study from the Canadian sub-Arctic." *Human Ecology* 6: 1-25.

_____ 1982. "Vicarious emotions and cultural restraint." *Journal of Psychoanalytic Anthropology* 5: 115-135.

_____ 1983. "Pet ideas: the domestication of animals, human behavior, and human emotions." In Aaron Katcher and Alan Beck (eds.), *New Perspectives on Our Lives with Companion Animals.* Philadelphia: University of Pennsylvania Press.

_____ 1990a. "Ambiguity, animals, and abuse." *Anthrozoos* 3: 222-223.

_____ 1990b. "The Hare and their dogs: human-animal bonds in an Arctic community. " *The World and I* 5: 642-653.

_____ 1991a. "Free shows and cheap thrills: staged deviance in the Arctic and the Bahamas." In Morris Freilich, Douglas Raybeck and Joel Savishinsky (eds.), *Deviance: Anthropological Perspectives.* New York: Bergin and Garvey.

_____ 1991b. "The ambiguities of alcohol: deviance, drinking and meaning in a Canadian native community." *Anthropologica* 33: 81-98.

_____ 1991c. *The Ends of Time: Life and Work in a Nursing Home.* Westport, CT: Greenwood Publishing.

Savishinsky, Joel S. and Susan B. Frimmer. 1973. *The Middle Ground: Social Change in an Arctic Community, 1967-1971.* Ottawa: National Museum of Man, National Museums of Canada, Mercury Publications No. 7.

_____ 1980. "The cultural context of drinking in a Hare Indian community." In K. Ishwaran (ed.), *Canadian Families: Ethnic Variations.* Toronto: McGraw-Hill Ryerson.

Savishinsky, Joel S. and Hiroko Sue Hara. 1981. "Hare." In Helm (ed., 1981).

Schwartz, Barry. 1968. "The social psychology of privacy." *American Journal of Sociology* 73: 741-752.

Scott, J.P. 1963. "The process of primary socialization in canine and human infants." *Monographs of the Society for Research in Child Development,* Serial No. 85, 28, No 1.

Selye, Hans. 1956. *The Stress of Life.* New York: McGraw-Hill.

Serpell, James. 1986. *In the Company of Animals: A Study of Human-Animal Relationships.* Oxford: Basil Blackwell.

Service, Elman R. 1962. *Primitive Social Organization.* New York: Random House.

_____ 1966. *The Hunters.* Englewood Cliffs, NJ: Prentice-Hall.

_____ 1971. *Primitive Social Organization.* 2nd ed. New York: Random House.

Sharp, Henry S. 1975. "Trapping and welfare: the economics of trapping in a northern Saskatchewan Chipewyan village." *Anthropologica* 17: 29-44.

_____ 1976. "Man : Wolf : Woman : Dog." *Arctic Anthropology* 13: 25-34.

_____ 1977. "The Caribou-eater Chipewyan: bilaterality, strategies of caribou hunting, and the fur trade." *Arctic Anthropology* 14: 35-40.

_____ 1978. "Comparative ethnology of the wolf and the Chipewyan." In Roberta L. Hall and Henry S. Sharp (eds.), *Wolf and Man: Evolution in Parallel.* New York: Academic Press.

_____ 1988. *The Transformation of Bigfoot: Maleness, Power, and Belief Among the Chipewyan.* Washington, DC: Smithsonian Institution Press.

Simmel, Georg. 1964. *Conflict and the Web of Group Affiliations.* Kurt H. Wolff and Reinhard Bendix, translators. New York: The Free Press.

Sindell, Peter. 1968. "Some discontinuities in the enculturation of Mistassini Cree children." In Norman Chance (ed.), *Conflict in Culture: Problems of Developmental Change Among the Cree.* Ottawa: Canadian Research Centre for Anthropology, Saint Paul University.

Slobodin, Richard. 1960a. "Some social functions of Kutchin anxiety." *American Anthropologist* 62: 122-133.

_____ 1960b. "Eastern Kutchin warfare." *Anthropologica* 2: 76-94.

_____ 1962. *Band Organization of the Peel River Kutchin.* Ottawa: National Museum of Canada, Bulletin No. 179.

_____ 1969. "Leadership and participation in a Kutchin trapping party." In Damas (ed., 1969a).

_____ 1970. "Kutchin concepts of reincarnation." *Western Canadian Journal of Anthropology* 2: 67-79.

Smith, D.G. 1968. "The Mackenzie Delta — domestic economy of the native peoples. A preliminary study." *Mackenzie Delta Research Project, Report No. 3.* Ottawa: Northern Co-ordination and Research Centre, Department of Indian

Affairs and Northern Development.

Smith, David M. 1973. *Inkonze: Magico-religious Beliefs of Contact-traditional Chipewyan Trading at Fort Resolution, NWT, Canada.* Ottawa: National Museum of Man, Mercury Series, Ethnology Division Paper 6.

_____ 1976. "Cultural and ecological change: the Chipewyan of Fort Resolution." *Arctic Anthropology* 13: 35-42.

_____ 1981. "Fort Resolution, Northwest Territories." In Helm (ed., 1981).

_____ 1985. "Big stone foundations: manifest meaning in Chipewyan myths." *Journal of American Culture* 8: 73-77.

_____ 1990. "The Chipewyan medicine fight in cultural and ecological perspective." In Robert Winthrop (ed.), *Culture and the Anthropological Tradition: Essays in Honor of Robert F. Spencer.* Washington, DC: University Press of America.

_____ 1992. "The dynamics of a Dene struggle for self-determination." *Anthropologica* 34: 21-49.

Smith, J.G.E. 1970. "The Chipewyan hunting group in a village context." *Western Canadian Journal of Anthropology* 2: 31-59.

_____ 1975. "The ecological basis of Chipewyan socio-territorial organization." In Annette M. Clark (ed., 1975).

_____ 1976. "Local band organization of the Caribou-Eater Chipewyan." *Arctic Anthropology* 13: 12-24.

_____ 1978. "The Emergence of the micro-urban village among the Caribou-eater Chipewyan." *Human Organization* 37: 38-49.

_____ 1979."Leadership among the Indians of the northern woodlands." In Robert Hinshaw (ed.), *Currents in Anthropology: Essays in Honor of Sol Tax.* The Hague: Mouton.

Smith, Lorne. 1972. "The mechanical dog team: a study of the ski-doo in the Canadian Arctic." *Arctic Anthropology* 9: 1-9.

Sommer, Robert. 1969. *Personal Space: The Behavioral Basis of Design.* Englewood Cliffs, NJ: Prentice-Hall.

Stack. Carol. 1975. *All Our Kin: Strategies for Survival in a Black Community.* New York: Harper and Row.

Steiner, Ivan D. 1970. "Strategies for controlling stress in interpersonal situations." In McGrath (ed., 1970a).

Sue, Hiroko. 1964. *Hare Indians and Their World.* Unpublished doctoral dissertation, Bryn Mawr College.

_____ 1965. *Pre-school Children of the Hare Indians.* Ottawa: Northern Co-ordination and Research Centre, Department of Northern Affairs and National Resources.

Symington, Fraser. 1965. *Tuktu, the Caribou of the Northern Mainland.* Ottawa: Canadian Wildlife Service, Department of Northern Affairs and National Resources.

Szasz, Kathleen. 1969. *Petishism: Pets and Their People in the Western World.* New York: Holt, Rinehart and Winston.

Tanner, Adrian. 1979. *Bringing Home Animals: Religious Ideology and Mode of Production of the Mistassini Cree Hunters.* St. John's, Newfoundland: Social and Economic Stduies No. 23, Institute of Social and Economic Research, Memorial University of Newfoundland.

Torrance. E. Paul. 1968. "Comparative studies of stress-seeking in the imaginative stories of preadolescents in twelve different subcultures." In Klausner (ed., 1968).

290   *The Trail of the Hare*

Turnbull, Colin M. 1961. *The Forest People.* New York: Simon and Schuster.

_____ 1968a. "The importance of flux in two hunting societies." In Lee and DeVore (eds., 1968).

_____ 1968b. "Discussion of resolving conflicts by fission." In Lee and De Vore (eds., 1968).

Usher, Peter J. 1971. *The Bankslanders.* 3 volumes. Ottawa: Northern Science Research Group, Department of Indian Affairs and Northern Development.

_____ 1972. "The use of snowmobiles for trapping on Banks Island." *Arctic* 25: 170-181.

Valentine, Victor F. and Frank G. Vallee (eds.). 1968. *Eskimo of the Canadian Arctic.* Toronto: McClelland and Stewart.

Vallee, Frank G. 1967. *Kabloona and Eskimo in the Central Keewatin.* Ottawa: Canadian Research Centre for Anthropology, Saint Paul University.

VanStone, James W. 1963. "Changing patterns of Indian trapping in the Canadian Subarctic." *Arctic* 16: 159-174.

_____ 1965. *The Changing Culture of the Snowdrift Chipewyan.* Ottawa: National Museum of Canada, Bulletin No. 209.

_____ 1974. *Athapaskan Adaptations: Hunters and Fishermen on the Subarctic Forests.* Chicago: Aldine.

Wah-shee, James J. 1974. "Preface." In Rene Fumoleau, *As Long as This Land Shall Last: A History of Treaty 8 and Treaty 11, 1870-1939.* Toronto: McClelland and Stewart.

Wallace, Anthony F.C. 1970. *Culture and Personality.* 2nd edition. New York: Random House.

Watkins, Mel (ed.). 1977. *Dene Nation: The Colony Within.* Toronto: University of Toronto Press.

Welsh, Ann. 1970. "Community patern and settlement pattern in the development of Old Crow Village, Yukon Territory." *Western Canadian Journal of Anthropology* 2: 17-30.

Wentzel, W.F. 1889. "Letters to the Hon. Roderic McKenzie, 1807-1824." In L.R. Masson (ed.), *Les Bourgeois de la Compagnie du Nord-ouest.* Premiere Serie. Quebec: A. Cote.

Wenzel, George. 1991. *Animal Rights, Human Rights: Ecology, Economy and Ideology in the Canadian Arctic.* Toronto: University of Toronto Press.

Weyer, Edward Moffat. 1969. *The Eskimos.* Hamden CT: Archon Books.

Whitaker, Ian. 1955. *Social Relations in a Nomadic Lappish Community.* Oslo: Samiske Samlinger, Bind II, Utgitt av Norsk Folkemuseum.

Willmott, W.E. 1960. "The flexibility of Eskimo social organization." *Anthropologica* 2: 48-59.

Wissler, Clark. 1957. *The American Indian.* 3rd edition. Gloucester, MA: Peter Smith.

Woodburn, James. 1968. "Stability and flexibility in Hadza residential groupings." In Lee and DeVore (eds., 1968).

Index